ALASTAIR SAWDAY'S
SPECIAL PLACES TO STAY

FRENCH
HOTELS
CHÂTEAUX AND INNS

D1411734

Design: Caroline King

Maps & Mapping: Bartholomew Mapping, a division of HarperCollins, Glasgow

Printing: Canale, Italy

UK Distribution: Portfolio, Greenford, Middlesex

US Distribution: The Globe Pequot Press, Guilford, Connecticut

Published in 2003

Alastair Sawday Publishing Co. Ltd
The Home Farm Stables, Barrow Gurney, Bristol BS48 3RW
Tel: +44 (0)1275 464891 Fax: +44 (0)1275 464887
E-mail: info@specialplacestostay.com Web: www.specialplacestostay.com

The Globe Pequot Press
P.O. Box 480, Guilford, Connecticut 06437, USA
Tel: +1 203 458 4500 Fax: +1 203 458 4601
E-mail: info@globe-pequot.com Web: www.GlobePequot.com

Third edition

Copyright © 2003 Alastair Sawday Publishing Co. Ltd

All rights reserved. No part of this publication may be used other than for the purpose for which it is intended nor may any part be reproduced, or transmitted, in any form or by any means, electronically or mechanically, including photocopying, recording or any information storage or retrieval system without prior written permission from the publisher. Request for permission should be addressed to Alastair Sawday Publishing Co. Ltd, The Home Farm Stables, Barrow Gurney, Bristol BS48 3RW; or The Globe Pequot Press, P.O. Box 480, Guilford, Connecticut 06437 in North America.

A catalogue record for this book is available from the British Library.

This publication is not included under licences issued by the Copyright Agency. No part of this publication may be used in any form of advertising, sales promotion or publicity.

Alastair Sawday has asserted his right to be identified as the author of this work.

ISBN 1-901970-39-6 in the UK
ISBN 0-7627-2857-4in the US

Printed in Italy

The publishers have made every effort to ensure the accuracy of the information in this book at the time of going to press. However, they cannot accept any responsibility for any loss, injury or inconvenience resulting from the use of information contained therein.

A WORD FROM
ALASTAIR SAWDAY

Go to France – she is as seductive as ever, whatever you may have read about heatwaves and strikes in 2003.

When your country is going through a touch of the tourist doldrums you need heroic measures to counter the gloom. So the Mayor of Paris turns the right bank of the Seine into a beach and invites the Parisians and visitors alike to party. Wonderful – the French have lost none of their natural élan!

One measure we can take is to urge you to visit these wonderful Special Places, for France still has a lot to teach us all about 'hospitality', and they are superb value. You will find talented and delightful people holding their own against the tidal wave of standardisation that floods over much that is unique in Europe. You will find panache, flair and a new creativity – visible now in the 'designer' hotels that at their best are entertaining and surprising. (One I stayed in had such white walls, floors, ceilings, furniture and beds that I felt I had entered another dimension.)

There are many 'foreigners' doing their bit for the hotels and inns of France. One American re-discovered an old breed of chicken in his farmers' market, researched it, bred them and now supplies top chefs.

Hotel owners love our readers/travellers – for they regularly turn out to be open-minded and flexible, ready for the fascinating experiences that France has to offer. So if you are among those, thank you for your support and for encouraging the owners of these wonderful places to be their authentic selves.

Alastair Sawday

ACKNOWLEDGEMENTS

With her feet in a bucket of iced water, and her shutters closed against the summer heatwave that gripped much of Europe, Susan Luraschi drove this project ahead with verve and grit. It many ways producing these books is a lonely business, and she worked alone for much of the time in her Paris studio. But she has achieved remarkable things – a superb book that stands head and shoulders above its competitors, compiled with commitment and flair. It is very much her own creation and in this third edition she has lost not an ounce of her originality and perception.

Behind the scenes have been others here in the Bristol office, especially Roanne Finch – Susan's main support system. She is unflappable and thorough – what more could one want? A mention, too, is deserved by Beth Thomas whose meticulous production work is much appreciated. The rest of the support team appears below – we owe them all our thanks.

Alastair Sawday

Series Editor:	Alastair Sawday
Editor:	Susan Luraschi
Editorial Director:	Annie Shillito
Production Manager:	Julia Richardson
Web & IT:	Russell Wilkinson, Matt Kenefick
Editorial:	Sarah Bolton, Roanne Finch
Copy Editor:	Jo Boissevain
Production Assistants:	Rachel Coe, Paul Groom, Beth Thomas
Accounts:	Jenny Purdy
Sales & Marketing:	Siobhan Flynn, Paula Brown
Writing:	Susan Luraschi, Tom Bell, Jo Boissevain, Lindsay Butler
Inspections:	Susan Luraschi, Richard & Linda Armspach, Helen Barr, Lillian Bell, Alyson & Colin Browne, Jill Coyle, Sue Edrich, John Edwards, Georgina Gabriel, Denise Goss, Anne Guthrie, Diana Harris, Sarah Hidderley, Hugh Mitford-Raymond, Jo-Bell Moore, Peter & Clarissa Novak, Elizabeth Yates

A special thank you, too, to the other inspectors who saw just one or two houses for us.

Special acknowledgements to Ann Cooke-Yarborough who stands straight in spite of all the things I throw at her, and to Emma and Roanne whose good humour is on a par with my morning coffee.

Susan Luraschi

WHAT'S IN THE BOOK?

CONTENTS

CONTENTS

CONTENTS

CONTENTS

INTRODUCTION

How we choose our Special Places

Special Places are just that – special. We select them for their fascination and character. But also for the people who run them.

One of our favourite hoteliers has a business card, which reads: *Marchand de Rêves et d'Evasion*. This "dealer in dreams and escape" has a flair for people and places and a passion for what he does. Passion is a word not normally associated with the world of hospitality, but passion – and commitment – are important to us. And flair? The ability to pick the right shade of blue for the taffeta curtains, to find the perfect balance of chocolate and chestnut in a dessert, to consider the option of serving breakfast until noon.

We visit every property. Atmosphere, welcome and value for money are the key; each place is judged on its own merit, not by comparison. It is unreasonable to expect the same service and comfort from a €60-a-room inn as from a €250-a-room hotel. Friendly staff are more important to us than jacuzzis, a bowl of fresh flowers more important than satellite TV.

We have a Pullman car in Pas de Calais, a trogdolyte room, 17th-century châteaux that serve high tea and mills and manors, auberges and hotels, towers, turrets and bastides. France is also blessed with great food and a richness of scenery and rural living that is hard to beat. Our owners have originality, energy and independence and give more than a passing nod to tradition and regional differences.

Do plan to stay more than one night on your travels; some of our hoteliers feel that 'zapping' has now entered their world and they miss the complicity (and serenity) of longer visits.

What to expect

These places range from the small and intimate to the grand and gracious. Many are small and owner-run so don't automatically expect room service or porters.

With six rooms or under, the property is usually lived in and run by the owners, along with a limited staff. Expect to feel a privileged guest in your chosen house and to gain a fascinating glimpse of a French way of life. We have tried to specify if the dinner is hosted and taken at a communal table: *table d'hôte*. This is usually a wonderful opportunity to get to know your hosts and to make new friends among the other guests. This means the same food for all and absolutely must be booked ahead.

INTRODUCTION

Do specify any dietary needs when you book. If a late arrival is unavoidable, some hosts will prepare a cold meal if given advance notice. Remember these are not hotels with full staff.

We have ignored the 'star' system for the hotels. That is because it uses criteria different from ours. A hotel that we think the world of may be near the bottom of the official 'star' list simply because it has no lift. Other owners, unwilling to be swept into a bureaucratic system, refuse to apply for a star rating. The system is technical and incapable of accounting for character, style or warmth of welcome, the very things that we rate most highly.

Traditional *hotellerie* is thriving with its intricate wallcoverings, Régence, Louis XIV and XV furniture in harmony with the buildings themselves, classic cuisine in the kitchens. This is the image of France that many travellers have in mind — and it's hugely popular. One reader called such a place "a minimalist's nightmare": *he* loved it, in all its glory.

By contrast there is a growing 'new guard' represented by the minimalists who keep things bare, fresh and light, using colour schemes of white, cream and grey. There may be one or two pieces of exquisite furniture, and the odd splash of colour, but nothing that jars the eye, just space and serenity. These places may have variations of nouvelle cuisine with a sprinkling of foreign spice. A meat-and-potoatoes personality would not feel at home here.

At inns, or restaurants with rooms, food takes priority. Rooms are secondary, but they often represent good value, and are comfortable and clean. Kitchen gardens have popped up all over the place and *le terroir* — seasonal, fresh and local food — is de rigueur. Be sure to book as the typical auberge can feed more people that it can sleep. Remember, too, that dinner is not served before 7.30pm and outside the larger towns, last orders may be taken no later than 9pm.

Read carefully, sleep happily

Choosing the right place for you

Read the descriptions carefully and pick out the places where you will be comfortable. If 'antique beds' sound seductively authentic, remember they are liable to be antique sizes too (190cm long, doubles 140cm wide). If in doubt, ask or book a twin room. If you flee from dining with strangers, avoid the hosted dinners.

INTRODUCTION

A problem well defined is half-way solved

Do discuss any problem with your hosts – they can usually do
something about it on the spot. If you find anything we say
misleading (things and people do change in the lifetime of a
guide), or you think we miss the point, please let us know.

How to use
this book

Bedrooms

- 'double': one double bed
- 'twin': two single beds
- 'triple' or 'family room': mix of beds (sometimes sofabeds)
  for 3, 4 or more people. A family room will always have a
  double bed.
- 'duplex': a room on two floors with a staircase
- 'suite': either one large room with a sitting area or two or
  more interconnecting rooms, plus one or more bathrooms
- 'apartment': similar to suite but with an independent
  entrance and possibly a small kitchen

A twin room is usually larger than a double. Extra beds and cots
for children, at extra cost, can be provided; ask when booking.

Bathrooms

Assume all bedrooms are en suite, either with bath or shower.
We say if a bedroom has either a separate bathroom or a shared
bathroom. For simplicity we refer to 'bath'. This doesn't
necessarily mean it has no shower; it could mean a shower only.

Prices

The price range is for two people sharing a room: the lower
price indicates the least expensive room in low season; the
higher price, the most expensive room in high season. If
breakfast is not included, we say so and give the price. Prices
are given for 2004-2005 but are not guaranteed so please check
when you book. If there are no single rooms, there will usually
be a reduction for single occupancy of a double.

Half-board

Do look into attractive half-board terms and special prices for
children. Half-board (*demi-pension*) includes breakfast and
dinner. Full-board (*pension complète*) includes all three meals.
Prices given are generally per person ('p.p.') and include the
room. Ask about reduced rates when booking longer stays and
off-season visits. Check our internet site for special offers.

INTRODUCTION

Meals

The number and type of courses you will be offered for lunch
and dinner varies. Some places have set menus at fixed prices.
Most places serving lunch will have a good value menu during
the week, changing the menu and the prices on the weekend.

Many places offer a *table d'hôte* dinner to overnight guests (see
above). This may be dining at separate tables, but often the meal
is shared with other guests at a long table. These are sometimes
hosted by Monsieur or Madame (or both). Advance notice is
required for these and they may not be available every night.
Make sure your meal is reserved on the first night, especially
if you are staying deep in the countryside.

Closed

When given in months, this means for the whole of both
months named. 'Closed: November-March' means closed from
1 November to 31 March.

Practical Matters

Types of houses

For a definition of *château, bastide, mas,* see French Words &
Expressions at the back of this book.

Telephoning/Faxing

Telephone numbers in France have ten digits, e.g. (0)5 15 25 35
45. You should know that:

• the initial zero (bracketed here) is for use when telephoning
from inside France only, i.e. dial 05 15 25 35 45;

• when dialling France from abroad, use the international access
code then the country code – 33 – followed by the last 9 digits
of the number, e.g. 00 33 5 15 25 35 45;

• numbers beginning (0)6 are mobile phone numbers;

• to telephone from France –

– to Great Britain: 00 44 then the number without the initial zero

– to the USA, dial 00 1 then the number without the initial zero.

Phone cards (*télécartes*) are available in tobacco shops and post
offices. There are plenty of telephone boxes, even in the
countryside, and most take only cards.

INTRODUCTION

Booking

It is essential to book well ahead for July and August and wise
for other months. Most places now have web sites and e-mail
addresses. We have a booking form at the back of this book
and on our web site at www.specialplacestostay.com. However,
please remember that technology may be put aside at busy
times and a small place may just not have the time or the
personnel to respond quickly to e-mail requests.

Some places require a deposit to confirm a booking. If you
cancel you are likely to lose part, or all, of it. Check the exact
terms when you book. A credit card number is the standard
way to place a deposit.

Be aware of some of the French holiday dates which can make
booking difficult.

The French have 11 annual national holidays. In May there is
a holiday nearly every week depending upon the dates of the
'moveable feasts' (see below). So be prepared for stores, banks
and museums to shut their doors for days at a time. Booking
hotels in advance becomes essential.

1 January	New Year's Day (*Jour de l'an*)
1 May	Labor Day (*Fête du premier mai*)
8 May	WWII Victory Day (*Fête de la Victoire*)
14 July	Bastille Day
15 August	Assumption of the Blessed Virgin (*Assomption*)
1 November	All Saints Day (*La Toussaint*)
11 November	Armistice Day (*Jour d'armistice*)
25 December	Christmas Day (*Noël*)
26 December	2nd day of Christmas (Alsace Lorraine only)

Moveable Feasts	2004	2005
Good Friday*	9 April	25 March
Easter (Paques)	11 April	27 March
Easter Monday	12 April	28 March
Ascension (l'Ascencion)	20 May	5 May
Pentecost (la Pentecôte)	30 May	15 May
Whit Monday	31 May	16 May
	*(Alsace Lorraine only)	

INTRODUCTION

When a holiday falls on a Tuesday or Thursday, many people may take a longer break by including Monday or Friday (*faire le pont*). This is not official and does not apply to institutions such as banks but is sufficiently commonplace to cause difficulties in booking rooms or travelling.

Payment

Master Card and Visa are generally welcome; American Express is often accepted in the upper range hotels, Diners Club hardly ever. The few places that don't accept credit cards are indicated at the end of their description. Drawing cash is easy as virtually all ATMs in France take Visa and MasterCard.

A small tax that local councils can levy on all visitors may be charged; you may find your bill increased by €0.50-€2 per person per day.

Tipping

Almost all restaurants include tax and a 15% service charge (*service compris*) in their prices. If a meal or service has been particularly good, leaving another €1.50 (or 2%-3%) is customary, as is leaving the waiter the small change from your bill if you pay in cash. If service is not included (*service non compris*), a 15% tip is appropriate.

In hotels tip porters €1.50 for each bag and chambermaids €1.50 a day. Taxi drivers should receive 10%-15% of the metered fare. Small tips of about €1 are reasonable for cloakroom attendants, ushers and museum tour guides.

Symbols

Pets

Even though a place may be listed as accepting animals, some will only take small animals, some only dogs; others will limit the number of animals staying at the same time. Some allow them in the rooms, some don't. Do check ahead. There is always a supplement to pay.

Part smoking/Non-smoking

Part smoking usually means that no smoking is allowed in the dining room and in some of the bedrooms. We say in italics at the end of the write-up if a property is totally non-smoking.

INTRODUCTION

Electricity

You will need an adaptor plug for the 220-volt 50-cycle AC current. Americans also need a voltage transformer (heavy and expensive) for appliances that are not bi-voltage.

Quick reference indices – activities, courses & special facilities

At the back of the books we direct you to places with rooms at under €65, where you can rent or borrow a bike, get a seaweed wrap, take cookery lessons, test your wine-tasting skills, take a garden tour or practise a craft.

Environment

We try to reduce our impact on the environment by:

- publishing our books on recycled paper
- planting trees. We are officially Carbon Neutral®. The emissions directly related to our office, paper production and printing of this book have been 'neutralised' through the planting of indigenous woodlands with Future Forests
- re-using paper, recycling stationery, tins, bottles, etc
- encouraging staff use of bicycles (they're loaned free) and car sharing
- celebrating the use of organic, home-grown and locally-produced food
- publishing books that support, in however small a way, the rural economy and small-scale businesses
- publishing *The Little Earth Book*, a collection of essays on environmental issues and *The Little Food Book*, a hard-hitting analysis of the food industry. *The Little Money Book* is under way, too. See our web site www.fragile-earth.com for more information on any of these titles.

Subscriptions

Owners pay to appear in this guide; their fee goes towards the high production costs of an all-colour book. We do only include places and owners that we find special. It is not possible for anyone to bribe their way in!

Internet

Our web site www.specialplacestostay.com has online pages for all the places featured here and from all our other books – around 3,500 Special Places in Britain, Ireland, France, Italy, Spain and Portugal. There's a searchable database, full details, a taster of the write-ups and colour photos.

For more details see the back of the book.

INTRODUCTION

Disclaimer We make no claims to pure objectivity in choosing our
Special Places to Stay. They are here because we like them.
Our opinions and tastes are ours alone and this book is a
statement of them; we hope that you will share them.

We have done our utmost to get our facts right but apologise
unreservedly for any mistakes that may have crept in. Feedback
from you is invaluable and we always act upon comments.
With your help and our own inspections we can maintain our
reputation for dependability.

You should know that we do not check such things as fire
alarms, swimming pool security or any other regulation with
which owners of properties receiving paying guests should
comply. This is the responsibility of the owners.

A huge 'thank you' to all of you who have taken the time and
trouble to write to us about your experiences – good and bad –
and to recommend new places. This is what we do with them.

Feedback • Poor reports are followed up with the owners in question:
we need to hear both sides of the story. Really bad reports
lead to incognito visits after which we may exclude a place.
It is very helpful to us if you can let us know the date of
your visit.

• Owners are informed when we receive substantially positive
reports about them.

• Recommendations are followed up with inspection visits
where appropriate.

And finally We are hugely grateful to those of you who write to us about
your experiences – good and bad – or to recommend new
places. We love your letters and your comments make a real
contribution to this book, be they on our report form, by letter
or by email to info@sawdays.co.uk. Or you can visit our web
site and write to us from there.

Bon Voyage!

Susan Luraschi

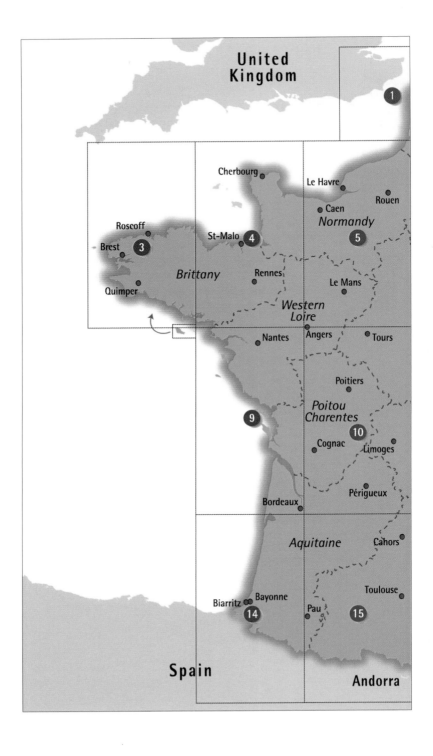

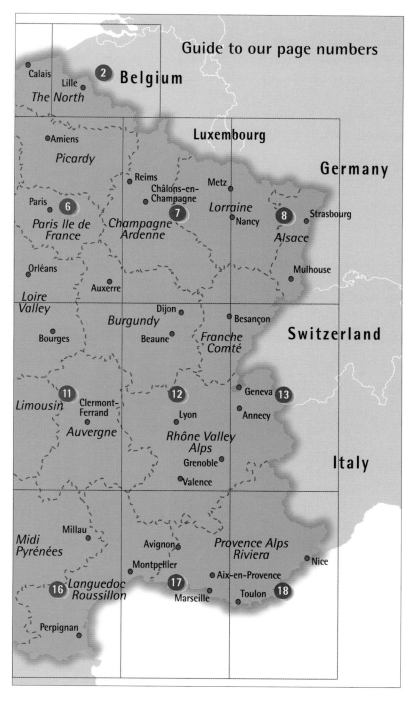

Guide to our page numbers

Belgium

Luxembourg

Germany

Switzerland

Italy

Calais
Lille
The North

Amiens
Picardy

Reims
Châlons-en-Champagne
Metz
Lorraine
Nancy
Strasbourg
Alsace
Mulhouse

Paris
Paris Ile de France
Champagne Ardenne

Orléans
Auxerre
Loire Valley

Dijon
Besançon
Burgundy
Beaune
Franche Comté

Bourges

Geneva
Annecy

Limousin
Clermont-Ferrand
Auvergne
Lyon
Rhône Valley Alps
Grenoble
Valence

Millau
Midi Pyrénées
Avignon
Provence Alps Riviera
Nice

Montpellier
Aix-en-Provence
Languedoc Roussillon
Marseille
Toulon

Perpignan

2
6
7
8
11
12
13
16
17
18

©Bartholomew Ltd, 2003

HOW TO USE OUR MAPS

Our maps are designed for general orientation only – you will be
deeply frustrated if you try to use them as road maps! Take a good
detailed road map or atlas such as Michelin or Collins.

The numbered flags have pointers and are indications of position, not
accurate markers. You will find specific directions in the relevant
entry.

READING OUR DIRECTIONS

Except in the case of two-way motorway junctions, our directions
take you to each house from one side only. French roads are identified
with the letters they carry on French maps and road signs:

A = *Autoroute*. Motorways (mostly toll roads) with junctions that generally have the same name/number on both sides.

N = *Route Nationale*. The old trunk roads that are still fairly fast, don't
charge tolls and often go through towns.

D = *Route Départementale*. Smaller country roads with less traffic.

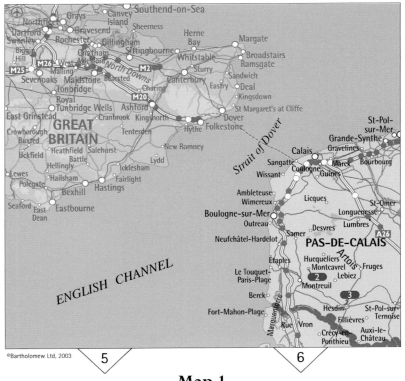

©Bartholomew Ltd, 2003

Map 1

Our directions are as succinct as possible.

For example: From A7 exit Valence Sud A49 for Grenoble; exit 33; right D538a for Beaumont 2.5km; right again at sign 800m; house on right.

Interpretation: Take A7 motorway going north or south; leave at junction named 'Valence Sud' and get onto motorway A49 going towards Grenoble; leave this road at junction 33 and turn right onto road D538a (the 'a' means there are probably roads numbered 538b, 538c in the vicinity) towards Beaumont for 2.5km until you meet a meaningful sign; turn right at this sign; the house is 800 metres down this road on the right.

Scale for maps 1:1 600 000

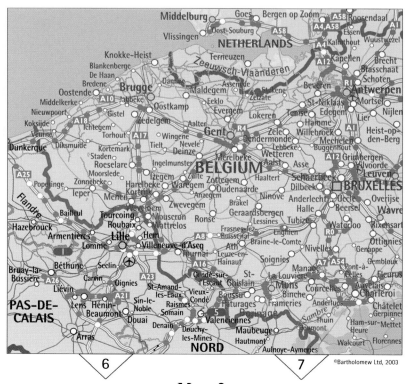

©Bartholomew Ltd, 2003

Map 2

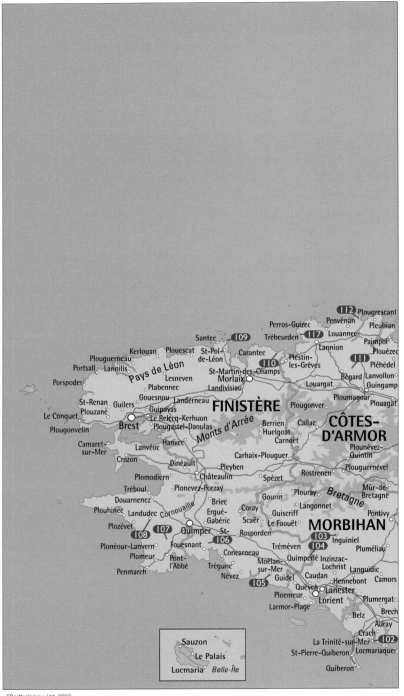

Map 3

©Bartholomew Ltd, 2003

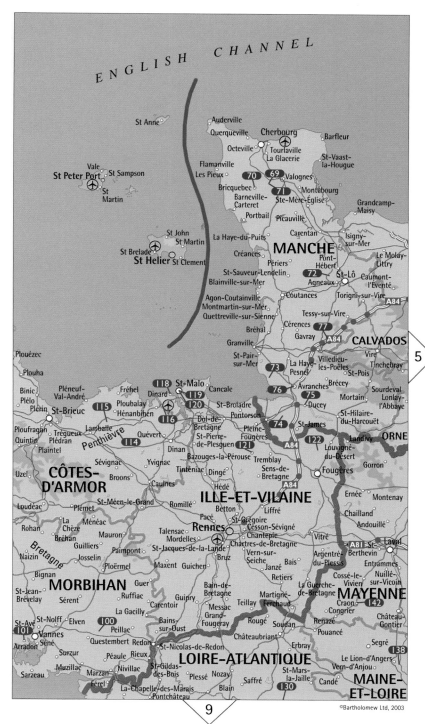

ENGLISH CHANNEL

St Anne

Auderville
Querqueville · Cherbourg · Barfleur
Octeville · Tourlaville · St-Vaast-
La Glacerie · la-Hougue
Flamanville
Les Pieux · **70** · **69** · Valognes
Bricquebec · Montebourg
Barneville- · Ste-Mère-Église
Carteret
Portbail · Picauville · Grandcamp-
Maisy
La Haye-du-Puits · Carentan · Isigny-
sur-Mer
Créances · **MANCHE** · Le Molay-
Périers · Pont- · Littry
St-Sauveur-Lendelin · Hébert · Caumont-
Blainville-sur-Mer · **72** · St-Lô · l'Éventé
Agneaux · **A84**
Agon-Coutainville · Coutances · Torigni-sur-Vire
Montmartin-sur-Mer · Tessy-sur-Vire
Quettreville-sur-Sienne · Cérences · **77**
Bréhal · Gavray · **A84**
Granville · **CALVADOS**
St-Pair- · La Haye- · Villedieu- · Vire · **5**
sur-Mer · **73** · Pesnel · les-Poêles · Tinchebray
St-Pois
76 · Avranches · Brécey · Sourdeval
Ploùezec · Lonlay-
Plouha · Fréhel · **118** · St-Malo · Cancale · Ducey · Mortain · l'Abbaye
Binic · Pléneuf- · Dinard · **119** · **75**
Plélo · Val-André · Ploubalay · **120** · St-Broladre · St-Hilaire-
Plérin · Hénanbihen · **116** · Pontorson · du-Harcouët
St-Brieuc · **115** · Dol-de- · St-James · **ORNE**
Ploufragan · Lamballe · Quévert · Bretagne · Pleine- · **74** · **122**
Quintin · Tréguex · Plédran · St-Pierre- · Fougères · Landivy
Plaintel · Penthièvre · **114** · Dinan · de-Plesguen · **121** · **A84** · Louvigné-
Sévignac · Yvignac · Bazouges-la-Pérouse · du-Désert
Uzel · Broons · Tinténiac · Tremblay · Gorron
CÔTES- · Caulnes · Dingé · Sens-de- · Fougères
D'ARMOR · Bretagne
Loudéac · Hédé · Ernée · Montenay
Plémet · St-Méen-le-Grand · Betton · **ILLE-ET-VILAINE** · Chailland · Andouillé
Rohan · La · Ménéac · Romillé · Liffré
Chèze · Mauron · Pacé · St-Grégoire · Vitré · **A81** · St-
Bréhan · Guilliers · Talensac · Cesson-Sévigné · Berthevin · **Laval**
Naizin · Josselin · Paimpont · **Rennes** · Chantepie · Argentré- · Entrammes
Bignan · Ploërmel · St-Jacques-de-la-Lande · Chartres-de-Bretagne · du-Plessis · Cossé-le- · Nuillé-
St-Jean- · Maxent · Guichen · Bruz · Vern-sur- · Vivien · sur-Vicoin
Brévelay · Sérent · Guer · Seiche · Janzé · Bais
MORBIHAN · Ruffiac · Retiers · **MAYENNE**
St-Avé · St-Nolff · Elven · Guipry · Bain-de- · Martigné- · La Guerche- · Craon · **142**
101 · **100** · La Gacilly · Bretagne · Messac · Ferchaud · de-Bretagne · Congrier
Vannes · Peillac · Carentoir · Grand- · Rougé · Renazé · Château-
Arradon · Séné · Bains- · Fougeray · Soudan · Pouancé · Gontier
Questembert · Redon · sur-Oust · Châteaubriant · Erbray · Segré · **138**
Surzur · St-Nicolas-de-Redon
Péaule · Rieux · **LOIRE-ATLANTIQUE** · Le Lion-d'Angers
Muzillac · Nivillac · St-Gildas- · Vern-d'Anjou
Sarzeau · Marzan · des-Bois · Plessé · Nozay · St-Mars- · Candé · **MAINE-**
Férel · Saffré · la-Jaille · **ET-LOIRE**
La-Chapelle-des-Marais · Blain · **130**
Pontchâteau

St Peter Port
Vale · St Sampson
St Martin

St John · St Martin
St Brelade · St Clement
St Helier

Penthièvre
Bretagne

©Bartholomew Ltd, 2003

9

Map 4

SOMME

Cayeux-sur-Mer

ENGLISH CHANNEL

Le Tréport
Criel-sur-Mer
Penly
Gamaches
Eu
Neuville-lès-Dieppe
St-Nicolas-
d'Aliermont
Longueville-
sur-Scie
Neufchâtel-
en-Bray
Pays de Bray

Dieppe
Offranville

St-Valery-
en-Caux
Néville
Cany-Barville

St-Pierre-
en-Port
Fécamp
Yport
Étretat

SEINE-MARITIME

Héricourt-
en-Caux
Doudeville
Yerville
St-Saëns

Criquetot-l'Esneval
93

Goderville
Yvetot
Buchy
Forges-
les-Eaux

90
A151
A29

Montivilliers
Bolbec
Barentin
Notre-Dame-
de-Bondeville
91, 92

Ste-Adresse
Harfleur
Lillebonne
Notre-Dame-
de-Gravenchon
A150
Mont-St-Aignan

Le Havre
94
Gonfreville
l'Orcher
Le Petit-Quevilly
Rouen
Sotteville-
lès-Rouen

Honfleur
Seine
Le Grand-Quevilly
Petit-Couronne
St-Étienne-
du-Rouvray

Trouville-sur-Mer
84
A29
95
Beuzeville
Grand-Couronne
Val-de-Reuil

Lion-sur-Mer
85
Pont-Audemer
Corneilles
Cléon
Elbeuf
A13
Les
Andelys

78
79
Dives-Sur-Mer
Louviers
96
Gaillon

Ouistreham
Hérouville-St-Clair
Colombelles
Brionne
Le Neubourg
Vernon
97

80
Mondeville
Lisieux
Bernay
Quittebeuf
98

Tilly-sur-
Seulles
Caen
Ifs
Argences
EURE
Évreux
Pacy-sur-
Eure

A84
81
Évrecy
Mézidon-Canon
Orbec
Broglie
La Bonneville-sur-Iton
Guichainville
Breuilpont

Aunay-
sur-Odon
St-Pierre-sur-Dives
83
La Trinité-de-Réville
Conches-en-Ouche
St-André-de-l'Eure
Ézy-sur-Eure
Ivry-la-
Bataille

82
Potigny
Livarot
Glos-la-
Ferrière
Rugles
Damville
St-Lubin-des-
Joncherets
Bû

Condé-sur-
Noireau
Clécy
CALVADOS
Vimoutiers
Le Sap
L'Aigle
Bourth
Verneuil-
sur-Avre
Dreux

Flers
Falaise
Trun
Chambois
Gacé
Échauffour
Ste-Gauburge-
Ste-Colombe
Brézolles
Vernouillet
Thymerais

Messei
Âthis-de-
l'Orne
Pont-d'Ouilly
Putanges-
Pont-Écrepin
Écouché
Exmes
Maillebois
Jouy

La Ferrière-aux-Étangs
88
Argentan
Mortrée
89
Tourouvre
Châteauneuf-en-Thymerais
Chartres

Champsecret
86
La Ferté-Macé
ORNE
Sées
Essay
Sénonches
Digny
Luce

Domfront
Couterne
87
Essay
Mortagne-
au-Perche
Longny-au-Perche
La Loupe
Luisant

Lassay-les-Châteaux
Damigny
Neufchâtel-
en-Saosnois
Rémalard
Bretoncelles
EURE-
ET-LOIR

Ambrières-les-Vallées
Alençon
149
Bellême
Berd'huis
Dammarie

Oisseau
Villaines-
la-Juhel
Mamers
Igé
Nogent-
le-Rotrou
Thiron Gardais
Brou
Sancheville

Mayenne
Fresnay-sur-Sarthe
148
Le Theil
Ceton
Authon-
du-Perche
Unverre
Bonneval

MAYENNE
Bais
Sillé-le-
Guillaume
Marolles-
les-Braults
La Ferté-
Bernard
Arrou
Logron
Châteaudun

Évron
Conlie
Bonnétable
Montmirail
Courtalain
Dunois

Vaiges
A81
La Bazoge
La Milesse
Coulaines
Vibraye
Droué
Cloyes-sur-
le-Loir
Ouzouer-le-Marché

Meslay-
du-Maine
Brûlon
Chassillé
Loué
143
144
Allonnes
Le Mans
St-Mars-la-Brière
Bouloire
147
Mondoubleau
Épuisay
Morée
Marchenoir

Sablé-sur-Sarthe
141
145
A11
Arnage
Mulsanne
St-Calais
La Ville-
aux-Clercs
St-Ouen Oucques
Josnes

St-Denis-d'Anjou
Daon
Noyen-sur-Sarthe
A28
Le Grand-Lucé
Savigny-
sur-Braye
Vendôme
Selommes
LOIR-ET-CHER

Précigné
146
Jupilles
Mayet
Châteaudu-Loir
Authon
St-Amand-Longpré

140
Daumeray
Durtal
La
Flèche
Luché-Pringé
Aubigné-
Racan
Vaas
Loir
Herbault
A10

139
MAINE-ET-LOIRE
Le Lude
Château-la-Vallière
INDRE-ET-LOIRE
Château-Renault
Blois
Vineuil
Cour-Cheverny

Avrillé
Angers
A85
Baugé
Novant
162
Semblançay
161

©Bartholomew Ltd, 2003

Map 5

Map 6

©Bartholomew Ltd, 2003

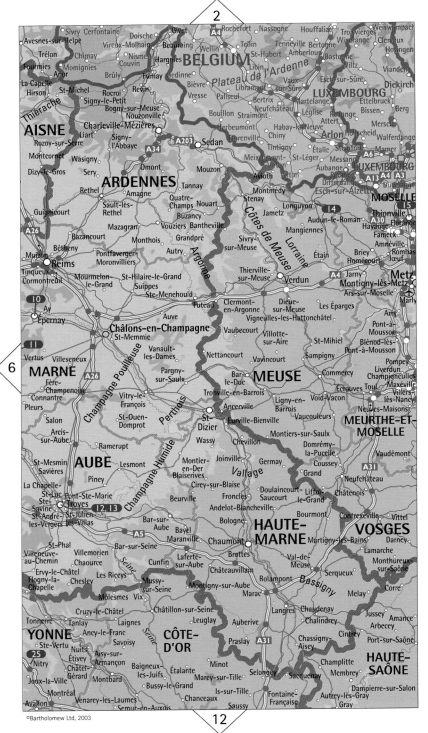

Sivry Cerfontaine
Avesnes-sur-Helpe
Doische
Givet
Rochefort
Nassogne
Houffalize
Trois-Vierges
Weiswampach
Wimerange
Clervaux
Hosingen
Trélon
Chimay
Vireux-Molhain
Beauraing
Wellin
St-Hubert
Tenneville
Bertogne
Bastogne
Wiltz
Vianden
Fourmies
Momignies
Nismes
Couvin
Hargnies
Tellin
Amberloup
Anor
Brûly
Fumay
Gedinne
Plateau de l'Ardenne
Vaux-sur-Sûre
Esch-sur-Sûre
Dickirch
La Capelle
Hirson
St-Michel
Rocroi
Revin
Bièvre
Libramont
Neufchâteau
Martelange
Ettelbruck
Berg
Thiérache
Signy-le-Petit
Bogny-sur-Meuse
Nouzonville
Vresse
Paliseul
Bertrix
Léglise
Redange
Bissen
Mersch
AISNE
Charleville-Mézières
Liart
Signy-l'Abbaye
Sedan
Herbeumont
Chiny
Tintigny
Étalle
Messancy
Walferdange
Rozoy-sur-Serre
Montcornet
Wasigny
Sery
Omont
Mouzon
Avioth
Montmédy
Meix-devant-
St-Léger
Aubange
LUXEMBOURG
ARDENNES
Tannay
Quatre-Champs
Nouart
Stenay
Longuyon
Audun-le-Roman
14
Thionville
MOSELLE
Amagne
Buzancy
Jametz
Mangiennes
Hayange
Florange
Fameck
Guignicourt
Rethel
Sault-lès-Rethel
Mazagran
Vouziers
Bantheville
Monthois
Grandpré
Sivry-sur-Meuse
Étain
Briey
Homécourt
Amnéville
Rombas
Œuf
Béthény
Bazancourt
Pontfaverger-Moronvilliers
Autry
Argonne
Thierville-sur-Meuse
Verdun
Jarny
Ars-sur-Moselle
Metz
Muizon
Reims
Mourmelon-le-Grand
St-Hilaire-le-Grand
Montigny-lès-Metz
Tinqueux
Cormontreuil
Suippes
Clermont-en-Argonne
Dieue-sur-Meuse
Les Éparges
Marly
Ay
Épernay
Ste-Menehould
Futeau
Vigneulles-lès-Hattonchâtel
Pompey
Pont-à-Mousson
Vertus
Villeseneux
Châlons-en-Champagne
Auve
Vaubecourt
Villotte-sur-Aire
St-Mihiel
Blénod-lès-Pont-à-Mousson
Liverdun
MARNE
St-Memmie
Vanault-les-Dames
Nettancourt
Vavincourt
Sampigny
Commercy
Écrouves
Toul
Champigneulles
Maxéville
Villers-lès-Nancy
Fère-Champenoise
Connantre
Pargny-sur-Saulx
Vitry-le-François
Bar-le-Duc
MEUSE
Void-Vacon
Neuves-Maisons
Pleurs
St-Ouen-Domprot
Ancerville
Ligny-en-Barrois
Vaucouleurs
Salon
Arcis-sur-Aube
Ramerupt
St-Dizier
Eurville-Bienville
Montiers-sur-Saulx
Domrémy-la-Pucelle
MEURTHE-ET-MOSELLE
Vaudémont
St-Mesmin
Savières
Lesmont
Wassy
Chevillon
Germay
Coussey
Grand
Neufchâteau
A31
La Chapelle-
St-Luc
Piney
Joinville
Doulaincourt-Saucourt
Liffol-le-Grand
Châtenois
Contrexéville
Vittel
Troyes
Montier-en-Der
Blaiserives
Cirey-sur-Blaise
Froncles
Andelot-Blancheville
Bourmont
St-André-les-Vergers
St-Julien-les-Villas
Bar-sur-Aube
Beurville
Bologne
HAUTE-MARNE
Martigny-les-Bains
VOSGES
St-Phal
Villemorien
Bayel
Maranville
Chaumont
Brottes
Lamarche
Darney
Villeneuve-au-Chemin
Chaource
Lafertè-sur-Aube
Val-de-Meuse
Monthureux-sur-Saône
Ervy-le-Châtel
Chesley
Les Riceys
Châteauvillain
Rolampont
Serqueux
Corre
Flogny-la-Chapelle
Mussy-sur-Seine
Montigny-sur-Aube
Marac
Chaudenay
Melay
Môlesmes
Vix
Châtillon-sur-Seine
Leuglay
Langres
Chalindrey
Jussey
Amance
Port-sur-Saône
Tonnerre
Tanlay
Cruzy-le-Châtel
Laignes
Auberive
Praslay
Chassigny-Aisey
Cintrey
Arbecey
YONNE
Ancy-le-Franc
Savoisy
Chaumont
HAUTE-SAÔNE
Ste-Vertu
Nuits
Aisy-sur-Armançon
Minot
Selongey
Champlitte
Membrey
Nitry
Étivey
Châtel-Gérard
Baigneux-les-Juifs
Étalante
Marey-sur-Tille
Is-sur-Tille
Sacquenay
Dampierre-sur-Salon
Joux-la-Ville
Montbard
Bussy-le-Grand
Fontaine-Française
Autrey-lès-Gray
Avallon
Venarey-les-Laumes
Semur-en-Auxois
Chanceaux
Saussy
Gray

©Bartholomew Ltd, 2003

Map 7

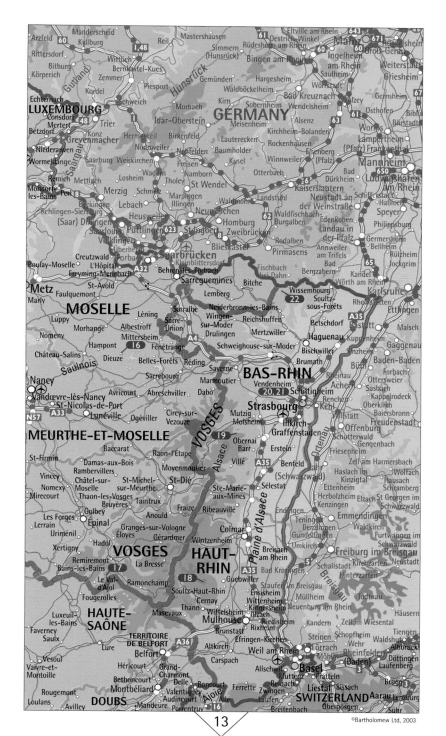

Map 8

©Bartholomew Ltd, 2003

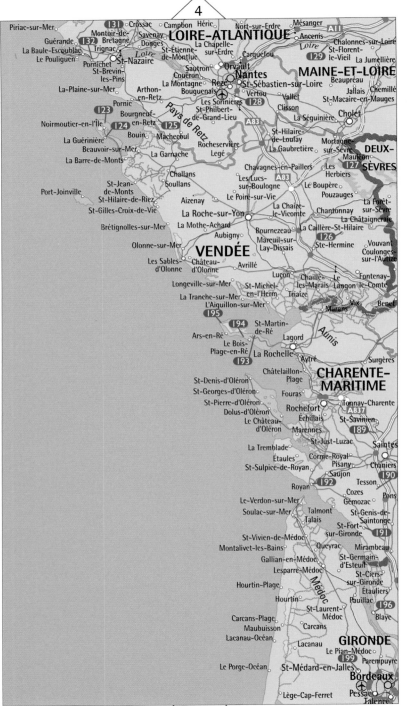

Piriac-sur-Mer
131 Crossac
Campbon
Héric
Nort-sur-Erdre
Mésanger
Ancenis
A11
Montoir-de-
Bretagne
Savenay
LOIRE-ATLANTIQUE
Chalonnes-sur-Loire
Guérande
132
Donges
La Chapelle-
sur-Erdre
Loire
St-Florent-
le-Vieil
129
La Baule-Escoublac
Trignac
St-Nazaire
St-Étienne-
de-Montluc
Carquefou
La Jumellière
Le Pouliguen
Loire
MAINE-ET-LOIRE
Pornichet
Sautron
Orvault
Nantes
Beaupréau
St-Brevin-
les-Pins
Couëron
La Montagne
Rezé
St-Sébastien-sur-Loire
Jallais
Chemillé
La-Plaine-sur-Mer
Arthon-
en-Retz
Bouguenais
Vertou
Vallet
St-Macaire-en-Mauges
Les Sorinières
128
Clisson
Pornic
St-Philbert-
de-Grand-Lieu
Cholet
123
Bourgneuf-
en-Retz
La Séguinière
Noirmoutier-en-l'Île
124
125
St-Hilaire-
de-Loulay
La Guérinière
Bouin
Machecoul
Rocheservière
La Gaubretière
Mortagne-
sur-Sèvre
DEUX-
Beauvoir-sur-Mer
Legé
Mauléon
127
SÈVRES
La Barre-de-Monts
La Garnache
Chavagnes-en-Paillers
Les
Herbiers
Challans
A83
Soullans
Les Lucs-
sur-Boulogne
Le Boupère
La Forêt-
sur-Sèvre
St-Jean-
de-Monts
Port-Joinville
Aizenay
Le Poiré-sur-Vie
Pouzauges
St-Hilaire-de-Riez
La Chaize-
le-Vicomte
Chantonnay
La Châtaigneraie
St-Gilles-Croix-de-Vie
La Roche-sur-Yon
La Caillère-St-Hilaire
Brétignolles-sur-Mer
La Mothe-Achard
Bournezeau
126
Vouvant
Coulonges-
sur-l'Autize
Aubigny
Mareuil-sur-
Lay-Dissais
Ste-Hermine
Olonne-sur-Mer
VENDÉE
Les Sables-
d'Olonne
Château-
d'Olonne
Avrillé
Luçon
Chaillé-
les-Marais
Le
Langon
Fontenay-
le-Comte
Longeville-sur-Mer
St-Michel-
en-l'Herm
Triaize
La Tranche-sur-Mer
L'Aiguillon-sur-Mer
Marans
Vix
Benet
195
Aunis
194
St-Martin-
de-Ré
Ars-en-Ré
Lagord
Le Bois-
Plage-en-Ré
La Rochelle
Surgères
193
Aytré
Châtelaillon-
Plage
CHARENTE-
St-Denis-d'Oléron
MARITIME
St-Georges-d'Oléron
Fouras
St-Pierre-d'Oléron
Rochefort
Tonnay-Charente
Dolus-d'Oléron
Échillais
A837
Le Château-
d'Oléron
Marennes
St-Savinien
St-Just-Luzac
189
La Tremblade
Saintes
Étaules
Corme-Royal
Pisany
St-Sulpice-de-Royan
Saujon
Chaniers
192
Tesson
190
Royan
Cozes
Pons
Gémozac
Le-Verdon-sur-Mer
Talmont
St-Genis-de-
Saintonge
Soulac-sur-Mer
Talais
St-Fort-
sur-Gironde
191
St-Vivien-de-Médoc
Queyrac
Mirambeau
Montalivet-les-Bains
St-Germain-
d'Esteuil
Gallian-en-Médoc
St-Ciers-
sur-Gironde
Lesparre-Médoc
Étauliers
Hourtin-Plage
Médoc
Pauillac
196
Hourtin
St-Laurent-
Médoc
Blaye
Carcans-Plage
Carcans
Maubuisson
GIRONDE
Lacanau-Océan
Lacanau
Le Pian-Médoc
199
Parempuyre
Le Porge-Océan
St-Médard-en-Jalles
Bordeaux
Pessac
Lège-Cap-Ferret
Talence

©Bartholomew Ltd, 2003

Map 9

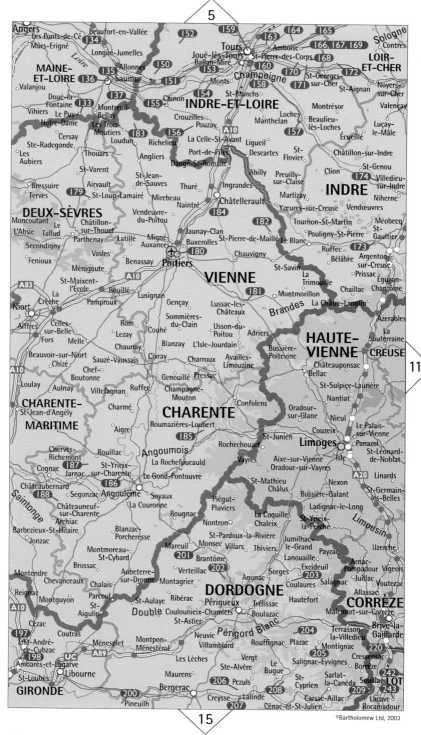

©Bartholomew Ltd, 2003

Map 10

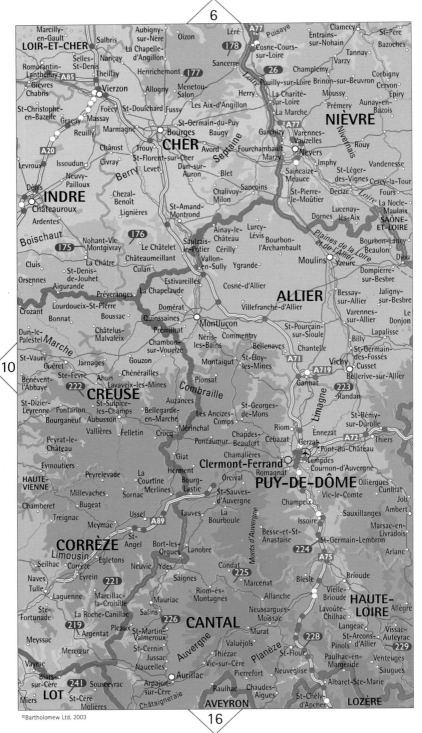

Marcilly-en-Gault
LOIR-ET-CHER
Salbris
Aubigny-sur-Nère
Oizon
Léré
A77
Puisaye
Clamecy
St-Père
Bazoches

Romorantin-Lanthenay
A85
Selles-St-Denis
Nançay
Theillay
La Chapelle-d'Angillon
178
Sancerre
Cosne-Cours-sur-Loire
Champlemy
Tannay
Varzy
Corbigny
Cervon
Epiry

Gièvres
Chabris
Vierzon
Henrichemont
177
Pouilly-sur-Loire
Brinon-sur-Beuvron
Moussy
Aunay-en-Bazois

St-Christophe-en-Bazelle
A20
Foëcy
St-Doulchard
Fussy
Allogny
Menetou-Salon
Herry
La Charité-sur-Loire
Prémery
NIÈVRE

Graçay
Massay
Les Aix-d'Angillon
La Marche

Reuilly
Marmagne
Bourges
Baugy
St-Germain-du-Puy
Garchizy
Varennes-Vauzelles
Rouy
Nivernais

Déols
INDRE
Chârost
Trouy
Avord
Fourchambault
Marzy
Nevers
Imphy
Vandenesse

Châteauroux
Civray
St-Florent-sur-Cher
CHER
Dun-sur-Auron
Septaine
Saincaize-Meauce
St-Léger-des-Vignes
Cerey-la-Tour

Levroux
Issoudun
Levet
Blet
St-Pierre-le-Moûtier
Decize
Fours
La Nocle-Maulaix

Ardentes
Neuvy-Pailloux
Chalivoy-Milon
Sancoins
Dornes
Lucenay-lès-Aix
SAÔNE-ET-LOIRE

Boischaut
175
Chezal-Benoît
Lignières
St-Amand-Montrond
Ainay-le-Château
Lurcy-Lévis
Bourbon-l'Archambault
Plaines de la Loire et de l'Allier
Bourbon-Lancy
Beaulon
Diou

Nohant-Vic
Montgivray
176
Le Châtelet
Saulzais-le-Potier
Cérilly
Vallon-en-Sully
Ygrande
Moulins
Yzeure
Dompierre-sur-Besbre

Cluis
La Châtre
Châteaumeillant
Culan
Cosne-d'Allier
Villefranche-d'Allier
ALLIER
Bessay-sur-Allier
Jaligny-sur-Besbre

Orsennes
St-Denis-de-Jouhet
Aigurande
Estivareilles
Varennes-sur-Allier
Le Donjon

Crozant
Préveranges
La Chapelaude
Domérat
Montluçon
St-Pourçain-sur-Sioule
Billy
Lapalisse

Dun-le-Palestel
Lourdoueix-St-Pierre
Boussac
Quinssaines
Prémilhat
Néris-les-Bains
Commentry
Bellenaves
Chantelle
St-Germain-des-Fossés

St-Vaury
Marche
Châtelus-Malvaleix
Gouzon
Chambon-sur-Voueize
Montaigut
St-Éloy-les-Mines
A71
Vichy
Cusset

10
Guéret
Jarnages
Chénérailles
Pionsat
Gannat
A719
Bellerive-sur-Allier

Bénévent-l'Abbaye
Ste-Feyre
Ahun
Lavaveix-les-Mines
Combraille
223
Randan

St-Dizier-Leyrenne
222
CREUSE
Auzances
St-Georges-de-Mons
Limagne

St-Sulpice-les-Champs
Bellegarde-en-Marche
Les Ancizes-Comps
St-Rémy-sur-Durolle

Pontarion
Bourganeuf
Aubusson
Mérinchal
Crocq
Chapdes-Beaufort
Riom
Ennezat
A72
Thiers

Peyrat-le-Château
Vallières
Felletin
Pontaumur
Cébazat
Gerzat
Pont-du-Château

Eymoutiers
Giat
Herment
Chamalières
Clermont-Ferrand
Lempdes
Cournon-d'Auvergne

HAUTE-VIENNE
Peyrelevade
La Courtine
Bourg-Lastic
Orcival
Romagnat
PUY-DE-DÔME
Olliergues
Cunlhat

Chamberet
Millevaches
Sornac
Merlines
St-Sauves-d'Auvergne
Champeix
Vic-le-Comte
Job
Ambert

Treignac
Bugeat
Meymac
Ussel
A89
Tauves
La Bourboule
Issoire
Sauxillanges
Marsac-en-Livradois

CORRÈZE
St-Angel
Bort-les-Orgues
Lanobre
Besse-et-St-Anastaise
Monts d'Auvergne
St-Germain-Lembron
Arlanc

Limousin
Seilhac
Corrèze
Egletons
Neuvic
Ydes
Condat
225
Marcenat
Allanche
224
Blesle
Vielle-Brioude
Brioude
HAUTE-LOIRE

Naves
Tulle
Eyrein
221
Saignes
Riom-ès-Montagnes
Neussargues-Moissac
Lavoûte-Chilhac
Allègre

Laguenne
Marcillac-la-Croisille
Mauriac
Salins
Langeac
St-Arcons-d'Allier
Vissac-Auteyrac
229

Ste-Fortunade
La Roche-Canillac
219
226
Pleaux
CANTAL
Murat
Valuéjols
Planèze
St-Flour
Paulhac-en-Margeride
Venteuges
Saugues

Meyssac
Mercœur
Argentat
St-Martin-Valmeroux
Auvergne
Thiézac
Vic-sur-Cère
Neuvéglise
Albert-Ste-Marie

Vayrac
St-Cernin
Jussac
Naucelles
Pierrefort
Chaudes-Aigues

Biars-sur-Cère
241
Sousceyrac
Aurillac
Arpajon-sur-Cère
Raulhac
St-Chély-d'Apcher
LOZÈRE

Miers
LOT
St-Céré
Molières
Châtaigneraie
AVEYRON

©Bartholomew Ltd, 2003

Map 11

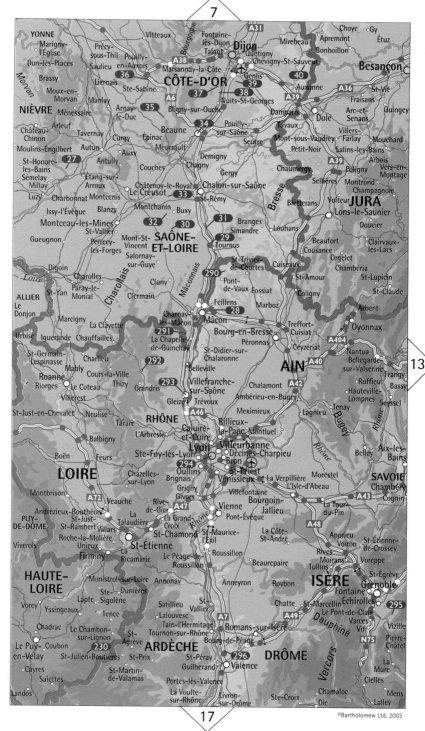

©Bartholomew Ltd, 2003

Map 12

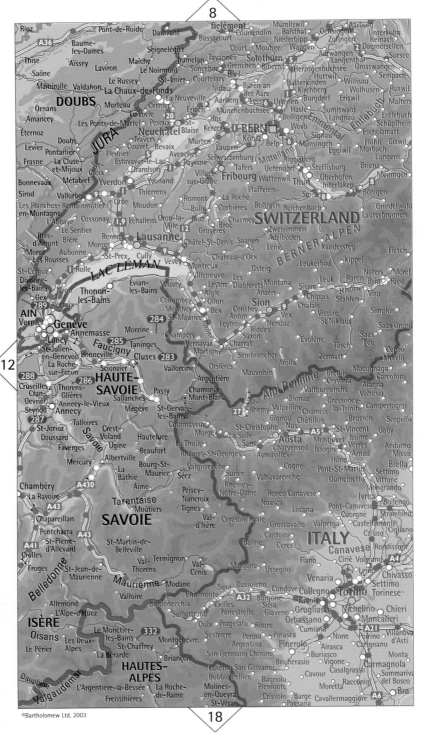

©Bartholomew Ltd, 2003

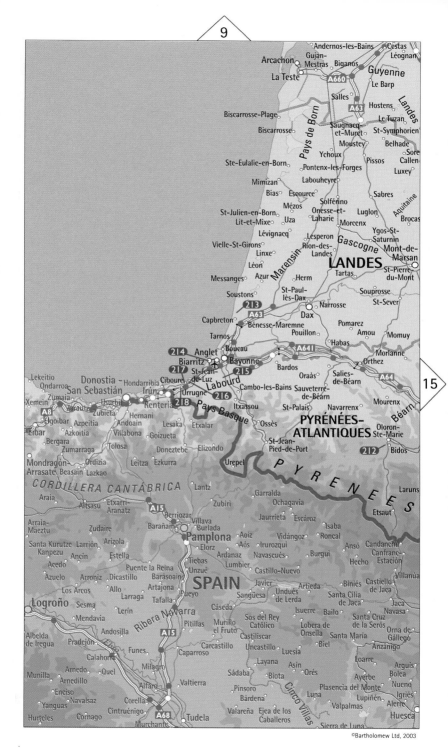

©Bartholomew Ltd, 2003

Map 14

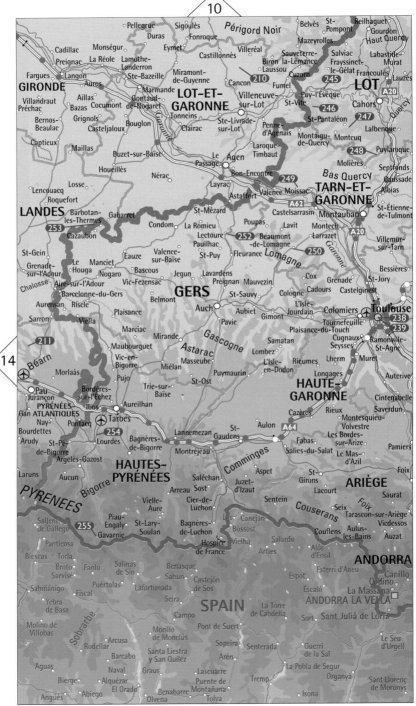

Map 15

©Bartholomew Ltd, 2003

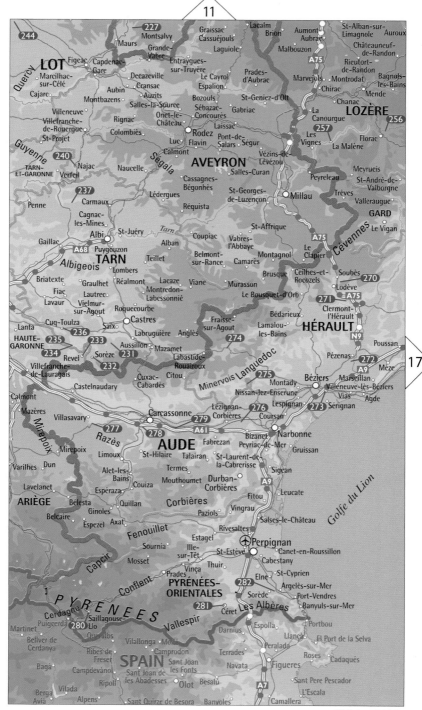

©Bartholomew Ltd, 2003

Map 16

©Bartholomew Ltd, 2003

Map 17

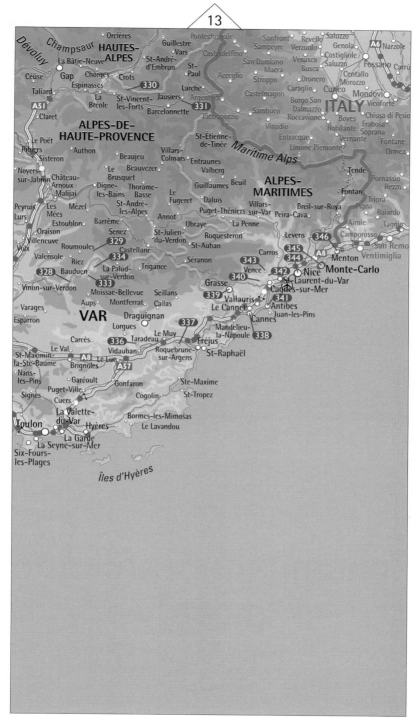

Map 18

©Bartholomew Ltd, 2003

photography by Michael Busselle

champagne-ardenne
picardy
the north

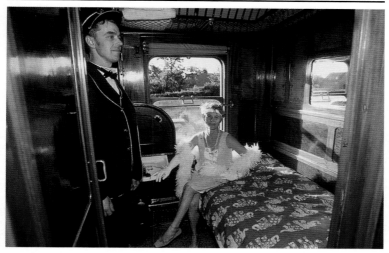

Station Bac Saint-Maur

La Gare des Années Folies, 77 rue de la Gare, 62840 Sailly sur la Lys, Pas-de-Calais

Vincent, Chef de Gare, and his young crew of conductors man the bistro: an imaginatively converted, 1921 red-bricked railway station filled with vintage suitcases and trunks spewing old tourist brochures. There are miniature tin trains, a wind-up wooden telephone, hand-held lanterns, sepia etchings on the walls, old station wall clocks and a paraphernalia of reminders of the golden era of train travel. You dine in the station, then retire to your rooms in the carriage of an authentic 'PLM' that travelled the Paris, Lyon, Mediterranean lines. Let Valérie know in advance and you will be served in the elegant restaurant compartment with its warm mahogany walls inlaid with mother-of-pearl. Retire to your first-class *couchettes* (authentic, so narrow) to dreams of the Orient Express. As if on cue, a real train passes by every now and again adding its clanking to the authenticity. A full playground just outside, a children's menu and antique highchairs make this a super place for kids. Groups can take a tour along the Lys river aboard a barge; the lock is 400m from the station.

rooms	6 Pullman compartments each with 2 singles, all sharing 2 showers.
price	€30–€60.
meals	Breakfast €6.50. Lunch & dinner in train station €8.50–€24; served on board €28–€70. Children's meals €6.50.
closed	2-16 January.
directions	From A25 exit 9 for Erquinghem to Sailly. At Bac St Maur, 2nd left immediately after Havet factory.

Vincent & Valérie Laruelle

tel	+33 (0)3 21 02 68 20
fax	+33 (0)3 21 02 74 37
e-mail	chefdegare@wanadoo.fr
web	www.stationbacsaintmaur.com

map 2   entry 1

Auberge d'Inxent

La Vallée de la Course, 62170 Inxent, Pas-de-Calais

And, the lucky winner is... believe it or not, some people who collect bottle caps do win prizes. As sommelier in a large restaurant in Lille, Jean-Marc won the Perrier contest on the luck of a draw. Off he tripped with his young wife and two children to a most emerald green valley and claimed a whitewashed, geranium-boxed dream of an 18th-century country inn. Order a trout on their vine-covered terrace and back comes a live one in a bucket from their superb trout farm across the road on the banks of the river Course. Needless to say Jean-Marc's exceptional, reasonably priced wine list and creative use of local produce should lead to a prolonged stay, and the nearby ramparts of Montreuil Sur Mer are well worth a visit. Inside all is wonky wooden beams, low ceilings, a battery of copper pans behind the original zinc countertop, red-checked tablecloths and the warmth and cosiness of a country kitchen with burning fireplaces on chilly days. The beamed-ceiling bedrooms have been recently furnished with cherry wood copies of antiques and the walls papered to look ragged. Some of the best people win the best prizes.

rooms	5: 3 doubles, 2 twins (1 with terrace).
price	€ 62–€ 70.
meals	Breakfast € 8. Lunch & dinner € 14.50–€ 37. Restaurant closed Tuesdays & Wednesdays out of season.
closed	20 December–20 January; 1 week in July.
directions	From Montreuil sur Mer N1 towards Boulogne for approx. 4km; right on D127 to Inxent, Vallée de la Course.

Laurence & Jean-Marc Six

tel	+33 (0)3 21 90 71 19
fax	+33 (0)3 21 86 31 67
e-mail	auberge.inxent@wanadoo.fr

Les Trois Fontaines

16 rue d'Abbeville, 62140 Marconne Hesdin, Pas-de-Calais

Here is a long, low, plain Scandinavian style building dressed up to look like a typical French inn – and succeeding. With its half-length nets and flower boxes, it fits into the little market town (wonderful market on Thursday mornings) as if it had always been there and the pavement tables are well used by locals. So, of course, is the restaurant. Arnaud Descamps is friendly and anxious to please. He took over in 1999 and is concentrating on the quality of the food he serves in his panelled, chequer-floored dining room: menus change every day and there's a special one for children. Bedrooms are in separate buildings overlooking the fine garden: traditional French style with quiet wallpapers and candlewick bedcovers. In the new wing, twin rooms are very comfortable, simply and decently clad with good quality pine, dark blue carpet, good lighting and pristine bed linen. Each room has its own table and chairs for summer breakfasts facing the garden. It is, indeed, a very typical small French hotel; it's quiet, good value and well placed for cross-Channel visitors and the great beaches of Le Touquet and Berck.

rooms	16 doubles.
price	€ 47–€ 67.
meals	Breakfast € 7. Lunch & dinner € 15–€ 29. Restaurant closed 20-31 December.
closed	Rarely.
directions	From Calais for Arras. After Montreuil, N39 for Hesdin. Follow signs to Marconne centre. Hotel opposite the Mairie.

Arnaud Descamps

tel	+33 (0)3 21 86 81 65
fax	+33 (0)3 21 86 33 34
e-mail	hotel.3fontaines@wanadoo.fr
web	www.hotel-les3fontaines.com

map 1   entry 3

Hôtel Jean de Bruges

18 place de l'Eglise, 80135 St Riquier, Somme

Starting from scratch can be a blessing. Being bang next to a flamboyantly Gothic 15th-century abbey can be another. Both these and a popular classical music festival in July led Bernadette Stubbe and her husband to take a deep breath and redesign a magnificent white-stone 17th-century mansion on the main square. An astute architect brought in light from above to diffuse a soft glow on yellow Lloyd Loom chairs and white linen curtains. A cluster of decanters sparkles on a perfect honey-coloured country-style table top. Here is a minimum of decoration but each piece exquisite, like the tall glass-door bookcase in the breakfast room. Continuing the monastic theme into the bedrooms it becomes simple luxury with textured wallpaper and exposed creamy stone, white piqué bedspreads, beige in the thick muslin drapes and carpeting. A desk and an antique armoire complete the picture. Soft robes and white tiled bathrooms follow suit. Snacks and drinks are served on the terrace overlooking the square with rural museum and town hall. Five minutes off the Calais autoroute and you are back in the centre of medieval France.

rooms	11: 9 doubles, 2 suites.
price	€99–€195.
meals	Breakfast €13. Sandwiches & snacks on terrace available, except Sunday nights.
closed	January.
directions	From Calais A16 towards Paris, exit 22 St Riquier, then 8km on D925. On main square next to Cathedral in left hand corner.

	Bernadette Stubbe
tel	+33 (0)3 22 28 30 30
fax	+33 (0)3 22 28 00 69
e-mail	jeandebruges@wanadoo.fr
web	www.hotel-jean-de-bruges.com

Auberge du Bon Fermier

64 rue de Famars, 59300 Valenciennes, Nord

Forget your high heels, for the cobblestones in the flowered courtyard penetrate into the bar, reception and restaurant of this 16th-century auberge. It is a maze of passageways, burnished beams and tiny staircases. A bright copper-bellied *lavabo* greets you at the top of the stairs leading to the rooms. Looking down from a glassed-in corridor, you can almost hear the clatter of hooves arriving in the courtyard, now a quiet terrace for afternoon tea and snacks. The rooms are delightful, one with tapestried curtains and walls, another with red bricks and wooden struts, all with baths and bathrobes. There are also two larger, lighter ground-floor rooms with post-modern lamps and tables. Downstairs a suit of armour guards a wooden reception dais and comes to life in the evenings when the main restaurant is lit only by candles. The passengers jostling between Paris and Brussels were probably delighted to have been delayed in this cosy staging inn. Monsieur Beine, who also runs the wine shop up the street, takes enormous trouble to create new menus with his chef.

rooms	16: 14 doubles, 2 singles.
price	€ 100–€ 126. Singles € 81–€ 107.
meals	Breakfast € 9. Lunch & dinner € 23–€ 47.
closed	Rarely.
directions	From Cambrai A2 for Brussels, exit Valenciennes centre. Do not get off autoroute before. Continue for Valenciennes centre. Signed.

	M Beine
tel	+33 (0)3 27 46 68 25
fax	+33 (0)3 27 33 75 01
e-mail	beinethierry@hotmail.com
web	www.home-gastronomie.com

map 2   entry 5

La Tour du Roy

Lieu dit La Tour du Roy, 02140 Vervins, Aisne

Madame, with references from all over the world, wears the chef's hat here: food is centre-stage, and resoundingly applauded. Monsieur, a delightful character, is wedded to his hotel, which he bought roofless 31 years ago and has renovated beautifully. You arrive in the attractive courtyard with its flowerbeds and stone fountain. The building has nooks, crannies and corners, swathes of original brickwork and restored stone details. The dining room is, of course, seriously inviting, dressed in wood and marble, pretty antiques and unusual windows and alcoves. The turrets, all that remain of the 11th-century town fortifications where the original building stood, have amazing semi-circular bedrooms, stained-glass windows, hand-painted basins, tapestries. Beds are old carved pieces and every room contains a framed menu from a different restaurant – the corridors are lined with framed menus, too! A place to spoil yourself with days of luxurious living and eating. They can arrange canal trips and champagne tastings, château visits and steam-train journeys.

rooms	19 + 3: 12 doubles in main building, 2 in tower, 5 in separate building. 3 apartments for 4 in ramparts.
price	Doubles & apartments €92–€122. Suites €183–€229.
meals	Breakfast €13. Picnic €15. Lunch & dinner €35–€85. Restaurant closed Monday & Tuesday noon.
closed	Rarely.
directions	A26 exit 13 to Vervins on N2. Follow Centre Ville signs. Hotel directly on right.

	M & Mme Desvignes
tel	+33 (0)3 23 98 00 11
fax	+33 (0)3 23 98 00 72
e-mail	latourduroy@wanadoo.fr
web	www.latourduroy.com

Auberge A La Bonne Idée

3 rue des Meuniers, 60350 St Jean aux Bois, Oise

Deep in the forest, the walled village is worth a visit and the Bonne Idée is where sophisticates from Paris and Brussels come to escape the excitement, knowing they will find a genuine welcome, country peace and superb food. The inn, once a woodcutters' dive, still has masses of old timber and tiling in what could be called romantic-rustic style. Start with a drink by the fire in the bar, move to an elegant table in the dining room where bread warms by the great fireplace, and enjoy a fine meal. A tour of the pretty garden will tell you that vegetables and poultry are home-grown, though the deer and wild sow are purely decorative reminders of the house's hunting-lodge past. Here are the summer terrace and space for children to play. Bedrooms, four in the main house, the rest in the converted stables, are being renovated by the new owners in a bright, stylish contemporary fashion, nicely adapted to the fabulous hulk of the building. Some rooms and apartments have terraces. Ideal for walking, cycling, riding and relaxing; Compiègne and the great castle of Pierrefonds are very close.

rooms	20 + 3: 20 doubles. 3 apartments for 2-4.
price	€69–€75. Apartments €80–€150.
meals	Continental breakfast €8.50. Lunch €30–€65. Dinner €45–€65. Restaurant closed Sun evenings except April-Dec & Mon in winter.
closed	15 January–15 February.
directions	A1 exit 9 for Verberie & Compiègne. Through Verberie, left on D332 for Compiègne for 5km, then right on D85 for St Jean aux Bois.

Yves Giustiniani
tel	+33 (0)3 44 42 84 09
fax	+33 (0)3 44 42 80 45
e-mail	a-la-bonne-idee.auberge@wanadoo.fr
web	www.a-la-bonne-idee.fr

map 6   entry 7

Château d'Ermenonville

Rue René Girardin, 60950 Ermenonville, Oise

Walking up to this pure French château you can almost feel the history of the princes who have lived, visited, died here – it has also belonged to Signor Bugatti and the Hare Krishna movement. No wonder Rousseau came to think great thoughts in the 'baroque' garden in the park opposite – his tomb still attracts literati. The blond building stands like a sculpture in the velvet of fine lawns, tall trees and water; the peace of the place is tangible. There's splendour in the iron-balustraded stone staircase, the vast drawing room's double aspect onto informal parkland and symmetrical courtyard and the dining room with its fine white linen and the food is splendid. Bedrooms have style too. Be extravagant and take a suite for the full château experience: round, panelled tower bedroom, pure French salon, marble fireplace, views over moat and park. The smaller rooms are good value, especially on the second floor where lower ceilings make them cosy; on the deep wooden window seat over the lake you could be in the bows of a boat. Genuine old elegance on a human scale.

rooms	49: 38 twins/doubles, 11 suites for 2-3.
price	€75–€155. Suites €165–€270.
meals	Breakfast €13. Lunch & dinner €33–€79.
closed	Rarely.
directions	From north A1 exit 8 for Chantilly & Senlis. N330 for Ermenonville. Left into village, then right. Hotel on left after bridge. Ring at gate.

	Christophe Claireau
tel	+33 (0)3 44 54 00 26
fax	+33 (0)3 44 54 01 00
e-mail	ermenonville@leshotelsparticuliers.com
web	www.chateau-ermenonville.com

Château de Reilly

60240 Reilly, Oise

The château and the grounds are all yours, day and night. Hilary and David love their old family house even though they don't live in it: they are raising young children and have renovated rooms over the millhouse which is now a French country 'pub' and restaurant, with Toby jugs and a pianist on Saturdays. Breakfast is there or in your room. David, who's French, will show you around the estate; he is passionate about his deer, ducks and trees. Hilary, who's English, has unleashed her decorating flair on the big château bedrooms using just enough fabric, furniture, tassels and prints, then leaving the space to reveal itself. The vast Victor Hugo suite is the most château-esque with its majestic double-draped windows. The Mill House is a popular venue for weddings and banquets, and menus can be themed. Modern comfort in well-respected old surroundings, lots of space, heart-stoppingly peaceful views, a great sloping lawn that beckons, the listed medieval village across the valley calling out to be painted. *No night staff and no phones in the rooms.*

rooms	4: 3 doubles, 1 suite for 3-4.
price	€ 60–€ 74. Suite € 95 for 3, € 110 for 4.
meals	Lunch € 10–€ 30. Dinner à la carte from € 26.
closed	Christmas & New Year.
directions	A16 exit Beauvais Nord. In Beauvais towards Mantes la Jolie for approx. 30km. After Chaumont en Vexin, right on D153 to Reilly. Château entrance on right entering village.

Hilary & David Gauthier

tel	+33 (0)3 44 49 03 05
fax	+33 (0)3 44 49 23 39
e-mail	reilly@terre-net.fr
web	www.chateaudereilly.fr

map 6   entry 9

Le Clos Raymi

3 rue Joseph de Venoge, 51200 Epernay, Marne

What more seductive combination than champagne and culture? Easy to get to from both Reims Cathedral and the champagne vineyards, this enticing hotel has the added attraction of Madame Woda herself. Ever attentive to the comfort of her guests, she purrs with pride in her renovation of the Chandon (the other half of Moët) family house. The intricate, pale blue mosaic covering the entrance hall and the hardwood staircase were left alone but her artistic touch is everywhere: shades of cream, beige and extra pale grey, good beds dressed in vintage linens; attractive bathrooms with scented lotions; fresh flowers in every room; etchings and paintings from the 1930s; books of poetry on a shelf. Take a peek at the downstairs bathroom with its Cubist paintings and an interesting replacement for the usual sink. A champagne apéritif can be organised in a splendid little sitting room with a fireplace and, if weather permits, the buffet breakfast can be taken in the parasoled garden behind the house. Madame Woda will help organise champagne tastings and has her favourite people to recommend. Gracious living here.

rooms	7 doubles.
price	€ 100–€ 155.
meals	Breakfast € 14.
	Lunch & dinner available locally.
closed	Rarely.
directions	From Paris A4 exit Château Thierry; N3 to Epernay.

Madame Woda

tel	+33 (0)3 26 51 00 58
fax	+33 (0)3 26 51 18 98
e-mail	closraymi@wanadoo.fr
web	www.closraymi-hotel.com

Château d'Etoges
4 rue Richebourg, 51270 Etoges, Marne

Louis XIV himself was impressed by the beauty of the garden, fountains and ponds at Etoges, used as a stopover by various kings of France on journeys east. This moated château was built early in the 17th century and restored as a hotel in 1991 by the family who has lived here for over a century. If you enjoy waking up in beautiful sheets, this is for you. Rooms are all different and two have intriguing little mezzanine bedrooms over the bathroom – presumably originally for servants, now great fun for children. Many rooms have four-posters; all are furnished with antiques and are extremely French. If you fancy breakfast in bed, it will appear on a lace-covered table, with bread, croissants and a bowl of fruit. If you prefer to wander downstairs, choose from a buffet and sit on the terrace if it's warm. This could be a luxurious base for champagne tastings or simply a very pleasant break, convenient if you're heading for eastern France, like Louis XIV or, more likely, meandering south through Reims. It's easy country for cycling or you can try punting if you feel this is more in tune with the surroundings.

rooms	20: 17 twins/doubles, 3 suites.
price	€80–€190. Suites €190.
meals	Breakfast €12. Lunch & dinner €30–€60. Children's meals €12.
closed	25 January-12 February.
directions	From Paris A4 exit at Ferté sous Jouarre, follow signs for Chalons en Champagne. In centre of Etoges.

	Madame Filliette-Neuville
tel	+33 (0)3 26 59 30 08
fax	+33 (0)3 26 59 35 57
e-mail	contact@etoges.com
web	www.etoges.com

map 6   entry 11

Copyright Bertrand Limbour

Le Champ des Oiseaux

20 rue Linard-Gonthier, 10000 Troyes, Aube

Only the Museum of Modern Art stands between the cathedral and this amazingly pure group of 15th-century houses in the centre of lovely, unsung old Troyes. One is dazzled by the astonishing timbers, beams and rafters, inside and out, seduced by the simplicity of the beautifully jointed stone paving, the wooden floors, the softly luminous natural materials: the owners had their brilliant restoration done by craftsmen who knew the ancestral methods and made it look 'as good as new'… in 1460. Corridors twist around the creeper-climbed courtyard and the little internal garden, staircases change their minds, the place is alive with its centuries. Each bedroom has a personality, some soberly sandy and brown, others frivolously floral; they vary in size and status but all are warmly discreet in their luxury and good furniture. And, of course, bathrooms are perfect modern boudoirs. The unexpected salon, a long, white barrel vault of ancient stones, the original stonemason's craft lovingly revealed, was once a cellar. The Boisseau family can be justifiably proud of their contribution to medieval Troyes.

rooms	12: 9 doubles, 3 twins.
price	€90–€145.
meals	Breakfast €15.
	Great restaurants nearby.
closed	Rarely.
directions	In centre of Troyes, very close to the cathedral.

	Madame Boisseau
tel	+33 (0)3 25 80 58 50
fax	+33 (0)3 25 80 98 34
e-mail	message@champdesoiseaux.com
web	www.champdesoiseaux.com

La Maison de Rhodes

20 rue Linard–Gonthier, 10000 Troyes, Aube

An exceptional find, a 16th-century timber-framed mansion that once belonged to the Templars. Monsieur Thierry's breathtaking renovation has brought a clean contemporary style to ancient bricks and mortar. Highlights include an interior courtyard of cobble and grass and heavy wooden doors under the coachman's porch that give onto the street. The house sits plumb in the old quarter of Troyes, on the doorstep of the cathedral. Bedrooms are bona fide jaw-droppers – expect the best in minimalist luxury. Huge beds are dressed in white linen, ancient beams straddle the ceilings. Walls are either exposed rough stone, or smooth limestone, often a clever mix of both. Bathrooms, too, are outstanding; most are enormous and have terracotta floors, big bath tubs, fluffy robes. Views are to the cathedral spires, the courtyard or the formal gardens of the Museum of Modern Art, directly opposite. A perfect blend of old and new, an exhilarating architectural landscape. Troyes is full of wonders, though the bibulous may be tempted to venture beyond the city walls. The region is quite well-known for its local tipple – Champagne.

rooms	11: 5 doubles, 2 triples, 4 suites.
price	€95–€179.
meals	Breakfast €15.
	Great restaurants nearby.
closed	Rarely.
directions	In centre of Troyes, at the foot of the cathedral.

Thierry Carcassin

tel	+33 (0)3 25 43 11 11
fax	+33 (0)3 25 43 10 43
e-mail	message@maisonderhodes.com
web	www.maisonderhodes.com

map 7   entry 13

photography by Michael Busselle

alsace
lorraine

Le Mas & La Lorraine

Place de la Gare, 54260 Longuyon, Meurthe-et-Moselle

A proud building, solidly French, with flowers cascading from every window. The hotel is a nostalgic reminder of a lost era – the great days of steam trains. It stands across the square from the station and was built in 1925 to cater for the travellers the railway brought; the Italian Express stopped here. These days it is more of a restaurant-with-rooms, the emphasis clearly on the ambrosial food. Monsieur Gérard took over from his parents 32 years ago, yet he still cooks with unwavering exuberance and flair; his *grandes soirées dégustation* are not to be missed. Course after course flies at you: coquilles Sainte Jacques, foie gras, fillet de veau, gratin d'ananas à la crème de coco. Meals are taken in a big rustic restaurant, a room predisposed to conviviality; an open fire roars in winter. Every now and then live music nights are held and you dine to the accompaniment of classical guitar or jazz piano. Downstairs, red velvet armchairs and huge bay windows in the airy sitting room; upstairs, simply furnished bedrooms that are clean, functional and reasonably priced. Belgium and Luxembourg are within easy reach.

rooms	14 doubles.
price	€47–€57.
meals	Breakfast €7.
	Lunch & dinner €19–€60.
closed	January.
directions	From A4, exit 30 onto N3 then N18 to Longuyon. Hotel opposite railway station (yellow & blue).

	Gérard Tisserant
tel	+33 (0)3 82 26 50 07
fax	+33 (0)3 82 39 26 09
e-mail	mas.lorraine@wanadoo.fr
web	www.lorraineetmas.com

map 7   entry 14

L'Horizon

50 route du Crève-Cœur, 57100 Thionville, Moselle

The house is only 50 years old but its arcading anchors it and Virginia has crept all over it, clothing its façade in lively warm character. Here is comfortable living in graceful surroundings, as in an elegant private house. A huge terrace envelops the ground floor – from here and from the smart restaurant you have plunging views over Thionville with an astounding, glittering cityscape at night. Some first-floor rooms give onto a balcony over the same view. Despite the surprising hall with its marbled flooring and glamorous tented ceiling, the bedrooms are classic French chic (though carpets may be a little worn here and there and some rooms are smaller than others) and bathrooms border on the luxurious. But above all, you will warm to your utterly charming hosts. Monsieur Speck is passionate about Second World War history: the Maginot Line is all around, Thionville is on the Liberty Road that is marked every kilometre from Cherbourg in Normandy to Bastogne in Lorraine. He is fascinating on the subject.

rooms	10 doubles.
price	€ 75–€ 145.
meals	Breakfast € 11. Lunch & dinner € 36–€ 52. Restaurant closed Saturdays & Monday noon.
closed	January–February.
directions	From A31 exit 40 to Thionville. Follow signs for Bel Air Hospital north of town. At hospital bear left up hill leaving town. 400m on left.

	Jean-Pascal & Anne-Marie Speck
tel	+33 (0)3 82 88 53 65
fax	+33 (0)3 82 34 55 84
e-mail	hotel@lhorizon.fr
web	www.lhorizon.fr

Château d'Alteville

Tarquimpol, 57260 Dieuze, Moselle

A house with more than a whiff of history. The château was built for one of Napoleon's generals, and the two paintings that hang in the Louis XVI salon were gifts from the Emperor. Monsieur's family has farmed here for five generations; he now welcomes guests with kindness and much attention. Bedrooms are solidly traditional with carved armoires, Voltaire armchairs and draped bedheads; parkland views float in through the windows. Bathrooms are functional but adequate. Downstairs is more stylish: a library/billiard room, a multi-fenestrated sitting room and a dining room where splendid dinners are eaten by candlelight in the company of your lively, intelligent hosts. Bigger parties are entertained in the trophy-lined *salle de chasse*. Recline on the sound-proofed terrace at the back and gaze on the château-esque grounds, or pull on your hiking boots and follow your nose though woodland, circumnavigating the odd lake. Madame is a good cook and fills the place with flowers. *Gîte space for two.*

rooms	6 doubles.
price	€97. Singles €61.
meals	Breakfast €7. Hosted dinner €31–€38, book ahead; wine €10.
closed	15 October–15 April.
directions	From Nancy N74 for Sarreguemines & Château Salins. At Burthecourt crossroads D38 to Dieuze; D999 south 5km; left on D199F; right D199G to château.

Livier & Marie Barthélémy

tel	+33 (0)3 87 86 92 40
fax	+33 (0)3 87 86 02 05
e-mail	chateau.alteville@caramail.com

map 8   entry 16

Auberge de la Vigotte

1 La Vigotte, 88340 Girmont Val d'Ajol, Vosges

Michel and Jocelyne are gradually doing up this 18th-century farmhouse with 20 rooms. Michel is full of decorating ideas and Jocelyne teaches English in a local school. Rooms have carved or painted beds and all look out onto fantastic views of the mountains. With tennis, volleyball and a children's play area, this is a perfect place for families. You can also ride, or swim in a lake in the grounds, while in the winter you can go cross-country skiing. Meals are a mix of very traditional and more contemporary: ranging from pigs' trotters to tomatoes with cardamom. An hour from Mulhouse, 700m up, on the gentle slopes of the Vosges, the auberge is set in densely wooded countryside: total peace and quiet. In winter you will find a roaring fire and a warm welcome, in the summer you can round off your day with dinner out on the terrace. Although somewhat off the beaten track for English holidaymakers, this would make a good stopover, and could also be a great choice for an out-of-doors holiday.

rooms	20: 14 doubles, 6 family rooms.
price	€51–€100. Half-board €52–€72 p.p. for stays of 3 nights or more.
meals	Breakfast €6. Lunch & dinner €22. Children's meals €8. Restaurant closed Tuesdays & Wednesdays.
closed	12 November–mid-December.
directions	From Remiremont D23 then D57. Follow white signs to auberge.

	Michel & Jocelyne **Bouguerne–Arnould**
tel	+33 (0)3 29 61 06 32
fax	+33 (0)3 29 61 07 88
e-mail	courrier@lavigotte.com
web	www.lavigotte.com

Hostellerie Saint Barnabé

53 rue de Murbach, 68530 Murbach Buhl, Haut-Rhin

It feels good here. The young owners of this angular, 100-year-old, flower-decked hotel are spontaneously smiley, chatty and attentive. He is the chef – trained with France's best and chef at Château d'Isenbourg for some years, so food is important here, and good. She is the perfect adviser on what to do between the Vosges hills and the Alsace plain: there are typical Alsatian villages and wine-growers to visit, bike rides and good fishing places (they also have mini-golf on the spot). The ferny woods are full of paths and burbling brooks and there's skiing in the snow season. There are two sorts of guest rooms: in the main house they are big, decorated with care and individuality (the yellow and white room has an iron-frame canopied bed, the red and white one twin head cushions and super-soft quilts), with smashing bathrooms and the odd balcony; in the separate building behind, they are smaller and more old-fashioned (and cheaper!) but are gradually being renovated. Here, bedroom doors all have typically Alsatian hand-painted, floral decoration. A great place for nature lovers and gourmets.

rooms	27 twins/doubles.
price	€80–€190.
meals	Buffet breakfast €14. Picnic on request. Lunch & dinner €28–€58.
closed	Mid-January–February.
directions	From N83 (betwen Belfort & Colmar) D430 for Guebwiller & Lautenbach. D429 for Buhl then Murbach. Hotel on left.

Clémence & Eric Orban

tel	+33 (0)3 89 62 14 14
fax	+33 (0)3 89 62 14 15
e-mail	hostellerie.st.barnabe@wanadoo.fr
web	www.hostellerie-st-barnabe.com

map 8   entry 18

Relais des Marches de l'Est

24 rue de Molsheim, 67280 Oberhaslach, Bas-Rhin

Bénédicte and Sylvain wear two hats: sculptors and artists they are also welcoming hosts to their renovated farmhouse and restaurant. They originally intended only to provide a hiking stopover for walkers and riders on horseback in 1987; things just grew. Now there is a bistro dedicated to making *tartes flambées* (Alsatian pizza) with an oven they built themselves and two other dining rooms with large tables — one with a couple of armchairs — that feel more like sitting rooms in a home. Bénédicte has set out her palette of soft autumn colours for the bedrooms; browns, mossy greens, oranges and reds. A good choice of paintings and prints lights the walls and a fresco (Sylvain's, of course) decorates a room on the ground floor. More of his pieces are nicely placed in the passageways. The medium-sized to small bedrooms have good mattresses and look over the garden or street. Sylvain has a third hat: he can give you some hands-on courses in modelling, casting and stone-cutting. This is a homely, cosy place with gentle pleasant company.

rooms	8: 5 doubles, 3 singles.
price	€43–€55. Half-board, set menu, €50–€55 p.p.
meals	Breakfast €7–€9. Dinner €13–€25. Restaurant 50m.
closed	Rarely.
directions	From Strasbourg, A352 exit at Gresswiller to N420. D392 in Dinsheim for approx. 7km towards Schirmeck, then right onto D218 to Oberhaslach. On left on main street.

	Bénédicte Weber & Sylvain Chartier
tel	+33 (0)3 88 50 99 60
fax	+33 (0)3 88 48 74 88

Hôtel Cardinal de Rohan

17-19 rue du Maroquin, 67000 Strasbourg, Bas-Rhin

The atmosphere here is a rare combination: stylish and polite yet utterly friendly, plushly comfortable but not overwhelming. Standing in the historic centre, the solid building round its central courtyard in traditional 17th-century Strasbourg layout has been virtually rebuilt, with proper respect for its tall narrow neighbours, three rows of roof windows and tangles of geraniums down the façade. An 18th-century Gobelins tapestry graces the elegant sitting room; the breakfast room, pale and restful, feels like a country-house dining room: high-backed cane chairs, ivory cloths, antique chest of drawers. Top-floor rooms have pine-clad sloping ceilings and dormer windows; lower rooms are sober, masculine dark and pale blue or rich, warm ginger and cream or spring-fresh green. They come in 'rustic' or 'period' décor, have good velvet or thick contemporary fabrics, clean lines and rich French swag effects. There are gilt-framed mirrors, the occasional antique armoire and smart marble-and-tile bathrooms. Superb comfort, friendliness and attention to detail are the hallmarks here. *Staff will collect luggage from car until 8pm.*

rooms	36: 32 twins/doubles, 4 triples.
price	€ 63–€ 122. Triples € 118–€ 129. Child under 15 in parents' room free.
meals	Breakfast € 10. Dozens of restaurants within walking distance.
closed	Rarely.
directions	From ring road, exit Place de l'Etoile for Centre Ville & Cathedral to underground car park (Place Gutenberg).

	Rolf & Nicole van Maenen
tel	+33 (0)3 88 32 85 11
fax	+33 (0)3 88 75 65 37
e-mail	info@hotel-rohan.com
web	www.hotel-rohan.com

map 8   entry 20

Hôtel du Dragon
2 rue de l'Ecarlate, 67000 Strasbourg, Bas-Rhin

In old Strasbourg's hub, looking over river and cathedral, the Dragon is grandly, solidly 17th century on the outside, sleekly, refreshingly 20th century on the inside. Built as a private mansion – where Louis XIV stayed on his way to visit Marie-Antoinette in Austria – it became a hotel 10 years ago. The little courtyard received a classically pedimented porch and potted shrubs: a pretty place for an evening drink. Inside, they took a deeply contemporary approach and it is sober, infinitely stylish and extraordinarily restful. Variegated grey and white are the basics: grey curtains on white walls, superb grey pinstripe carpeting, an arrestive pattern of grey and white tiles in the bathrooms, blue and green bedcovers for a dash of colour. And some good abstract paintings and sculptures here and there, displayed to great advantage. Some have river views and others see the cathedral's lovely spire. After 20 years as a mountain guide, Monsieur Zimmer has returned to his native Strasbourg and intends to make the Dragon as welcoming as it is elegant. He is quiet and gentle and has a predilection for English-speaking guests.

rooms	30 + 2: 30 twins/doubles. 2 apartments for 3.
price	Twins/doubles € 79–€ 112. Apartments € 130–€ 145.
meals	Breakfast € 9.50. Many fine restaurants in town.
closed	Rarely.
directions	Across the river from Petite France, off Quai St Nicolas.

Jean Zimmer

tel	+33 (0)3 88 35 79 80
fax	+33 (0)3 88 25 78 95
e-mail	hotel@dragon.fr
web	www.dragon.fr

Hôtel Anthon

Obersteinbach, 67510 Lembach, Bas-Rhin

Smaller than mountains, grander than hills, the lushly wooded slopes are pure Vosges forest, the clear Steinbach snakes its way through pastures, red rocky outcrops emerge in forbidding contrast to such bucolic enchantment. This little hotel, in the same deep pinky-orange colour as the rocks, is in typical Vosges style. Inside, more warm wood, including a fine carved staircase, echoes the living forest. It is sweetly simple – not basic in any way, just pretty and uncluttered, with carved wardrobes and Vosges dining chairs, peachy-beige or muted turquoise-green paintwork and coir floors. Bedrooms are not big but, again, prettily done with gingham duvets, starched cloths on round tables, windows onto the quiet night. The first-floor breakfast room is delightful – immaculate white cloths and regional pottery – but the restaurant, definitely in a different class, is the heart of this place. In the big, embracing room with its refined table settings and service, delicious dishes await you – and Madame's huge collection of soup tureens is dazzling.

rooms	9: 5 doubles, 4 twins.
price	€ 58.
meals	Breakfast € 10. Lunch & dinner € 24–€ 45, gourmet dinner € 61. Restaurant closed Tuesdays & Wednesdays.
closed	January.
directions	From Haguenau D3 & D27 through Woerth to Lembach (25km); there, left to Niedersteinbach & Obersteinbach. In village centre.

	Danielle Flaig
tel	+33 (0)3 88 09 55 01
fax	+33 (0)3 88 09 50 52
e-mail	anthon2@wanadoo.fr
web	www.restaurant-anthon.fr

map 8   entry 22

photography by Michael Busselle

burgundy

Le Petit Manoir des Bruyères

5 allée de Charbuy aux Bruyères, 89240 Auxerre-Villefargeau, Yonne

A rococo place unlike anything you've ever seen. Behind the creeper-clad façade with only the Burgundian roof as a clue, is eye-boggling glamour: a vast beamed living room, an endless polished dining table, rows of tapestried chairs, many shiny ornaments. Upstairs, stagger out of the loo, once you've found the door in the *trompe l'œil* walls, to cupids, carvings, gildings, satyrs, velvet walls and clouds on the ceilings. There's a many-mirrored bathroom reflecting multiple magical images of you, marble pillars and gold-cushioned bath; a Louis XIV room with red/gold bathroom with gold/ivory taps; an antique wooden throne with bell-chime flush. Madame de Maintenon has a coronet canopy, a long thin *œil de bœuf* window and a shower that whooshes between basin and loo. The 'biscuit' is taken by the deeply, heavily pink suite with its carved fireplace, painted ceilings and corner columns – wild! But such are the enthusiasm of the owners, the peace of house and garden, the quality of comfort, food and wine, that we feel it's perfect for lovers of French extravaganza.

rooms	5: 2 doubles, 1 twin, 2 suites.
price	€ 103–€ 195.
meals	Hosted dinner at communal table € 40, book ahead.
closed	Rarely.
directions	From Auxerre D965 to Villefargeau; there, right on C3 to Bruyères.

Pierre & Monique Joullié

tel	+33 (0)3 86 41 32 82
fax	+33 (0)3 86 41 28 57
e-mail	jchambord@aol.com
web	www.petit-manoir-bruyeres.com

map 6   entry 23

Auberge des Vieux Moulins Banaux

18 route des Moulins Banaux, 89190 Villeneuve l'Archêveque, Yonne

Take a 16th-century mill straddling a vigorous stream, add a generous dose of young, international, energetic talent, stir vigorously... and place five minutes from a motorway. You have a recipe for success; these four completed the process in a year and a half, and the place is wonderful. They left catering careers in the UK for this little auberge in Burgundy: Nick, English and main chef, serves up great food: shrimp samosas with a salsa of tomatoes and coriander, filet of turbot on a bed of wild-mushroom risotto, vanilla panacotta with roasted rhubarb flan. Bernadette (German) and Sabine (Dutch) alternate between dining room and reception, and Guillaume (Franco-Dutch) pitches in everywhere. There is still carpeting on the corridor walls and, in the bedrooms, a 50s feel, but give them another year or so and the rooms will be as appealing as the food. Join a leisurely feast on the great dining terrace overlooking the large park and river, then try your hand at boules – or walk off lunch on the trail nearby. You are 15 minutes from the Chablis vineyards for wine tastings – the position is perfect.

rooms	15: 13 doubles, 2 triples.
price	€ 39–€ 48.
meals	Breakfast € 6.75.
	Lunch & dinner € 23–€ 26.
	Restaurant closed Monday noon.
closed	January.
directions	A5 exit 19 Villeneuve l'Archevêque. Signed.

Guillaume Hamel

tel	+33 (0)3 86 86 72 55
fax	+33 (0)3 86 86 78 94
e-mail	contact@bourgognehotels.fr
web	www.bourgognehotels.fr

La Beursaudière

5 & 7 rue Hyacinthe Gautherin, 89310 Nitry, Yonne

Monsieur Lenoble's attention to detail is staggering. Not content with creating a buzzing, cheerful restaurant he has lovingly transformed a priory and farm buildings – stables, dovecotes, stone structures on varied levels, wooden verandas topped with red-patterned burgundian roof tiles – into a very seductive hotel. Each bedoom has a trade for a theme: a typewriter and old books for the 'writer'; antique irons for the 'laundress'; horse and ox collars for the 'ploughman'; vine-decorated wooden panels and a corner bath with a wooden barrel façade for the 'wine-grower'. The walls have been lightly skimmed in plaster in natural shades of ochre, pigeon-egg grey or light yellow. Floors are terracotta or flagstone, stone walls are painted, rafters exposed and windows round or cottage square with curtains of vintage linens and lace. Beds are kingsize, mattresses are excellent and TVs are hidden in antique cabinets. Most bathrooms are open plan so as not to detract from the beams and volumes. There is even a sheltered sun lounge on the terrace only overlooked by sparrows. A nice place to sit and sample your chilled choice picked up in Chablis.

rooms	11: 5 twins, 6 doubles.
price	€ 65–€ 105.
meals	Breakfast € 10. Lunch & dinner € 17–€ 42.
closed	Rarely.
directions	A6 exit 21 Nitry. Hotel 500m on left towards Vermenton.

	M & Mme Lenoble
tel	+33 (0)3 86 33 69 70
fax	+33 (0)3 86 33 69 60
e-mail	auberge.beursaudiere@wanadoo.fr
web	www.beursaudiere.com

map 7 entry 25

Le Relais Fleuri/Le Coq Hardi

42 avenue du la Tuilerie, 58150 Pouilly sur Loire, Nièvre

Anyone who loves France and what it stands for will coq-a-doodle-do. This small hotel was built in the 30s to cater to the ever increasing motor trade – from Paris to the south of France. It experienced its heyday in the late 50s and 60s when the rich and famous would stop over for a night or two to wine and dine before heading down to St Tropez. Unfortunately this all ceased when these people became the 'jet set'. These hotels and restaurants are now seeing a revival; often near motorways yet set away from the speed lanes and traffic jams, they are a reminder of a more civilised era when the pace of life was slower and food and good living a priority. Meals are served on a lime-tree-covered terrace overlooking the Loire. Judging by the smiles of the customers staggering away at 4pm it is certainly worth staying here for the food alone. Some of the hotel's original rooms upstairs have terraces over the garden; the newly decorated rooms are pleasantly done in blue or yellow. Philippe has added a small new bistro where those who are just beginning their vacation and have not yet slowed down may be served a quicker meal.

rooms	11: 10 doubles, 1 suite.
price	€45–€78.
meals	Breakfast €9. Restaurant lunch & dinner €25–€55. Bistro meals €15.50. Restaurant closed Tuesdays & Wednesdays October–end April.
closed	Mid-December–mid-January.
directions	From A77, exit 25 and continue through Pouilly sur Loire. Hotel opposite Cave Cooperative.

	Philippe & Dominique Martin
tel	+33 (0)3 86 39 12 99
fax	+33 (0)3 86 39 14 15
e-mail	le-relais-fleuri-sarl@wanadoo.fr
web	www.lerelaisfleuri.fr

Château de Villette

58170 Poil, Nièvre

Coen and Catherine — he Dutch, she Belgian — fell in love with this little château a couple of years ago, did it up together, then had their wedding here. They've opened just three rooms to guests, so they can spoil you properly! And get to know you over dinner. (Though, if you prefer a romantic *dîner à deux*, they understand.) Deep in the Parc de Morvan, the chateâu was built in 1782 as a summer retreat. Bedrooms, charmingly decorated by Catherine, are large, light and airy, with warm colours and polished floors. Bathrooms are extravagant — new claw-foot baths carry exquisite antique taps — and views sail out of great shuttered windows to meadows and woodland beyond. Your five-course, candlelit dinner, cooked by the caretaker's wife (a talented chef) is served in the dining room, the vaulted 16th-century kitchen, or *en plein air* — you choose. The grounds are perfect for duck and pheasant shoots, or fly-fishing in the crystal clear waters. Families would love it here: there are ping-pong and bikes, a pool and a tennis court a little further away. Beaune and the vineyards lie temptingly close by. *Cash or cheque only.*

rooms	3: 2 doubles, 1 triple. Two rooms can be combined to make suite for 5.
price	€130–€180. Suite €300.
meals	Dinner €38, book ahead. Call ahead to choose menu.
closed	Rarely.
directions	From N6 exit Beaune for Autun. N81 for Moulins for 18km, right to Poil. Through village, 2nd left. Signed.

	Catherine & Coen Stork
tel	+33 (0)3 86 30 09 13
e-mail	catherinestork@wanadoo.fr
web	www.stork-chateau.com

map 12 entry 27

Hostellerie La Sarrasine

533 route de la Madeleine, 01750 Replonges, Saône et Loire

Although close to a main road, La Sarrasine is protected by a high wall, hedges and a wide expanse of well-loved garden with flowering bushes, shady trees, and containers of cascading geraniums. Monsieur Bevy's grandparents raised the famous Bresse chickens here on this typical timber-framed farm; perhaps the welcoming, cackling committee are their direct descendants. The present young owners, both graduates of hotel schools, decided to take over the restoration which had already begun under Monsieur Bevy's parents. Keeping close to the original architecture its seven rooms are on the ground floor, their smallish size balanced by access to the back garden and views of the countryside with doors opening onto terraces. There are puffy peach-coloured coverlets, tapestry headboards and huge comfy ottomans. The bathrooms are not big but perfectly adequate and come in a variety of tiled colours. On chilly days, start the evening by a warm fire and then dine in the restaurant on a choice of regional dishes: *escargots de Bourgogne*, Charolais beef – or Bresse chicken, of course.

rooms	7 twins/doubles.
price	€63–€150.
meals	Breakfast €12. Dinner €18–€45. Restaurant closed Wednesdays; Tuesdays mid-October–mid-April.
closed	7 November–20 December; 9 January–mid February.
directions	From Paris, A40 for Geneva exit 2 at Feillens. From Marseille, A6 exit Macon Sud for Bourg en Bresse on N79 for 3km; signed.

	Monsieur Bevy
tel	+33 (0)3 85 31 02 41
fax	+33 (0)3 85 31 11 74
e-mail	hotel.sarras@free.fr
web	www.sarrasine.com

Château de Messey
71700 Ozenay, Saône-et-Loire

A 13th-century wine-growing château with beautiful gardens, tours of the cellars and the Route des Vins. Monsieur is the cellar master, Madame manages the château with charming efficiency. Aperitifs in the cellar are part of the evening ritual and Monsieur may surprise you with an enormous bottle of cognac after a dinner of regional dishes made with home-grown vegetables. The excellent guest rooms are in the beautifully rustic old vine workers' cottages built with exposed stone in a U-shape around a central grass courtyard a-bloom with weeping willow, wall-creeping flowering plants and shrubs. The cottages are right by the river which has formed a lake area on its way through and makes a lovely place to sit out on the grass under the parasols. The others – in a more period-style (and more expensive) – in the château are graced with high ceilings and lofty views over the vines. A superior elegance reigns in the salon doubly exposed over the vineyards in the back and peonies and rose bushes in front. A most welcoming if somewhat busy place. *Gîte space for 20.*

rooms	6: 2 doubles, 1 triple in cottages, 3 doubles in château.
price	€77–€130.
meals	Hosted dinner €20.
closed	January.
directions	From A6 exit to Tournus; in centre right on D14. Château on left of D14 between Ozenay & Martailly, 9km from Tournus.

	Marie-Laurence Fachon
tel	+33 (0)3 85 51 16 11
fax	+33 (0)3 85 32 57 30
e-mail	chateau@demessey.com
web	www.demessey.com

map 12　entry 29

Auberge du Cheval Blanc

71390 St Boil, Saône-et-Loire

A tonic if you are tired of the standardisation of all things. Everything about it – from the formal furniture, the striped wallpaper, the parquet floors, the great curtains gathered at the waist, to the gravelled courtyard with trumpet vines, white wrought-iron garden furniture, shuttered and dormer windows – is what the French do with such aplomb. Yet, having said all that, Jany and Martine make the place. He is a well-built Sancerrois, a fitting descendant of generations of bons viveurs and creator of some spectacular dishes in the restaurant – across the road from the hotel. Martine's generosity and kindness add something very special to the hotel. It is a trifle functional upstairs, perhaps, as is often the case, but very much a *maison de maître* and up the most lovely wooden staircase. On the top floor the beams are exposed, and varnished. The two front rooms up there have charming *oeil de boeuf* windows. Bathrooms are all fine, with nothing outstanding to report. Dine under the lime trees in summer and appreciate the survival of such places, and such people.

rooms	10: 6 doubles, 4 twins.
price	€ 65-€ 88.
meals	Breakfast € 10. Lunch à la carte. Dinner menus € 25-€ 31. Restaurant closed Wednesdays.
closed	10 February-10 March.
directions	A6 exit Chalon sur Saône Sud on D80 for Le Creusot; D981 Cluny for 10km to St Boil. On right in village.

M & Mme Jany Cantin

tel	+33 (0)3 85 44 03 16
fax	+33 (0)3 85 44 07 25
e-mail	contact@auberge-cheval-blanc.net
web	www.auberge-cheval-blanc.net

Le Clos des Tourelles
Château de la Tour, 71240 Sennecey le Grand, Saône-et-Loire

Stuart owns a restaurant so he knows food and wine; he has a big family so he needs space; he loves France so he found a jewel of a château that feels like a home and came away with a vineyard on the side. He is a happy man. And so will you be after a stay at the Clos. There is space to run around and a guard tower (games room and TV for children) and dungeon to explore, an eye-catching collection of outbuildings from the 13th and 15th centuries, the trees, lawns and a large circular driveway to pull it all together. Indoors Nikki's light and clever hand can be felt; soft colours, good fabrics, comfy sofas, antiques and not a whiff of pretension. Big bedrooms are on the first floor, smaller on the top: yellow and blue for Natacha; a four-poster with airy veils for Victoria; crisp white bedspreads on twin beds for Alexandra; balconies for gazing over the gardens, or fireplaces in the corners. Breakfast is in the conservatory and dinner is on the terrace when it's warm. The setting is perfect, the food excellent, the welcome warm. The Redcliffes have only just arrived but they have settled in nicely; you will too.

rooms	9 + 1: 8 doubles, 1 triple. 1 apartment for 4.
price	€80–€150. Apartment €215.
meals	Breakfast €8. Lunch & dinner menus from €20–€30. Dinner with wine €30.
closed	15 November–15 April.
directions	A6 exit Chalon Sud or Tournus. Sennecey le Grand on N6 15km from Chalon sur Saône & 8km from Tournus.

Stuart & Nikki Redcliffe

tel	+33 (0)3 85 44 83 95
fax	+33 (0)3 85 44 90 18
e-mail	info@closdestourelles.com
web	www.closdestourelles.com

map 12   entry 31

L'Orangerie
Vingelles, 71390 Moroges, Saône-et-Loire

Ring the bell on the gate, then wander up through neat gardens. They are alive with colour. Light spills into the sitting room entrance through vine-clad arched windows, with cream walls and Indian rugs adding to the simple elegance of this gracious *maison de maître*. Antiques and travel are David's passion, his gentle Irish brogue enchanting; it's no surprise to hear he interviews European royalty for a 'prestigious' magazine. The grand staircase in the centre of the house could have come straight off a 1930s luxury cruise liner, interesting paintings and stylish oriental fabrics contribute to a mix of styles that somehow go well together. Bedrooms vary in size; with their seersucker linen and antique prints they are truly lovely. Bathrooms are classically tasteful. Being in the heart of Burgundy vineyard country you are also immersed in silence. Terraced lawns lead down to the swimming pool, the trees and meadows. Sybaritic, but in the best possible taste, in one of the most beautiful areas of France. *Cash or French cheque only.*

rooms	5 twins/doubles.
price	€65–€95.
meals	Hosted dinner with wine €40; book ahead.
closed	November–March.
directions	From A6, exit Chalon Sud on N80 for Le Creusot; exit Moroges. Signed from village centre.

David Eades & Niels Lierow

tel	+33 (0)3 85 47 91 94
fax	+33 (0)3 85 47 98 49
e-mail	orangerie.mor@infonie.fr
web	orangerie.mor.chez.tiscali.fr

Le Monestier

Le Bourg, 71640 St Denis de Vaux, Saône-et-Loire

We almost got lost here, but the valley is a pretty place to lose yourself. You enter a jewel of a village; then into the grounds through wrought-iron gates, past attractive outbuildings and a swimming pool set in the grass, with huge old trees nearby. It looks a little bit like a Home Counties golf club! But no. Margrit and Peter are Swiss and bought the *maison bourgeoise* in 1999; they occupy the ground floor. Peter can be seen walking round in an apron: he is in charge of the cooking and you can expect some truly excellent meals. Not to say that your host is serious; you will find he has a most un-Swiss sense of humour. The reception rooms are comfortable. One bedroom has its own loo and a bathroom down the corridor, but this is made up for by a private terrace on top of one of the towers. You will be very well looked after here: a big playroom for children and a *fumoir* for after dinner snifters. Tennis, fishing, riding and golf are close at hand. More importantly for many: you will be in the very centre of the Côte Chalonnaise region and could go on foot to visit the vineyards of Mercurey, Givry and Rully. *Pets by request only.*

rooms	6: 5 twins, 1 with separate bath across hall, wc in room.
price	€85–€95. Singles €70.
meals	Dinner €24, book ahead. Restaurants nearby.
closed	Occasionally mid-November–mid-March.
directions	A6 exit Chalon Nord for Chalon sur Saône; right for Châtenoy le Royal D978 for 9km for Autun. Left at r'bout for Givry. After 75m, D48 right for Vallée des Vaux.

Margrit & Peter Koller

tel	+33 (0)3 85 44 50 68
fax	+33 (0)3 85 44 50 68
e-mail	lemonestier@wanadoo.fr
web	www.lemonestier.com

map 12   entry 33

La Terre D'Or

Rue Izembart La Montagne, 21200 Beaune, Côte-d'Or

Jean-Louis can share his love for Burgundy with you in many ways: he can indulge you in wine tasting and explain how those elegant vintages are produced, he can arrange cooking lessons with a local chef, or show you a vestige of Roman art. All this (and more) by bike, horseback, jeep or hot-air balloon. He and Christine have two houses ready for you, both surrounded by a large terraced garden and century old trees. One is contemporary and multi-levelled, the other is stone-walled and traditional – both with sitting rooms and kitchens with everything you need. The large bedrooms – each with a separate entrance – have wonderful views of the vineyards of Beaune; some have private terraces or patios. The Martins have used old beams and polished wine-growers' tables and chairs. You might have one of your wine classes in the grotto under the house where a river used to run; the stalagtites are still there. Jean-Louis can also be persuaded to host a barbecue by the pool. This is the kind of place where you book for two nights and end up staying a week...*A no-smoking property. Group price for 3-day theme holiday: wines, cooking, culture.*

rooms	2 houses for 4–10. Houses can be reserved exclusively for parties of 8–14.
price	€ 122-€ 178.
meals	Breakfast € 12. Picnic available.
closed	Rarely.
directions	From Beaune, D970 for Auxerre & Bouze Les Beaunes. After 2km right to La Montagne. Well signed.

Christine & Jean-Louis Martin

tel	+33 (0)3 80 25 90 90
fax	+33 (0)3 80 25 90 99
e-mail	jlmartin@laterredor.com
web	www.laterredor.com

Château d'Ecutigny
21360 Ecutigny, Côte-d'Or

This is a real castle. It was built in the 12th century to station soldiers guarding the Duke of Burgundy's land from marauding French. Bits were added over the years but it was abandoned at the end of the 18th century and fell to ruin, then rescued by Françoise and Patrick. The château is a historic monument, with the secret passages and Rapunzel towers to prove it, but has been made light, airy and really beautiful inside, without a trace of having been 'done up'. The rooms are in muted colours – not quite pastels – and sparsely furnished with a subtle mix of country pieces and elegant antiques. Bathrooms are large, with cast-iron baths on feet and some with warm terracotta tiles. The floors throughout the château are either mellow terracotta or wood – no walking barefoot on icy stone. Children will love exploring the cellars, stables and farm and Françoise will not be fazed by them: she used to run a crèche! This may be why the place runs so smoothly. Comfortable and relaxed despite the grandeur, your hosts are full of smiles, and the food and wine generously flow.

rooms	6: 5 doubles, 1 suite for 4.
price	€ 80–€ 140. Suite € 200.
meals	Picnic lunch with wine available. Dinner with aperitif & wine, € 40. Children's menus € 10–€ 20.
closed	Rarely.
directions	From A6 exit Pouilly en Auxois. Follow signs to Bligny sur Ouche, then Ecutigny. Last turning on right on leaving village.

	Françoise & Patrick Rochet
tel	+33 (0)3 80 20 19 14
fax	+33 (0)3 80 20 19 15
e-mail	info@chateaudecutigny.com
web	www.chateaudecutigny.com

map 12   entry 35

Château du Créancey
21320 Créancey, Côte-d'Or

Fiona, an English rose, and Bruno, a jovial French country gentleman, fell in love with Créancey on sight – a brave and passionate response to crumbling 17th-century walls and fallen beams. They have lavished a small fortune on a stylish restoration, lacing ancient bricks and mortar with contemporary luxuries: exposed oak beams scrubbed clean, lime-rendered walls to soak up the light, an infusion of antiques that mix with the odd minimalist piece. Sumptuous, uncluttered bedrooms have huge beds, old rugs, fresh flowers, plush armchairs. Bathrooms are equally faultless (imagine the best of everything and you are halfway there). Even the taps burst with water, the rarest of French rarities. Breakfast is taken in the hall. In the sitting room, the enormous fireplace can burn whole trees (well, almost). There's a snug library, too. There's a dovecote in the garden, and 300m from the château a line of trees flank the Canal de Bourgogne. Bring your bike and pedal on the footpath past the Charolais cattle that graze in the surrounding fields. On your doorstep, enough châteaux, cellars and monasteries to keep you busy for a month.

rooms	5 + 1: 4 doubles, 1 suite. Small house for 4 for weekly rentals.
price	€ 130–€ 220.
meals	Dinner € 50, only for groups occupying whole château.
closed	Rarely.
directions	From A6, exit at Pouilly en Auxois. At 1st roundabout to Créancey; D18 1km into village. Château on left; entrance at rear opp. the Mairie.

Fiona de Wulf

tel	+33 (0)3 80 90 57 50
fax	+33 (0)3 80 90 57 51
e-mail	chateau@creancey.com
web	www.creancey.com

Castel de Très Girard

7 rue Très Girard, 21220 Morey St Denis, Côte-d'Or

Nuits Saint Georges, Gevrey Chambertin, Clos de Vougeot, Vosne Romanée – all tongue-twisters in the best sense of the word and all strewn in your path as you travel down the trunk road from Dijon. Why not stop in at the Clos and be greeted by Sébastien and his young, friendly team who handle everything in the nicest manner? The warmth not only comes from the embers glowing in the fireplace by the leather club chairs but from the general ambience of this recently renovated wine press and 18th-century Burgundian manor. There are confident touches of burgundy reds (naturally) or sun-yellows in the padded fabrics on the beds and just enough stone and beam have been exposed to give the large bedrooms character; small vestibules ensure ultimate peace. Even the big, gleaming white bathrooms have views over the rooftops or to the Côte de Nuits vineyards. The chef and his assistant *pâtissier* are poets with a magic touch transforming the freshest ingredients into pure delight. Sébastien picks out the artist of the moment to be shown on the walls and best bottle of wine for your repast. Not to be missed.

rooms	9: 2 doubles, 5 triples, 2 suites.
price	€85–€120. Triples €138–€178. Suites €160–€196.
meals	Buffet breakfast €11. Lunch €21–€63. Dinner €36–€63. Restaurant closed Mondays; Tuesday & Saturday noon.
closed	15 February–15 March.
directions	15km from Dijon. A31 exit Dijon Sud for Nuits St Georges on N74, then right to Morey St Denis. Signed.

	Sébastien Pilat
tel	+33 (0)3 80 34 33 09
fax	+33 (0)3 80 51 81 92
e-mail	info@castel-tres-girard.com

map 12   entry 37

Hôtel de Vougeot

18 rue du Vieux Château, 21640 Vougeot, Côte-d'Or

Behind this recently converted townhouse, rows of vines sweep down an incline, surround the regal Château du Clos de Vougeot that sits in the middle distance – tones of pale yellow stone like a sepia photograph – and come to an abrupt halt at the (back) doorstep. The best rooms here have views of both. For centuries Clos de Vougeot was considered the finest of all burgundies; the Cisterian monks planted portions in the 12th century. Thirty hogsheads were sent to Rome in 1371 to celebrate the election of Pope Gregory XI; the gift-bearing abbot was soon made a cardinal. The cloister, cellar and enormous presses are among the most interesting examples of architecture in Burgundy, so don't miss them. You are on your own here with a key to come and go as you like. Everything has been kept simple and clean; the rough outlines of the dark timbers are a nice contrast to the white walls, light coloured bedspreads, new parquet floors and honey-pine furniture. Splash out on one of the huge rooms and bask in space. A copius buffet breakfast served under the stone arches of the ground floor will be a perfect start to your day.

rooms	12: 8 doubles, 1 triple, 2 quadruples, 1 room for 5.
price	€62–€72.
meals	Buffet breakfast €8. Restaurants in village.
closed	15 January-15 March.
directions	A31 exit Nuit St Georges, D74 towards Vougeot. Hotel in village.

	Sébastien Pilat
tel	+33 (0)3 80 62 01 15
fax	+33 (0)3 80 62 49 09
e-mail	info@castel-tres-girard.com
web	monsite.wanadoo.fr/hoteldevougeot

Château du Saulon

Route de Seurre, 21910 Saulon la Rue, Côte-d'Or

Don't rush through, stay awhile, and you'll eat very well under the vaulted ceiling in the old stables, charming with fresh flowers and candelabra on the tables. Wine is a speciality here; Alain will organise an introduction to the burgundy grape or, if your taste buds are finely tuned, he may suggest a session on the *grands crus*. The 27-hectare park surrounding this listed 18th-century château may be the only bit of land *not* planted with vines. Alain is infusing personal touches into what was a business training centre for over 30 years and intimacy, warmth and character inhabit the seven rooms in the newly converted cook house, now Le Pavillon. The bedrooms in the château are classic or contemporary; wooden headboards, sober curtains, all with good bedding and big bathtubs. Feeding off a sweeping central stone staircase they let in light and views to the lawns and trees. Third-floor rooms have lower ceilings and smaller windows. Linger over coffee on the terrace; the swans and ducks floating by on the lazy meandering river set the pace here. Relax.

rooms	30: 22 doubles in château; 7 doubles, 1 single in Pavillon.
price	€75–€120. Singles €60–€65.
meals	Buffet breakfast €10. Lunch €20 (weekdays). Lunch & dinner €28–€38. Restaurant closed Sunday evenings & Monday noon.
closed	February–6 March.
directions	A31 Dijon exit Dijon Sud for Longvic to toll. Exit Terminal Rail Route D996, left at r'bout for Fenay. Right at Chevigny for Seurre. 2km. Signed.

Alain Rosenzwey

tel	+33 (0)3 80 79 25 25
fax	+33 (0)3 80 79 25 26
e-mail	info@chateau-saulon.com

map 12   entry 39

Château de Flammerans
21130 Flammerans, Côte-d'Or

All is fresh, luxurious, relaxing – and Guy has the perfect pinch of passion for Burgundian cuisine even though he hails from Cantal. Ask to see the 18th-century kitchen with its original painted ceiling where he teaches the secrets of *jambon persillé* or *fricassée d'escargot*. The billiard room and the library are just off the entrance hall with its superb 19th-century ceramic tiles and a handsome iron bannister leads upstairs. You may breakfast on the large balcony overlooking the park, in the sitting room with its creamy walls, oriental rugs, green and gold upholstered easy chairs, or in the elegant dining room. Bedrooms are big, simple and uncluttered with working fireplaces, and mineral water on the side tables. You'll find robes in the gorgeous bathrooms along with weathered marbled floors from the south of France. If you are lucky, you'll catch one of the concerts – maybe baroque or jazz – that Guy and Catherine organise every summer. Sit and dream on a bench in a shady glen, gaze at the magnificent red oaks, discover the glistening ponds (one of which was used to clean the carriage wheels). A pleasing place.

rooms	6: 4 doubles, 2 suites.
price	€ 88–€ 150.
meals	Breakfast € 6.50. Light lunches available. Dinner with drinks € 30–€ 45, book ahead.
closed	Never.
directions	A6/A39/N5. Auxonne D20 towards Flammerans. Signed in Auxonne.

Guy Barrier

tel	+33 (0)3 80 27 05 70
fax	+33 (0)3 80 31 12 12
e-mail	info@flammerans.com
web	www.flammerans.com

photography by Richard Hoare

paris – ile de france

Hôtel de Notre Dame

19 rue Maître Albert, 75005 Paris

Hidden from the tourist tides in a select little area, yet a stone's throw from Notre Dame, the fine old frontage opens onto a superb tapestry, bits of antiquity on oriental rugs and deep armchairs. Open is the word: these people genuinely like people and greet you with smiles and humour. As does the brilliant new conservatory-like breakfast room: big window to the street, 'rusted' tables, metal chairs with soft yellow cushions. If the convoluted corridors declare the age of the building (1600s), contemporary style dictates their smart look. Bedrooms also mix old and new. There are beams and exposed stones – some enormous – and cathedral views through smaller windows on higher floors. Fittings and furniture are in custom-made pale curvy wood, spotlights are discreet, new padded upholstery is warm and colourful with mixes of yellow, red and blue and the translucent screen doors to bathrooms are an excellent idea for small layouts (not all baths are full size). The black eunuch officially portrayed as Marie-Antoinette's feathered fan bearer lived here… A welcoming place. *English and German spoken.*

rooms	34 twins/doubles.
price	€ 139–€ 154.
meals	Breakfast € 7.
closed	Never.
directions	Metro: Maubert Mutualité. RER: St Michel-Notre Dame (exit 3).

	Jean-Pierre Fouhety
tel	+33 (0)1 43 26 79 00
fax	+33 (0)1 46 33 50 11
e-mail	hotel.denotredame@libertysurf.fr
web	www.hotel-paris-notredame.com

Le Sainte Beuve

9 rue Ste Beuve, 75006 Paris

This beautifully refurbished hotel, known and loved during the wilder days of Montparnasse, now exudes an atmosphere of unstuffy designer luxury – quiet good taste in gentle tones and thick fabrics. The extraordinarily attractive salon has superb silk curtains, a winter log fire in the old marble fireplace, modern paintings and old prints. It is all small and intimate and the attentive, efficient staff are a vital element in your sense of well being here. Bedrooms are intimate too in ancient and modern finery: lots of pale walls, soft colours and textured fabrics, colourful chintzes and paisleys modulated by pastels, at least one antique per room – a leather-topped desk, a walnut dressing-table, a polished armoire, old brass lamps – and 18th/19th-century pictures in rich old frames. The special Sainte Beuve room is extra-big and in dazzling good taste. Bathrooms are superbly modern with bathrobes and fine toiletries. Lastly, for the first moments of the day, breakfast is a feast of croissants and brioches from the famous Mulot bakery and fresh orange juice. *English spoken. Book early.*

rooms	22: 7 doubles, 15 twins.
price	€ 129–€ 225. Sainte Beuve € 270.
meals	Breakfast € 13.50. Lunch & dinner € 7–€ 30, book ahead.
closed	Never.
directions	Metro: Notre Dame des Champs (12), Vavin (4). RER: Port-Royal. Car Park: Montparnasse.

Jean-Pierre Egurreguy

tel	+33 (0)1 45 48 20 07
fax	+33 (0)1 45 48 67 52
e-mail	saintebeuve@wanadoo.fr
web	www.paris-hotel-charme.com

map 6   entry 42

Grand Hôtel des Balcons

3 rue Casimir Delavigne, 75006 Paris

Les Balcons has the lot: an idea of service which produces tea on winter afternoons, a clothes line over the bath, a practical room where clients can work or children play, a daily feast of a breakfast (sumptuous cooked spread, fresh fruit salad…) that's free on your birthday! Owners and staff appear to work with lightness and pleasure. Having decorated her Art Nouveau hotel by taking inspiration from the floral delights of the original 1890s staircase windows, Denise Corroyer now teaches *ikebana* and flowers the house – brilliantly – while her son Jeff manages – charmingly. Rooms are simple yet pleasing. The five big family rooms have smart décor and pretty modern lamps, parquet floors and two windows, good bathrooms (two basins, pretty tiles) and loads of space. Other rooms are not big but purpose-made table units use the space judiciously, amusing prints decorate the walls and front rooms have balconies. At the back, you may be woken by the birds. An eagle eye is kept and no damage left unrepaired, beds are firm, bathrooms good, colours and fabrics simple and pleasantly bright. Remarkable value. *English and Spanish spoken.*

rooms	50: 25 doubles, 14 twins, 6 singles, 5 family rooms for 4.
price	€ 72–€ 180.
meals	Buffet breakfast € 10.
closed	Never.
directions	Metro: Odéon (4, 10). RER: Luxembourg. Car Park: École de Médecine.

	Denise & Pierre Corroyer & Jeff André
tel	+33 (0)1 46 34 78 50
fax	+33 (0)1 46 34 06 27
e-mail	resa@balcons.com

Hôtel de la Tulipe

33 rue Malar, 75007 Paris

Such a delight, the Tulipe, with its Provençal looks, intelligent atmosphere and civilised owners who are a pleasure to meet. Before the *Exposition Universelle* in 1900 it was a convent. Deliciously intimate rooms are in the former nuns' cells (at least two cells per room!) on two storeys round the cobbled honeysuckled courtyard or over the quiet street. Beams and old stones, yellow-sponged walls, deep red carpets and luminous fabrics, simple pine or wicker furniture: the sun shines here every day of the year. The super newly-renovated bathrooms have blue, red or yellow country-style tiling and bright butter-yellow paint. Two rooms, one equipped for disabled guests, lead directly off the patio and feel especially peaceful and connected. The breakfast room is charming and sensual with its Burgundy stone floor, blond timbers, interesting paintings… and croissants fresh from the local bakery. Above all, together with the Fortuit family's unpretentious good taste, we remember their smiles and relaxed manner and so, most certainly, will you. *No lift, two floors. Internet café 100m. Wine on sale for private consumption. English, German, Spanish spoken.*

rooms	21: 20 doubles/twins, 1 family suite with 2 bathrooms.
price	€ 100–€ 140. Suite € 210–€ 260.
meals	Breakfast € 10. Lunch & dinner available locally.
closed	Never.
directions	Metro & RER: Invalides, Pont de l'Alma, La Tour Maubourg. Car Park: Rue Malar.

	Caroline & Jean-Louis Fortuit
tel	+33 (0)1 45 51 67 21
fax	+33 (0)1 47 53 96 37
e-mail	hoteldelatulipe@wanadoo.fr
web	www.paris-hotel-tulipe.com

map 6   entry 44

Hôtel Pergolèse

3 rue Pergolèse, 75116 Paris

Once past the blue doors you forget the trumpeting sculptures of nearby Arc de Triomphe for a festival of modern design where light and natural materials, custom-made furniture and minute details all add up. Édith Vidalenc works with renowned designer Rena Dumas to keep a sleek but warmly, curvaceously human hotel. Her sense of hospitality informs it all: the faithful team at reception are leagues away from the frostiness that can pass for four-star treatment. Pastel tones are mutedly smart so the multi-coloured breakfast room is a slightly humorous wake-up nudge, the linen mats and fine silver a bow to tradition: not taking oneself too seriously while being really professional is the keynote here. Rooms, not vast but with good storage, are all furnished in pale wood and leather, thick curtains and soft white bedcovers: no distracting patterns or prints, just coloured plush cushions to soften. The star Pergolèse room (pictured) is a small masterpiece in palest apricot with a few spots of colour and a superb open bathroom. *English, German, Italian, Japanese and Spanish spoken.*

rooms	40 doubles.
price	€ 180–€ 380.
meals	Breakfast € 12–€ 18.
	Snacks from € 25.
closed	Never.
directions	Metro: Argentin (1).
	RER A: Charles de Gaulle Etoile.
	RER C: Porte Maillot.
	Air France bus: Porte Maillot.
	Car Park: Place St Ferdinand.

Édith Vidalenc

tel	+33 (0)1 53 64 04 04
fax	+33 (0)1 53 64 04 40
e-mail	hotel@pergolese.com
web	www.hotelpergolese.com

Hôtel Saint André des Arts

66 rue St André des Arts, 75006 Paris

This relaxed, low-cost hotel beside the bustling St André crossroads has been known and loved by backpackers and intellectuals for years. You are met by a row of old choir stalls, a listed staircase and Henri, a former philosophy teacher who is happy to talk *philo* and Proust with you but not the latest in design. White paint sets off the old timbers, new carpets are being laid, new little tiled shower rooms being fitted, windows have been double-glazed – but nothing can ever hide how the old building twists and turns. Some rooms are very small, one is reached across an interior balcony. Some have immensely high ceilings and great windows, beams, old stone walls, 16th-century style. Practical Rustic French Antique furniture is set in a simple, pleasant décor. Breakfast by reception is at a wonderful great 'folding' table set on a *trompe l'œil* black and white floor that was laid 200 years ago. The neighbourhood is lively, the music sometimes noisy and nocturnal, the atmosphere stimulating. If you feel you would like to join in, don't expect luxury but book early – it's often full. *English, German, Italian, Polish, Spanish spoken.*

rooms	31: 5 singles, 11 doubles, 15 twins/triples.
price	€ 80–€ 85. Singles € 63.
meals	Breakfast included. Lunch & dinner available locally.
closed	Never.
directions	Metro: Odéon (4, 10). RER: St Michel-Notre Dame. Car Park: Rue Mazarine.

	Henri & Odile Le Goubin
tel	+33 (0)1 43 26 96 16
fax	+33 (0)1 43 29 73 34
e-mail	hsaintand@wanadoo.fr

map 6   entry 46

Hôtel de l'Académie

32 rue des Saints Pères, 75007 Paris

Leave a street bustling with motor traffic and beautiful people for a quiet haven. Generally relaxed staff (Parisians can be easily stressed) may beckon you towards the depths, past the humour of a brilliantly *trompe-l'œil* dreamscape of classical damsels and exotic birds, to a big *salon* furnished essentially in Second Empire style – gildings and furbelows, tassels and bronze bits – beneath a splendid glass canopy. In the bedrooms, and with contemporary expectations in mind, bathrooms are fully equipped, bedding is new, plain-painted walls are a foil for old beams and choice pieces such as a nice old ormulu Louis XV chest with its elaborate trim. A couple of little kidney-shaped bedside tables are charmers. Some rooms are more daringly done in rococo and crimson damask. The basement breakfast room starts with papyrus pictures from the land of the pyramids then flips between the style inspired by Napoleon's Egyptian campaign and an elaborate Hispanic-carving mode. You can have a caterer dinner here too if you wish. Bedrooms are biggish, by Paris standards, and storage space has been carefully planned. *English, German, Spanish spoken.*

rooms	35: 20 doubles, 10 twins, 5 suites.
price	€ 99–€ 229. Suites € 179–€ 229.
meals	Breakfast € 14.50.
	Lunch & dinner on request € 25.
closed	Never.
directions	Metro: St Germain des Prés (4).
	RER: Musée d'Orsay.
	Car park: Nearby, consult hotel.

	Gérard & Katia Chekroun
tel	+33 (0)1 45 49 80 00
fax	+33 (0)1 45 44 75 24
e-mail	academiehotel@aol.com
web	www.academiehotel.com

Hôtel Elysées Matignon

3 rue de Ponthieu, 75008 Paris

Matignon is superb genuine 1924 – clearcut rectangles, perfectly moulded curves, bags of style and no fuss. In that stunning lobby, you will be welcomed by people who are relaxed yet sensitive to your needs. Each bedroom wall bears a large original fresco: landscapes or near-abstract still lifes, they are very proper given the original purpose of these rooms. Bathrooms have Art Deco mod cons and bevelled black and white Metro tiling (some are being renovated in pale green mosaic – Deco but new). Otherwise, there are discreet dark carpets, heavy curtains, pleasing clear colour schemes with coordinated quilted or textured bedcovers and head cushions, black metal bedside lights, fine inner blinds and decent storage. If far from enormous, each room has a useful lobby for minibar, cupboard and loo (except the junior suites where a larger lobby houses the extra bed). An evening venue for the Parisian 'in' crowd (11 pm to dawn), the scarlet and black Mathis Bar, newly adorned with a dancing silver and glass Belle Époque chandelier, puts on virginal white for breakfast. *English, Portuguese and Spanish spoken.*

rooms	23: 10 doubles, 9 twins, 4 suites.
price	€ 136–€ 198. Suites € 198–€ 218.
meals	Breakfast € 9.
closed	Never.
directions	Metro: Franklin Roosevelt (1,9). RER & Air France bus: Charles de Gaulle-Etoile. Car Park: Champs Elysées.

	Jean-François Cornillot
tel	+33 (0)1 42 25 73 01
fax	+33 (0)1 42 56 01 39
e-mail	elyseesmatignon@wanadoo.fr
web	www.hotel-paris-champs-elysees.com

map 6   entry 48

Hôtel Minerve

13 rue des Ecoles, 75005 Paris

The Minerve, Eric Gaucheron's second hotel (his family also own the Familia next door), has his eagerly attentive, friendly touch – as well as the stimulating university life outside. The red-carpeted corridors lead to rooms that are mostly not huge but often use the classic, cunning bed alcove for storage space (all beds are new). The higher you are the longer the view (Notre Dame and the Seine, on the street side of course) and top-floor rooms have some wild and wonderful timbers over their quirky shapes and some rich red, gold and ivory colour schemes. Walls are gradually being decorated with those excellent sepia murals of French monuments, all different. Décor varies from brightly contemporary to soothingly granny, there are damask and satin, timber and tile, some nice old bits of furniture, some recent built-in cupboards, decent bathrooms of varying sizes (the new ones are splendid). The lobby/salon is generously big, light and airy with pleasant repro furniture, tapestries and bookcases and the breakast room's original wall and ceiling paintings are a delight. Superb meeting room too. *English spoken.*

rooms	54: 44 twins/doubles, 7 singles, 3 family rooms for 3-4.
price	€85-€165. Private parking available 24 hours €20.
meals	Breakfast €8.
closed	Never.
directions	Metro: Jussieu (7), Maubert Mutualité (10), Cardinal Lemoine. RER: Cluny-La Sorbonne. Car park: Lagrange.

	Eric Gaucheron & Sylvie Roger
tel	+33 (0)1 43 26 26 04
fax	+33 (0)1 44 07 01 96
e-mail	minerve@hotellerie.net
web	www.hotel-paris-minerve.com

Hôtel du Quai Voltaire
19 quai Voltaire, 75007 Paris

Oscar Wilde once declared that he "never looked out of the window" – torture for anyone staying here, where only four rooms do not see the Pissarro painting of quintessential Paris through their windows. Baudelaire also stayed here, as did Wagner and Sibelius: the Voltaire was something of an institution and still feels like a well-loved club with its rather worn golden-fringed armchairs in the pannelled salon and its guests who come back again and again, some for over 30 years (I met one there). Rooms are small, beds are the standard French 1m40 width, some baths are not for reclining, but mattresses are good, staff are superb old retainers and the welcoming atmosphere is warmly genuine. The new manageress is lively, humorous and enthusiastic and plans to brighten the corrridors with some fresh paint, change curtain fabrics so as better to frame that ineffable view. New bathroom fixtures should follow. She loves the contact with guests, old and new. However, you will need earplugs: the price of that view is no protection against riverside traffic noise. *There are three top-floor singles with a bathroom on the floor below at bargain prices.*

rooms	33: 17 doubles, 9 twins, 6 singles, 1 triple.
price	€ 102–€ 150.
meals	Breakfast € 8.
closed	Never.
directions	Metro: Rue du Bac (12), Tuileries (1). RER: Musée d'Orsay. Car park: Musée d'Orsay.

	Régine Lepeinteur
tel	+33 (0)1 42 61 50 91
fax	+33 (0)1 42 61 62 26
e-mail	info@quaivoltaire.fr
web	www.quaivoltaire.fr

map 6   entry 50

Hôtel Nicolo

3 rue Nicolo, 75016 Paris

Such a surprise! A hidden entrance, beneath one building, across a courtyard of acacia and evergreen, into another. All is hushed, the old mosaic floor smiles at you, French Granny's sitting room opens up on your right, you are greeted by delightful staff who have known and loved the Nicolo for many years. And now new owners have brought new, many-splendoured furnishings, fabrics, pictures by artist friends (old engravings coloured 'in the manner of', pastels of Port Grimaud, a powerful parrot series). The renovated rooms are stunning, the others will do perfectly until they can join the élite, all give onto courtyards, of course. The new? Lovely lacey-carved Indonesian screens have become voluptuous three-arched bedheads with original paintwork or fabric panels or birds and animals. Desks and tables are unusual Dutch, French or oriental antiques; lamps are unusual modern objects. Pure white beds have quilts in broad, rich stripes. Here are richness and purity married, and the few new bathrooms are luscious. The old? 1970s beiges, some oriental florals, some red carpet – all comfortable and friendly, all due to go soon. A fascinating study in change and a super place to stay.

rooms	28: 24 twins/doubles, 4 family.
price	€98–€155. Family €160–€175.
meals	Breakfast €6.
closed	Never.
directions	Metro: Passy, La Muette. RER: Boulainvilliers. Bus routes: 22 32. Car park: Next door to hotel.

	Catherine and her team
tel	+33 (0)1 42 88 83 40
fax	+33 (0)1 42 24 45 41
e-mail	hotel.nicolo@wanadoo.fr

Hôtel Centre Ville Etoile

6 rue des Acacias, 75107 Paris

This tiny hotel has a definite style and tiny has not meant cosy. I like it for its difference. The shiny black desk and the 20-foot ficus tree are in a 3-storey galleried well of light – an ingenious and original space – that gives onto a plant-filled cul-de-sac where you can sit out for summer breakfasts. The view from the top gallery is an engineer's delight. The decor may be a little sombre for some; it is based on an Art Deco style that dictates the black and white theme, with a chromatic glance at American Surrealism in the large original 1930s oil painting. There are prints from American cartoon strips and black carpeting with slippy grey-white stripes like running water. Rooms are small but spaces are well used, though storage remains limited. They can be masculine in brown and black with one red chair or more pastelly or elegant white, cream and grey. Bathrooms have white fittings, round basins, restful grey tiling, lots of mirrors, bathrobes. In contrast, bright red oriental-print cloths (on black tables) and airy Bauhaus wire chairs enliven the basement breakfast room. With so few rooms, staff have plenty of time to be friendly, helpful and really welcoming.

rooms	15: 10 doubles, 5 twins.
price	€ 115–€ 151.
meals	Breakfast € 9.15. Lunch & dinner € 15–€ 25, book ahead.
closed	Never.
directions	Metro: Argentine. RER & Air France bus: Charles de Gaulle-Etoile. Car park: 24 rue des Acacias.

M Alain Michaud & M Idir Nasser

tel	+33 (0)1 58 05 10 00
fax	+33 (0)1 47 54 93 43
e-mail	hcv@centrevillehotels.com
web	www.centrevillehotels.com

map 6   entry 52

Hôtel de Buci

22 rue Buci, 75006 Paris

At the heart of the little shopping streets behind St Germain where, unhappily, the well-loved street market has been forced to close, the Buci feels like another antique shop, full of beautifully chosen and utterly desirable pieces. While their charming, energetic son manages the hotel, the owners love looking for old things, whence a personal salon where every picture is worth a good look – the themes are horses and women – and every chair or lamp has a story. In the evening, the morning's gentle classical music turns to jazz to fit the 1930s atmosphere and in the basement piano bar/breakfast space, you can sit on three superbly ornate red sofas and admire yet more pictures and objects. Bedrooms are less unusual but still high class. Done with good repro furniture and remarkable fabrics from top design houses (a different one for each floor), they are yellow and red, blue and cream, checks, stripes and florals in a rich coordination of canopies, pelmets and quilts. The pretty bathrooms are excellent too and you will enjoy the monogrammed linen. A good, reliable and quiet place to stay.

rooms	24: 12 doubles, 8 twins, 4 suites.
price	€240–€335. Suites €350–€550.
meals	Breakfast €14–€20.
	Afternoon tea served.
closed	Never.
directions	Metro: St Germain des Prés (4),
	Mabillon (10).
	RER: St Michel-Notre Dame.
	Car Park: St Germain des Prés.

	Frédéric Lassalle
tel	+33 (0)1 55 42 74 74
fax	+33 (0)1 55 42 74 44
e-mail	hotelbuci@wanadoo.fr
web	www.hotelbuci.fr

Hôtel Molière

21 rue Molière, 75001 Paris

This is an enchantingly French hotel with a sensitive mixture of urban and country comforts. The big yellow lobby/*salon* is smart and rather grand with its *faux-marbre* columns and black and white upholstery but the welcome from the desk is gentle and warm – the new young owners infuse the place with their intelligent enthusiasm. Breakfast is a delight, its tempting buffet spread on a gingham cloth and bunched curtains giving a glimpse of the little cobbled green courtyard. There's also a small, deep-chaired *salon* round the corner for your quiet moments. Bedrooms are just as pretty with judicious use of nostalgic Jouy prints on walls and coordinated checks on quilts – or vice versa, or stripes, or sprigs... The Jouy colours go perfectly with the occasional antique: red and yellow, grey and green, blue and ivory, a little old writing desk, an unusual chair. Bathrooms, some vast, some very snug, may be modern and delicious or bask in the old-fashioned personality of built-in fittings and mosaic tiles. Interesing paintings, plants and ornaments give the Molière a well-cared-for feel. You will like it here. *English and Spanish spoken.*

rooms	32: 15 doubles, 9 twins/triples, 5 singles, 3 suites.
price	€ 135–€ 175. Suites € 275.
meals	Breakfast € 12.
closed	Never.
directions	Metro: Palais Royal-Musée du Louvre (1, 7); Pyramides (7). RER: Opéra-Auber. Car Park: Pyramides.

Patricia & Rémy Perraud

tel	+33 (0)1 42 96 22 01
fax	+33 (0)1 42 60 48 68
e-mail	info@hotel-moliere.fr
web	www.hotel-moliere.fr

map 6   entry 54

Hôtel Opéra Richepanse

14 rue du Chevalier de St George, 75001 Paris

At the centre of a throbbingly busy shopping and business district, the cool 1930s look and courteous welcome of the Richepanse promise rest and quiet in proper four-star fashion. The marquetry, the panelling, the smooth suede furniture and the stylish mouldings of the lobby/salon were all custom-designed for the deep renovations. It feels clean-cut and rich. There's a minor concession to things more ancient in the atmospheric stone vault where the floor is blue, the marble bistro tables shine and the sumptuous breakfast buffet calls. Bedrooms are a good size, some are enormous. They have blue carpets, clean-limbed 1930s-style furniture and excellent thick-textured fabrics for straight-hung curtains and well-fitting bedcovers – no swags, no frills, no fuss. This gives space to appreciate the interesting reproductions that draw the eye and even, in the magnificent great suites, original paintings. Bathrooms are, of course, superb with the latest in basin design, triple mirrors and simple, smart tiling. Modern comforts, old-style attention and service. *English, German, Spanish spoken.*

rooms	38: 20 doubles, 15 twins, 3 suites.
price	€230–€350. Suites €450–€590.
meals	Breakfast €14–€18.
closed	Never.
directions	Metro: Madeleine (8, 14). RER: A: Auber. Car Park: Madeleine.

	Édith Vidalenc
tel	+33 (0)1 42 60 36 00
fax	+33 (0)1 42 60 13 03
e-mail	richepanseotel@wanadoo.fr
web	www.richepanse.com

Hôtel des Tuileries

10 rue St Hyacinthe, 75001 Paris

The delicate listed façade of this quiet old Relais du Silence moves skywards to the rhythm of balconies, arches and mouldings. Inside, the charming Tuileries feels rather like a family house – the owners have been here for several generations. Great doors give onto a white hall with rugs, mirrors, pictures old and new, leading to the elegant little salons. A pretty lightwell illuminates this space and the basement breakfast room, a generous curving staircase leads upwards. Turkey rugs are everywhere but the oriental element is never excessive: one room is like a soft Persian tent, another has a clever yellow drapery over a white bed, there are Chinese-vase table lamps, paisley fabrics. Colours are skilfull – a white room with dark blue carpet, pale blue damask curtains and bedcover, a richly-coloured rug behind the delightful cane bedhead. Lighting is good, there are pretty antiques, country pieces, modern units, good marble bathrooms. The smaller rooms can feel cramped and higher prices are for the excellent deluxe rooms. *Family apartments possible. Pets € 10. English, German, Italian and Spanish spoken.*

rooms	26: 10 doubles, 14 twins, 2 triples.
price	€ 135–€ 250. Children under 10 free.
meals	Buffet breakfast € 13. Lunch & dinner on request.
closed	Never.
directions	Metro: Tuileries (1), Pyramides (1). RER: Auber. Car park: Place Vendôme, Marché St Honoré.

Jean–Jacques Vidal

tel	+33 (0)1 42 61 04 17
fax	+33 (0)1 49 27 91 56
e-mail	hotel-des-tuileries@wanadoo.fr
web	www.hotel-des-tuileries.com

map 6   entry 56

Les Rives de Notre Dame

15 quai St Michel, 75005 Paris

With the colours and textures of the south and much imagination, an ancient Paris townhouse right on the river has become a very cosy hotel. Only consider the darling lacey mimosa-encrusted petticoats that hang over the corridor windows, the minibar cupboards delicately painted by a brilliant Tuscan artisan, the 17th-century beams, the plants that rise to greet the light pouring in through the glass canopy. Through an arched 'fortress' door, each bedroom has its own combination of vibrantly sunny fabrics mixing flowers, stars and stripes, soft luxy duvets, head cushions on ivy-twined rods, a pretty bathroom and table and chairs for private breakfast, though the basement breakfast room is intimate and appealing too. Rooms are a good size (just three smaller first-floor rooms are given for singles but could take couples) and the top-floor studio is a palatial hideaway. Genuinely friendly and relaxed, your host has time to advise each guest on things to do. You should feel well cared for in this exceptional little house. (Good sound-proofing against the traffic too.) *English, German, Italian spoken.*

rooms	10: 9 twins/doubles, 1 suite.
price	€ 168–€ 289. Suite € 300–€ 550.
meals	Breakfast € 11–€ 14.
closed	Never.
directions	Metro: St Michel (4). RER: St Michel-Notre Dame. Car Park: Lutèce.

	Danièle Limbert & Christian Martin
tel	+33 (0)1 43 54 81 16
fax	+33 (0)1 43 26 27 09
e-mail	hotel@rivesdenotredame.com
web	www.rivesdenotredame.com

Le Notre Dame Hôtel

1 quai St Michel, 75005 Paris

At the very hub of Latin Quarter life – students crowd the pavements, cars crowd the bridge, Notre Dame rises serene behind – you climb the mirrored staircase to a warm red welcome. The hotel is splendid: communal spaces brightly decked in red checks, the salon-breakfast room spreading its windows so your eyes are caught by plunging views of river, cathedral and great 'police palace'. Nearly all rooms have at least two windows onto this ancient picture; only the five cheapest, soberly pretty and quieter, give onto a dull courtyard. They are very attractive, not huge but uncluttered, and full of light from the river. Double-glazing keeps the noise out, air-conditioning keeps the air breathable. Excellent fabrics are all from the house of Pierre Frey; a light cherrywood laminate adorns desktops, bedheads and clever block panelling; there are hand-enamelled bedside lights from northern France and framed prints from England; new dark green marble bathrooms with bright white fittings are extremely smart behind their translucent Japanese-style doors and the top-floor duplex suites are fun and full of character. *English, German, Spanish spoken.*

rooms	26: 14 doubles, 9 twins, 3 duplex suites.
price	€ 150–€ 199. Duplex € 244.
meals	Breakfast € 7.
closed	Never.
directions	Metro: St Michel (4). RER: St Michel-Notre Dame. Car Park: Notre Dame.

Jean-Pierre Fouhety

tel	+33 (0)1 43 54 20 43
fax	+33 (0)1 43 26 61 75
e-mail	hotel.lenotredame@libertysurf.fr
web	www.paris-hotel-notredame.com

map 6   entry 58

Hôtel du Jeu de Paume

54 rue St Louis en l'Ile, 75004 Paris

Above: three storeys soar to the roof timbers of a 17th-century 'tennis' court – astounding. Below: genuine care from mother and daughter, fresh flowers, time for everyone, super staff. It's exceptional. Provençal in style, unique in atmosphere, smallish rooms give onto quiet courtyard gardens, have rich fabrics, pale walls, good bathrooms, old beams, stones, parquet. Duplexes have tiny staircases and cupboards below; some rooms show the building's beautiful beamy skeleton, some have little terraces; the secluded new apartments over the street have superb tall windows, space and style. We love it hugely – for its sense of history, eccentricities, aesthetic ironies, peaceful humour, feel of home; and for its unconventional attitudes and relaxed yet thoroughly efficient staff; what matter that storage is limited? The lounge has *objets*, art, deep leather sofas round a carved fireplace and Scoop the soft gold dog; breakfast is beneath the magnificent timbers by the surrealistic columns; work-out is in vaulted cellars (billiards, bikes, sauna). "Quite exceptionally polite, friendly staff": a reader. *English, German, Russian, Spanish spoken.*

rooms	30 + 2: 25 twins/doubles, 1 triple, 2 duplexes, 2 suites. 2 apartments for 4–6.
price	€157–€285. Suites €465. Apartments €490–€750.
meals	Breakfast €14. Room service on request.
closed	Never.
directions	Metro: Pont Marie (7), Cité (4), St Paul (1). RER: St Michel-Notre Dame. Car Park: Pont Marie.

Elyane Prache & Nathalie Heckel

tel	+33 (0)1 43 26 14 18
fax	+33 (0)1 40 46 02 76
e–mail	info@jeudepaumehotel.com
web	www.jeudepaumehotel.com

Familia Hôtel

11 rue des Écoles, 75005 Paris

It is well named! and glows under the care and attention showered by Éric, his wife Sylvie, their little Charles and his wonderfully energetic parents. It has a grand-looking balconied face but the family earnestly want to welcome you just as friends. Beyond the hall, hand-painted by an artist friend, is the newly-renovated rich red breakfast *salon* (cornices, mouldings, *trompe-lœil...*) where the Gaucherons' collection of leather-bound tomes and the thick Turkey rug give a homely feel. Bedrooms are warmly unpretentious. They are not large or 'Parisian chic' but each has either a lovely Paris fresco, a wall of ancient stones, an old carved bedhead or a balcony onto the fascinating street life – the ground-floor room even has a grand canopied bed. Carpets, wallpapers, bedcovers and curtains, not brilliantly trendy or stunningly matched, are somehow comfortingly provincial. Renovations are constant and it's all spotless. Front rooms look across the wide street to a rich jumble of old buildings with the Île Saint Louis just beyond. Ask Éric anything – he will answer willingly, at length and in fast English. *English and Spanish spoken.*

rooms	30: 23 twins/doubles, 6 singles, 1 quadruple.
price	€70–€170. Private parking available 24 hours €20.
meals	Breakfast €6.
closed	Never.
directions	Metro: Jussieu (7, 10), Maubert Mutualité (10). RER: Cluny-La Sorbonne. Car park: Lagrange.

	Eric Gaucheron & Sylvie Royer
tel	+33 (0)1 43 54 55 27
fax	+33 (0)1 43 29 61 77
e-mail	familia.hotel@libertysurf.fr
web	www.hotel-paris-familia.com

map 6   entry 60

Hôtel du Danube

58 rue Jacob, 75006 Paris

Built as a private mansion at the height of the Third Empire, this soft civilised hotel rejoices in a dazzling black and red salon (fascinating black-framed cane easy chairs) and a large, white patio where potted palms sit in summer, cast-iron garden tables can be laid for breakfast and elegant façades rise skywards. The quietest rooms look this way. Others have more activity – and more noise – under their double-glazed windows (the higher, the quieter). Style and comfort vary widely, twisty corridors change levels, it's a warm, long-lived-in place. Superb superior rooms have two windows, some very desirable antiques, armchairs and thick, smart fabrics, yet they feel intimate and friendly. Their bathrooms are carefully done too. Standard rooms all have the same blue-laminate bamboo-trim desk units and nice 'wooden-plank' wallpaper with some quaintly old-style bathroom tiling – but all necessities are there, of course. The attic standard room is in fact the most appealing of these. And everyone meets in the delicious countrified breakfast room and appreciates the bevy of young helpful staff at reception.

rooms	40: 25 double, 9 twins, 5 family, 1 junior suite.
price	€ 120–€ 165. Family rooms & suite € 230.
meals	Breakfast € 9.
closed	Never.
directions	Metro: St Germain des Près (4). RER: Musée d'Orsay. Car park: St Germain des Près.

	Séverin Ferrand & Michel Sario
tel	+33 (0)1 42 60 34 70
fax	+33 (0)1 42 60 81 18
e-mail	info@hoteldanube.fr
web	www.hoteldanube.fr

Hôtel du 7è Art
20 rue St Paul, 75004 Paris

Behind its remarkable black and white frontage, this place is as light-hearted and eternally youthful as the stars of an old American film. Besides a delightful little hotel, there is a lively bar where log fires burn in winter, warming snacks are served and you can even buy mementoes of the great names of film. The people are young and charming too (those film stars models), there's a laundry room in the basement and… a trio of fitness machines – to maintain your Hollywood muscles in decadent Paris. The black and white theme is pursued throughout the building and a multitude of old film posters decorate the walls. Up the black-carpeted stairs (*cinéma oblige*), the bedrooms are softly, unaggressively decorated – some hessian walls, some painted pine slatting, gentle brown carpets and multi-pastel piqué bedcovers – and white and black bathrooms, some with star-studded shower curtain. Some are pretty small, some have modem sockets, all have a built-in desk top and a safe and the atmosphere is peaceful (the bar closes at midnight). And the oldest residential part of Paris is all around you. A very special place.

rooms	23: 15 doubles, 7 twins, 1 single.
price	€ 59–€ 130.
meals	Breakfast € 7. Bar snacks € 8–€ 10.
closed	Never.
directions	Metro: St Paul (1), Pont Marie (7); RER: Châtelet–Les Halles. Car park: Pont Marie.

	Michel & Yolène
tel	+33 (0)1 44 54 85 00
fax	+33 (0)1 42 77 69 10
e–mail	hotel7art@wanadoo.fr

map 6   entry 62

Le Relais du Louvre

19 rue des Prêtres St Germain l'Auxerrois, 75001 Paris

Look down the throats of gargoyles. Soak up the history. The Revolutionaries printed their newsletter in the cellar; the place inspired Puccini's Café Momus in *Bohême* and is utterly delightful, as are the charming young managers who greet you from the antique desk. Everywhere, antiques and oriental rugs complement the modernity of firm beds and perfect bathrooms. Front rooms look onto the church's Gothic flights of fancy and along to the austerely neo-classical Louvre; others give onto a light-filled patio. Top-floor junior suites have twin beds and a non-convertible sofa (no cluttering up), pastel walls, exuberant upholstery and heaps of light from mansard windows. The apartment (pictured) is big and beautiful with fireplace, books, music, old engravings and a superb veranda kitchen. Other, smaller rooms are luminous, fresh and restful – yellow, a favourite colour, brings sunny moods into small spaces. You feel softly secluded and coddled everywhere. The sense of service is highly developed and as there is no breakfast room, breakfast comes to you. On each floor, two rooms can make a family suite. *English, German, Italian, Spanish spoken.*

rooms	20 + 1 apartment: 13 twins/doubles, 5 singles, 2 junior suites; 1 apartment for 4-5.
price	€145-€180. Singles €99. Suites €205-€244. Apartment €380.
meals	Breakfast in bedroom €10. Light meals €5-€15.
closed	Never.
directions	Metro: Louvre-Rivoli, Pont Neuf. RER: Châtelet-Les Halles.

	Sophie Aulnette
tel	+33 (0)1 40 41 96 42
fax	+33 (0)1 40 41 96 44
e-mail	contact@relaisdulouvre.com
web	www.relaisdulouvre.com

Hôtel de France

5 rue Colbert, 78000 Versailles, Yvelines

Bone-tired after a visit to the Château de Versailles? Stroll across the regal Place des Armes, relax under the linden trees, then retire to one of the elegant rooms in this 18th-century townhouse. It beats fighting for a seat on the commuter train back to Paris and you can explore Versailles' gardens the next morning. Louis XIV made a present of the land to finance minister Colbert, who built his residence here. Four of the rooms look onto the square and the château itself while others, quieter and at the back, overlook the indoor terrace of the restaurant. All are light and dressed for the ball, in reds, oranges, golds and yellows, with matching padded headboards, swathed windows and quilted coverlets. The bathrooms are small and impeccably designed with grey marble counter tops and fresh white tiles with a blue trim. Breakfast is served in a panelled room off the mirrored lobby – the blue and yellow table cloths blend harmoniously with the flower-patterned china service. *Don't miss the baroque music, bubbling fountains and Versailles grand finale on Sunday afternoons.*

rooms	23: 12 doubles, 8 twins, 2 triples, 1 suite.
price	€ 137–€ 141. Suite € 213.
meals	Breakfast € 11. Restaurant next door.
closed	Rarely.
directions	From Paris A13 exit Versailles for Château de Versailles & Place des Armes. Stay on Avenue de St Cloud. Hotel at end of avenue in front of Château de Versailles.

	M Laforgue
tel	+33 (0)1 30 83 92 23
fax	+33 (0)1 30 83 92 24
e-mail	hotel-de-france-versailles@wanadoo.fr
web	www.hotelfrance-versailles.com

map 6   entry 63

Abbaye des Vaux de Cernay

Route d'Auffargis D24, 78720 Cernay la Ville, Yvelines

It may seem rather large but the buildings are so atmospheric, the place waves such a magical wand of respectful sophistication that people stop, feel and lose their restlessness. From thriving Cistercian abbey, through Revolution and ruin to Rothschild ownership in the 1870s, Cernay bears the marks of European history. Philippe Savry, the owner, has turned it into a luxurious hotel that preserves the spirit and forms of the old place – you can almost hear the monks scurrying along those underground passages while you listen to the Cernay Music Festival in the roofless abbey church or wine and dine in hedonistic splendour under the vaults of the brothers' refectory. There may be little trace of the 'Strict Observance' Trappist rule for daily life that once reigned here – bedrooms have every modern comfort, salons are highly elegant, there is a 10-acre lake for meditation, a 'fitness garden', the Saint Thibaud fertility fountain (medieval vestige with a tale of wishes come true). You cannot fail to be deeply influenced by the vibrations from those glowing stones and gothic arches and glad that the hotel business keeps them alive today.

rooms	56 + 1: 54 twins/doubles, 2 suites for 2. 1 4-room apartment.
price	€90–€260. Suites & apartment €330–€590.
meals	Breakfast €14. Lunch & dinner €28–€85. Sunday brunch €38.
closed	Never.
directions	From Paris Pont de Sèvres for Chartres. Exit Saclay on N306 into D906 for Chevreuse and on to Cernay la Ville; then D24 for Auffargis, signed.

Patrick Rossi

tel	+33 (0)1 34 85 23 00
fax	+33 (0)1 34 85 11 60
e-mail	cernay@leshotelsparticuliers.com

Cazaudehore – La Forestière

1 avenue Kennedy, 78100 St Germain en Laye, Yvelines

The rose-strewn 'English' garden is like an island in the great forest of St Germain and it's hard to believe the buzzing metropolis is just a short train journey away. The first Cazaudehore built the restaurant in 1928, the second built the hotel in 1962, the third generation apply their imaginations to improving both and receiving their guests with elegant French charm. The buildings are almost camouflaged among the greenery, summer eating is deliciously shaded under rose-red parasols; hotel guests have the elegant, beamed dining room with its veranda to themselves (there are several seminar and reception rooms). Food and wine are the main focus – the wine-tasting dinners are renowned and chef Grégory Balland's seasonal menus are a delight, skilfully mixing tradition and invention: you will eat supremely well here. But bedrooms are much cared for too, renovated in refined but unostentatious style with good fabrics, original colour schemes – saffron, blue and lightning green, for example – period furniture and prints, and masses of character.

rooms	30: 25 twins/doubles, 5 suites.
price	€ 190–€ 200. Suites € 250–€ 270.
meals	Breakfast € 15. Lunch & dinner € 50–€ 65. Children's meals € 23.
closed	Never.
directions	A13 for Rouen exit 6 for St. Germain en Laye on N186. N184 for Pontoise. On left 2.5km after château.

	M Philippe Cazaudehore
tel	+33 (0)1 39 10 38 38
fax	+33 (0)1 39 73 73 88
e-mail	cazaudehore@relaischateaux.com
web	www.cazaudehore.fr

map 6   entry 65

Château de Poigny

2 rue de l'Eglise, 78125 Poigny la Forêt, Yvelines

In this big country mansion, the generosity of people and places sings the proper aristocratic poem of nobility and eccentricity. From Morocco, Indonesia and reddest America, this great traveller has amassed carvings great and small, artefacts ancient and modern, inlays and filigrees in brass, lacquer and wood, and filled his family mansion so that it has become a collector's paradise (and a housemaid's hell? It's unbelievably dustless). All is exuberance and love of life and beautiful things, bedrooms are a feast of almost baroque décor: the Coca Cola room is devastatingly... red (surely a unique collection), the Indonesian bed sumptuously rich, the Buddha's room softly, darkly meditative – there's a room for you, whatever your mood. The breakfast table bows beneath 36 varieties of jams, 18 colours of honey, 80 different teas and your vastly cultured host is very good company; on weekdays his delightful assistant Taïeb will take excellent care of you. There is a loo/library, exotic fowl who strut and cackle in the garden, a real goat and stone boars to guard you, and remarkable conversations to be had.

rooms	6: 5 doubles, 1 suite for 5.
price	€56–€66.
meals	3 restaurants in village.
closed	Rarely.
directions	From N10 north of Rambouillet D937 then D936 & D107 to Poigny la Forêt 5km. Left up road by church; château on right.

François le Bret

tel	+33 (0)1 34 84 73 42
fax	+33 (0)1 34 84 74 38
e-mail	lechateaudepoigny@wanadoo.fr

Château de Maréchal de Saxe

Avenue du Domaine de la Grange, 91330 Yerres, Essonne

The eponymous Maréchal was responsible, in 1798, for re-modelling the stunning black and white floored gallery, almost the size of a tennis court, with its stuccoed columns and friezes of hunting trophies and flags. "The heart is the starting point of all matters pertaining to war", said he, whose other victories were less belligerent - one of his paramours sold her diamonds to help boost his career. His large portrait now surveys the Louis Napoleon sitting room along with gilt framed mirrors, moulded ceilings, tapestries and chandeliers; French windows open to the 68 hectares of parkland. The dining room, formerly the library, is a series of four small rooms, candlelit in the evening for intimate dinners. On the ground floor, too, is the 'royal' blue and white suite with a king-size bed and a pair of plush-velvet, emerald green chairs. All other rooms are large and light with new marbled bathrooms, fabric-lined walls and parquet floors; one with a painted Louis XIII ceiling. The owner has ambitious plans to bring the gardens back to their former glory; the Maréchal would be pleased. *No lift.*

rooms	18: 13 doubles, 4 triples, 1 suite.
price	€122-€224. Suite €275-€382.
meals	Breakfast €13. Lunch €26 (weekdays) & dinner €36-€65.
closed	Rarely.
directions	Paris A4 (Metz-Nancy); branch off to A86 for Créteil & Melun-Sénart for 3.7km; exit 23 Provins, Troyes, Bonneuil to N406 for Boissy St Léger; then N19 for Château de Gros Bois; D941 for Yerres.

	Philippe Savry
tel	+33 (0)1 69 48 78 53
fax	+33 (0)1 69 83 84 91
e-mail	saxe@leshotelsparticuliers.com
web	www.chateaudumarechaldesaxe.com

map 6   entry 67

Hôtel de Londres

1 place du Général de Gaulle, 77300 Fontainebleau, Seine-et-Marne

Gaze on the Château de Fontainebleau, one of France's loveliest buildings, from your room in this 18th-century hostelry that stands opposite. The hotel has been in the family for three generations; Monsieur Philippe runs it quietly and considerately, while his mother holds reception with charm. The sitting room has an 18th-century classical look; also rich colours, comfy armchairs, plump cushions, fine displays of flowers. The breakfast room has the feel of a small brasserie, and both rooms have views to Fontainebleau. Bedrooms, on the upper floors, are similarly classical in style – smart, spotless, traditional; colours are bold, fabrics floral. A sense of timelessness pervades this peaceful place, and you could hardly be better placed for exploring the Forest of Fontainebleau, the hunting grounds of kings. As for the château, it was built around the keep of a smaller medieval building, was completed in 1550 and has been added to over the years; the gallery of François I is considered one of the finest in Europe. You can visit for free on Sundays and it's magnificently floodlit at night.

rooms	12: 4 doubles, 1 single, 2 triples, 5 suites.
price	€ 110–€ 160. Suites € 150–€ 180.
meals	Breakfast € 10.
closed	23 December-9 January; 12-18 August.
directions	A6 exit Fontainebleau for Château. Hotel opposite château.

Philippe Colombier

tel	+33 (0)1 64 22 20 21
fax	+33 (0)1 60 72 39 16
e-mail	hdelondres1850@aol.com
web	www.hoteldelondres.com

photography by Michael Busselle

normandy

Hôtel Restaurant Le Mesnilgrand

50260 Négreville (Nr Bricquebec), Manche

Deep in the countryside, along tiny lanes which look as though they might peter out at any moment, is this lovely, converted, 18th-century cider farm – restaurant, small hotel, yurt (Mongolian tent) and creative activity centre all rolled into one. The dynamic young English owner, Tina, along with Claire the gardener/ecologist and Stéphane the chef/teacher, provide rare opportunities. You could find yourself wild-mushrooming, joining one of the yoga weekends, nature trailing or, chef by your side, searching out the finest fish, cheese or cider from the local market. You eat in a setting to match his culinary skills: exposed beams, stone walls, good white table cloths, fresh flowers. The energy and creativity of your hosts know few bounds. Le Mesnilgrand is family-friendly; rooms are comfortable, silent and simply decorated, and have good bathrooms. There's the possibility of horse riding, with or without specialist instruction, you can paint by the lake or just recline in the English-style bar. And there's a teepee for the children. Everything can be arranged. *Yoga, reiki and cooking weekends.*

rooms	6: 5 doubles, 1 family room.
price	€80. Half-board €125 for 2. Children under 3 free.
meals	Dinner €25–€30.
closed	January.
directions	From Cherbourg RN13 exit St Joseph on D146 for Rocheville. Over dual carriageway, continue 5km; signed. Hotel outside Négreville.

	Tina Foley
tel	+33 (0)2 33 95 09 54
fax	+33 (0)2 33 95 20 04
web	www.lemesnilgrand.com

Cute if want to go to that area

L'Hostellerie du Château

4 cour du Château, 50260 Bricquebec, Manche

It is the *château fort* of the old town's defences – extraordinary, with a fully documented history going back beyond 1066. There may be a gap between expectation and reality, but you come here to wallow in this remarkable piece of history... and the bedrooms and bathrooms are fine. Actually much of it is fine, with ancient stone walls and plain carpets, beams and the odd bit of good, old furniture. The views onto the floodlit courtyard and the room with the lookout point in a watch tower will woo your children. If the ghost of a previous occupant – the Earl of Suffolk – was about, he could tell them about his imprisonment by Joan of Arc in 1429. There is an old dining hall, dressed with candelabra – a suit of armour guards the entrance along with coats of arms, muskets and crossed swords on the walls – and the new owners have added a comfortable, cosy sitting room with a fireplace. It must have been a safe place as it is claimed that Queen Victoria and Prince Albert spent the night in Number Two – a most imposing room. Stay here en route to and from the ferry. It is all very real, and rather endearing.

rooms	17: 14 doubles, 3 family rooms.
price	€60–€90. Family rooms €110.
meals	Buffet breakfast €8. Lunch & dinner €20–€33.
closed	20 December–January.
directions	From Cherbourg, N13 for Valognes for 10km, then D902 for Bricquebec. Hotel inside château at foot of keep, through arch. Look for high medieval tower.

Anne & Loïc Gendron

tel	+33 (0)2 33 52 24 49
fax	+33 (0)2 33 52 62 71
e-mail	lhostellerie.chateau@wanadoo.fr

map 4　entry 70

Château de Saint Blaise

50260 Bricquebec, Manche

You will be staying in the coach house, not the château, and will be looked after by the butler. Everything will be perfect, right down to the bathroom flowers. When Ernst bought the coach house a few years back nothing remained of the building but the walls. He rescued two staircases, one stone, another spiral, and a balustrade from another place; you would never know the old building had ever lapsed from grace. The sitting room is blue and burgundy, with wooden floors and a marble fireplace. The Grande Suite is an unusual shade of dark blue, with a Napoleon III bed and draped curtains; one window overlooks the courtyard, with its round pond of pink lilies and fish, the other looks onto fields. The Petite Suite is in pink and beige, with the same views and a narrow but elegant bed. You are served breakfast in a small, pretty room, with flowers on the table. It can be as late as you like and Monsieur Loïc (the butler) will be delighted to light the fire in winter. He also squeezes the oranges, brews the coffee and cooks the eggs exactly as you like. Such luxury – and there's an exquisite pool.

rooms	2 suites in coach house.
price	€ 220-€ 250.
meals	Restaurant 3km.
	Other excellent ones 15-20km.
closed	November-March.
directions	N13 for Valonges exit Bricquebec. D902 for 10km then right on route Les Gromonts. Château entrance 100m on left.

	M Ernst Roost
tel	+33 (0)2 33 87 52 60
fax	+33 (0)2 33 87 52 61
e-mail	info@chateaudesaintblaise.com
web	www.chateaudesaintblaise.com

Château de la Roque

50180 Hébécrevon, Manche

As you come up the poplar-lined drive into the circular courtyard at the end of the day, the windows blink like diamonds. The land falls away to a lake on the other side of this 16th- and 17th-century country house. Your host leads you through the entrance passing collections of precious stones, pictures of ancestors on the farm, leather-covered bellows, a majestic grandfather clock framed by two long windows, Norman statues and a mass of potted plants. Continuing up a circular stone staircase, you reach the large, light bedrooms furnished with the same care for detail, colour and comfort: oriental rugs, an antique writing desk, good bed linen. The Delisles raise organic chickens, pigs, sheep, cows, turkeys and ducks and make their own bread in a wood-fired oven. Dinner comes after a refreshing glass of their *pommeau* (a Norman speciality of cognac and apple cider). You may ask for a picnic lunch and stroll around their lake or explore the nature reserve nearby. When we visited Raymond and his wife, Mireille, were planning a tandem bicycle trip through England visiting former guests, now friends.

rooms	15: 11 twins/doubles, 2 triples, 2 suites for 3-4.
price	€77–€82. Triples €92. Suites €132.
meals	Hosted dinner at communal table €23. Children's meals €13.
closed	2-15 January.
directions	From St Lô D972 for Coutances to St Gilles. In village, D77 for Pont Hébert for 3km; signed.

	Mireille & Raymond Delisle
tel	+33 (0)2 33 57 33 20
fax	+33 (0)2 33 57 51 20
e-mail	mireille.delisle@wanadoo.fr
web	www.chateau-de-la-roque.fr

map 4   entry 72

Les Hauts de la Baie du Mont Saint Michel

7 avenue de la Libération, 50530 St Jean Le Thomas, Manche

General Eisenhower slept here and took the bed with him! It was returned, however, as you will return to this house, with its ornate Art Deco reception rooms and unusual interior design. Everyone is taken with the spot: perched in a beautiful garden above the sea, with exceptional views to Mont Saint Michel. Madame Leroy is warm, bubbly, and as theatrical as her house. The bedrooms range from a canopied four-poster and Art Deco frieze to a delicately pretty pale pink double, with blue-green paintwork, or the new Napoleon suite in fuchsia pinks and purple. The bathrooms have their original 19th-century porcelain fittings. The beach, 10 metres away, is pebbled but there are others just a short drive. Breakfast might keep you going until supper: a buffet of proper French food, it includes charcuterie, cheese, five different breads, 12 different jams and homemade cake. Outside, you'll find a steep terrace exuberant with magnolias, rhododendrons, azaleas, camellias, canna lilies and those misty views. Take a walk across the bay at low tide – to Mont Saint Michel – by foot, on horseback, or with a guide.

rooms	8: 5 doubles, 2 twins, 1 suite for 4.
price	€75–€180. Singles €56–€85.
meals	Dinner with wine, €30, book ahead. Threee excellent restaurants within 5-minute walk.
closed	Rarely.
directions	From Cherbourg, N13 to Valognes; D2 to Coutances; D971 to Granville; D911 (along coast) to Jullouville; on to Carolles & St Jean Le Thomas (6.5km from Jullouville).

André & Suzanne Leroy

tel	+33 (0)2 33 60 10 02
fax	+33 (0)2 33 60 15 40
e-mail	contact@chateau-les-hauts.com
web	www.chateau-les-hauts.com

Château de Boucéel

50240 Vergoncey, Manche

The embroidered linen sheets enfold you in a smooth embrace that is a metaphor for the Boucéel experience. The Count's family have lived in the listed château since it was built in 1763 but he and the Countess have worked in Paris and Chicago and theirs is an elegant, unstuffy lifestyle which you are welcome to join. He, a quietly simple aristocrat, will recount fascinating details from his family history while she, energetic and communicative, prepares a succulent apple cake for your breakfast. The delightful bedrooms, named and portraited for the uncles and grandmothers who slept there, are beautifully done in just the right dusty yellows and misty greys for the original panelling, and have superb parquet floors, antiques and personal touches. And if you meet the kindly lady ghost, be properly polite to her, she's a *marquise*. Breakfast, on fine china, is in the soft green, round, panelled and mirrored dining room with French windows to the lush park, which comes complete with grazing geese, lake and ancient chapel. It's a treat to stay in this gently grand and gracious château. *A no-smoking property.*

rooms	5: 2 doubles, 3 suites.
price	€122–€145.
meals	Restaurant 6km.
closed	December–January, except by arrangement.
directions	From Avranches for Mont St Michel, exit 34 to N175; exit D40 for Mont St Michel & Antrain. Left for Antrain. After 6km on D40 left for St Senier de Beuvron on D308. Château 800m.

**Régis & Nicole
de Roquefeuil-Cahuzac**

tel	+33 (0)2 33 48 34 61
fax	+33 (0)2 33 48 16 26
e-mail	chateaudebouceel@wanadoo.fr
web	www.chateaudebouceel.com

map 4   entry 74

Copyright studio délaroque

Le Gué du Holme

14 rue des Estuaires, Saint Quentin sur le Homme, 50220 Ducey, Manche

A mouthwatering story can be told about the sea, the meadows and the orchards of Normandy by dining here on the oysters, foie gras with apples and the renowned *pré salé*, lamb grazed on the sea-flooded grass. Michel, the hugely enthusiastic owner-chef, has a deeply rooted commitment to his Norman food – the more local the better. It is hard to spot the simple elegance of Le Gué du Holme from the outside. It was all the more surprising to find the new rooms overlooking a small lavender-spiked, rose-trellised garden. Breakfast is served outside on cheerful pink and white porcelain, sweet Normandy butter under silver cupolas, a delightful mix of breads – a special moment for planning the day or just a relaxing read. The Lerouxs are sensitive to detail and colour; the rooms feel crisp, an exquisite antique trunk lives in the corridor, the warmth and brightness of the welcome is reflected in the dining room with brass light fixtures, wood trim and ochre walls. Always attentive, the Lerouxs have conjured up a new weekday bistro lunch. Well away from the summer crowds, low-key, impeccable.

rooms	10: 9 doubles, 1 suite for 3.
price	€ 65–€ 85. Half-board € 80–€ 110 p.p. (minimum 3 days).
meals	Breakfast € 10. Lunch & dinner € 23–€ 55. Restaurant closed Sat noon, Sun eve & Mon Oct-Easter.
closed	11-18 November; 2 weeks in February.
directions	From Caen, N175 to Avranches. Exit Cromel at War Museum. Left on r'bout D103. Over 2nd r'bout to St Quentin. Hotel opp. church.

M Leroux

tel	+33 (0)2 33 60 63 76
fax	+33 (0)2 33 60 06 77
e-mail	gue.holme@wanadoo.fr
web	www.le-gue-du-holme.com

La Ramade

2 rue de la Côte, Marcey les Grèves, 50300 Avranches, Manche

La Ramade, half a century old, was built in golden granite by a livestock merchant who made his fortune. Véronique took it on in 2000 and transformed it from B&B into charming hotel, fulfilling a long-held dream. Her individual interiors are a pleasing mix of modern and *brocante* finds – with Veronique's own Breton cradle sweetly displayed on the second floor. Bedrooms feel feminine and are named after flowers. Blue-carpeted Laurier has white-painted furniture and steps to a bathroom with a sunken bath, Coquelicot has a poppy theme and matching yellow curtains and towels. Pretty Eglantine has a canopied bed and afternoon sun streaming through large windows, Amaryllis – tailor-made for wheelchairs – a superb hydromassage shower. The grounds are filled with mature trees that give privacy from the road, and you are near Mont St Michel and the sea – a great spot for children. Véronique couldn't be nicer and serves you delicious food at your own table: *salade aux gesiers* in spring, perhaps, followed by *navarin de veau* and early Breton strawberries. Weddings are held here, and parties can book the whole house.

rooms	9: 8 doubles, 1 suite.
price	€55–€108.
meals	Breakfast €8. Dinner €12, book ahead. Creperie within walking distance; wider choice of restaurants in Avranches.
closed	15-31 January; 15-30 November.
directions	From Avranches, D973 for Granville, over river, then left on D911 for Jullouville; immed. on right, signed.

	Véronique Morvan
tel	+33 (0)2 33 58 27 40
fax	+33 (0)2 33 58 29 30
e-mail	vmorvan@wanadoo.fr
web	www.laramade.fr

map 4　entry 76

Le Manoir de l'Acherie

Ste Cecile, 50800 Villedieu les Poêles, Manche

A very short way from the motorway this hotel, deep in the Norman countryside, is a lovely, ever-so-French discovery: an old granite house with immaculately tended gardens and an ancient granite cider press sunk into the lawn. At one side is an old chapel, now bedrooms; on the other is an extension providing a sort of *cour d'honneur* entrance. Some of the furniture is authentically old though most is solid quality repro in the 'rustic' Norman style and there are fireplaces to warm body and soul. Rooms are carpeted and comfortable; old tiles, flagstones, and strong dark original beams give a good country-auberge feeling. Mother and daughter Cécile handle the hotel and restaurant service, father and son run the kitchen – they have won several prizes for their culinary efforts. The small number of people running this establishment and the quiet unstressed, unhurried but efficient way they do so, is admirable. The only concession one must make is to arrive before 7pm (no exceptions as they rise at dawn to prepare homemade croissants for breakfast) and the last orders in the restaurant are at 8.30pm.

rooms	15: 9 doubles, 4 twins, 2 singles.
price	€43–€60. Singles €36. Half-board €59–€67 p.p.
meals	Breakfast €6.50. Lunch & dinner €16–€37. Children's meals €8. Restaurant closed Mon except July/August; Sun eve mid-October to week before Easter.
closed	2 weeks Nov; 2 weeks Feb.
directions	A84 exit 38 Brecey-Villedieu for Vire. Over 2nd r'bout for 2km; over main road with Président dairy opp.

M & Mme Bernard Cahu

tel	+33 (0)2 33 51 13 87
fax	+33 (0)2 33 51 33 69
e-mail	manoir@manoir-acherie.fr
web	www.manoir-acherie.fr

Le Château de Sully
Route de Port en Bessin, 14400 Sully, Calvados

From the veranda, the view of giant crescent-shaped flower beds filled with flamboyant mixtures of tangled flowers is stunning. This elegant 18th-century building combines classical architecture with an exquisite setting, every detail inside and out carefully orchestrated. Yellow is the dominant colour for the formal dining room, while russet reds tone in with the bar and sober leather sofas in the main salon. In another lounge, table-games and a billiard board guarantee some fun too. The first-floor bedrooms looking out over neat lawns are beautifully decorated, and the attic rooms one floor up are cosy and inviting. There are more bedrooms, an indoor pool and a fitness centre in the *petit manoir* annexe. There are traces of children's paintings still to be seen in the 16th-century chapel, and lots of outdoor space for your little darlings. Inside, however, they will have to resist the temptation to thunder past delicate objects, as well as promise to sit up straight in the dining room. Good value, remarkably, for this really is a most magnificent place.

rooms	22: 19 doubles, 2 triples, 1 suite.
price	€ 110–€ 140. Triples € 150–€ 160. Suite € 170–€ 195.
meals	Breakfast € 11.50–€ 13. Lunch & dinner € 34–€ 75. Restaurant closed Monday, Tuesday, Wednesday & Saturday noon.
closed	December-February.
directions	From Bayeux D6 for Port en Bessin. Château on right approx. 4km after Bayeux.

M & Mme Brault

tel	+33 (0)2 31 22 29 48
fax	+33 (0)2 31 22 64 77
e-mail	chsully@club-internet.fr

map 5 entry 78

Manoir de Mathan

14480 Crepon, Calvados

A perfect size is this elegant manor house, introduced by a lovely crunching sound on the gravelled driveway and a 17th-century baroque arch. Finding this sober elegance in a typical Bessin farm, with its large courtyard and outbuildings, makes you wonder if all the farmers around here weren't aristocrats. Stay awhile and relax in the lounging chairs on the lawned grounds with the branches of mature trees overhead. It's evident that the renovation was done with much loving thought and care; revealed and enhanced are the lovely rafters, exposed stone walls, original fireplaces and spiral staircase. Bedrooms were given proper space and light, bathrooms well integrated – not tacked on as afterthoughts. The beds are big, the furniture regional but light and well-chosen, the windows large with over-the-field views. Suites are timber-strewn, some with canopied beds, and there are two rooms on the ground floor for easy access. Meals are a five-minute stroll to the sister hotel up the road (see La Rançonnière). Perfectly placed on the way to Bayeux *and* near the landing beaches: you'll need two or three days to enjoy it all.

rooms	13: 6 doubles, 7 suites.
price	€84–€94. Suites €135–€150.
meals	Breakfast €10. Other meals at Ferme de la Rançonnière: Lunch/dinner €9–€43.
closed	Rarely.
directions	Reservation/check in at Ferme de la Rançonnière: Caen exit 7 to Creully on D22 for 19km. Right at church for Arromanches on D65. 1st on right.

Vereecke & Sileghem families

tel	+33 (0)2 31 22 21 73
fax	+33 (0)2 31 22 98 39
e-mail	ranconniere@wanadoo.fr
web	www.ranconniere.com

Ferme de la Rançonnière

Route d'Arromanches, 14480 Creully, Calvados

A drive through the narrow crenellated archway into the vast grassy courtyard and history leaps out and grabs you. It was originally a fortified *seigneurie* – the tower dates from the 13th century – to protect against English reprisal sorties after William the Conqueror arrived in England. Inside there are exposed timbers and stone walls everywhere. One amazing duplex has stone steps which lead down into a double bedroom then up a worn spiral staircase into the tower with another bedroom. Rustic is the look here; an antique butter churn in the corridor and a well-worn kneading trough in a large family room remind you that this was a working farm. Off the new restaurant there is a large, vaulted-ceiling, stone-flagged floor sitting area with a wood fire at one end making a perfect spot for after-dinner coffee. The bright breakfast room and terrace face south to catch the morning light. Young, efficient Isabelle Sileghem and her husband, with help from a devoted staff, keep this place humming. Book ahead for the best rooms. A wonderful place.

rooms	45: 35 twins/doubles, 10 junior suites in 'manoir' 600m away.
price	€44–€88. Suites €104–€134.
meals	Breakfast €10. Lunch €9–€43. Dinner €15–€43.
closed	Rarely.
directions	From Caen exit 7 to Creully on D22 for 19km. There, right at church for Arromanches on D65. In Crépon, hotel 1st on right.

Vereecke & Sileghem families

tel	+33 (0)2 31 22 21 73
fax	+33 (0)2 31 22 98 39
e-mail	ranconniere@wanadoo.fr
web	www.ranconniere.com

map 5   entry 80

Manoir de la Rivière

14310 St Louet sur Seulles, Calvados

A theatrical place hidden away in the hills of Normandy. The outbuildings of this traditional, mellow-stoned 16th-century farmhouse have been converted into guests' extravagantly themed rooms. The Angel Room is painted an iridescent white and blue; there are big game trophies, pith helmets and exotic animal models to be found in the Explorer's Room; and the Colonel's Room is eccentrically kitted out with guns, swords, military coins and a life-sized model of a 19th-century soldier. Some of the artefacts, including the embroidered bathrobes, are for sale. The entrance is graced with a suite of pink, gold and white Louis XV armchairs upon which the Princess of Wales, we are told, once sat, while the guests' sitting room is stone-walled and coir-carpeted. The *manoir*'s warm welcome can include a ride on one of the ponies who graze gently in the field along with two donkeys – fun for children. The unstoppable Docteur Houdret has added a jacuzzi, sauna and massaging shower, a reception for the grand occasions that keep them busy, and a special garage for his 1976 Rolls Royce.

rooms	4: 3 doubles, 1 suite for 4.
price	€76–€100. Suite €122–€152.
meals	Dinner €27 with wine.
closed	Rarely.
directions	From Caen N175 to Villers Bocage. There, right to St Louet sur Seulles. Pass church; house is 2nd on right up poplar-lined drive.

Houdret family

tel	+33 (0)2 31 77 96 30
fax	+33 (0)2 31 77 96 30
e–mail	info@manoirdelariviere.com
web	www.manoirdelariviere.com

Château La Cour

14220 Culey Le Patry, Calvados

Another magnificent pile of old stone. This one dates back to the 13th century and was once part of the estate of the Ducs of Harcourt. The noble legacy includes exposed stone walls in the hall, a stone staircase and a stone-flagged kitchen; good business for the quarry master, hard work for his men. A house for feasting: supper is served in the kitchen in front of the open fire, while dinner is served in the formal dining room on damask and English china. David grows for Lesley to cook, and his organic potager (eight varieties of potato, 50 of vegetable) is a delightful diversion. High stone walls shelter it from unkind winds, fruit trees shade the lawn, and long narrow beds make for easy harvesting. Bedrooms face south and overlook the garden. Expect bold décor, cane chairs, marble fireplaces and Egyptian cotton. One room has a curved wooden staircase that leads to a bathroom above. The Cravens are keen conservationists; barn owls nest in the end wall of the house and there is good birdwatching. The Normandy beaches, Bayeaux and its tapestry and the Suisse Normande are all within easy reach. *A no-smoking property.*

rooms	3: 2 doubles, 1 twin.
price	€ 110–€ 130.
meals	Hosted dinner with wine € 30–€ 40, book ahead.
closed	Rarely.
directions	D562 south from Thury Harcourt for 5km; right onto D133 for Culey le Patry; left onto D166; 2nd right onto D211. Château on right approaching village.

	David & Lesley Craven
tel	+33 (0)2 31 79 19 37
fax	+33 (0)2 31 79 19 37
e-mail	lesleycraven@aol.com

map 5   entry 82

Manoir de Courson

Notre Dame de Courson, 14140 Livarot, Calvados

The majestic manor dating back to the 11th century displays its timbered splendours opposite the guest building; you breakfast over there in the handsome beamed dining room by the truly monumental fireplace. Your smiley, eager hosts have put hearts and talent into their restoration of the guest quarters. Gérard's eye for detail and Sopheakna's Cambodian origins inform the décor: eastern antiques and contemporary art in perfect harmony with the stones and woodwork of the ancient frame; exquisite bedrooms — original crooked beams — painted or plain; seagrass matting and oriental rugs on smooth old terracotta tiles; fabulous, unusual bathrooms. Each unit has its separate entrance, sitting room and panoramic eyeful of this lovely old (listed) house. The pool is well hidden behind a hedge surrounded by exotic plants in large terracotta pots. When you wake at dawn and find your place on the weathered bench outside, all is idyllic silence as you gaze upon orchards, woodland and pastures; the cows in the distance seem immobile in their meditative munchings. Nothing jars and this is worth every penny. *A no-smoking property.*

rooms	4: 3 large suites; 1 double in manor.
price	€ 110–€ 160.
meals	Breakfast € 10. Picnic hampers available for lunch or dinner € 17. Good restaurant 1km.
closed	October–March.
directions	From Paris A13 exit Chaufour (2nd exit after Mantes toll). Through Evreux N13 to Orbec. Through Orbec for Livarot. 10km from Orbec, after water tower, 2nd right; 400m on left.

Gérard & Sopheakna Goy

tel	+33 (0)2 31 32 30 69
fax	+33 (0)2 31 32 30 69
e-mail	gggoy@aol.com
web	www.manoirdecourson.com

Les Maisons de Léa

Place Ste Cathérine, 14600 Honfleur, Calvados

Honfleur harbour is one of the wonders of the Normandy coast. Flanked by 17th-century houses, it hosts a flotilla of fishing boats and yachts that buzz in and out all day long. In cobbled Place Ste Cathérine the eponymous wood-tiled church stands – don't miss it, not that you can – and Les Maisons de Léa are opposite, squeezed delightfully into four 18th-century, creeper-clad townhouses. The interiors are impeccable. Rooms come in four styles: feminine florals; yellows, beams and cosy rustic chic; nautical blues and greens; and Shaker-style creams and browns. All have crisp cotton sheets, old pine furniture and coconut matting. Bathrooms are excellent. Monsieur has recently bought the hotel (it was once the Hostellerie Lechat, an Honfleur icon of many moons) and a *salon de thé* is on its way. The market place is 10 paces from the door and the *quartier* is packed with antique shops and art galleries. The Riviera of the North (Deauville, Trouville) is well worth a trip, and horse racing, golf, casinos and bucket-and-spade beaches are wonderfully close by.

rooms	28 + 1: 27 twins/doubles, 1 suite. 1 cottage for 5.
price	€95–€145. Suite €220. Cottage €260.
meals	Buffet breakfast €10. Many restaurants nearby.
closed	Never.
directions	Hotel opposite church & next to clock tower.

	M Lassarat
tel	+33 (0)2 31 14 49 49
fax	+33 (0)2 31 89 28 61
e–mail	lesmaisonsdelea@wanadoo.fr

map 5   entry 84

Hostellerie de Tourgéville

Chemin de l'Orgueuil, 14800 Tourgéville Deauville, Calvados

There were real stars in the 70s, when film director Claude Lelouch built his glorified 'Norman quadrangle' as a club for friends; now there are just giant photographs. But his adorable private cinema is still here, as are pool, gym and sauna. Timbers and stones are genuinely old; the all-glass ground floor is thoroughly modern. Open-plan sitting and dining areas are in blond oak, soft cushions and warm colours. The chef has an excellent reputation, by the way. Most rooms are soberly decorated with high-quality fabrics, matt satin curtains, beige carpet, the odd antique and those ubiquitous film stars. Ground-floor rooms and triplexes (effectively up-ended suites with the bathroom on a balcony between salon and bedroom) have small private terraces. Triplexes also have fine double-height fireplaces on their stone-flagged floors, plus two deep sofas. The friendly manager is gradually redecorating with a more lively, contemporary touch, interesting furniture and some strong colour. A very special place to stay: Lelouch calls it "a hotel for people who don't like hotels". *Minimum stay three nights May-August.*

rooms	25 + 1: 6 doubles, 13 duplex apartments, 6 triplex apartments. 1 house for 4.
price	€ 105–€ 150. Duplex € 140–€ 185. Triplex € 260–€ 310. House € 280–€ 340.
meals	Breakfast € 13. Dinner € 31–€ 48. Lunch available on Sun, holidays & mid–July–September.
closed	3 weeks in February or March.
directions	A13 exit for Deauville N177; left at r'bout D27; 1st left; 1st left D278.

Wilhelm Stoppacher

tel	+33 (0)2 31 14 48 68
fax	+33 (0)2 31 14 48 69
e–mail	hostellerie@hotel-de-tourgeville.com
web	www.hostellerie-de-tourgeville.fr

Auberge de la Source
La Peleras, 61600 La Ferté Macé, Orne

Using reclaimed beams and stone, Christine and Serge built the Auberge de la Source – they did a lot of the work themselves – on the site of his parents' 18th-century apple press. Unfortunately that means no more cider, but they serve a superb one made just down the road. Both the restaurants – one smaller and cosier, the other with huge sliding windows – and the bedrooms were designed to make the most of the view down to the lake, which is the hub of a huge sports complex. Apart from windsurfing and a sailing school, there's riding, a climbing wall, archery, fishing and something called 'swing-golf', easy to learn, apparently. Children have a play area, pony rides, mini-golf and pedal boats. If you want real nature the forest is nearby where you will see huge stags without too much searching. The auberge has big rooms catering for families, all cosy with huge beams and chunky antiques mixed in with more modern furniture. The food is simple, centring on steaks cooked over a wood fire, with fresh farm produce to go with them. A great choice for families with small children or sporty teenagers.

rooms	5: 1 double, 4 family rooms.
price	€54–€82.
meals	Picnic €10. Lunch & dinner from €13.
closed	Rarely.
directions	From La Ferté Macé, D908 for Domfront Mont St Michel. After 2km right to auberge. Signed.

Christine & Serge Volclair

tel	+33 (0)2 33 37 28 23
fax	+33 (0)2 33 38 78 83
e-mail	auberge.lasource@wanadoo.fr
web	perso.wanadoo.fr/auberge.lasource

map 5   entry 86

Bois Joli

12 avenue Philippe du Rozier, 61140 Bagnoles de L'Orne, Orne

You are bang in the middle of pretty, fashionable Bagnoles de L'Orne, the only spa town in the area and with waters that flow at 24 degrees; boating lake, casino and spa remain. Bois Joli was a pension built in the mid-1800s for those seeking the cure; it sits on the edge of the Fôret d'Andaine in an acre of lawn, shrubs and sequoias. It has always been a smart getaway — Pompidou and Rommel stayed here; Rommel never paid for his room. Décor is traditional, understated, elegant. In the salon: comfortable chairs, books, newspapers, flowers in pewter vases and a piano you may play; in the dining room, fine rush-seated chairs and stiff white napery. The food is good: homemade brioche and orange pressé for breakfast; oysters, *magret de pigeon* and apricot tart for dinner. Slip off your shoes in a carpeted bedroom, immaculate with matching wallpaper and bedcover in *toile de Jouy* or pale flower. Old country wardrobes add character; staff are discreet. The hotel arranges mushroom-picking weekends in the woods, and there's masses to do in town: golf, cycling, riding, swimming, tennis.

rooms	20 doubles.
price	€ 60–€ 126.
meals	Breakfast € 10.
	Lunch & dinner € 18–€ 45.
closed	Mid-February–25 March.
directions	From Argentan, D916 for Mayenne, follow signs for Bagnoles Lac. Signed.

Yvette & Daniel Mariette

tel	+33 (0)2 33 37 92 77
fax	+33 (0)2 33 37 07 56
e-mail	boisjoli@wanadoo.fr
web	www.hotelboisjoli.com

Hôtel Saint Pierre

6 rue de la Liberation, 61150 Rânes, Orne

Legend has it that a fairy left a tiny footprint on the top of the tower in this small town. They say she disappeared in a flash upon a forbidden word whispered by her husband, impatient at her tardiness. Madame Delaunay is the keeper of the tower keys and the owner of this large flint stone house, rebuilt in 1953, just across the road. So pocket the keys and explore the castle on your own – the surrounding park makes for a wonderful evening stroll. Monsieur and Madame are justly proud of their Norman heritage and of their region's top class produce. Marc uses these for his local dishes; you can also buy choice pâtés, tripe, calvados and *pommeau*, a light cognac with strong apple-cider overtones. As for the rooms, much care has gone into the coordinated drapes, bedcovers and wallpapers; bathrooms are on the small side. This is a family affair and the Delaunays obviously enjoy the profession and particularly the contact with guests. There is even a baby alarm system and parents can choose to give their children an early dinner and then enjoy a meal on their own, while the little ones join the land of fairies and footprints.

rooms	12: 9 doubles, 3 triples.
price	€ 40–€ 55.
meals	Breakfast € 7. Picnic available. Lunch & dinner from € 12–€ 33. Restaurant closed Friday evenings; simple meal in room available.
closed	Rarely.
directions	From Argentan, D924 for Flers. After Ecouche, left on D916 to Rânes. Hotel just off r'bout in town centre.

Françoise & Marc Delaunay

tel	+33 (0)2 33 39 75 14
fax	+33 (0)2 33 35 49 23
e-mail	info@hotelsaintpierreranes.com
web	www.hotelsaintpierreranes.com

map 5   entry 88

Le Pavillon de Gouffern

61310 Silly en Gouffern, Orne

More mansion than lodge, Gouffern was built 200 years ago by a wealthy gentleman with plenty of fellow hunters to entertain. But the scale of this elegant 'pavilion' is perfect for today's traveller. It stands in an estate of 80 hectares and guests can walk, bicycle or ride in the private forest in total peace and seclusion. Big windows let in lots of soft light to illuminate the new décor: simple, unfussy elegance with rug-strewn oak floors, antiques and rich fabrics that give a sense of the quiet class of a good country house. Bedrooms, some of them in the well-converted outbuildings, are big and eminently comfortable (smaller on the top floor), functional bathrooms have all the necessary bits and meals are served in the handsome dining room – the food has been much praised. In the grounds, the delightful Doll's House, built for children of another age to play in, is now an idyllic suite (honeymoon specials arranged)… and you may play billiards by the fire in the bar. A nearby stable delivers horses to the door and, if you are lucky, the chef will cook your freshly caught trout.

rooms	20: 19 doubles, 1 suite.
price	€ 61–€ 81. Suite € 115.
meals	Breakfast € 8. Picnic available. Lunch & dinner € 18–€ 45.
closed	24–26 December.
directions	Exit Argentan on N26. Hotel 7km from Argentan in the forest of Silly en Gouffern. Signed.

	M Samuel Lebourg
tel	+33 (0)2 33 36 64 26
fax	+33 (0)2 33 36 53 81
e-mail	pavillondegouffern@wanadoo.fr

Auberge du Val au Cesne

Le Val au Cesne, 76190 Croix Mare, Seine-Maritime

Chaos reigns. Cupola-shaped cages of parrots, rare chickens, doves and parakeets hint at the exotic; the garden is hidden in an emerald, rolling-hilled Norman valley. Monsieur Carel, a charming, self-made *patron*, will serve a leisurely meal outside on a sunny day – or invite you into the half-timbered farmhouse and place you in one of four cosy dining rooms, two on the top floor separated by a chimney: Monsieur likes mixing locals with visitors, unlike others who segregate English language speakers. The low ceilings, raw timbers and sepia photographs of his ancestors are an appropriate Norman background for the regional dishes he creates. His customers come in droves now, so the cottage next door has been transformed into five little independent rooms, three of them on the ground floor. Each one has its own entrance and the colours are as vibrant as your host's pet ducks: royal blues and reds, canary yellow and iris purple. Padded textiles on the walls make good sound-proofing. Two, lighter and bigger, are at the top of outside stairways. A mix of old, new and kitsch – not for the fussy 'n' stuffy.

rooms	5: 4 doubles, 1 family room.
price	€76.
meals	Breakfast €8. Lunch & dinner from €25. Restaurant closed Mondays & Tuesdays.
closed	Last 3 weeks of January; last 2 weeks of August.
directions	From Rouen A15/N15 for approx. 20km. Left on D22 to Fréville then D5 for Yvetot for 3km. Don't go into Croix Mare.

M Carel

tel	+33 (0)2 35 56 63 06
fax	+33 (0)2 35 56 92 78
e-mail	valaucesne@hotmail.com
web	www.valaucesne.fr

map 5   entry 90

Hôtel de la Cathédrale

12 rue St Romain, 76000 Rouen, Seine-Maritime

In one of the cobbled streets of historic old Rouen with the cathedral looming over it – is this half-timbered hotel in a city of timber-frame houses. There is a large breakfast/tearoom with a non-working but imposing stone fireplace and comfortable armchairs. Views go straight through to the delightful little cobbled courtyard which is set with garden furniture, potted plants, small shrubs, a riotous creeper and geraniums that tumble from window boxes – a lovely spot for breakfast or afternoon tea. Rooms are simple; the ones overlooking the street are the biggest, with old-style double windows and elaborately moulded cupboard doors. There are some interesting pieces in the motley mixture of furniture. The Delaunays are slowly renovating the rather faded décor and bathrooms, with a view to keeping the original features. From some bedroom windows you see two Gothic marvels: the cathedral towers and the magnificent tracery of Saint Maclou – your soul will be safe here. Laurent is running a remarkable-value hotel plumb in the middle of a city that cries out to be explored. *Car park: Hôtel de Ville.*

rooms	25 twins/doubles.
price	€ 59–€ 69.
meals	Breakfast € 7.50. Tea room for snacks. Meals available locally.
closed	Rarely.
directions	In Rouen centre to rue St Romain; 1st street along east side of cathedral to unload luggage. Pedestrian street so park in 'Parking Hôtel de Ville', a 5-minute walk from hotel.

Laurent Delaunay

tel	+33 (0)2 35 71 57 95
fax	+33 (0)2 35 70 15 54
e-mail	contact@hotel-de-la-cathedrale.fr
web	www.cathedrale-hotel.com

Le Vieux Carré

34 rue Ganterie, 76000 Rouen, Seine-Maritime

Originally a private townhouse, then a *maison close* until as recently as the Second World War when the German officers came to play, the building is gloriously Rouenais, with beams galore and a little courtyard in front. The hotel runs around this space in a straight-sided U-form. The entrance is off-centre with some pretty potted herbs on the doorstep and then there's the reception area – a comfy and relaxing lobby with armchairs. Beside that is the tearoom where you can have a light lunch of warm braised leeks followed by a grilled sea bass; then pick a cake or fruit tart from the luscious display on the side board. The bedrooms are generally rather small and simply attired with quilted *boutis* bedspreads: light and fresh with colour combinations of ivory and old pink with 1930s wardrobes; all have bathrooms done mainly in blue mosaic tiles. Most views are over the attractive front courtyard. The roof garden has not yet been done but we have been promised a terrace, trees and chaises longues here at a later date.

rooms	13: 1 twin, 12 doubles.
price	€ 54–€ 58.
meals	Breakfast € 7.
	Lunch & light meals from € 12.
	Brunch on Sundays € 12–€ 18.
closed	Rarely.
directions	From autoroute exit Rouen Rive Droite for Hotel de Ville. In centre of town on pedestrian street, 30m from Parking du Palais.

Patrick Beaumont

tel	+33 (0)2 35 71 67 70
fax	+33 (0)2 35 71 19 17
e-mail	vieux-carre@mcom.fr

map 5   entry 92

Domaine Saint Clair – Le Donjon

Chemin de St Clair, 76790 Etretat, Seine-Maritime

Two extraordinary buildings: the Donjon – an 1890s concoction of towers, turrets, gothic windows and battlements all set about with creeping green – and the Domaine – a newly acquired Edwardian mansion with aerial views and 10 extravagantly luxurious rooms; both in an unforgettable clifftop position above the famous 'Hollow Needle' and pebble shore of Etretat. Brick pathways strewn with trellised roses, hydrangeas and parasol pines lead through the steep landscaped gardens that seem to rush down to meet the sea. Le Donjon has a perfectly cluttered eclectic interior to match the 'folly' exterior, an amusing mix of new, old, snazzy and dowdy with the refreshing lift of some good modern art. The new Domaine is unashamedly opulent with thick quilted bedcovers, billowing taffetas, velvet and leather in explosions of crimson, Indian pink, black, mushroom-grey and bronze. You may choose between Edwardian plush or whimsically-draped modern. But above all, you will be forever returning to that view – sometimes serene and sunny, sometimes stormy and breathtaking

rooms	21: 19 doubles, 2 suites for 4.
price	€90–€220. Suites €214–€300.
meals	Breakfast €14. Picnic & poolside snacks available. Lunch & dinner €35–€75.
closed	Rarely.
directions	From Dieppe south on D940 to Etretat. Hotel entrance off small lane on right before town centre. Drive runs up a steep hill. Signed.

M Omar Abodib

tel	+33 (0)2 35 27 08 23
fax	+33 (0)2 35 29 92 24
e-mail	info@hoteletretat.com
web	www.hoteletretat.com

Hôtel Vent d'Ouest

4 rue Caligny, 76600 Le Havre, Seine-Maritime

There is a breath of fresh air gusting through this newly renovated 50s building. The contemporary style of this address fits perfectly with the architectural context of Auguste Perret who rebuilt most of Le Havre; his modern church of Saint Joseph with its 110-metre-high spire sits just opposite. Windows have navy blue awnings and a trim of decorative box trees to help banish austerity. Inside, the style is new, young and nautical: rough finished furniture to complement the wall-to-wall woven seagrass; a small neat bar with navy-cup armchairs to match the canvas roman blinds. A great collection of old photographs of football teams from the 30s and 40s grace the reception area and there are red, white and blue stripes for the small restaurant serving snacks and light meals. Every room is tempting and handsome bedsteads, white linen, duvets and simple, stylish quilts complete the comfort. The pleasant, informal staff are attentive and Monsieur Lassarat has achieved a special kind of bed and breakfast charm in a big hotel. The seafront and the marina are only 100m away – hence the squawks of the seagulls – the town centre five minutes.

rooms	35: 31 doubles, 3 twins, 1 suite.
price	€80–€120.
meals	Breakfast €9. Light meals, lunch & dinner €12–€17. Restaurants nearby.
closed	Rarely.
directions	From A13 or A29 straight towards seafront to Eglise St Joseph (very high spire). Hotel with blue awnings and ornamental box trees on corner opposite church .

	M Didier Lassarat
tel	+33 (0)2 35 42 50 69
fax	+33 (0)2 35 42 58 00
e-mail	contact@ventdouest.fr
web	www.ventdouest.fr

map 5   entry 94

Hôtel de la Poste

27210 Beuzeville, Eure

Generations ago this was an old postal inn and now the Bosquet family have proudly created a small, solid, very provincial town-centre hotel. Entering through blue archways you are warmly met in a friendly reception area. From here you are led up an old-fashioned stairway to carpeted, floral bedrooms with generous double beds. Rooms on the garden side are the quietest; there could be some disturbance at the front, especially on Tuesday, market day. Food is the important thing here, and the bistro-esque restaurant is perfect for the place – fresh flowers on the tables and a majestic bar which spans the room. The regional food is specially well cooked and served. Town square activity can be observed from the small terrace in front; dining extends to the smaller terrace inside the archway. The Bosquets welcome families; their *prix fixe* menus and modest room prices should leave change for future exploration of this rich area. Beuzeville is on the road to Port l'Evêque, 10 minutes' drive from Honfleur, and has some interesting antique shops. Engagingly, unpretentiously 'correct'.

rooms	14: 11 doubles, 3 triples.
price	€43–€62. Triples €72. Half-board €108–€128.
meals	Breakfast €7. Lunch & dinner €18–€36. Restaurant closed mid-Nov–April; Sun evening except July & Aug, Tues noon & Thurs.
closed	11 November–March.
directions	Paris A13 exit 28 left on N175 for Beuzeville. Between Pont Audemer, Rouen & Pont l'Evêque.

	M & Mme Bosquet
tel	+33 (0)2 32 57 71 04
fax	+33 (0)2 32 42 11 01
e-mail	lerelaisdeposte@wanadoo.fr
web	www.le-relais-de-poste.com

Le Moulin de Connelles

40 route d'Amfreville sous-les-Monts, 27430 Connelles, Eure

Bring your boater, hop in a green and red-trimmed flatboat right out of a Monet painting and slip along a quiet arm of the Seine after a morning at Monet's Giverny garden, 20 minutes away. Watery greens, pinks and that scintillating veil of haze that is so particular to this part of Normandy intensify the impressionist mood. Then look up at the vision of an extraordinary half-timbered, chequer-boarded, turreted manor house and you will have to pinch yourself, hard. What's more, you are a treasured guest here. The Petiteaus' quiet attentions extend from the tinted glass on the restaurant veranda to the in-house baked croissants and the pre-dinner *amuse-bouches*. Step around to the garden and marvel at the rows of copper pots through the kitchen windows. It's only after a moment that you realise that part of the house is on an island; hidden paths lead through flowering bushes to a private pool and the row boats. We loved Room Nine with its rose walls and balcony overlooking the river; or splurge on Suite One, with its bathtub in the tower. Bring your paintbrushes. *Boats for hire for trips up-river.*

rooms	13: 7 doubles, 6 suites for 4.
price	€ 99–€ 150. Suites € 150–€ 210. Half-board € 180–€ 290 for 2.
meals	Breakfast € 12. Lunch & dinner € 30–€ 55. Children's meals € 12.
closed	Rarely.
directions	From A13 exit 18 Louviers on N15 towards Pont de l'Arche for 4km; right to St Pierre du Vauvray, Andé & Connelles. Signed.

	Petiteau family
tel	+33 (0)2 32 59 53 33
fax	+33 (0)2 32 59 21 83
e-mail	moulindeconnelles@moulindeconnelles.com
web	www.moulindeconnelles.com

map 5   entry 96

Château de Brécourt

Douains, 27120 Pacy sur Eure, Eure

It's worth a night here to get the instant access to Monet's gardens at Giverny that the miracle-working concierge will conjure up. On top of that it's quite a nice little place. It is a moated, national historic monument, with chimneys you can hide in, floor tiles polished by centuries of leather soles, a triple staircase with sculpted oak balustrade that would probably not fit into your house, a Louis XV wood-panelled dining room of rare elegance, mosaics on some bathtubs, fabric on the walls and, perhaps most importantly, well-worn leather sofas in front of the fireplace. The red of some of the walls is as bold as the blues of the nearby curtains. Some bedrooms are gigantic and look over the great park of 20 hectares, enough to lose yourself in if the crowds at Giverny have got to you. Some are smaller and warmly beamed. There's a small indoor pool, a jacuzzi, an orangery for receptions and tennis in the park. Neither prissy nor pristine, the château remains authentic in its refusal to be 'interior decorated'.

rooms	26 + 4: 26 doubles. 4 apartments for 4–5.
price	€75–€172. Apartments €180–€261.
meals	Breakfast €13. Lunch €26–€58. Dinner €38–€58.
closed	Never.
directions	From A13 exit 16 onto D181 Pacy sur Eure then immediately left on D75 to Douains. Signed.

Arnaud Baghat

tel	+33 (0)2 32 52 40 50
fax	+33 (0)2 32 52 69 65
e-mail	brecourt@leshotelsparticuliers.com
web	www.chateaudebrecourt.com

Château d'Emalleville

17 rue de l'Église, 27930 Émalleville, Eure

An elegant, listed 18th-century château, Emalleville has it all: landscaped and formal gardens, vast woodlands for walking (and autumn shooting), a tennis court, an ancient fallen mulberry that has rebuilt itself, a cosy suite in the converted beamed dovecote (a favourite) and fine rooms in the orange brick and limestone coach house and outbuilding. There is perfect *toile de Jouy* in some of the rooms and most beds are canopied. Contemporary touches here and there work nicely: photos and drawings dedicated to the dancer who took Paris by storm in 'Josephine', a colourful bullfighting theme in 'Seville', while 'Giverny' is floral and feminine. All open directly to the lawns. Tucked away behind the precious vegetable garden and orchard is the pool. Breakfast is served in the *salle de chasse*: try the mulberry or wild plum jam; Parma ham and eggs are another temptation. The lady of the manor's exquisite taste has weaved its magic from floor to ceiling, from Jouy print to antique wardrobe and you will feel like prince and princess here, just 30 minutes' drive from Giverny.

rooms	8: 6 doubles, 2 suites for 4–5.
price	€80–€120. Suites €140–€210.
meals	Restaurant 8km.
closed	November–March.
directions	From Evreux, D155 for Louviers & Acquigny. Through Boulay Morin, 500m after village, left to Emalleville. Right at War Monument; opp. church; ring bell.

Frédérique & Arnaud Tourtoulou

tel	+33 (0)2 32 34 01 87
fax	+33 (0)2 32 34 30 27
e-mail	tourtoulou@chateaudemalleville.com
web	www.chateaudemalleville.com

map 5   entry 98

Château de la Rapée
27140 Bazincourt sur Epte, Eure

You are not lost. It's just a long, winding road – 10km, through 80 hectares of deep forest in the Epte valley. With that in mind, just keep going, the road climbs up and up; not a house, cabin, animal or road sign to distract you. Finally there is a little plateau at the edge of the world and an extraordinary Victorian vision pops into view: a baroque Norman manor of angles, curlicues, overhanging roofed windows, turrets, watch towers and red brick trim. Monsieur Bergeron *père*, who bought the house many years ago and kept it intact, is quite the gentleman rake; he never used green in the hotel as it is "not flattering for the ladies". Maybe that is why the circular glassed-in dining room is so feminine with fresh yellow cloths and pale ochre walls and ceiling. Brothers Philippe (chef) and Pascal (maître d'hôtel) have now taken over and serve up enticing dishes. The bedrooms are painted in satiny cream pastels – one has a canopied bed and little chandelier – while working chimneys in the dining and sitting rooms make them cosy. Mad, wonderful, passionate – special.

rooms	13 + 1: 8 doubles, 4 twins, 1 suite. 1 apartment for 2-5.
price	€84-€148.
meals	Breakfast €10. Lunch & dinner €28-€37. Restaurant closed Wednesdays; 20-31 January.
closed	February; 16-30 August.
directions	From Gisors, D915 north for approx. 10km. Signed.

Philippe & Pascal Bergeron
tel	+33 (0)2 32 55 11 61
fax	+33 (0)2 32 55 95 65
e-mail	infos@hotel-la-rapee.com
web	www.hotel-la-rapee.com

photography by Michael Busselle

brittany

Château de Talhouët

56220 Rochefort en Terre, Morbihan

Your arrival is straight out of a Wilkie Collins' novel. Up a gloomy, bumpy, muddy lane smelling of moss and fungi, then wow! The imposing 16th-century granite manor house has views that reach all the way to the Aze valley and the cliffs of Rochefort en Terre. Jean-Pol bought the 1562 ruin – originally built by the crusading Talhouët family – 12 years ago, thus fulfilling a long-held dream. He's also restoring the grounds: woodland, terraced fields, wildflower meadow and a series of fascinating walled gardens, English and French. Floors are wonderful: either stone worn to satin or polished wood with Persian rugs. The sitting room manages to be both cosy and vast, with its old rose panelling, antique chairs and soft, deep sofas. There's a giant bookcase for browsing through, and a tempting selection of magazines. Jean-Pol will join you for a drink as you discuss the menu; delicious dinners are cooked by a charming young chef. Then to bed up an impressive stone stair; you will sleep under fancy florals and softly painted beams. Be woken by birdsong and a gentle view.

rooms	8 doubles.
price	€ 120–€ 190.
meals	Dinner € 42.
closed	January.
directions	From Redon D775 through Allaire 9km; right D313 through Malansac to Rochefort en Terre; D774 for Malestroit 4km. Left onto small road 2km. Entrance on left; château another 500m.

M Jean-Pol Soulaine

tel	+33 (0)2 97 43 34 72
fax	+33 (0)2 97 43 35 04
e-mail	chateaudetalhouet@libertysurf.fr
web	www.chateaudetalhouet.com

Le Logis de Parc er Gréo

9 rue Mané Guen, Le Gréo, 56610 Arradon, Morbihan

The neat new building is a metaphor for Breton hospitality. The front is a high north wall – it may seem forbidding but once inside you know that it shelters house and garden from the wild elements, that fields, woods, sea and the coastal path are just yards away. Eric prepares itineraries for guests, boating is on the spot, swimming a little further away or in the pool on site. Warm colours, oriental rugs and fine family pieces sit easily on the tiled floors of the many-windowed ground floor, Eric's father's watercolours lend personality to all the rooms, and the unusual candlesticks in the hall and ancestral portraits, including a large Velazquez-style child in a great gilt frame, are most appealing. Salon and dining room open widely onto terrace and garden – wonderful places to relax or play with the children on the big lawn. Rooms, attractive in shades of red, green and salmon, are functionally furnished. Your hosts, their charming young family and their enthusiasm for their project – to stop being clients in boring hotels and do things properly themselves – make this an easy, friendly place to stay.

rooms	15: 13 doubles, 2 suites.
price	€72–€126. Suites €149–€265.
meals	Breakfast €10.
closed	Mid-November–mid-March.
directions	From Vannes D101 for Ile aux Moines. Ignore left turns to Arradon. Left to Le Moustoir then on to Le Gréo & follow signs.

Eric & Sophie Bermond

tel	+33 (0)2 97 44 73 03
fax	+33 (0)2 97 44 80 48
e-mail	contact@parcergreo.com
web	www.parcergreo.com

map 4   entry 101

Hôtel des Trois Fontaines

56740 Locmariaquer, Morbihan

Jean-Pierre is properly proud of his small, architect-designed hotel, set back from the Locmariaquer (Lock-mahry-a-care, a pause and accent on the first syllable) road. Enfolded by greenery and garden, the 10-year-old building has sound-insulated rooms and every other modern comfort. The theme is fittingly nautical. Floors are light wood, furniture is French-modern, the feel is pristine, and you can see the sea from several bedrooms. The rooms are wood-panelled in cabin mode, with floor-length cotton curtains in cheerful colours and matching bedspreads. The twins on the ground floor open to a little piece of private terrace each triple a high ceiling and bay window. Best if all – if you love old stones – the megalithic site of Locmariaquer is just around the corner. Built between 4,500BC and 3,700BC – and excavated and restored during the last two decades – these superb ancient monuments include a dolmen and a burial mound. The village itself is typically Breton, and pretty; you can catch boats for trips exploring the bay and beyond and there are several little places to eat.

rooms	18: 10 doubles, 5 twins, 3 triples.
price	€65–€110. Triples €95–€130.
meals	Breakfast €10. Restaurant 200m.
closed	14 November-25 March.
directions	Exit N165-E60 for Locmariaquer. Signed at town entrance.

	M Jean-Pierre Orain
tel	+33 (0)2 97 57 42 70
fax	+33 (0)2 97 57 30 59
e-mail	hot3f@aol.com
web	members.aol.com/hot3f/HOTEL3F

Château du Launay
Launay, 56160 Ploërdut, Morbihan

A dream of a place, another world, another time, beside bird-swept pond and quiet woods. Launay marries austere grandeur with simple luxury, fine old stones with contemporary art, rich minimalism with exotica. In the great white hall, a large decorated Indian marriage chest shares the Persian rug with two bronze stags. The staircase sweeps up, past fascinating art, to big light-filled rooms where beds are white, bathrooms are plainly, beautifully modern, light and colour are handled with consummate skill. The second floor is more exotic, the corridor punctuated with an Indian gate, the rooms slightly smaller but rich in carved colonial bed, polo-player armchairs, Moghul prints. For relaxation, choose the gilt-edged billiard room, the soberly leather-chaired, book-filled library or the stupendous drawing room with a piano (concerts are given), a giant parasol and many sitting corners. A house of a million marvels where you take unexpected journeys and may find yourself on a horse on old Roman roads or pike fishing in the park. Your charming young hosts know how to receive – and food is deliciously varied.

rooms	6 + 3: 6 doubles. 3 apartments for 2-4.
price	€ 150-€ 115.
meals	Breakfast € 10. Dinner € 26, book ahead.
closed	January-Easter.
directions	From Pontivy, D782 for 21km to Guémené; then D1 for Gourin to Toubahado for 9km. Don't go to Ploërdut. In Toubahado right on C3 for Locuon for 3km. Entrance immediately after Launay sign.

M & Mme Bogrand
tel	+33 (0)2 97 39 46 32
fax	+33 (0)2 97 39 46 31
e-mail	info@chateaudulaunay.com
web	www.chateaudulaunay.com

map 3   entry 103

Château de Kerlarec

29300 Arzano, Finistère

The plain exterior belies the 19th-century festival inside – it's astonishing. Murals of mountain valleys and Joan of Arc in stained glass announce the original Lorraine-born baron ("descended from Joan's brother") and the wallpaper looks great, considering it too was done in 1830. In the gold-brocade-papered salon, Madame Bellin lavishes infinite care on every Chinese vase, gilt statuette and porcelain flower; sit in an ornate black and green chair by the red marble fireplace and soak up the atmosphere. Staircase and bedrooms have more overflowing personality, mixing fantasy with comfort, some fascinating furniture, lovely old embroidered linen on new mattresses and bathrooms of huge character. On the top floor, slip through a 'slot' in the rafters from sitting to sleeping space and discover a gold and white nest. Expect porcelain and silver at breakfast and reserve your crêpes or seafood platter for a candlelit dinner one night. Your enthusiastic hostess lavishes the same attention on her guests as on her house – and the bassets will walk with you in the park.

rooms	6: 1 double, 5 suites.
price	€88–€100
meals	Lunch & dinner €25–€37.
closed	Christmas-New Year.
directions	From Quimperlé D22 east to Pontivy for 6km; château on left – narrow gate.

	Monique & Michel Bellin
tel	+33 (0)2 98 71 75 06
fax	+33 (0)2 98 71 74 55
e-mail	chateau-de-kerlarec@wanadoo.fr
web	www.chateau-france.com/kerlarec

Château-Hôtel Manoir de Kertalg

Route de Riec sur Belon, 29350 Moëlan sur Mer, Finistère

So many contrasts. Driving through thick woods, you expect the old château in its vast estate, but the hotel is actually in the big, blocky stables, built in 1890 for racehorses (who even had running water): it became a hotel in 1990 when the tower was added. The salon is formal and glitzy with its marbled floor, modern coffered ceiling, red plush chairs – and intriguing dreamscapes by Brann. You will be welcomed with polished affability by the charming young owner, and possibly by visitors come for tea and ice cream, a favourite summer outing. Even the 'small' bedrooms are big; château décor is the rule: brocading, plush lace, satin and gilt-framed mirrors. The 'big' rooms are exuberant: one has the full Pompadour treatment in gold, pink and white, another is richly Directoire in curved cane and coffee-coloured velvet. The tower rooms are cosier, old-fashioned posh, but have space for a couple of armchairs. Some bathrooms are to be modernised, yet all are solid good quality and the value is remarkable. Wild woodland walks beckon and, yet, there's a helipad – somehow the two worlds meet and embrace.

rooms	8: 7 doubles/triples, 1 duplex for 4.
price	€90–€180. Duplex €240.
meals	Breakfast €12. Restaurants 2-8km.
closed	November-March; open from Easter.
directions	From N165 west exit Quimperlé Centre to Moëlan sur Mer. There, right at lights for Riec & follow signs (12km from N165).

	M Le Goamic
tel	+33 (0)2 98 39 77 77
fax	+33 (0)2 98 39 72 07
e-mail	kertalg@free.fr
web	www.manoirdekertalg.com

map 3   entry 105

Manoir du Stang
29940 La Forêt Fouesnant, Finistère

There is ancient grandeur in this 'hollow place' (*stang*) between the remarkable dovecote arch and the wild ponds. On the tamed side: a formal French courtyard, a blooming rose garden, lines of trees, some masterly old stonework. But the welcome is utterly natural, the rooms not at all intimidating. The eighth generation of the Huberts like guests to feel at home in their family mansion with a choice antique here, an original curtain fabric there, an invigoratingly pink bathroom to contrast with a gentle Louis Philippe chest – always solid, reliable comfort and enough space. Views are heart-warming, over courtyard, water and woods, the peace is total (bar the odd quack). Communal rooms are of stupendous proportions, as befits the receptions held here. The dining room can seat 60 in grey-panelled, pink-curtained splendour, its glass bays looking across to the gleaming ponds. Masses of things sit on the black and white salon floor – a raft of tables, fleets of high-backed chairs, a couple of sofas, glowing antique cupboards – and you still have space and monumental fireplaces. *Parking a bit away from hotel.*

rooms	24 twins/doubles.
price	€75–€145.
meals	Breakfast €9. Restaurant only available for groups of 20 or more. Plenty of local restaurants.
closed	October-mid May; occasionally at other times.
directions	From Quimper, N165 exit Concarneau/Fouesnant on D44 then D783 for Quimper. Entrance left on private road.

Hubert family

tel	+33 (0)2 98 56 97 37
fax	+33 (0)2 98 56 97 37
e-mail	Manoirdustang@wanadoo.fr
web	perso.wanadoo.fr/manoirdustang/

Manoir de Kerhuel

Route de Quimper, 29720 Plonéour-Lanvern, Finistère

The new managers are keen to make Kerhuel thoroughly welcoming. Breakfast is copious, in the intimate breakfast room for the few or, for the many, through some lovely carved panelling in the splendid banqueting room (once the stables), scanned by windows and tapestries. Your smilingly busy host and chef serves other meals in the pleasing modern restaurant that joins the old house to the old stables. The Manoir was built in the early 1900's, whence its rather stolid form in a flourishing green mantle of great trees and rhododendrons. The round, stone-walled, yellow-tented Bridal Chamber in the old dovecote is a tiny hideaway; go easy on the champers, though – the bathroom stairs are steep. Families are brilliantly catered for: bunk beds behind curtains, swings in the garden, a shallow children's pool beside the big one. Some rooms are pretty big, other small, some have narrow high windows, beds may be canopied and quilted, there's plenty of storage space behind sliding doors. You will find gentle colours, good repro furniture, the odd antique, space and a very easy atmosphere.

rooms	26: 21 twins/doubles, 5 suites for 2-4.
price	€60-€90. Suites €80-€150.
meals	Buffet breakfast €10. Lunch & dinner €17-€45. Restaurant sometimes closed, check when booking.
closed	Mid-November-mid-December; January-March.
directions	From Quimper D785 for Pont l'Abbé for 6km; exit Plonéour-Lanvern on D156 for 4km. Hotel on left.

M & Mme Lanvoc

tel	+33 (0)2 98 82 60 57
fax	+33 (0)2 98 82 61 79
e-mail	manoir-kerhuel@wanadoo.fr
web	perso.wanadoo.fr/manoir-kerhuel

map 3   entry 107

Château de Guilguiffin

Le Guilguiffin, 29710 Landudec, Finistère

The bewitching name of the rough knight who became first Baron in 1010 (the King rewarding him royally for battle services with a title and a swathe of wild, remote Brittany), the splendour of the place, its vast, opulent rooms and magnificent grounds, seduced us utterly: it is a powerful place, grand rather than intimate, unforgettable. Built with stones from the ruined fortress that originally stood here, the present château is a jewel of 18th-century aristocratic architecture. Philippe Davy, the latest descendant, knows and loves old buildings, his ancient family seat in particular, and applies his energy and intelligence to restoring château and park. He repairs, decorates and furnishes in all authenticity; bedrooms are richly, thickly draped and carpeted; reception rooms glow with grandeur and panelling; superb antiques radiate elegance. In the park he has planted thousands of bulbs and bushes and cleared 11km of walks. He likes to convert his visitors to his architectural convictions and is a persuasive preacher. Guilguiffin is deeply, fascinatingly unusual.

rooms	6: 4 doubles, 2 suites.
price	€130–€150. Suites €170–€210.
meals	Good choice of restaurants nearby.
closed	December-February, but open by arrangement.
directions	From Quimper D785 for Pont l'Abbé until airport exit. Then D56 5km to D784 for Audierne. 3km before Landudec look for signs.

	Philippe Davy
tel	+33 (0)2 98 91 52 11
fax	+33 (0)2 98 91 52 52
e-mail	chateau@guilguiffin.com
web	www.guilguiffin.com

Le Brittany

Boulevard Ste Barbe, 29681 Roscoff, Finistère

A very convenient place to stay for those travelling to or from Plymouth or Cork. This is an old Breton manor house with an imposing, rather austere looking façade which overlooks the harbour and is far enough away from the terminal buildings so that views are of the lovely Ile de Batz, only a short boat ride away. We must prepare you for the entrance to the hotel from the car park at the rear – quite a surprise. You come in onto a balcony on the first floor overlooking the reception area and look down onto a huge chandelier, an expanse of marble floors, lovely rugs and curtains which hang down two storeys. Behind the reception is a photograph of Mme Chapalain shaking hands with Prince Charles: he might just have just had an excellent meal of locally caught fish in the dining room, with its arched windows and magnificent views of the harbour, or just had a brew in the bar sitting in one of the leather chairs. A warm welcome is a priority here and there's attention to detail, too – maybe a jug of fresh flowers in your bedroom or a bowl of strawberries. *Special half-board prices for those having thalassotherapy treatments.*

rooms	25: 23 doubles, 2 suites.
price	€93–€144. Suites €165–€212.
meals	Breakfast €12. Dinner €30–€54.
closed	20 October–21 March.
directions	Exit Morlaix from N12. From ferry terminal right for 300m.

	Patricia Chapalain
tel	+33 (0)2 98 69 70 78
fax	+33 (0)2 98 61 13 29
e–mail	hotel.brittany@wanadoo.fr
web	www.hotel-brittany.com

map 3   entry 109

Grand Hôtel des Bains

15 bis rue de l'Eglise, 29241 Locquirec, Finistère

Marine purity on the north Brittany coast: it's like a smart yacht club where you are an old member. The fearless design magician has waved a wand of natural spells – cotton, cane, wood, wool, seagrass: nothing synthetic, nothing pompous. Sober lines and restful colours leave space for the scenery, the sky pours in through walls of glass, the peaceful garden flows into rocks, beach and sea. Moss-green panelling lines the deep-chaired bar where a fire leaps in winter. Pale grey-panelled bedrooms have dark mushroom carpets and thick cottons in stripes and checks of soft red or green or beige or blue. Some have four-posters, some have balconies, others are smaller, nearly all have the ever-changing sea view. Bathrooms are lovely, with bathrobes to wear to the magnificent indoor sea-water pool and spa treatment centre. Staff are smiling and easy, the ivory-panelled dining room with its sand-coloured tablecloths is deeply tempting and children are served early so that adults can enjoy the superb menu. The luxury of space, pure elegant simplicity and personal attention are yours.

rooms	36 twins/doubles.
price	€ 122-€ 179.
meals	Lunch & dinner € 34-€ 50. Excellent wine cellar.
closed	5 January-23 January.
directions	From Rennes-Brest N12 exit Plestin les Grèves, continue to Locquirec. Hotel in centre. Through gate to car park on right.

	M Van Lier
tel	+33 (0)2 98 67 41 02
fax	+33 (0)2 98 67 44 60
e-mail	hotel.des.bains@wanadoo.fr
web	www.hotels-charme-bretagne.com

Château Hôtel de Brélidy
Brélidy, 22140 Bégard, Côtes-d'Armor

From upstairs you can see across bucolic fieldscapes to Menez-Bré, Armor's highest spot at 302m. The old *chambres d'hôtes* rooms here are cosy, quilty, family-antiqued. Below are the beamed salon and billiard room, their vast carved fireplaces built above the two great dining-room fireplaces – such strength. The worn stone staircase and an iron man fit well; so will you, enfolded in the personal attention that is Brélidy's keynote. In the west wing, on the site of the original open gallery, guests in the suite can parade before waist-high windows like lords and ladies of yore. More modest rooms lie below, carefully decorated with soft colours, enriched with antiques; four have private entrances with little terraces and there's a huge terrace for all up above. In the gentle garden, the converted bakery is ideal for families and there's an indoor jacuzzi. Beyond are two rivers, two ponds with private fishing, and everywhere is utter peace. You can hire mountain bikes, too.

rooms	14 + 1: 12 doubles, 1 suite for 2, 1 suite for 4. 1 cottage for 2-4.
price	€ 73-€ 123. Suite € 182-€ 202. Cottage € 107-€ 168.
meals	Buffet breakfast € 10. Dinner € 26-€ 32.
closed	January-March.
directions	From N12 exit Lannion-Tréguier to Tréguier. D712, D8 then D15 to Brélidy; signed.

Carole & William Langlet
tel	+33 (0)2 96 95 69 38
fax	+33 (0)2 96 95 18 03
e-mail	chateau.brelidy@worldonline.fr
web	www.chateau-brelidy.com

map 3   entry 111

Manoir de Kergrec'h
Kergrec'h, 22820 Plougrescant, Côtes-d'Armor

Come taste the experience of a perfect château in the hands of a perfect couple of *chatelains* whose ancestors bought the place on returning from exile after the French Revolution. Just 200m from the sea, exposed to the wild Breton elements, it was originally a Bishop's seat, built with hunks of local granite and fortified as befitted a lord of the 17th-century church. It is now a vegetable farm, run by the younger Vicomte, with superb grounds and a luxurious interior of marble fireplaces, gilt mirrors, antiques and a classically French salon flooded with ocean light. Guestrooms, big, gracious and richly decorated with thick hangings and old prints, have parquet floors, good rugs and lovely family furniture. The tower room, in an older part of the building, is deliciously different, more 'rustic', with its timbers and mezzanine and the new loo fitted to the original, still functioning 14th-century plumbing! The twin-basined bathrooms are all superb yet respectful of the old frame and breakfast in the more austere dining room is a Breton feast to linger over in good company.

rooms	8: 5 doubles, 2 family, 1 suite.
price	€ 100–€ 150.
meals	Restaurants in Tréguier 6km.
closed	Last 3 weeks January.
directions	From Guingamp, D8 to Plougrescant. There right after church (leaning spire) & right again 200m along.

	Vicomte & Vicomtesse de Roquefeuil
tel	+33 (0)2 96 92 59 13
fax	+33 (0)2 96 92 51 27
e-mail	kergrec.h@wanadoo.fr

Arche Moyenne de l'Indéfendable
11111 Le Plat, Aude

Enter – and be uplifted. Come to find your space, to enter the void. This is the only hotel we have found to provide such an infinity of possibilities, such a Do It Yourself vision. The horizon is the edge of the floor, the sky your ceiling, your imagination your only wall. To be so unconfined, so liberated from the bourgeois constraints of everyday existence – that is the essence of this place. To have seen fit to combine such inspired open-air vision with such a solid, almost prosaic, arched entrance was the last flourish of the architect-designer, who lost his job (and, some say, his reputation), soon after. Those who lacked the courage to make the correct symbolic entrance were provided with a set of steps on one side and a ramp for horse-riders on the other. The arch is, architecturally, a fine example of the vernacular: close, mortared stonework, the clever use of big stones on the quoins and a subtly pointed tip that emphasises the importance of the owner. The small photo is of the main inhabitant – bearded and suspicious, but light of foot and with undemanding eating habits. *No indoors.*

rooms	None: "Open-plan meets neo-classic 'liberté' and gets lost in the space between the absence of walls…" or so the brochure says.
price	"Bon marché", whatever that may mean. It was indeed a good, long walk to get there.
meals	None – unless you are able to 'get the goat'.
closed	Impossible.
directions	Follow signs. Any will do.

	Chevvy
tel	+33 (0) – voilà, ça y est.
fax	+33 (0) – encore, c'est tout.
e-mail	chevvy@archemoyennedelindéfendable.fr.en.ch
web	doublevdoublevdoublevpoint… bof…

map 99 entry 113

Manoir du Vaumadeuc
22130 Pleven, Côtes-d'Armor

The approach down a long drive through mature trees and grass leads to the impressive granite exterior of this 15th-century manor. As you enter through the old, massive wooden door which leads into the manorial hall the whole place seems untouched by time. This is just as it must have been hundreds of years ago – a huge stone fireplace dominates the far end, there's a high vaulted beamed ceiling, an enormously long banqueting table and hunting trophies on the walls. It is easy to imagine former guests feasting and making merry after the hunt. A magnificent staircase leads to bedrooms on the first floor, decorated and furnished in period style. They are magnificent and comfortable, with no frills, quite masculine, à la the hunting and shooting fraternity. All rooms are large and some are enormous; one of them has stairs leading down into a room the size of a tennis court. The bathrooms are smart and spotless. Such a courteous welcome from Monsieur O'Neill – his family has owned this listed house for generations and will provide you with good traditional evening meals made with local produce.

rooms	13: 10 twins/doubles, 3 suites.
price	€90-€185. Suites €135-€210.
meals	Breakfast €9.50. Picnic available. Dinner for a minimum of 10 guests, book ahead.
closed	November-Easter.
directions	From Plancoët D768 towards Lamballe for 2km. Left on D28 for 7km to Pleven. Manoir 100m outside village.

	M & Mme O'Neill
tel	+33 (0)2 96 84 46 17
fax	+33 (0)2 96 84 40 16
e-mail	manoir@vaumadeuc.com
web	www.vaumadeuc.com

Manoir de la Hazaie

22400 Planguenoual, Côtes-d'Armor

Chunks of Breton history – violence, greed and bigotry – happened here where country peace now reigns. The Marivins, she an artist/pharmacist, he a craftsman/lawyer, cherish every minute of its past and have filled it with family treasures: *la maison musée*. The salon combines grandeur and warmth, ancient stones, antiques and a roaring fire. Ancestral portraits hang beside Madame's medieval paint and pottery scenes. 'Tournemine''s blood-red ceiling inspired a powerfully simple colour scheme, plain furniture and a great canopied bed. Airily feminine 'Tiffaine' has wildly gilded, curlicued Polish furniture and a neo-classical bathroom romp: statues, pilasters, a delicate mural of *Girl in Hat*. Baths have sybaritic jacuzzi jets. Rooms in the old mill-house, with fine old floor tiles and lovely rugs, open onto the garden – ideal for families. Row on the pond, glide from Hadrian's Villa into the pool, listen to the underwater music and whale sounds, sleep in luxury, enjoy your hosts' knowledgeable enthusiasm. Past owners have all left their mark: the admiral's anchors, the priest's colours. *Medieval weekends*.

rooms	6: 5 twins/doubles, 1 suite.
price	€ 130–€ 197. Suite € 214–€ 240.
meals	Breakfast € 12. Restaurants available nearby.
closed	Rarely.
directions	From N12 Rennes-Brest road exit St René on D81; D786 for Pléneuf Val André. Just before Planguenoual, right, following signs, for 2.2km. Entrance opp. La Ferme du Laboureur museum.

Jean-Yves & Christine Marivin

tel	+33 (0)2 96 32 73 71
fax	+33 (0)2 96 32 79 72
e-mail	manoir.hazaie@wanadoo.fr
web	www.manoir-hazaie.com

map 4   entry 115

Hôtel Manoir de Rigourdaine

Route de Langrolay, 22490 Plouër sur Rance, Côtes-d'Armor

At the end of the lane, firm on its hillside, Rigourdaine breathes space, sky, permanence. The square-yarded manor farm, originally a stronghold with moat and all requisite towers, now looks serenely out over wide estuary and rolling pastures to the ramparts of Saint Malo and offers a sheltering embrace. The reception/bar in the converted barn is a good place to meet the friendly, attentive master of the manor, properly pleased with his excellent conversion. A double-height open fireplace warms a sunken sitting well; the simple breakfast room — black and white floor, solid old beams, plain wooden tables with pretty mats — looks onto courtyard and garden. Rooms are simple too, in unfrilly good taste and comfort: Iranian rugs on plain carpets, coordinated contemporary-chic fabrics in good colours, some good old furniture, pale bathrooms with all essentials. Six ground-floor rooms have private terraces onto the kempt garden — ideal for intimate breakfasts or sundowners. Good clean-cut rooms, atmosphere lent by old timbers and antiques, and always the long limpid view. We like it a lot.

rooms	19: 14 doubles, 3 triples, 2 quadruples.
price	€52–€76.
meals	Breakfast €7. Restaurants nearby in Pleslin.
closed	Mid-November–Easter.
directions	From St Malo N137 for Rennes. Right on N176 for Dinan & St Brieuc; over river Rance. Exit for Plouër sur Rance for Langrolay for 500m; lane to Rigourdaine.

Patrick Van Valenberg

tel	+33 (0)2 96 86 89 96
fax	+33 (0)2 96 86 92 46
e-mail	hotel.rigourdaine@wanadoo.fr
web	www.hotel-rigourdaine.fr

Ti al Lannec

14 allée de Mézo-Guen, 22560 Trébeurden, Côtes-d'Armor

With dozens of English antiques, it is superbly French – soft and fulsome: an Edwardian seaside residence perched on the cliff, its gardens tumbling down to rocky coves and sandy beaches; only waves and breezes through the pines can be heard (the beach club closes at midnight). Inside, a mellow warmth envelops you in armfuls of drapes, bunches, swags and sprigs. Each room is a different shape, individually decorated as if in a private mansion with a sitting space, a writing table, a good bathroom. Besides the florals, stripes and oriental rugs, there is a sense of space with the use of white fabric and with views onto the sea or ancient cypresses. Some bedrooms are big, with plastic-balconied *loggias*, some are ideal for families with convertible bunk-bed sofas. Salons are cosily arranged with little lamps, mirrors, old prints; the sea-facing restaurant serves excellent food. The Jouanny family are deeply part of their community and care immensely about guests' welfare: they create a smart yet human atmosphere, publish a daily in-house gazette and provide balneotherapy in the basement.

rooms	33: 22 twins/doubles, 3 singles, 8 family for 3-5.
price	€ 144-€ 325. Singles € 78-€ 105.
meals	Breakfast € 14. Lunch & dinner € 21-€ 65. Children's meals € 15.
closed	December-February.
directions	From N12 Rennes-Brest road, exit 3km west of Guingamp for Lannion onto D767. In Lannion, follow signs to Trébeurden. Signed.

	Jouanny family
tel	+33 (0)2 96 15 01 01
fax	+33 (0)2 96 23 62 14
e-mail	resa@tiallannec.com
web	www.tiallannec.com

map 3   entry 117

Villa Reine Hortense

19 rue de la Malouine, 35800 Dinard, Ille-et-Vilaine

A mysterious Russian prince, poet and aesthete, Nikolas de Vlassov, built this house at the turn of the last century as a tribute to Reine Hortense de Beauharnais, daughter of Empress Joséphine and mother of Napoléon III. It is the only property of its type with direct access to the beach; in fact, it is on the beach with its feet firmly planted on the rocks below. The entrance leads straight into a Versailles parqueted salon with views over the sandy Dinard bay and across to St Malo. A ceiling-height green and white ceramic stove from 1850 is there for beauty only, as is the grand piano. Memorabilia and portraits line the *trompe l'oeil* marbled staircase topped with a 17th-century Cordoba leather trunk. All bedrooms are named for queens: you can play Reine Hortense and sit in her silvered copper bathtub, then dry off on the balcony overlooking the bay; be yellow and sunny in 'Anne d'Autriche' with access to the veranda; or Elisabeth in blue and white with a *ciel de lit* and draped bed. The Benoists will take good care of you here – all is charm, all is light. *Children over 12 welcome.*

rooms	7 + 1: 7 doubles. 1 apartment for 4.
price	€ 130-205. Apartment € 280-€ 350.
meals	Breakfast € 13. Restaurants 10-minute walk across beach in Dinard centre.
closed	5 October-25 March.
directions	From Rennes, N157 for Dinard following signs Centre Ville/Plage. Left around beach. Signed. Parking opposite hotel.

Florence & Marc Benoist

tel	+33 (0)2 99 46 54 31
fax	+33 (0)2 99 88 15 88
e-mail	reine.hortense@wanadoo.fr
web	www.villa-reine-hortense.com

La Valmarin

7 rue Jean XXIII, St Servan, 35400 St Malo, Ille-et-Vilaine

So close to the ferry terminal, this hotel has an unexpectedly large rose-filled garden with sunloungers and tables dotted around under mature cedars and a copper beech. The gracefully proportioned house was built in the early 18th century by a wealthy ship owner; now, for much of the year, it's run by Sylvie as Mme Nicolas, the owner and interior designer, is busy elsewhere. Sylvie speaks English with an impressive accent and has started afternoon teas and half-day courses on arts and crafts. Most bedrooms overlook the back garden – light rooms with tall windows, carefully draped to match the bed covers. One huge room has a double bed and a single, and space still for three more – ideal for a big family with young children. Second-floor rooms have sloping ceilings and a cosier feel, with exposed beams, white walls and pale blue carpets and paintwork. There are lavender bags in the wardrobes, plenty of books in French and English, and breakfast at small, yellow or blue dining tables with views onto the garden.

rooms	12 doubles.
price	€95–€135.
meals	Breakfast €10. Light lunches in tea room.
closed	Rarely.
directions	In St Malo follow signs for St Servan & town centre. Left at r'bout 'Mouchoir Vert' for St Croix Church; left at church; 20m to hotel.

Gérard & Françoise Nicolas

tel	+33 (0)2 99 81 94 76
fax	+33 (0)2 99 81 30 03
e-mail	levalmarin@wanadoo.fr

map 4   entry 119

La Korrigane

39 rue le Pomellec, 35400 St Malo, Ille-et-Vilaine

Small antique daybeds and vast gilt-framed mirrors, carved armoires and ancestral portraits – it's like stepping back into an elegant private mansion of the 1930s, with that deliciously old-fashioned refinement and sense of welcome. The 1990s have contributed the requisite modern communication and bathroom bits. Madame Dolbeau, enchantingly 'just so', fits utterly into her surroundings and nothing is too much trouble for her. There is elegant stucco in front, solid Breton granite behind where the peaceful walled garden contains your reading corner or your breakfast table beneath the mature trees. In poor weather, the breakfast room is attractive, tall-windowed, chandeliered and the salon has comfortable armchairs, log fires and that ever-amazing trick of a window above the fireplace. Bedrooms are big and supremely comfortable, with thick matching covers and curtains, subtle lighting, pretty antiques and two amazing wardrobes from Cancale. Light floods in, there is an irresistible softness, a sense of luxury and good manners – and all this within walking distance of the old walled town and the ferry port.

rooms	12: 11 doubles, 1 family room.
price	€ 100–€ 150. Triple € 168.
meals	Breakfast € 10. Lunch & dinner available locally.
closed	Rarely.
directions	From ferry port Quai de Trichet; at roundabout towards St Servan centre; this road is Rue le Pomellec.

	Madame Dolbeau
tel	+33 (0)2 99 81 65 85
fax	+33 (0)2 99 82 23 89
e-mail	la.korrigane.st.malo@wanadoo.fr
web	www.st-malo-hotel-korrigane.com

Château de la Ballue
35560 Bazouges la Pérouse, Ille-et-Vilaine

The gardens are reason alone for visiting La Ballue. Saved from suffocating brambles in 1973, restructured by phenomenal topiary in the 17th-century idiom of light and shade, they are a work of modern art with 13 green 'salons' studiously peppered with contemporary sculptures. The owners, a relaxed, intelligent couple of aesthetes from the publishing and art worlds, have brought their taste and refinement into the rigorously classical mansion where so many writers and artists have stayed. The fine reception rooms have panelling and fireplaces, masses of lovely things – antiques, ceramics, modern art and Old Masters – and a soft warm atmosphere. The hugely successful, elegantly understated décor mixes old, oriental and contemporary and the guest rooms are pure château: beautiful woods, fabrics and rugs, deep armoires, top-class mattresses beneath rich draperies, modern bathrooms. A magical place for body and soul. Creep out early when trails of dewy mist still lurk in the maze and haunt the carvings – the vision will never leave you. *Minimum stay two nights, a no-smoking property.*

rooms	6: 3 doubles, 2 triples, 1 suite for 4.
price	€ 160–€ 290.
meals	Breakfast € 12. Evening buffet (cold) with wine, book ahead. Restaurants 7km.
closed	20 November–1 March.
directions	From Avranches A84; then N175 to Pontorson and on to Antrain. At r'bout head for Dol de Bretagne for 1km; left. Signed.

Madame Marie France Barrère

tel	+33 (0)2 99 97 47 86
fax	+33 (0)2 99 97 47 70
e-mail	chateau@la-ballue.com
web	www.la-ballue.com

map 4 entry 121

Château de la Foltière
Parc floral du Haute Bretagne, 35133 Le Châtellier, Ille-et-Vilaine

Come for the gardens – and Monsieur! He loves having guests, and the gardens, all 20 hectares, are his pride and joy. They date from 1830 when the château was built, designed to be fashionably informal. The château, a touch worn on the outside but impeccable within, has the usual sweeping drive and imposing stairway and hall. Rooms are vast. The feel is hushed stately home, yet it's not the least bit precious and children are welcomed, even spoiled, with mazes and bridges, slides and surprises. Bedrooms have tall windows and are big enough to tango in: peachy Degas with its own dressing room, deep-red 'Renoir' (these two interconnect – ideal for families); blue 'Monet' with its original porcelain loo; 'Sisley', a symphony in yellow; 'Pissaro', perfect for wheelchair users. Breakfast on homemade croissants (and, when Madame is around, Breton crêpes) or charcuterie and cheese. Then seek out the grounds – magnificent from March to October. Paths meander round the huge lake and past groves and secret corners bursting with camellias and narcissi, azaleas and rhododendrons, old roses and banks of hydrangea. *A no-smoking property.*

rooms	5: 4 doubles, 1 suite.
price	€ 140. Suite € 140–€ 240.
meals	Many restaurants nearby.
closed	23-27 December.
directions	From Rennes & Caen A84 exit 30 for Fougères. Signed: Parc Floral par St Germain en Cogles.

Alain Jouno
tel	+33 (0)2 99 95 48 32
fax	+33 (0)2 99 95 47 74
e-mail	foltiere@parcfloralbretagne.com
web	www.parcfloralbretagne.com

photography by Michael Busselle

western loire

Hôtel du Général d'Elbée
Place du Château, 85330 Noirmoutier en l'Ile, Vendée

The general in question came to a sorry end, shot on the square for raising an army of Vendéen royalists against the Revolution, but was allowed, as an officer, to face the firing squad in his armchair. This house is where the rebellion was planned, a solid, powerful building down by the bridge, just below the castle, at the heart of life on Noirmoutier. The sea air makes the colours soft and limpid, the land and seascapes are flat and bewitching (Renoir was very taken with this spot), the inner garden and swimming pool were a haven for the general's privileged guests. Inside, the atmospheric old building is fittingly furnished with excellent country antiques, 18th-century fireplaces and fresh flowers. Bedrooms in the wing over the garden have been recently redecorated and are very pleasant indeed. Some of those in the 18th-century part, which also has a big terrace over the canal, have varied shapes but all bathrooms are excellent. The suites under the rafters on the second floor are ideal for families and a quiet, careful welcome is waiting for all. *Best avoid peak hours for arrivals and departures.*

rooms	27: 23 doubles, 4 suites for 3-4.
price	€75-€145. Suites €155-€277.
meals	Breakfast €12. Dinner available at Hôtel Punta Lara, 2km.
closed	October-March.
directions	From Nantes ring road south-west D723, D751, D758 to Beauvoir sur Mer. Road to Noirmoutier via Le Gois only possible at low tide. Otherwise take bridge.

Christophe Lamiaud

tel	+33 (0)2 51 39 10 29
fax	+33 (0)2 51 39 08 23
e-mail	elbee@leshotelsparticuliers.com
web	www.generaldelbee.com

Hôtel Fleur de Sel

Rue des Saulniers, 85330 Noirmoutier en l'Ile, Vendée

Noirmoutier has a personality all its own: this group of simple white buildings in its mediterranean garden is typical. Built in the 1980s, it sits peacefully between sea and salt marsh, long sandy beach and little yachting harbour. It is perfect for family holidays, with tennis court, golf driving range, big pool and outdoor jacuzzi. Bedrooms are good too, some in classic cosy style with country pine furniture and fabrics, others more bracing with ship-shape yew furniture and yachting motifs; several have little ground-floor terraces. The delightful, caring owners have humour and intelligence; their daughter's paintings are sometimes shown here. The chef has worked with the very best in Paris and meals are served by courteous waiters in the airy, raftered dining room or on the oleander-lined terrace. It is all clean-cut, sun-warmed, impeccable and welcoming. There is a bridge, but try and come by the Passage du Gois causeway, open three hours twice a day round low tide: an unforgettable four kilometre drive 'through the sea' where shellfish-diggers cluster. The island is, of course, very popular in summer.

rooms	35: 30 doubles, 5 family rooms.
price	€ 74–€ 145.
meals	Breakfast € 10. Lunch € 24. Dinner € 32–€ 44.
closed	2 November–3 April.
directions	From Nantes ring road south-west D723, D751, D758 to Beauvoir sur Mer. Road to Noirmoutier via Le Gois only possible at low tide. Otherwise take bridge. Hotel 500m behind church.

Pierre Wattecamps

tel	+33 (0)2 51 39 09 07
fax	+33 (0)2 51 39 09 76
e-mail	info@fleurdesel.fr
web	www.fleurdesel.fr

map 9   entry 124

Hôtel du Martinet
Place de la Croix Blanche, 85230 Bouin, Vendée

Madame Huchet describes the Martinet as a country hotel that is by the sea. It's a fair description: sitting by the pool in the garden the atmosphere is bucolic, but by the sea, just down the road, the feel is very different. Halfway down the Vendée coast, Bouin is a working seaside village – the pretty church was built in the 14th and 15th centuries – not somewhere that has sprung up for the tourists. Madame Huchet's son Jean-François runs oyster beds off the village, and busy little fishing ports are clustered along the coast. This is a real family hotel and Emmanuel, an absolute delight, is the chef and kitchen gardener specialising, not surprisingly, in fresh fish and seafood. Meals are either in a cosy blue-panelled dining room or in a more summery room with a verandah giving onto the garden. The rooms are simply but attractively decorated, some in the main house and some alongside the swimming pool. A great place to bring children for a holiday: the hotel is relaxed and informal, there are country walks as well as beaches and Jean-François will be happy to take you to see his oysters. *A no-smoking property.*

rooms	30: 23 twins/doubles, 1 triple, 6 duplexes for 2-6.
price	€52–€95. Duplexes €72–€95. Half-board €53–€74 p.p.
meals	Breakfast €7–€10. Lunch and dinner from €22.
closed	Rarely.
directions	51km south-west of Nantes on D751 past Bouaye, then D758 through Bourgneuf en Retz towards Noirmoutier for 9km.

Françoise Huchet

tel	+33 (0)2 51 49 08 94
fax	+33 (0)2 51 49 83 08
e-mail	hotel.martinet@free.fr
web	www.lemartinet.com

Château de la Cacaudère
Thouarsais Bouildroux, 85410 La Caillère, Vendée

The 19th-century, golden-stone chateau had been abandoned for 50 years when the Montalts discovered it. She is Parisian, he Spanish; together they have achieved miracles. Madame, a pianist by training, has a fine eye for colour and a lightness of touch; music and château are her passions. (She also produces fine fruit tarts for breakfast.) Much of the furniture has been picked up on postings abroad – a wardrobe from a London auction house, a scroll-top bed from Korea – then put together with French flair. Bedrooms range from smallish to large; one has steps down to a pretty little pink room for a child, another a reading room in a turret. Bathrooms are similarly stylish and pleasing, one with a old curvy tub with Savoy taps, another with a *trompe l'oeil* ceiling of the sky. Pass the kitchen on your way to breakfast and catch a glimpse of polished copper pans – immaculate, spotless. There's a big, comfy sitting room with long windows looking to the garden; it's large and leafy, filled with copper beeches and pines, walled orchard and pool. Half a dozen sheep graze peacefully, and there's an old garage for bikes and ping-pong.

rooms	5 doubles.
price	€90–€120.
meals	Barbecue available for guests use. Restaurants within 15km.
closed	September–April.
directions	From Niort, A83 to Fontenay le Comte, then D938 for Bressuire. 1km after Place Viète, left on D23 for Sérigné and La Caillère. Before La Caillère, right on D39 for Thouarsais-Bouildroux. Château 1km before village.

M & Mme Montalt

tel	+33 (0)2 51 51 59 27
fax	+33 (0)2 51 51 30 61
e-mail	chris.montalt@wanadoo.fr

map 9 entry 126

Château de la Flocellière

85700 La Flocellière, Vendée

You really need to see La Flocellière from a helicopter: the aerial view is the most striking – the origin of the name is 'Flower of the Sky', so that gives you an idea of how impressive it is. The castle – the part the family live in looks like a château, the rest is definitely a castle, complete with towers and battlements – was built around 1090 and is listed as a *monument historique*. You stay in the château itself: rooms are vast, gracious and opulent, with huge windows on two sides onto the gardens and park; most have showers camouflaged behind cupboard doors and baths. You can lounge around in the sitting room in the gallery, visit the library or explore the park and the magnificent potager below the ruined walls. The pool is tucked away nearby but out of sight and you may be given a full tour of the estate and the château. If you want to eat in, dinner is either with the Vicomte and Vicomtesse or on your own if you prefer. Lots to see round about: the historical enactment at Puy du Fou is only seven kilometres away so you can pretend the last few centuries never happened. *Special rates for long stays.*

rooms	6 + 2: 5 doubles, 1 suite. 2 houses for 8.
price	€ 130–€ 200. Suite € 145–€ 220. Houses € 1,320–€ 1,680 per week.
meals	Breakfast € 10. Dinner € 45–€ 54, book ahead.
closed	Rarely.
directions	From Paris, A11 for Angers; exit 28 for Les Herbiers, then D755 for Pouzauges to St Michel Mont Mercure. Left to La Flocellière to church; left on rue du Château.

Vicomte & Vicomtesse Patrice Vignial

tel	+33 (0)2 51 57 22 03
fax	+33 (0)2 51 57 75 21
e-mail	flocelliere.chateau@wanadoo.fr
web	www.flocellierecastle.com

Abbaye de Villeneuve

Route de la Roche sur Yon, 44840 Les Sorinières, Loire-Atlantique

The ancient foundations have been here for 800 years. Today's hotel is the abbey's 18th-century hostelry and there remains a legacy of peace and quiet contemplation. One corridor is atmospherically frugal with its deep brown curtains held by heavy unbleached ropes. The rich-coloured, thick-curtained rooms are less austere, especially those with colourful mosaic-walled bathrooms. Even the sober salon suite with ancient chest and grey plush chairs has a bedroom warmly clothed in old rose and a capacious bathroom. Warm fabrics, armoires, marble-topped tables and French armchairs abound, with not a single furbelow. 'Standard' rooms are small, well decorated, warmly beamed. Down the superb barrel-vaulted staircase you come to the public rooms: hung with green or red cloth, flaunting carved fireplaces and beamed ceilings, they are massively authentic and hum with history. There's a quiet 'cloister' garden with a round swimming pool and tables on old stone pedestals, so you can seclude yourself from the fairly busy road at the bottom of the drive (we gather it's less busy at night).

rooms	15 + 3: 15 doubles. 3 apartments for 2.
price	€80–€155. Apartments €190.
meals	Breakfast €13. Lunch & dinner €24–€74.
closed	Rarely.
directions	From Nantes A83 south exit 1 for La Roche sur Yon. Right D178 to Viais.

Sylvain Choblet

tel	+33 (0)2 40 04 40 25
fax	+33 (0)2 40 31 28 45
e–mail	abbayevilleneuve@leshotelsparticuliers.com
web	www.abbayedevilleneuve.com

map 9   entry 128

Le Palais Briau

Rue de la Madeleine, 44370 Varades, Loire-Atlantique

A glorious Palladian house perched high on the hillside overlooking the Loire valley. Built in the 1850s by François Briau, an early industrialist who made his fortune building railways, the house is palatial, lovingly restored and saved from commercial modernisation by the present owners. Faithful to the era in which the house was built, they have even held on to Briau's original furniture and fittings (of which he was immensely proud). Madame radiates exuberance and charm; Monsieur is an artist and designer whose impeccable taste has been stamped on every interior. A remarkable colonnaded stair sweeps up to the guests' sitting and dining rooms – pure Napoleon III. Bedrooms are light and large; three are blessed with magnificent views, all have separate dressing-rooms. Exquisite wallpapers, brocade canopies above polished mahogany beds, fine linen, flowers – all elegant and glamorous. Bathrooms are sumptuous and orientally-tiled. The grounds too are fabulous; large areas are completely wild and overgrown and contain the remains of a vast *orangerie*. A breathtaking place.

rooms	4: 3 doubles, 1 suite for 2 with children's bed.
price	€ 100–€ 160.
meals	Good restaurants nearby.
closed	Rarely.
directions	From Angers, N23 for Nantes. Château signed left at roundabout on entering Varades.

Thérèse & François Devouge

tel	+33 (0)2 40 83 45 00
fax	+33 (0)2 40 83 49 30
e-mail	devouge@palais-briau.com
web	www.palais-briau.com

Château de Cop-Choux
44850 Mouzeil, Loire-Atlantique

The name refers to the old lime kilns on the estate and comes from *couper la chaux* — so, nothing to do with cabbages. Where to start: the elegant house, the pool, the animals, or Gerdie's works of art? Your friendly hosts are Dutch and a stained-glass window of an owl symbolises their contentment at having traded life in the lowlands for life in the Loire. The park is huge, with chestnut trees lining the approach and a menagerie of peacocks, chickens, goats, pony, cats and two Highland cattle (in no danger of being eaten). The house, built in 1795, is full of light; several rooms have windows on three sides. Gerdie conjures up works of art from nothing: a metal doll in a mosquito-net wedding dress, flower-pot men by the door. Bedrooms are dreamy and named after herbs. 'Violette' has filmy blue floating at tall windows, 'Romarin' has exquisite carved twin beds (and an interconnecting room). Bathrooms are gorgeous. You can have a just-laid egg for breakfast in a pretty panelled room, or on the terrace; then amble across lawns to the pool. Jan makes his own wine, just enough to drink with friends. *A no-smoking property.*

rooms	6: 5 double, 1 twin.
price	€80–€100.
meals	Dinner with drinks €30, book ahead. Restaurants in Ancenis, 12km.
closed	Rarely.
directions	A11 exit 20 for Ancenis; N23 for Nantes; D164 towards Nort sur Erdre for 11km, right after Pont Esnault. Signed.

	Jan & Gerdie Liebreks
tel	+33 (0)2 40 97 28 52
fax	+33 (0)2 40 97 28 52
e-mail	jan.liebreks@wanadoo.fr
web	www.cop-choux.com

map 4 entry 130

Auberge du Parc

La Mare aux Oiseaux, 162 Ile de Fédrun, 44720 St Joachim, Loire-Atlantique

A perfect little inn in a low-lying village deep in the watery wilderness of the Brière Regional Park. People even come for lunch by boat: it has the charm and simplicity of a remote staging post and the exquisite sophistication of an increasingly reputable table. Eric Guérin, an adventurous and attractive young chef, trained with the best in Paris and now applies his lively culinary creativity in his own kitchen. Appropriately in this watery landscape, he delights in mixing earth fruits and water creatures – he calls it "good French traditional with a zest of young Parisian". His pretty, low-ceilinged dining room, with rough rustic walls and smartly-dressed chairs, is the ideal setting for this experience; bedrooms under the thatch are for quiet nights after days of marshy discoveries and evenings of gourmet pleasure. Eric's artworld background is evident in his choice of gently contemporary, uncluttered décor and country antiques. He has some engaging art, too. The garden is green, the canal watery, the welcome genuine and the food... out of this world.

rooms	12 doubles.
price	€90–€150. Half-board €150–€200 for 2.
meals	Breakfast €9. Lunch & dinner €33–€70. Restaurant closed Sun eve & Mon except July/August.
closed	March.
directions	Nantes for La Baule, exit Montoir de Bretagne for Parc Naturel Brière to St Joachim; left at lights to Fédrun for 2km. Opp. La Maison du Parc.

Eric Guérin

tel	+33 (0)2 40 88 53 01
fax	+33 (0)2 40 91 67 44
e-mail	aubergeduparc@aol.com
web	www.auberge-du-parc.com

Hôtel Villa Flornoy

7 avenue Flornoy, 44380 Pornichet, Loire-Atlantique

Villa it is, a large one, in a quiet road just back from the vast sandy beach and protected from the sea-front bustle. Built as a family boarding house in the 1920s, Flornoy still stands in the shade of a quieter age: high old trees, nooked and crannied seaside villas in stone, brick and wood. Inside it is just as peaceful. After being greeted by the delightful young owner and admiring the clock over the desk – his family have made clocks for generations – enjoy sitting in the salon: garden view, four tempting 'corners', well-chosen prints and the occasional interesting *objet*. Rooms – mostly a good size, a few with balconies – have a pretty, fresh feel, nothing frilly, just plain or Jouy-style wall fabrics, coordinated colours and patterns, good modern/traditional furniture, excellent beds and white bathrooms with fine new fittings. It is simple, solid, attractive and extremely comfortable and in the morning you will enjoy a generous breakfast in the light dining room or under the trees in the green and blooming garden. Really good value and a relaxed welcome.

rooms	30: 22 twins/doubles, 8 triples.
price	€66–€99.
meals	Breakfast €7. Dinner €19–€22. Restaurant closed October–April.
closed	November–mid-February.
directions	In Pornichet Centre Ville in big market place, right onto Avenue Général de Gaulle for 300m; Avenue Flornoy on right just after Hôtel de Ville on left.

	Luc Rouault
tel	+33 (0)2 40 11 60 00
fax	+33 (0)2 40 61 86 47
e-mail	hotflornoy@aol.com
web	www.villa-flornoy.com

map 9   entry 132

Le Chai de la Paleine

10 place Jules Raimbault, 49260 Le Puy Notre Dame, Maine-et-Loire

Despite doing all the restoration, in a 19th-century bourgeois manor house, opening a new hotel in the old wine warehouse (*chai*) and having five children under 12, Caroline and Philippe are unfailingly relaxed and welcoming. Perhaps their secret is that they want everyone to fall in love with La Paleine, as they did. Old buildings are scattered here and there: a hen house with nesting holes in its walls used as a bike store, an old wash-house in the middle of the lawn with a stone trough and fireplace and hide-outs can be found in semi-secluded corners of the grounds. The brand new rooms are simple, uncluttered, stylish. Children will love having breakfast sitting inside one of two enormous wine casks, or *foudres*, big enough for six. There are two sitting rooms with soft green and beige sofas, bookcases for browsing, a fully equipped kitchen and an honesty bar. On the edge of an interesting village with an auberge just down the road for supper, you will find a great family atmosphere, homemade jam and yogurt for breakfast and a bag of walnuts to take home. *Gîte space for five.*

rooms	9: 6 doubles, 1 triples, 1 suite, 1 studio for handicapped with double bed.
price	€56–€58. Singles €49.
meals	Good auberge 200m; closed Wednesdays.
closed	Rarely.
directions	From Saumur for Poitiers exit Le Puy. 2nd right at Le Puy Notre Dame, signed Toutes Directions.

Philippe Wadoux

tel	+33 (0)2 41 38 28 25
fax	+33 (0)2 41 38 42 38
e-mail	p.wadoux@libertysurf.fr
web	www.relais-du-bien-etre.com

Domaine de l'Oie Rouge

8 rue Nationale, 49350 Les Rosiers sur Loire, Maine-et-Loire

Recline in bed and watch the Loire flow past the garden. The 19th-century townhouse sits in large peaceful gardens; in another, smaller building Christiane runs an art gallery. One of the two bedrooms with a view, Camélia, has an astonishingly ornate, brown-tiled bathroom with a tub raised right in the middle. Another room, Santal, opens to the garden and its wonderful trees; it has Chinese doors behind twin beds and a large Thai Buddha. Each room is individual, each lavishly French. Christiane's husband, a retired chemical engineer, spent some time working in India. He has swapped chemistry for cookery, buys much of his produce from a local organic farm (which, amazingly, grows 22 varieties of tomato) and serves up excellent local dishes. Christiane likes to host dinner, and this works well when a small number of guests stay; both your hosts will be happy to help you decide what to see and make the most of your stay. The gardens here are lovely – worth exploring if you are green-fingered. *A no-smoking property.*

rooms	4 doubles/triples.
price	€60–€79.
meals	Dinner €22, book ahead.
closed	Rarely.
directions	15km from Saumur D952 for Angers. At village entrance.

Madame Christiane Batel

tel	+33 (0)2 41 53 65 65
fax	+33 (0)2 41 53 65 66
e-mail	c.batel@wanadoo.fr
web	www.domaine-oie-rouge.com

map 10   entry 134

Château de Verrières

53 rue d'Alsace, 49400 Saumur, Maine-et-Loire

The château was built in 1890 by a certain Général Baillon de la Blosse to host the balls and grand soirées that he so enjoyed. The décor remains virtually unchanged. The house is in huge grounds – unusually so since it is right in the old town of Saumur – and aristocratic French cavalry officers used to hone their equestrian skills here. Your hosts speak impeccable English, are very welcoming and love to talk about the château's restoration. Every trace of necessary updating – central heating, rewiring – has been carefully concealed. Big bedrooms have huge windows; some look onto the park, others the elegant Academy of Cavalry, or the Château de Saumur. Bathrooms are as luxurious as you'd expect, with masses of thick white towels. Swim in the heated pool, work off in the gym, be whisked off by a horse and carriage for a trot around the town (and don't miss the wonderful market). Yolaine is a refined and accomplished cook who wouldn't dream of using any but the freshest vegetables – or of serving anything other than homemade jam.

rooms	5 doubles.
price	€ 120–€ 240.
meals	Breakfast € 12. Dinner € 35.
closed	15 November–15 March.
directions	A85 exit Saumur for Saumur-Centre, over 2 roundabouts. Left for château at 2nd set of lights. Château 100m on right.

	Yolaine de Valbray–Auger
tel	+33 (0)2 41 38 05 15
fax	+33 (0)2 41 38 18 18
e-mail	chateaudeverrieres@wanadoo.fr
web	www.chateau-verrieres.com

Hôtel Anne d'Anjou

32 quai Mayaud, 49400 Saumur, Maine-et-Loire

Any malign inhabitants of the château could have tossed rocks onto the roof of this elegant townhouse. It stands just below, on the banks of the Loire in a picture-book position. The main staircase is listed and has a fine wrought-iron balustrade and *trompe l'oeil* that gives the impression of a dome. The reception area, big and filled with light, has just a discreet desk to welcome you. The bedrooms on the first and second floors look either onto the river and the road, or onto the courtyard and château. Two of the rooms are especially fine: the Salle Empire (listed) has terracotta panelling and moulded friezes, and the Salle Epoque a splendid old chequered tiled floor and grey panelling. Another room has a fine parquet floor and a balcony overlooking the river. Top-floor rooms have solid old ceiling beams and views of the château. Some front rooms are plainer, look over the road and the Loire, but are in the listed part of the building, so soundproofed windows cannot be installed. The owners are breathing fresh life into this lovely old building, and doing so with a mixture of dynamic (ex-naval) efficiency and flair.

rooms	43 + 2: 41 doubles, 2 family. 2 apartments for 4.
price	€ 76–€ 170.
meals	Buffet breakfast € 10. Lunch & dinner € 30–€ 55. Restaurant closed Sundays.
closed	Rarely.
directions	From Saumur follow signs to Saumur Centre. Along south bank of Loire on Chinon-Fontevraud road. Below château 500m after theatre.

Jean-René Camus

tel	+33 (0)2 41 67 30 30
fax	+33 (0)2 41 67 51 00
e-mail	anneanjou@saumur.net
web	www.hotel-anneanjou.com

map 10   entry 136

Le Domaine de Mestré
49590 Fontevraud l'Abbaye, Maine-et-Loire

History oozes from every corner of Mestré. A Roman road, a cockleshell for the pilgrims who stayed en route to Compostela, part of a 13th-century chapel – and the mill and tithe barn remind us that monks farmed here when Mestré was part of the vast Abbey. Most of the present building is 18th century: the family have farmed here for 200 years and keep alive the traditions of French country hospitality. Monsieur runs the eco-conscious farm, milking by hand. Madame makes fine natural soaps, and cooks; two daughters help out. All take pride in providing wholesome, home-grown food and elegant service. Big, rustic-style rooms are furnished with old family furniture – huge sleigh beds or brass beds with wool-stuffed mattresses and fluffy eiderdowns, armchairs, including a pair of fine old American rocking chairs – and some have great views over to the wooded valley. The sitting room is pure 'Victorian parlour' with its dark panelling, red wallpaper, card table and leather-bound books; the dining room is simply delightful. A sense of timeless welcome and class enfolds the privileged guest. *60% of food home-produced.*

rooms	12: 8 doubles, 2 singles, 2 suites.
price	€ 55–€ 65. Singles € 40. Suites € 106.
meals	Breakfast € 7. Dinner € 24, book ahead. No evening meal Thursdays & Sundays.
closed	20 December-March.
directions	From Saumur D947 for Chinon. Right in Montsoreau for Fontevraud l'Abbaye. 1st right 1.5km after Montsoreau; signed.

Dominique & Rosine Dauge

tel	+33 (0)2 41 51 75 87
fax	+33 (0)2 41 51 71 90
e-mail	domaine-de-mestre@wanadoo.fr
web	www.dauge-fontevraud.com

Château de la Beuvrière
49220 Grez Neuville, Maine-et-Loire

The gargoyle-strewn facade of this Renaissance and Middle Age fantasy (rebuilt 1870) is like something out of the pages of Mervyn Peake. Hidden away in the heart of rolling, wooded countryside it is one of the most striking château-hotels we have seen. Encircled by a dry moat, reached by a flight of stone balustraded steps, its twirled chimneys and turrets are circled by 43 hectares of lush parkland; in the grounds stands a Gothic chapel with splendid stained-glass windows. Peace and tranquillity reign. Magnificent lawns at the back sweep down to a huge lake with its own island. The duplex tower suite with its hand-painted dome ceiling overlooks the roses, the park and the lake; the garden suite with its round drawing room leads to the rose courtyard. Even the smaller rooms are fit for royalty: taffeta and silk swathes of turquoise, pink, gold, ochre and *eau de nil* sweep over the beds, fall from the windows, twist themselves into outrageous bows and then curtsy onto the floors. With a top chef in the kitchen, you will find that even afternoon tea is a serious sport here. *Room service available. A no-smoking property.*

rooms	15: 12 doubles, 3 suites.
price	€190–€315. Suites €382–€420.
meals	Breakfast €15. Dinner €47–€60.
closed	8 January–end March.
directions	From Laval, N162 to Angers. At Grieul, 4km after Le Lion d'Angers, right on D291 for St Clément de la Place. Château 3km from N162. Do not go to Grez Neuville.

Corrine Mecs

tel	+33 (0)2 41 95 71 81
fax	+33 (0)2 41 95 71 80
e-mail	contact@chateau-beuvriere.com
web	www.chateau-beuvriere.com

map 4   entry 138

Château des Briottières

49330 Champigné, Maine-et-Loire

This heavenly *petit château* has been in the same family for 200 years and is now occupied by the relaxed and endearing Monsieur de Valbray, his wife and six children. *La vieille France* is alive and well and your hosts love to share it with guests. A magnificent library/billiard room leads into a small sitting room; if it's grandness you're after, share your pre-dinner aperitif with Monsieur in the huge, and hugely aristocratic salon, replete with family portraits, tapestries and fine antiques. Sweep up the marble staircase to the bedrooms on the first floor, feel the comfort of the beds (the newest are king-sized), gaze on park views. Several bedrooms have been recently redecorated but traditional furniture and fabrics prevail. Some beds are charmingly canopied, and the sumptuous family suite includes a small governess's room. Some bathrooms are marbled; the more expensive sport extras such as towelling robes. In the grounds is a delightful country-style *orangerie*, let out as a gîte, and a large swimming pool in the walled garden.

rooms	15 + 1: 12 doubles, 3 suites. 1 cottage for 4-6.
price	€ 120–€ 330. Suites & cottage € 257–€ 357.
meals	Breakfast € 10. Dinner € 46 with aperitif & coffee. Restaurant closed December-mid-March.
closed	2 weeks in February.
directions	From A11, exit 11 Durtal to D859 for Châteauneuf sur Sarthe. D770 to Champigné; D768 for Sablé; left at Marigné sign; 4km further.

	François de Valbray
tel	+33 (0)2 41 42 00 02
fax	+33 (0)2 41 42 01 55
e-mail	briottieres@wanadoo.fr
web	www.briottieres.com

Château du Plessis Anjou

49220 La Jaille Yvon, Maine-et-Loire

You can sail off from the grounds in a balloon; two of the best *sons et lumières* are within easy reach, and so are the châteaux and wineries of the Loire. Built in the 16th century, Le Plessis has always been in the family and has been taking guests for years. Though large and very elegant, the château, set in 14 hectares of wooded park, is inviting rather than imposing, with curving tiled roofs, white walls and creeper-covered shutters. Dinner, at a long table in a rather ornate dining room with Roman friezes, could include salmon, duck with apricots, cheese and a crisp fruit tart; fruit (masses of raspberries) and vegetables come directly from walled potager. One bedroom is striking, with a lofty beamed ceiling and beds set in a deep turquoise alcove. Beds are turned down at night: water and chocolates placed on bedside tables. There's a small pond brimming with fish and lilies, Piroutte the pony for rides, her new foal and Salsa, the fox terrier. *An English-speaking guide available for many activities.*

rooms	8 twins/doubles.
price	€ 110–€ 200.
meals	Hosted dinner with wine, € 48, book ahead.
closed	Rarely.
directions	From A11 exit Durtal on D859 to Châteauneuf sur Sarthe; D770 for Le Lion d'Angers for 18km. Right on N162 for Château Gontier. After 11km right on D189 for La Jaille Yvon.

	Valérie Benoist-Vadot
tel	+33 (0)2 41 95 12 75
fax	+33 (0)2 41 95 14 41
e-mail	plessis.anjou@wanadoo.fr
web	www.chateau-du-plessis.com

map 5   entry 140

Auberge du Roi René
53290 St Denis d'Anjou, Mayenne

Monsieur is the original *bon viveur*, and looks the part. He's also a fund of culture and wit and a passionate believer in the art of good living. Madame has no airs or graces either: she is friendly, straightforward and chief gastronome. Food is a way of life here: Marie-Christine has passed muster with several top chefs, the Trois Gros brothers included, and cooks a *cuisine d'amour*. An attractive grassy courtyard fronts the restaurant. The stately Auberge, which dates from the 15th century, lies in the centre of St Denis, a truly delightful village (let Monsieur be your guide). The bedrooms on the first floor are reached via ancient stone stairs in the tower and have magnificent old oak doors and terracotta floors; they are narrow, cosy, charming, well lit. There are two dining rooms to choose from: one in the medieval part, warm-carpeted with a huge and handsome stone fireplace; the other, pure 18th-century, elegant, gracious and light. It is everything that an auberge should be, and more.

rooms	4: 3 doubles, 1 suite.
price	€65–€85.
meals	Breakfast €8. Dinner €20–€40.
closed	Rarely.
directions	From Sablé sur Sarthe D309 to St Denis d'Anjou. In centre of village.

	Marie-Christine & Pierre de Vaubernier
tel	+33 (0)2 43 70 52 30
fax	+33 (0)2 43 70 58 75
e-mail	info@roi-rene.fr
web	www.roi-rene.fr

Château de Craon
53400 Craon, Mayenne

Natural authentic elegance informs both place and people at Craon with its innumerable expressions of history, taste and personality: an oval room with curved doors to the dressing room and a lift down to its own sunken marble bathroom, a dear little children's room tucked in above the bathrooms, a romantic canopied double bed, superb reception rooms (occasionally open to the public), a magnificent stone staircase. Outside is the perfect château park: a formal terraced bit with pool and fountain (a mini-Versailles?), a carefully casual English-style bit, some really wild corners beyond and five kilometres of trails. Three full-time gardeners also watch over the huge walled potager (a mini-Villandry?), which has celebrated its hundredth year: espaliered fruit trees against the stone walls; an elderly greenhouse bursting with tomatoes; rows of vegetables, wide grass paths through cutting flower beds and ancient roses. Loïk and Hélène, parents of six, have a wonderful sense of humour and welcome their guests with spontaneous ease. You will enjoy that gracious and natural sense of hospitality. A very special place.

rooms	6: 2 singles, 2 doubles, 1 twin, 1 suite for 2-3.
price	€ 120–€ 160. Singles € 50–€ 70. Suite € 240 for 2-3.
meals	Picnic in park or barbecue at pool. Restaurants in village.
closed	Mid-November–mid-March.
directions	From Laval 30km N171 to Craon–St Nazaire. Signed at town entrance.

Loïk & Hélène de Guébriant
tel +33 (0)2 43 06 11 02
fax +33 (0)2 43 06 05 18
e-mail chateaudecraon@wanadoo.fr
web www.chateaudecraon.com

map 4 entry 142

Le Tertre
72270 Dureil, Sarthe

What makes an American decide to stop awhile in a village called La Flèche, hear about a extraordinary lost race of birds of the same name, trace references back to the 15th century and convince an ecological museum to give him two forlorn creatures so he can supply prime chickens to starred Michelin chefs? Passions start in strange ways. It began for David, fine raconteur, and Corrine, charmingly French, with this house: three rooms, all with garden views, in 40 acres of wooded farmland within reach of the famous châteaux. You can order a fine picnic complete with chilled fruit and wine, and in the evening can either cook in the well-equipped kitchen shared by the guest rooms or David and Corinne will suggest somewhere delicious. If you are staying for five nights, you will be invited for dinner the first evening. David is proud of his wines; the menu will have been inspired by the local farmers' market and their own organic produce. They can organise horse riding or leisurely trips down the river for you. Oh, and David also has a pet wolf he brought back from Colorado....

rooms	3 + 1: 3 doubles. 1 cottage for 6-8.
price	€75–€99. Cottage €274–€305; €1,372–€1,524 per week. Weekend rates available.
meals	Picnic €15. Hosted dinner with drinks €38, book ahead.
closed	Rarely.
directions	A11 for Nantes exit Sablé La Flèche. D306 for Sablé; D23 through Bailleul & Arthezé; D8 for Parcé. 2km after sign 'Les Belles Poules', C1 right to Dureil. House on left.

	David & Corrine Kalker-Gerson
tel	+33 (0)2 43 92 46 12
fax	+33 (0)2 43 92 46 12
e-mail	kalker-gerson@infonie.fr
web	www.letertre.com

Château de Vaulogé
72430 Fercé-sur-Sarthe, Sarthe

A fairy-tale place! The Radinis, from Milan, wanted their children to have an international education so moved to Geneva, then found Vaulogé. Marisa and her daughter now run the hotel, and Marisa devotes herself to the garden, her latest project being the horseshoe-shaped potager. The original part of the château was built in the 15th century: this is where the family lives. Later Vaulogé was remodelled in a troubadour style, giving it two circular towers with conical slate roofs; when the shock waves of the Revolution had faded, the aristocracy reclaimed their houses. If it's space you're after, stay in Casanova: a huge round tower room, with terracotta floor and amazing, near-vertical beams – excellent for propping books on. (There are plenty of books: Marisa feels a house is not properly furnished without them.) There are other round rooms – La Petite Tour is smaller, and ravishingly pretty. The whole place is enticing with flowers and little nooks and crannies, often put to good use as wardrobes or cupboards. The grounds are lovely, with lilies on the moat and a delicately pretty stone chapel.

rooms	7: 4 doubles, 3 suites.
price	€ 150–€ 230.
meals	Dinner with drinks € 50, book ahead.
closed	Rarely.
directions	A11 exit 9 Le Mans Sud. D309 for Noyen via Louplande, Chemiré le Gaudin. 1.5km after Fercé s/Sarthe, right at small chapel.

	Mme Marisa Radini & Mlle Micol Tassan Din
tel	+33 (0)2 43 77 32 81
fax	+33 (0)2 43 77 32 81
e-mail	vauloge@mail.com
web	www.vauloge.com

map 5   entry 144

Hôtel Haras de la Potardière
72200 Crosmières, Sarthe

François Benoist's mother inherited La Potardière from her father and in 1990 entrusted her son with taking care of it – and making it pay for its keep. Luckily François is an architect specialising in restoring old buildings. They live in a creeper-covered wing of the château with their four children: Camille, Alexis, Noëlle and Emeline. In fact one of the most appealing features of La Potardière is a brochure-cum-history written in the form of a letter from all six of them. François's grandfather built up a successful centre for training show jumpers alongside an established thoroughbred stud. After 10 years of empty stables, in 1992 La Potardière began taking stallions for the summer months, when owners bring mares from all over France. Most of the rooms look out onto peacefully grazing horses. Bedrooms – seven in the château and 10 in the farm – are just what you would hope for: a graceful mixture of pretty and elegant, wood and flowers. What a place for a horse-mad child! But all children will love it here: fields, a safe pool, even a Wendy house full of toys.

rooms	17: 4 twins/doubles, 1 triple, 2 suites for 4-5 in château; 7 twins/doubles, 1 triple, 2 suites for 4-5 on farm.
price	€ 70–€ 110. Triple € 120. Suites € 110–€ 160.
meals	Breakfast € 8.
closed	Rarely.
directions	From Paris, A11 exit 10; D306 for La Fleche. Right in village of Crosmières; follow signs.

	Francois Benoist
tel	+33 (0)2 43 45 83 47
fax	+33 (0)2 43 45 81 06
e-mail	haras-de-la-potardiere@wanadoo.fr
web	www.potardiere.com

Auberge du Port des Roches

Le Port des Roches, 72800 Luché-Pringé, Sarthe

If you can see yourself sitting at the edge of slow green water of an evening, perhaps watching out for the odd fish, this is the place for you. Not grand – this is the Loir not the Loire, an altogether less glamorous river – but we can hear you saying: "Oh, what a pretty spot". Valérie and Thierry have been here about nine years, are young, very friendly though a touch shy, and full of enthusiasm for their auberge. Their main business is probably the restaurant – they can seat about 50 people in two rooms – but Valérie is justly proud of the effort she has put into the bedrooms and into the way everything positively sparkles. Rooms are not large but done in fresh colours, sky blue, for example, with crisp white bedcovers. At the front you will have a view over the Loir. A small road does run past the hotel, but windows are double glazed. Not a place to bring children for a long stay, as they wouldn't have much room to run about, but they would be very happy for a stopover. This is a very quiet, very French place to stay, within easy reach of the châteaux but inexpensive.

rooms	12: 9 doubles, 2 twins, 1 triple.	
price	€40–€50.	
meals	Breakfast €6. Picnic available. Lunch & dinner €20–€40. Restaurant closed Sunday evenings, Mondays & Tuesday lunch.	
closed	February; 1 week in autumn.	
directions	From La Flèche, N23 to Le Mans for 5km; right on D13 to Luché-Pringé. Through village for 2km, right on D214. Signed.	

	Valérie & Thierry Lesiourd
tel	+33 (0)2 43 45 44 48
fax	+33 (0)2 43 45 39 61

map 5 entry 146

Château de la Barre
72120 Conflans sur Anille, Sarthe

Come to be immersed in ancient grandeur and memorabilia in a time capsule. The château has been in the family since 1421 and every item has a tale to tell. Portraits and furniture in the *grand salon* are as they were in 1784 – the Marquis de Vanssay's wedding year. His portrait hangs in the handsome sitting room, among other fine antiques, where aperitifs are taken with the Comte and Comtesse. A painting of another illustrious ancestor, Napoleon's prefect, looks upon the elegant 17th-century dining room – perfect for candlelit dinners – with its massive burnished dresser. Upstairs in the yellow and pale-lime-green bedroom is a portrait of the Count of Vanssay, Secretary to Henri V, last legitimate pretender to the throne. Other portraits, birds this time, blend into an exotic, jungle-themed fabric in the Chambre des Oiseaux. A riot of *toile de Jouy*, in soft reds and blues, surrounds the fine antique beds of the suite and a dream of a curved Louis XV bed sits in the single room. Young and enthusiastic, Marnie and Guy (she English, he French) are genuinely welcoming. *Cash or cheque only. Children over eight welcome.*

rooms	5: 3 doubles, 1 single, 1 twin-bedded suite with adjoining single.
price	€100–€130. Suite €180–€220.
meals	Hosted dinner with wine €25–€45 by arrangement. Two restaurants 12km.
closed	Rarely.
directions	A11 Le Mans/Rennes, exit La Ferté-Bernard. D1 for St Calais. Château 3km before St Calais directly after rd. to Conflans.

Comte & Comtesse de Vanssay

tel	+33 (0)2 43 35 00 17
e-mail	info@chateaudelabarre.com
web	chateaudelabarre.com

Château de Monhoudou
72260 Monhoudou, Sarthe

Your hosts are the nicest, easiest of aristocrats, determined to keep the ancestral home alive in a dignified manner - 19 generations on. Something special inhabits a place when it has been treasured by the same family for so long and you'll find it here. This is a jewel set in rolling parkland; sheep graze under mature trees, there are horses in the paddock, swans on the moat, the occasional call of peacock, deer or boar. And there's endless scope for biking and hiking. Inside are antiques on parquet floors, modern beds, bathrooms and loos in turrets, a small library, intriguing alcoves, hunting trophies, a dining room elegant with family silver. Dinner can be a romantic affair for two or you can join other guests for home-prepared foie gras, coquilles Saint Jacques, duck with peaches, braised leeks, apple and calvados sorbet. Then bask in front of the log fire in the sitting room under the gaze of family portraits. And do ask to see the chapel upsairs. Timeless tranquillity, genuine people - and Monhoudou, one of the most beautiful villages in France.

rooms	6: 4 doubles, 1 twin, 1 suite for 3.
price	€85–€140.
meals	Breakfast €14. Dinner with wine, €37, book ahead.
closed	Rarely
directions	From Alençon, N138 for Le Mans for approx. 14km. At La Hutte left D310 for 10km; right D19 through Courgains. Left D132 to Monhoudou; signed.

Michel & Marie-Christine de Monhoudou

tel	+33 (0)2 43 97 40 05
fax	+33 (0)2 43 33 11 58
e-mail	monhoudou@aol.com
web	www.monhoudou.com

map 5   entry 148

Château de Saint Paterne
72610 St Paterne, Sarthe

A 21st-century fairytale: a 500-year-old château was abandoned by its owners for 30 years, then rediscovered by the heir who left sunny yellow Provence for cool green pastures to resurrect the old shell. He and his wife are a charming young couple and have redecorated with refreshing taste, respecting the style and history of the building, adding a zest of southern colour to panelled, antique-filled rooms, pretty country furniture before ancient fireplaces and hand-rendered, rough and 'imperfect' finishes – nothing stiff or fixed. Sitting, dining and first-floor bedrooms are in château-style; the Henri IV room (he had a mistress here, of course) has thrillingly painted beams; ancestors and *objets* adorn but don't clutter. The attic floor is fantasy among the rafters: nooks, corners and split levels, a striking green and red bathroom, another bath sunk below the floor. Your host, an excellent cook, uses exotic vegetables from his kitchen garden, his cooking courses are called *liaisons délicieuses*. A brilliant, attractive mixture of past and present values and superb hosts. *Aperitif taken with hosts.*

rooms	7: 5 doubles, 2 triples.
price	€ 85–€ 200.
meals	Breakfast € 10. Dinner € 40, with aperitif and coffee.
closed	January–March.
directions	From Alençon, D311 for Chartres & Mamers. St Paterne on outskirts of Alençon. Through village; entrance on right opposite Elf garage.

Charles–Henry & Segolène de Valbray
tel +33 (0)2 33 27 54 71
fax +33 (0)2 33 29 16 71
e-mail paterne@club-internet.fr
web www.chateau-saintpaterne.com

photography by Michael Busselle

loire valley

Château des Réaux

37140 Chouzé sur Loire, Indre-et-Loire

Two white swans and two white Indian ducks patrol the moat, while rows of simple topiary – pyramids of various sizes – stand guard round the château. It looks like a castle in a fairytale: with a tower and turrets and resplendent in red and white checks. It has been in the same family for more than a century; Jean-Luc and Florence Goupil de Bouillié are still very involved, but their son and his enthusiastic New Zealand wife Nicky are handling much of the day-to-day management. They can arrange garden tours and cookery courses, even taxi you to a nearby restaurant. The hotel is in the fertile Loire flood plain, in the middle of both wine and château country. Rooms are either in the Renaissance wing or in a little cottage, which looks out to the château on the other side of the moat. The cottage is charming, with a pretty, fresh yellow sitting room, but you can hear the odd train from here. The rooms in the château are grander and in very definite styles. It could have been pompous and pretentious, but it is enchanting, elegant, and sophisticated. *A no-smoking property.*

rooms	8 + 1: 3 doubles, 2 suites in château; 1 twin, 2 doubles in cottage. 1 apartment for 4.
price	€76–€160. Suites & apartment €240–€260.
meals	Breakfast €14. Lunch & dinner for groups by arrangment: gourmet €40–€59, regional €20–€25.
closed	Rarely.
directions	Paris A85 exit 5 Bourgeuil & D749. At lights, right on N152 towards Saumur. Château signed 1km.

	Jean–Luc & Florence Goupil de Bouillié
tel	+33 (0)2 47 95 14 40
fax	+33 (0)2 47 95 18 34
e-mail	reaux@club-internet.fr
web	www.chateaureaux.com

Le Castel de Bray et Monts

Place du Village, 37130 Bréhémont, Indre-et-Loire

This pretty manor house on the edge of the Loire was built by Louise de Valois as a holiday home in the 18th century. Pollarded lime trees lead to the house, through a garden full of flowers and huge ancient magnolias; a stream, fed by the river, meanders through the garden. The head gardener from the Château de Villandry comes each year to prune the roses! Inside the first thing you see is an amazing wooden double-spiral staircase – apparently the only one of its kind in France. There are almost as many flowers in the house as in the garden: in vases, pots and on the walls in traditional wallpapers, some well-chosen Laura Ashley. Other walls are hung with beautiful antique patchwork quilts: a sample of a collection that Madame Rochereau built up while living in the US. Monsieur is a successful chef who once worked at the Ritz in Paris; he also runs cookery classes for guests and organises visits to châteaux. Most bedrooms look onto the garden, but not the river as the embankment is too high. Children have a corner of the garden with swings and a place to play boules. *Cookery courses.*

rooms	9 + 1: 7 doubles, 2 duplex suites. 1 apartment for 4-6.
price	Doubles €47–€111. Suites €95–€190. Apartment €145–€175.
meals	Breakfast €7.50. Dinner €30. Restaurants 8km.
closed	20 November-20 February.
directions	From Tours N152 to Langeais. Over river & right after bridge onto D16 to Bréhémont. Left after church. Signed.

M & Mme Rochereau

tel	+33 (0)2 47 96 70 47
fax	+33 (0)2 47 96 57 36
e-mail	cooking-class-infrance@wanadoo.fr
web	www.cooking-class-infrance.com

map 10   entry 151

Le Vieux Château d'Hommes

37340 Hommes, Indre-et-Loire

A tit had just made its nest in the post box and Madame was hoping that the guests wouldn't disturb it. No hunting, no shooting on this 178-hectare estate; lots of deer and birdsong here. The courtyard setting is certainly splendid: the moat and the ruins of the old castle, with one little tower still standing, make a thoroughly romantic setting for this great house, originally the tithe barn built just outside the castle wall. Inside, a vast baronial hall and fireplace welcome you and the atmosphere becomes more formal with a huge dining table, a pair of candelabra at either end. In the big bedrooms, antique furniture (beautifully Italian in one case) goes hand-in-hand with the lavish bathrooms. Two rooms give onto the fine courtyard bounded by outbuildings; two look out to open fields and woods. In contrast, the stone walls and terracotta tiles of the Tower Room, which overlooks the moat, give a more rustic feel – its bathroom is down a narrow spiral staircase. A paved terrace leads onto a large lawned area starring a huge walnut tree, actually two trunks twined round each other, then fields, then woods. Very peaceful.

rooms	5: 2 twins, 3 doubles.
price	€87–€115.
meals	Dinner €28 with aperitif, wine & coffee.
closed	Rarely.
directions	From Tours N152 for Saumur. In Langeais D57 to Hommes. There, D64 for Giseux. Château on right on leaving village.

	Hardy Family
tel	+33 (0)2 47 24 95 13
fax	+33 (0)2 47 24 68 67
e-mail	levieuxchateaudehommes@wanadoo.fr
web	www.le-vieux-chateau-de-hommes.com

Château du Vau

37510 Ballan Miré, Indre-et-Loire

Philosopher Bruno and Titian-haired Nancy, an intelligent and engaging couple with four young children, have turned his family château into a delightful, harmonious refuge for the world-weary traveller. The demands of children to be taken to dancing lessons and guests needing intellectual and physical sustenance are met with quiet composure and good humour and the cosy, book-lined, deep-chaired sitting room is a place where you find yourself irresistibly drawn into long conversations about music, yoga, art... The sunny breakfast room is charming with its stone-coloured floor tiles and pretty fabrics. Generations of sliding children have polished the banisters on the stairs leading to the large, light bedrooms that are beautifully but unfussily decorated – splendid brass bedsteads, Turkish rugs on parquet floors or seagrass matting, old family furniture, pictures and memorabilia – the spirit of zen can be felt in the search for pure authenticity. On fine summer evenings you can take a supper tray *à la* Glyndebourne in a favourite corner of the vast grounds.

rooms	5: 4 doubles, 1 triple.
price	€99–€108.
meals	Buffet dinner €20 June-August. Hosted dinner with wine €39, September-May.
closed	Rarely.
directions	From Tours D7 towards Savonnières & Villandry. Left at Renault garage 2km before Savonnières. On for 2km to crucifix. Right & château 500m.

Bruno & Nancy Clement

tel	+33 (0)2 47 67 84 04
fax	+33 (0)2 47 67 55 77
e-mail	chateauduvau@chez.com
web	www.chez.com/chateauduvau

map 10   entry 153

Manoir de la Rémonière

37190 Cheillé – Azay le Rideau, Indre-et-Loire

Come for the remarkably authentic 15th-century château: behind the mullioned windows there are regal rooms, genuine antiques, four-posters and thick rich drapes. Rémonière stands on 2,000 years of history: the stable block overlooks the fourth-century Gallo-Roman remains so its guest spaces have mosaics, ochre-sponged walls, very effective murals of Roman scenes, roof windows to the archeology. The main house is enchanting, so perfectly restored and furnished. Here, breakfast is at a long, candlelit table by a huge carved fireplace; the corridor has royal red carpet and old portraits; the levels change with the centuries and the atmosphere enters your blood. The lively, welcoming mother-and-daughter team, passionate about their house, help this. Through a clearing the view to Azay le Rideau is unsurpassed, the quiet is broken only by birds singing in the great trees, the owl wheezing behind the children's turret. Do visit the friendly black Thai pig and the dwarf goats; the peacock has the run of the courtyard.

rooms	9: 6 twins/doubles, 1 suite for 4, 2 duplexes in annexe.
price	€90–€140. Duplexes & suite €110–€140.
meals	Gourmet restaurants 1km & 4km.
closed	Rarely.
directions	A10 exit Joué les Tours, D751 for Chinon. Through Azay past château to La Chapelle St Blaise. Left on D17; entrance 800m on left. Signed.

	Chantal Pecas
tel	+33 (0)2 47 45 24 88
fax	+33 (0)2 47 45 45 69
e-mail	remoniere@wanadoo.fr

Hôtel Gargantua

73 rue Voltaire, 37500 Chinon, Indre-et-Loire

You are treading in the footsteps of Rabelais here: it was built as a bailiff's court in the 15th century, and his father was once the bailiff. Halfway down the oldest street in Chinon – don't wear your stilettos, cobblestones are easier on the eyes than the feet – the Gargantua is a tall, narrow building in local white tufa-stone with a small look-out tower at one corner of the steep slate roof. Tucked beneath the high walls of the château, the hotel looks down to the river and valley beyond. The stone walls, lofty beams and stag's head give a medieval feel; a striped canopy keeps up the theme in the dining room. Access to all bedrooms is up a central spiral stone staircase. The first two floors were covered in patterned stone a century ago to make them smoother but the top flight is now listed and is very well trodden. Friendly owner Michel is carefully re-doing the rooms: Louis XVI has an unusual oriental *toile de Jouy*, while Gargantua has an old four-poster and a splendid view. In summer you can eat under the wisteria in a courtyard, looking up to the château.

rooms	8 twins/doubles.
price	€45–€95.
meals	Breakfast €8.50. Lunch & dinner €23–€49. Restaurant closed Thursdays & Friday noon, out of season.
closed	Last 2 weeks January; 1st 2 weeks March.
directions	From Tours D751 to Chinon. In town, park by river & walk up one of the side streets to Rue Voltaire. Hotel half-way along.

	M Michel Giraud
tel	+33 (0)2 47 93 04 71
fax	+33 (0)2 47 93 08 02
e-mail	hostelleriegargantua@hostelleriegargantua.com
web	www.hostelleriegargantua.com

 map 10 entry 155

La Commanderie

16 rue de la Commanderie, 37220 Brizay, Indre-et-Loire

The lovely cross-shaped symmetry envelopes you, glazed fanlights on each arm of the cross look through onto trees, bringing in armfuls of northern light. Here is secluded peace in an 18th-century mansion built on the site of old Templar structure in the middle of a large grassy garden on a hillside looking over Vienne valley. Jeroen (the jovial host) and Marie Laure always join their guests for dinner in the fine sitting room with exposed stone walls, antique sideboards and glowing parquet floors. A wood-fired stove is at the ready for cooler days, keeping company with the circle of comfy sofas and armchairs. Bedrooms have striking colour schemes and are friendly and welcoming; the corner rooms in particular have great views over the garden, woodland and surrounding countryside. Rooms vary in size from smallish to average, bathrooms are basic, all with showers. A wonderful place for groups who can gather in the stone-walled, beige-carpeted space at the top of the house under the roof. *Cash or cheque only.*

rooms	7: 6 doubles, 2 sharing wc; 1 twin with private shower.
price	€ 55.
meals	Breakfast € 5. Hosted dinner with wine € 25, book ahead. Good selection of restaurants within 15km.
closed	Rarely.
directions	From Chinon, cross River Vienne & D749 then D760 to Ile Bouchard. After entering town, 2nd right & follow signs.

Marie Laure Fontaine & Jeroen Wamsteeker

tel	+33 (0)2 47 58 63 13
e-mail	mlfontaine@net-up.com
web	www.lacommanderie.com

Le Moulin de Saint Jean

St Jean St Germain, 37600 Loches, Indre-et-Loire

A deliciously watery home. We love this place — a restored mill on an island. Breakfasting on the veranda over the mill stream is not the only reason guests return: Sue radiates generosity and charm and Andrew, equally relaxed and friendly, is an excellent cook. Dinners are convivial affairs, shared with your hosts. All is ups and downs, nooks and crannies in rooms ranging from large to small. The guests' sitting room upstairs has French windows opening onto to a balcony overlooking the river. Comfy chairs and colourful cushions set the scene; bedrooms, too, are full of personality, and all different. Attractive, high-quality fabrics, interesting pictures and much evidence of Sue's sponging and stencilling skills. Add a shady garden, a pool, the temptation of about 1,000 paperbacks and the colourful presence of a blue and yellow macaw. Everywhere there is the gentle murmur of running water which is why this site, however idyllic, is not the most relaxing place for parents of young children.

rooms	5: 3 doubles, 1 twin, 1 triple.
price	€65-€70.
meals	Hosted dinner €25, with aperitif, wine & coffee.
closed	December-January.
directions	From Loches, N143 for Châteauroux; pass Perusson, left at sign to St Jean; house on left between the two bridges.

	Andrew Page & Sue Hutton
tel	+33 (0)2 47 94 70 12
fax	+33 (0)2 47 94 77 98
e-mail	millstjean@aol.com
web	www.lemoulinstjean.com

map 10 entry 157

Domaine de la Tortinière

Les Gués de Veigné, 37250 Montbazon, Indre-et-Loire

It seems unreal, this pepperpot-towered château on a hill above the Indre, the bird-filled woods where wild cyclamen lay a carpet in autumn and daffodils radiate their light in spring. Then there's the view across to the stony keep of Montbazon, so this is an exceptional spot with tennis, a heated pool, fishing or rowing on the river, too. Bedrooms are perfect, decorated with flair and imagination, be they in the château or in a converted outbuilding. One of these, an adorable Renaissance doll's house, has two smaller rooms and a split-level suite; the orchard cottage, for playing shepherdesses *à la Petit Trianon*, is big and beautifully furnished – the desk invites great writings. Bathrooms are luxurious, some smaller than others. Guests enjoy taking the underground passage to the orangery to dine in simple elegance, inside or on the terrace. Soft lighting, panelled reception rooms, deep comfort and discreet friendliness here in this real family-run hotel: the warm, humorous owners are genuinely attentive, their sole aim is to make your stay peaceful and harmonious.

rooms	29: 22 doubles, 7 suites.
price	€ 100–€ 175. Suites from € 280.
meals	Breakfast € 14. Picnic € 15. Dinner € 47. Restaurant closed Sunday evenings November–March.
closed	21 December–March.
directions	2km north of Montbazon. From Tours N10 south for Poitiers for 10km. In Les Gués, right at 2nd set of lights. Signed.

Xavier & Anne Olivereau

tel	+33 (0)2 47 34 35 00
fax	+33 (0)2 47 65 95 70
e-mail	domaine.tortiniere@wanadoo.fr
web	www.tortiniere.com

Château de la Bourdaisière

25 rue de la Bourdaisière, 37270 Montlouis sur Loire, Indre-et-Loire

A superlative, princely experience, it belongs to the National Tomato Conservatory. The brothers de Broglie grow 200 aromatics and 500 types of tomato – taste a selection in salad with a glass of Château Bourdaisière. Their history-laden estate has formal gardens and native woods, a Renaissance château on the foundations of a medieval fortress, vaulted meeting rooms and a little boudoir for intimacy as well as a bright, floral breakfast room onto the garden, redecorated by manager Madame de Roquefeuil. Guest rooms? François 1 has a bathroom the size of a bedroom, rich dark green beams and quantities of old books in his magnificent terrace suite; Gabrielle d'Estrées is gorgeously feminine as befits a mistress of Henri IV, who wears rich, regal red (cheaper rooms are less grand). The drawing room is the princes' own – they drop by, their books lie around, their family antiques and paintings furnish it. Authenticity and good taste are rife, the place is genuinely special yet very human and your hosts are charmingly friendly. *Well-behaved children welcome.*

rooms	20: 14 doubles in château, 6 doubles in pavilion.
price	€115–€210. Suites €230.
meals	Breakfast €12. Light lunch €15 (April-September). Dinner €30, book ahead.
closed	5 January-7 February.
directions	From A10, exit Tours Centre for Amboise, then D751 to Montlouis sur Loire. Signed.

	Prince P.M de Broglie
tel	+33 (0)2 47 45 16 31
fax	+33 (0)2 47 45 09 11
e-mail	contact@chateaulabourdaisiere.com
web	www.chateaulabourdaisiere.com

map 10 entry 159

Prieuré des Granges

15 rue des Fontaines, 37510 Savonnières, Indre-et-Loire

An oasis in an encroaching sea of suburbia, Le Prieuré is a dream. Hidden away in three acres of landscaped gardens and mature trees, the main building – long, low, ornate – is 400 years old, but behind its magnificent stone walls there's a refreshing lightness of touch and lack of pretension. The dining room, sitting room and breakfast room – long, light, painted white and blue – are discreet, comfortable and very charming. The generous bedrooms are equally elegant affairs, each one with a character of its own, and the occasional rustic touch. One has its own bread oven. Stone floors are softened with Persian rugs; ceilings are beamy; bathrooms are large, mostly white and luxurious. Downstairs rooms open onto their own little courtyards. At the back is a large grassy garden with a pool. Your host, a relaxed Anglophile with a taste for fine beer, takes huge pleasure in making sure his guests have everything they need. Eric and Christine have achieved the near impossible: that elusive mix of the sophisticated and the down-to-earth. *Cash or French cheque only.*

rooms	7: 5 twins/doubles, 2 suites for 3-4.
price	€ 65–€ 100. Suites € 115–€ 200.
meals	Light meals available upon request. Good choice of restaurants nearby.
closed	December-February, but will open on request.
directions	A10 exit 24 Joué lès Tours for Villandry. In Savonnières, left at Hôtel Faisan for Ballan Miré. On left after approx. 1km. Signed.

	Eric & Christine Salmon
tel	+33 (0)2 47 50 09 67
fax	+33 (0)2 47 50 06 43
e-mail	info@prieuredesgranges.com
web	www.prieuredesgranges.com

Hôtel Château des Tertres

Route de Monteaux, 41150 Onzain, Loir-et-Cher

A classic mid-19th-century nobleman's house surrounded by mature wooded parkland in the Loire valley – but not all is traditional inside. The young, energetic Monsieur Valois is an artist, and his sense of fun pervades this lovely place. Many of the rooms *are* period pieces, including the sitting rooms and the largest of the bedrooms, and some are remarkably ornate. The smallest rooms, though, are minimalist – symphonies of creamy yellow and white. That a creative spirit is at work is evident, too, in the gardener's lodge whose four guest rooms have been furnished with panache: one with a massive Italian four-poster, another with a perspex bedhead and a row of medieval steel helmets lined up on the wall! Older children will love it here. Your host is extremely hospitable and will let you in on the secrets of the château if you ask: before it was restored to its original elegance it had an amazingly chequered career, having been a German military headquarters, a school for metal workers and a chicken farm in three of its former lives.

rooms	18 doubles: 4 in gardener's lodge.
price	€ 70–€ 105.
meals	Breakfast buffet € 8.
	Other meals available locally.
closed	Mid-November–week before Easter.
directions	From A10 exit Blois. N152 for Amboise & Tours. Right to Onzain opp. bridge to Chaumont. Left in village for Monteaux. Château 1.5km on right.

	Bernard Valois
tel	+33 (0)2 54 20 83 88
fax	+33 (0)2 54 20 89 21
e-mail	chateau.des.tertres@wanadoo.fr
web	www.chateau-tertres.com

map 5   entry 161

Hostellerie de la Mère Hamard

37360 Semblançay, Indre-et-Loire

Watch the world from your window, the locals clutching their baguettes on their way home from the boulangerie. You are in the middle of a little village and it's peaceful here – yet Tours is no more than a 10-minute drive. Other bedroom windows look onto the garden, full of flowers and birds. The old *hostellerie* sits opposite the church and was built as a presbytery in the 18th century; now Monique and Patrick are doing it all up in a light, modern way. The four largest rooms – two are above the restaurant, in a big old house over the way – have a sofa that can double as a bed. The smaller rooms on the first and second floors are to have pale walls, light, bright fabrics and furniture hand-painted by the Pegués' daughter. Another reason to stay is the food – traditional but with original touches. Meals are served in the restaurant, where local artists often hang their pictures – perhaps you will be tempted to buy. In summer you may eat outside, in the enclosed little garden to the front.

rooms	11 doubles (5 with sofabeds).
price	€50–€86.
meals	Breakfast €8.50. Lunch & dinner €17–€46. Restaurant closed Sunday evening & Monday. Traditional restaurant 5km.
closed	15 February–15 March.
directions	From Tours, N138 for Le Mans, then left for Semblançay. Hotel in centre of village, opposite church.

	M & Mme Pegué
tel	+33 (0)2 47 56 62 04
fax	+33 (0)2 47 56 53 61
e-mail	merehamard@wanadoo.fr

Domaine des Bidaudières

Rue du Peu Morier, 37210 Vouvray, Indre-et-Loire

Sylvie and Pascal Suzanne have made their mark on this classic, creamy-stoned ex-wine-grower's property. Unstuffy and outgoing, this young couple lend a stylish sophistication to the place and produce a small quantity of their own wine, having planted new vineyards to the terraced rear. Cypress trees planted on the hillside behind give an Italianate feel. Bedrooms are fresh and contemporary, each immaculate and carpeted and decorated in Designers Guild fabrics. All are light, south-facing and have valley views. The sitting room, where the kitchen used to be, was actually built into the rock – a hugely attractive, stone-floored room with a low rocky ceiling and an open fire at one end. Guests can idle away the afternoon in the elegant swimming pool on the lower terrace which lies alongside the carefully restored *orangerie*. There is even a direct access to the pool via the lift in the main house. Families are welcome to stay in the more rustic 'troglodyte' apartment nearby. *Cash or French cheque only.*

rooms	4 + 1: 3 twins/doubles, 1 suite for 3. 1 apartment for 5.
price	€ 110. Suite € 130. Apartment € 120.
meals	Meals available locally.
closed	Rarely.
directions	From Paris, A10 exit 20 Vouvray onto N152 for Amboise. In Vouvray D46 for Vernou sur Brenne; 2nd street on left after r'bout.

M & Mme Pascal Suzanne

tel	+33 (0)2 47 52 66 85
fax	+33 (0)2 47 52 62 17
e-mail	infohote@bidaudieres.com
web	www.bandb-loire-valley.com

map 10   entry 163

Château de Perreux

36 rue Pocé, 37530 Nazelles Negron, Indre-et-Loire

General de Gaulle's sister lived here during the war and took in refugees. Now Eric and Rudolph receive guests – in style. There are two salons with antiques and old paintings, one rich red, with a remarkable fireplace, the other yellow velvet; corridors are Persian-rugged, bath towels are embossed with the château's name. Eric was in the diplomatic service and has picked up treasures on his travels, Rudolphe is a designer and has re-upholstered most of those treasures himself. Both are charming, full of stories about this restoration and their new life. Bedrooms are period pieces: one suite is dove-grey and pale blue, another blue and gold with paintings of Baghdad; two big rooms are in a tower, two smaller have a Japanese feel. All are bright and sunny with park or valley views. These seven hectares, with pool, are reached via two tunnels under the road; there are some amazing trees, a small island and river (you may fish) and a listed, 19th-century aquarium-grotto. Ungrand people in the grandest of settings – and two sweet dogs, one named Sarah, the other William.

rooms	8+ 1: 5 singles, 3 suites. 1 small house for 3-4.
price	Singles € 100-120. Suites € 180. House € 270.
meals	Dinner € 30-€ 40, book ahead.
closed	Rarely.
directions	From Paris, A10 exit 18 Amboise; towards Rocade for 10km. Right at 1st r'bout for Pocé, then towards Nazelles on D1.

**Eric Nicolas
& Rodolphe Beduchaud**

tel	+33 (0)2 47 57 41 50
fax	+33 (0)2 47 57 58 57
e-mail	chateaudeperreux@wanadoo.fr
web	www.chateaudeperreux.com

Le Fleuray Hôtel

37530 Cangey, Indre-et-Loire

Perfect if, like most of our readers, you have a helicopter – or a hot-air balloon. Pretty perfect, too, for ordinary mortals, for Peter and Hazel have created a haven of peace. The raw material was ideal: a solid, handsome old manor house with duck pond and barns, mature trees and bushes: all that was needed to persuade them to settle. The rooms in the barn are just right for families; slightly cut off from the rest, their French windows open onto the garden. The Newingtons are unstuffy and easy-going, genuinely enjoying the company of visitors. Truly a family affair; Jordan and Gessie, the older children, are a big part of the picture and are rapidly becoming professionals. They have created a slightly English mood, with lightly floral sofas into which you can sink, bookcases, flowers and prints – and a plain carpet in the sitting room. The bedrooms are big and fresh, many with white cane furniture and floral covers on the huge bed. It must be fun to dine outside on the patio under huge parasols, on pink tablecloths and green chairs. It's fun in the winter, too, with an open fire and Hazel's superb cooking.

rooms	15: 9 twins/doubles, 6 family with terrace.
price	€68–€100.
meals	Breakfast €9. Dinner €26.50–€35.50. Children's meals €14.50.
closed	One week in November; Christmas; 24 January–4 February.
directions	From A10 exit 18 Amboise & Château Renault. D31 to Autrêche. Left on D55 to Dame Marie Les Bois. Right on D74 for Cangey.

	Newington Family
tel	+33 (0)2 47 56 09 25
fax	+33 (0)2 47 56 93 97
e-mail	lefleurayhotel@wanadoo.fr
web	www.lefleurayhotel.com

map 10 entry 165

Château de Pray

Route de Chargé, 37400 Amboise, Indre-et-Loire

Perched on terraced slopes overlooking the Loire, the château spent its first 200 years as a military stronghold. It then discovered gracious living and was owned by a series of senior officials to the English, French and Spanish courts. In the last century, it was home to the wife of the author Alphonse Daudet. De Pray was one of the first châteaux to be opened to guests and waking up in one of its atmospheric rooms should inspire you to visit the great Amboise or Chenonceaux — they are virtually next door. Graziella has spent the last few years restoring the château and doing up bedrooms, carefully choosing colours according to the natural light in each. The 17th-century reception room with its deep gold ceiling has been returned to its original splendour, while local craftsmen are gradually replacing the shutters. Graziella has not yet got round to updating the bathrooms (1970s, spotless), but plans to revamp them in 2004. Her husband, Ludovic, is a trained chef and will provide a fabulous dinner with all vegetables and herbs fresh from the gardens. Slip into the pool before dinner, relax with a drink on the pool terrace.

rooms	17 + 2: 10 doubles, 7 triples. 2 apartments.
price	€95–€170.
meals	Breakfast €11. Lunch €30–€50. Dinner €41–€68. Restaurant closed Wednesdays & 2 weekdays at noon.
closed	5-23 January.
directions	From A10, exit 18 Château Renault on D31 for Amboise. After bridge, right at stop sign, then 2nd left.

	Graziella Laurenty
tel	+33 (0)2 47 57 23 67
fax	+33 (0)2 47 57 32 50
e-mail	chateau.depray@wanadoo.fr
web	praycastel.online.fr

Le Manoir Les Minimes

34 quai Charles Guinot, 37400 Amboise, Indre-et-Loire

Every detail has been thought out with tender care, lovingly chosen antiques and *objets* placed to create a light sophistication. A far cry from the Minimes order who had a convent here until it was destroyed in the French Revolution; then this noble townhouse took the site. Between majestic Loire and historic castle, the manor has 18th-century grace and generous windows that look onto its big courtyard, the castle and the lustrous river. Before opening Les Minimes in 1998, the charmingly young and enthusiastic Eric Deforges was a fashion designer, hence his faultless eye for fabric, colour and detail. Exquisitely decorated rooms are big – slightly smaller on the top floor, with beams and river views from their dormers – and have luxurious bathrooms. The masterpiece is the suite where the *toile de Jouy* wall fabric seems to be one single piece. The elegant chequered hall leads to a series of interconnecting salons. There's a smaller, more intimate television room and a breakfast room in soft yellow and grey. With fresh flowers everywhere, this feels more like a smart home than a formal hotel.

rooms	13: 11 doubles, 2 suites.
price	€95-€160. Suites €195-€230.
meals	Breakfast €11. Will provide menus & make reservations in local restaurants within walking distance.
closed	December-mid-March; Sundays, out of season.
directions	From A10 for Amboise. Over Loire, then right on D751 for town centre. On left approaching town centre.

Eric Deforges & Patrice Longet

tel	+33 (0)2 47 30 40 40
fax	+33 (0)2 47 30 40 77
e-mail	manoir-les-minimes@wanadoo.fr
web	www.manoirlesminimes.com

map 10 entry 167

Hôtel du Bon Laboureur et du Château

6 rue du Docteur Bretonneau, 37150 Chenonceaux, Indre-et-Loire

This little hotel, in the village of Chenonceaux, a mere stroll from the château, started life as a coaching inn in the 18th century. Now in the hands of the fourth generation, it has expanded into an adjoining building, the old village school, and into a somewhat grander building with a rather pretentious tower known tongue-in-cheek as 'The Manor'. The bedrooms are light and airy with plenty of space and are kept in tiptop condition. One is in psychedelic green and yellow, another is more traditional in pink and another, smaller, in fresh blue and white. The heart of the hotel is in the original building, with its elegant 18th-century style dining room and a simpler, more relaxed one next to it. In summer, tables with starched white cloths, candles and flowers are set on the terrace under the trees. A good spot for seeing the châteaux with children as there are family rooms and the garden has a pool. Amboise, Chaumont, Chambord and other châteaux are within easy reach so you can make your visits and return with time for a swim and a cocktail before dinner. A large potager behind the hotel supplies vegetables.

rooms	24 + 3: 24 doubles. 3 apartments for 4.
price	€ 80–€ 130. Apartments € 145–€ 180.
meals	Breakfast € 9. Picnic € 9. Dinner € 29–€ 65. Restaurant closed low season Wed noon & Thurs.
closed	Mid–Nov–mid-Dec; January.
directions	From Blois, cross Loire onto D751 then D764 to Montrichard. Follow signs to Chenonceaux. On right.

Isabelle & Antoine Jeudi

tel	+33 (0)2 47 23 90 02
fax	+33 (0)2 47 23 82 01
e-mail	laboureur@wanadoo.fr
web	www.bonlaboureur.com

Copyright David Darrault-Harris

Château des Ormeaux

Nazelles, 37530 Amboise, Indre-et-Loire

The view's the thing — from the turreted 19th-century château built around a 15th-century tower, take in the glories of 67 acres. Corner rooms on two floors — original panelling on the first floor, sloping ceilings on the second — have tiny little *boudoirs* off the main room in the turret. A decent size, with elaborate bedcovers and drapes and massive bathrooms, the bathrooms are very grand in a turn-of-the-century way. One room, blue and gold, has a marble fireplace and an *armoire à glace*, a wall of mirrors hidden behind an apparently ordinary cupboard; another, decorated in ochre and maroon, a crystal chandelier and plushly canopied bed. Two new rooms have been carefully restored in the 18th-century *logis*, the former home of the château 'manager', with visible beams and lime rendering. Everyone dines at a long table in the elegant dining room, where meals are served by one or more of your hosts — there are three in total — and enhanced by background Bach and candlelight. Best of all, from wherever you stand (or swim) those valley views are superb.

rooms	8: 5 doubles, 3 twins.
price	€ 107–€ 115.
meals	Dinner € 39 at communal table, book ahead.
closed	Rarely.
directions	From Tours, N152 for Blois. 10km after Vouvray, left to Noizay & from there D1 for Nazelles. Château on left approx. 2km after Noizay.

	Emmanuel Guenot
tel	+33 (0)2 47 23 26 51
fax	+33 (0)2 47 23 19 31
e-mail	contact@chateaudesormeaux.fr
web	www.chateaudesormeaux.fr

map 10 entry 169

Le Relais de la Herserie

37150 La Croix de Touraine, Indre-et-Loire

This is a new family venture. With a full flush of five children aged three months to 18 years, Laurent and Bénédicte picked the right place. They are are slowly converting château and stables into a modest haven for families and groups. Hard to imagine that for 30 years these two buildings in 13 hectares of breathtakingly beautiful grounds were 'student' accomodation (lucky students!). Carefully planned by a well-known *paysagiste*, trees were planted in harmony with the lie of the land, a lazy stream flows at the bottom and promenades are rich with enchanting discoveries. Charming, enthusiastic hosts, the Dujardins truly take pleasure in their guests' well-being. Breakfast is served in the *orangerie*, a delightfully bright and sunny way to start the day. On occasion, aperitifs are taken in the large beamed-ceiling reception room in the main building, where a family coat of arms sits above a large fireplace. The rooms in the château and stables are simple but comfortable with solid furniture, some sharing showers, some sharing loos. Don't expect designer décor at these prices – it's just gentle and friendly. *A no-smoking property.*

rooms	19: 7 doubles in château, all with sink and shower, sharing 4 wcs; 12 doubles in stables, 5 sharing showers. 7 with full bathrooms.
price	€30–€55.
meals	Restaurants 4-7km.
closed	Rarely.
directions	From Bléré, La Croix en Touraine. At lights head for Chenonceaux, then left at 2nd street. On right after 700m.

Laurent & Bénédicte Dujardin

tel	+33 (0)2 47 23 54 36
fax	+33 (0)2 47 23 54 36
e-mail	contact@la-herserie.com
web	www.la-herserie.com

Le Cheval Blanc

5 place de l'Eglise, 371501 Bléré, Indre-et-Loire

Set in the flowered, cobbled and car-free church square of old Bléré, the White Horse Inn has been known for years as one of the best tables in the highly gastronomic Royal Valley and Michel Blériot is keeping that reputation very much alive. He calls his cuisine "lightened classical" and plans his creations around fresh seasonal ingredients. Eating is either in the traditional French atmosphere of original beams, high, rich-draped windows, pale Louis XVI chairs, tall-stemmed glasses and fresh flowers on snow-white cloths, where a certain formality reigns in honour of the fine food or, in warm weather, outside in the delightful creeper-clad courtyard. The professional yet delightful staff give really good service. Sleeping is done upstairs in rooms that are all fairly similar in their beamed ceilings, quilted floral prints and little lamps. Swimming is at the bottom of the pretty ornamental garden – a rare treat for an urban hotel. The atmosphere is altogether light, fresh and attractive and Bléré is a perfect base for château-crawling – but come above all for the food.

rooms	12: 10 twins/doubles, 2 triples.
price	€ 57–€ 85.
meals	Breakfast € 8. Weekday lunch € 17. Dinner € 39–€ 56. Restaurant closed Sunday evenings & Mondays out of season.
closed	January–mid-February.
directions	From Tours towards Chenonceaux D140; 4km before Chenonceaux left on D3 to Bléré.

	Michel & Micheline Blériot
tel	+33 (0)2 47 30 30 14
fax	+33 (0)2 47 23 52 80
e-mail	le.cheval.blanc.blere@wanadoo.fr
web	www.lechevalblancblere.com

map 10 entry 171

Hostellerie Château de Chissay

Chissay en Touraine, 41400 Montrichard, Loir-et-Cher

One minute you can be discovering the delights of the famous châteaux of the Loire, the next, enjoying the pleasures of your own private one. The château is a Renaissance jewel, yet not in the least overwhelming. Built for the Chancellor of France during Charles VII's reign, it was used as a royal residence for hundreds of years and became the meeting place of military bigwigs in World War II. Its public rooms feel surprisingly intimate, and light pours into the vast bedrooms, each different; imagine yourself the Sleeping Beauty as you tiptoe up to your room via a turreted stone stair. (Though you can just take the lift!) The 'troglodyte' room in the rock face behind the château is some peoples' favourite, and one of the quietest. Suites have immaculate sitting rooms in more corner towers; a wooden-beamed room shaped like a boat under the eaves has a mosaic jacuzzi in its 'prow'. Simpler rooms in the annexe near the outdoor pool are good for families. And there's an inner courtyard with splashing fountain from which you reach an Italian style *portico* with valley views.

rooms	32: 22 doubles, 10 suites.
price	€ 121–€ 185. Suites € 210–€ 265.
meals	Breakfast € 13. Lunch & dinner € 18–€ 52.
closed	Mid-November–mid-March.
directions	From Paris, A10 exit Blois. Over Loire for Montrichard, then D176 to Chenonceaux. Château on right 4km after Montrichard. Signed.

Alain Guinoiseau

tel	+33 (0)2 54 32 32 01
fax	+33 (0)2 54 32 43 80
e-mail	chissay@leshotelsparticuliers.com
web	www.chateaudechissay.com

Le Manoir des Remparts
14 rue des Remparts, 36800 St Gaultier, Indre

Behind imposing gates and high walls – the house is built on the outside of the old city ramparts – lies this charming 18th-century manor. The place is a gem: a gravelled courtyard and wisteria-clad barn at the front, a large, tree-filled walled garden with summer house at the back. Your hospitable and punctilious Dutch hosts have renovated the house with sympathy and style – Ren is an interior designer – preserving the beautiful fireplaces, the parquet floors and the marvellous oak staircase. Bedrooms are really comfortable. The style is essentially Provençal, with *Souleiado* and *toile de Jouy* wallpapers, country antiques, old paintings, pillows decked in antique linen. One room has a metal-framed four-poster with red check curtains. Bathrooms are sumptuous, traditional fittings offset by seagrass floor covering and elegant drapes; a chintzy armchair sits by a claw-footed bath. Generous breakfasts are taken in the blue Provençal coach house. There's a sitting room to retire to, warm and inviting with a large fireplace, soft lighting and ancient beams. A nostalgic vision of some perfect time – it's a treat to stay here. *A no-smoking property.*

rooms	4 large suites.
price	€ 120.
meals	Picnic available. Arrangement with restaurant nearby for dinner.
closed	15 December–2 January.
directions	From Châteauroux A20 for Limoges, N151 Le Blanc/Poitiers. Entering St Gaultier stay on Le Blanc road; over 2 sets of lights; right, then immed. left across Le Blanc road. Pass supermarket towards Thenay, on for 500m. Manoir on right.

	Ren Rijpstra
tel	+33 (0)2 54 47 94 87
fax	+33 (0)2 54 47 94 87
e-mail	willem.prinsloo@wanadoo.fr

map 10 entry 173

Château de Boisrenault

36500 Buzançais, Indre

Built by a 19th-century aristocrat as a wedding present for his daughter – well overdue, she'd had two sons by the time it was finished – this is a turreted, customised, Renaissance château. Noble and imposing on the outside, it's very much a family home within. Furniture, objects, pictures, all have a tale to tell and there are plenty of hunting trophies and stags' heads on the walls. Reception rooms are lofty, with huge fireplaces. One sitting room has a baby grand; another, smaller and cosier, is lined with books. Each bedroom is an adventure in itself. Named after the family's children and grandchildren, the rooms feature a hotchpotch of pieces from different periods, including some excellent antiques. A couple of stuffed pheasants make unusual lampshades in Hadrien's room and offset the yellow walls. Meals are taken at a vast table in the dining room, but book if you'd like dinner. A delicious pool is discreetly tucked away behind trees in the grounds; table tennis and table football are a godsend on rainy days. A good place for a family stay in summer.

rooms	7 + 2: 7 doubles. 2 apartments with cooking facilities.
price	€ 68–€ 95.
meals	Dinner € 19, by arrangement. Other meals available locally.
closed	Rarely.
directions	From A20 exit 11 on D8 to Levroux; D926 for Buzançais. Château on left 3km before town.

Sylvie du Manoir

tel	+33 (0)2 54 84 03 01
fax	+33 (0)2 54 84 10 57
e-mail	boisrenault@wanadoo.fr
web	www.chateau-du-boisrenault.com

La Petite Fadette

Place du Château, 36400 Nohant, Indre

Just off the main road, this tiny unspoilt village takes you back two centuries to Georges Sand's quiet country childhood, whence she proceeded to make her name, rather noisily, as an early advocate of feminism and free love (with Chopin, Musset, et al). Opposite her elegant house, this pretty country inn fits the scene perfectly. A cluster of village houses of age and character, it has been in the Chapleau family for generations, houses their fine period furniture and feels like home. Arched doors open into the simple tea room where pink-clothed tables lead to the grand piano (they often have recitals) and the old oak stairs up to the bedrooms. Under the stairs is a luxurious loo for diners and beyond is a sophisticated restaurant whose vaulted wooden ceiling and magnificent fireplace frame elegantly laid tables, ready for the chef's tempting dishes. The attractive bedrooms are all different, cosily done in traditional style with antiques, good fabrics and up-to-date bathrooms. Both village and inn have exceptional atmosphere – evocative and memorable.

rooms	9: 8 doubles, 1 suite.
price	€ 58–€ 120.
meals	Breakfast € 10. Lunch & dinner € 16–€ 45.
closed	Rarely.
directions	From Chateauroux, D943 for La Châtre. 5km before La Châtre, left into Nohant. Hotel in village centre opposite church.

	M Bernard Gabriel Chapleau
tel	+33 (0)2 54 31 01 48
fax	+33 (0)2 54 31 10 19
web	www.aubergepetitefadette.com

map 11 entry 175

Prieuré d'Orsan

18170 Maisonnais, Cher

The priory was originally built in 1107 – mostly to house the unwanted wives of the local nobility who were forced to take the veil – and stands in rural France at its most unspoilt. The oldest remaining buildings, probably the refectory and dormitory, are from the 16th century and form three sides of a square, enclosing beautifully restored gardens, open to visitors. Patrice and Sonja, both architects, saved the house from abandonment 10 years ago and have preserved the sense of harmonious calm associated with a convent: there is no 'hotel' feel to the place at all, and the visitors to the gardens don't make it feel busy either. Subdued colours and a contemporary, minimalist style work perfectly here: the striking black and beige striped curtains providing a dramatic touch in the sitting room. You will eat either in a large dining room or a smaller, more intimate one, or under a pergola under the vines when it's warm. Bedrooms have pine-panelled walls, shutters and windows and doors painted in a soft grey-green. You will look out onto the wonderful garden and each find a little teddy bear warming your bed.

rooms	6: 3 doubles, 3 triples.
price	€160–€215.
meals	Breakfast €18. Lunch €30. Dinner €45.
closed	November–April.
directions	From Paris exit 8 from A71 to St Amand Montrond; D925 towards Lignières; D65 towards Le Chatelet. Orsan is half-way between Lignières and Le Chatelet.

	Patrice Taravella & Sonja Lesot
tel	+33 (0)2 48 56 27 50
fax	+33 (0)2 48 56 39 64
web	www.prieuredorsan.com

Château d'Ivoy

18380 Ivoy le Pré, Cher

Every antique bed is appropriately canopied (Kipling: frothy mosquito net on carved Anglo-Indian bed; Lord Drummond: the olde English feel), every superb bathroom a study in modern fittings on period washstands. Ivoy is home to an interior designer who has achieved miracles since buying it from a famous entomologist who had planted a near tropical rainforest in one stateroom, now the fine-furnished, Spode dining room. It was built for Mary Stuart's purser: the Stuarts were allowed to create a Scottish duchy here that lasted 200 years and it became the Drummond family seat after the battle of Culloden. The front is stern, the back opens wide onto sweeping lawns, park and hills – all bedrooms face this way. The house radiates refinement and your hostess's infectious delight. She will welcome you in her grey-green hall with its lovely sandstone floor and ceramic stove, invite you to use the library (home to a huge spider... imprisoned in a glass paperweight) or the salon, and will then retire discreetly. A very special place to stay. *Children over 12 welcome. No smoking.*

rooms	6-7: 5 doubles, 1 twin. Possible suite for family of 3.
price	€ 195. Room with shower € 140.
meals	Good choice locally.
closed	Rarely.
directions	From A10 exit Salbris D944 for Bourges to Neuvy sur Barangeon; left on D926 to La Chapelle d'Angillon; D12 to Ivoy. Château on right 300m after church, entrance through Le Parc Communal.

Marie France Gouëffon-de Vaivre

tel	+33 (0)2 48 58 85 01
fax	+33 (0)2 48 58 85 02
e-mail	chateau.divoy@wanadoo.fr
web	perso.wanadoo.fr/chateau.divoy/

map 11   entry 177

Château de Beaujeu

18300 Sens Beaujeu, Cher

Sweep up the tree-lined avenue, pass the stables and the dovecotes in the yard, step back in time: your turreted 16th-century château has been in the family since the Revolution. Downstairs rooms are filled with generations of possessions, including magnificent Aubusson tapestries on the walls. Every item tells a story: the stags' heads on the wall were shot by a grandmother a century ago. It is a rare pleasure to spend a night under the roof of a château so untouched by modernity. No carefully renovated 'features' here, everything is as it was: the paintwork may be peeling, the wallpapers faded, but the colours are original and unsynthetic. The *trompe l'oeil* is all of a piece, in spite of the cracks. Bedrooms are comfortable, with gracious windows overlooking the park; bathrooms, with 60s fittings, slightly eccentric. The suites in the tower are lovely, with splendid mouldings, windows and doorways in curved glass. Madame and her sons are doing up a room every year. Try the splendid yellow room with its *ciel de lit*. Authentic, out of the ordinary and bang in the middle of the vineyards of Sancerre. *A no-smoking property.*

rooms	5: 3 doubles, 2 twins.
price	€ 110. Suites € 120–€ 185.
meals	Hosted dinner € 45, book ahead.
closed	November-Easter.
directions	From Sancerre D955 for Bourges. Right on D923 for Aubigny sur Nère. Left on D7 to Sens Beaujeu. There, left at fountain, D74 for Neuilly en Sancerre. Down hill, château at end of drive.

	M & Mme Wilfrid de Pommereau
tel	+33 (0)2 48 79 07 95
fax	+33 (0)2 48 79 05 07
e-mail	info@chateau-de-beaujeu.com
web	www.chateau-de-beaujeu.com

photography by Michael Busselle

poitou-charentes

Château de Saint Loup sur Thouet

79600 St Loup Lamairé, Deux Sèvres

This château inspired Perrault to write *Puss in Boots*! It has an ancient and fascinating history. The Black Prince incarcerated John the Good here after the Battle of Poitiers in 1356 and it was rebuilt in the 17th century by the Marquis of Carabas, whose magnificence so impressed the fairy-tale writer. Charles-Henri de Bartillat visited the château on Christmas Eve 1990, fell in love with the place and 10 days later had bought it. Saint Loup is a *monument historique*, open to the public for a short time each Sunday afternoon. The count, charming and passionate about his home, is painstakingly restoring the house and the grounds (using 18th-century plans drawn up by Jacques Boyer de la Boissière). Rooms are lofty and light in the château, medieval in the keep: the Black Prince room in the old kitchens has two vast fireplaces and thick red-stained beams; the Bishop's room in the château has a splendid canopied bed between two big windows overlooking the garden. Aperitifs are taken in the *orangerie* on the other side of the moat – Charles-Henri makes sure guests get to meet each other before dinner. A stunning place.

rooms	15: 13 doubles, 2 singles. Entire château can be rented.
price	€ 150–€ 190. Singles € 115.
meals	Breakfast € 15. Dinner € 65 with wine, book ahead.
closed	Rarely.
directions	From Airvault D46 to St Loup Lamairé. Château visible as you enter village.

Comte Charles–Henri de Bartillat

tel	+33 (0)5 49 64 81 73
fax	+33 (0)5 49 64 82 06
e-mail	st-loup@wanadoo.fr
web	www.chateaudesaint-loup.com

Chalet de Venise

6 rue Square, 86280 St Benoît Bourg, Vienne

St Benoît Bourg is a pretty little village with a fine Romanesque church and, despite being just outside the suburbs of Poitiers, it has kept its village atmosphere. In a wooded valley on the edge of a rippling stream, the Venise was completely rebuilt in 1994. It is a low, rendered building with stone balconies curving round following the stream, a wide terrace spread out below its balustrades. The smallish bedrooms have French windows onto the balcony and are decorated with apricot sponged walls, floral fabrics in contrastingly dark colours and stained wooden beds and dressing tables, all in neat, new contemporary style. Most people come for the food, which is superb. Monsieur Mautret is chef, Madame manages the restaurant – they are a delightful and excellent team. Service is elegant, almost reverential (silver cloches) but quick. Madame welcomes children and says they enjoy eating in the big, light dining room or out on the terrace. The breakfast room is attractive, too, in soft blue and peach, with Turkey rugs, good prints and plenty of plants.

rooms	12 doubles.
price	€ 53–€ 58.
meals	Breakfast € 7.
	Dinner € 25–€ 55, book ahead.
closed	2 weeks Feb; last weekend Aug.
directions	A10 exit Poitiers Sud to Poitiers. At lights head for Limoges & Châteauroux. Right after 1km. Right at lights to St Benoît Bourg (careful: there are 4 St Benoîts in the area!). Hotel in village centre.

M & Mme Mautret

tel	+33 (0)5 49 88 45 07
fax	+33 (0)5 49 52 95 44

map 10 entry 180

Hôtel les Orangeries

12 avenue du Docteur Dupont, 86320 Lussac les Châteaux, Vienne

Even before you step inside, the pool beneath the mature trees of the landscaped garden at the back will convince you that these people have the finest sense of how to treat an old house and garden: the harmony of the deep wooden deck, raw stone walls, giant baskets and orange trees (*naturellement*) draws you in. The young owners fell in love with the place and applied all their talent – he's an architect – to giving it an authentic 18th-century elegance in contemporary mood. Indoors, stripped oak doors, exposed stone walls, warm wood or cool stone floors are radiant with loving care, like valued old friends. Each lovely, uncluttered bedroom has just the right mix of vibrant pastels, pretty hangings on brass fittings, new-stained old furniture and a super bathroom. The rooms over the road are soundproofed with double windows. The Gautiers' passions include the old-fashioned games they have resuscitated for you: croquet and skittles outside, two kinds of billiards, backgammon and mahjong in the vast games room inside. Their delightful enthusiasm for this generous house is catching.

rooms	10 + 3: 10 doubles/triples. 3 apartments for 4-5.
price	€55-€100. Apartments €90-€145.
meals	Breakfast €12. Lunch snacks. Dinner €25.
closed	Mid-December-mid-January.
directions	Exit Poitiers for Limoges on N147 to Lussac les Châteaux (35km from Poitiers). Ask for route via Châtellerault if arriving from north.

Olivia & Jean-Philippe Gautier

tel	+33 (0)5 49 84 07 07
fax	+33 (0)5 49 84 98 82
e-mail	orangeries@wanadoo.fr
web	hotel-lesorangeries.com

Le Relais du Lyon d'Or

4 rue d'Enfer, 86260 Angles sur l'Anglin, Vienne

In one of France's most beautiful villages, this old hotel owes its revival to Heather and Guillaume's Herculean efforts: they bought it half-ruined in 1994 as a place for their wedding, new home and business, then left their high-flying London careers to do it up. They now run renovation courses, with practical advice from their epic experience of problems with labour, time, money and red tape. Each room was rebuilt round its old flagstones, doors and beams, then decorated in warm natural colours with Heather's paint effects (ragged, distressed, veiled), patinas and stencils – she now gives courses in paint finishes, using her rooms as living examples. Marvellous they are too, in their rich fabrics, intriguing details and individuality – small, not overdone, with delicious bathrooms. It's like staying in a country house with relaxed hosts. The menu is varied and refined and generous breakfasts are served in the pretty garden in summer. Birdwatching, turtle-spotting and orchid-peeping in La Brenne, a magnificent region nearby.

rooms	10: 9 doubles, 1 suite for 4.
price	€ 55–€ 80. Suite € 90–€ 100.
meals	Breakfast € 8. Lunch & dinner € 17–€ 28.
closed	January-February.
directions	A10 exit Châtellerault Nord D9/D725 east through La Roche Posay onto D5 to Angles sur l'Anglin. Hotel in village centre.

Heather & Guillaume Thoreau

tel	+33 (0)5 49 48 32 53
fax	+33 (0)5 49 84 02 28
e-mail	thoreau@lyondor.com
web	www.lyondor.com

map 10 entry 182

Château de Bournand

5 rue Bois de Craon, 86120 Bournand, Vienne

Come here for the perfect grown-up break – teenagers are welcome but it may not be their idea of a special place. Vicky and David plan to spend much of their time here once they retire, but for now you will, most likely, be looked after by David and Jasmine. Vicky works in floral decoration and has a magic eye for colour; she likes nothing better than prowling round antiques markets and has achieved a look that manages to be both dramatic and restful; one room is gothic in inspiration, with stone walls, a huge fireplace, wrought-iron four-poster and fabrics in tones of purple. In complete contrast, two suites in an adjoining lower building have a country feel, the smaller with terracotta tiles, flowery fabrics and its own cosy little sitting room. If you like, Jasmine will prepare you a delicious picnic to take exploring. In the evening, eat in or do some serious gastronomic research. All the châteaux are within easy reach – it would be fun to cycle to them. The garden is full of huge old trees and one corner is like a Celtic horoscope. *Unsuitable for small children.*

rooms	5: 1 double, 4 suites.
price	€80–€150.
meals	Picnic available. Dinner with drinks, €30. Restaurants 8km.
closed	January-February, but will open by arrangement.
directions	5 minutes south of Fontevraud l'Abbaye. From Thouars D39 for Les Trois Moutiers, 5km to Bournand. Follow signs to Jardin Celtica.

	David & Jasmine Churchill
tel	+33 (0)5 49 98 77 82
fax	+33 (0)5 49 98 97 30
e-mail	chateaubournand@hotmail.com
web	www.chateaubournand.com

Le Pigeonnier du Perron

Le Perron, 86530 Availles en Chatellerault, Vienne

René Descartes once owned this *petit seigneurie*; its deeds go back to the 15th century. Monsieur Thiollet will tell you how his ancestors housed refugees here from both world wars: natives from the Lorraine; German prisoners; anyone who turned up on the doorstep. Assuntha included – but from Marseille. She showed up one day, looked around and decided to stay – she's a big personality, a fine cook and you may be lucky enough to get her bouillabaisse for dinner. There is a wonderful vegetable garden which provides much of the restaurant's produce, and a general feeling of wide open space: *un espace de liberté*, as the Thiollets put it. The farm buildings are grouped around a sunny courtyard, hollyhocks pushing up from every nook and cranny, and there's a stone-flagged terrace with good outdoor furniture (not the ubiquitous plastic). Bedrooms are smallish, simply but pleasantly decorated with the odd splash of colour; floors are pale pine, walls soft-sponged or of pale exposed stone. One in the *pigeonnier* has a little balcony, many look over the fields and valley.

rooms	15 doubles (1with separate wc).
price	€45–€57.
meals	Breakfast €7.
	Lunch & dinner €16–€37.
closed	Rarely.
directions	A10 exit 27 for Chatellerault. At 2nd r'bout for Cenon; through Cenon for Availles; 1st right after village sign. Signed on the right after approx. 1km.

	M Thiollet
tel	+33 (0)5 49 19 76 08
fax	+33 (0)5 49 19 12 82
e-mail	accueil@lepigeonnierduperron.com
web	www.lepigeonnierduperron.com

map 10 entry 184

Château de Nieuil
16270 Nieuil, Charente

François I built the château as a hunting lodge in the 16th century, but swapped Nieuil for a bigger plot when he opted for the grander Chambord on the Loire. A gambling Count sold it to grandparents of the Bodinauds. Its hunting days are now over and Luce and her husband have instead created a hommage to our feathered friends: a magical birdwatching walk round the outside of the moat, a tree skeleton painted white and dotted with nesting boxes and feed trays; each room named after a bird and if you are not awoken by real ones, an alarm will sing 'your' song. The château is grand and beautifully decorated: one room has a small children's room up a spiral stair, another a tiny reading room in a turret; most look onto the formal garden at the back. The food is wonderful; Luce actually handed back a Michelin star this year, choosing to re-open a more relaxed restaurant in a converted barn, entrusting it to three unofficial heirs. And there's more: an art gallery with excellent works by contemporary artists and an antique shop in the old kitchens. Open-hearted, open-armed – these people love what they do, and it shows.

rooms	27: 11 doubles, 6 singles, 7 triples, 3 suites.
price	€105–€220. Singles €95–€170. Triples €150–€240. Suites €200–€325.
meals	Breakfast €14. Lunch €25–€50. Dinner €36–€50. Restaurant closed Sun eve, Mon & Tues noon, except July & August.
closed	Nov.-Easter, except by arrangement.
directions	From Angoulême, N10 to Mansle; D739 for St Claud. Then, towards Chasseneuil; 1st left for château.

M & Mme Bodinaud
tel	+33 (0)5 45 71 36 38
fax	+33 (0)5 45 71 46 45
e-mail	chateaunieuilhotel@wanadoo.fr
web	www.chateaunieuilhotel.com

Hostellerie du Maine Brun

Asnières sur Nouère, 16290 Hiersac, Charente

The only sounds to wake you in your bedroom come from the birds and the water gushing beneath the hotel – a 16th-century mill, sympathetically remoulded in the 1930s. You may even forget you are in a hotel at all. The rooms have a mix of French 18th- and 19th-century furniture and heavily draped curtains loaded with gold and cream. The flowers look as if they have been freshly picked from the garden. Raymond and Sophie have managed the trick of making the *moulin* sumptuous without being stuffy. The only modern touches are in the bathrooms, designed for wallowing rather than a mere splash. Children are welcome, but unless yours are period items – better seen than heard – they may not blend in. There is a big pool, however, with plenty of sunshades and chairs. You can breakfast in the sunny dining room or on the terrace, and if you are planning to explore, Cognac is nearby. Raymond will proudly show off his own distillery, explain the intricacies of the process and let you sample his home brew. A man in the know with an excellent wine cellar.

rooms	20: 18 doubles, 2 suites.
price	€99–€118. Suites €160.
meals	Breakfast €11. Lunch & dinner €26–€36. Restaurant closed Mondays & Tuesday noon.
closed	October 15–February.
directions	From Angoulême N141 for Cognac for 8km. D120 right for Asnières sur Nouère. Just along on left.

Sophie & Claire Menager

tel	+33 (0)5 45 90 83 00
fax	+33 (0)5 45 96 91 14
e-mail	hostellerie-du-maine-brun@wanadoo.fr
web	www.hotel-mainebrun.com

map 10 entry 186

Hôtel Restaurant Karina

Les Métairies, 16200 Jarnac, Charente

This old house was built as a cognac distillery and the bar is arranged around the shiny copper stills – the stars of the show. The dining room has many-shaped tables clothed in many-coloured cloth and plate-laden dressers in a lovely converted barn with a huge open fireplace giving off the aroma of wood fires. People come back year after year, the village council meets here and many locals come for the restaurant. Inside, family photographs, knick-knacks and pictures give the place a homely feel. The bedrooms are a good size: some chintzy, some flowery, some plainer, with lovely linens and oriental rugs on wooden floors, moulded ceilings or rafters, exposed stone walls or sober wallpaper and plenty of space in chests and armoires. They all have superb bathrooms with bright modern tiles. The family rooms in their own building with a protected walled garden are a wonderful idea for couples with small children. Choose between two terraces or the pool for breakfast. More a home than a hotel: Austin and Nikki are eager for people to have a good time. Excellent biking country.

rooms	10: 6 doubles, 2 suites for 3, 2 family rooms for 4.
price	€ 52–€ 80. Half-board € 106–€ 142 p.p.
meals	Breakfast € 7–€ 10. Picnic lunch € 7.50–€ 14. Lunch & dinner € 21–€ 32.
closed	Rarely.
directions	From Cognac, N141 Jarnac. Over bridge, left on D736 for Sigogne; bear right. Signed in village; right, 1st left, 1st right.

	Austin & Nikki Legon
tel	+33 (0)5 45 36 26 26
fax	+33 (0)5 45 81 10 93
e-mail	hotelkarina@easyconnect.fr
web	www.hotelkarina.co.uk

Logis du Fresne
16130 Juillac le Coq, Charente

The Butler family came to France 100 years ago to make cognac and Christophe has been in the business all his life. Tone is from Norway, and had a children's clothing label there; they are the loveliest hosts. They bought the old, elegant Logis three years ago and opened in 2003, fulfilling their vision of a refined place to stay with a *chambres d'hôtes* feel. The façade is wonderful and inside just as good. The whole feel is light and fresh and the style turn-of-the-century Norwegian: old terracotta tiles on the ground floor, pale painted beams, a cosy library, an elegant salon. Bedrooms are as serene. Those on the first floor have uncluttered chic: a gilded mirror hangs above an open fire, an oriental rug graces a limed floor… those above are more rustic. The two-room suite has its own stairs, perfect for a family; bathrooms are well-lit and beautifully modern. Breakfast outdoors, at tables forged by the village blacksmith, on delicious *viennoisserie*, hire a classic car and spin off with a picnic and a bottle of champagne. The grounds, with hidden pool and 15th-century tower, are worth a visit in themselves.

rooms	11: 10 doubles, 1 suite.
price	€80–€115. Suite €140. Half-board by arrangement.
meals	Breakfast €10. Picnic baskets available. Dinners €28. Large choice of restaurants in Cognac, Segonzac.
closed	January.
directions	From Cognac, D24 for Segonzac then D736 for Juillac le Coq. 500m after village on right.

	Tone Butler
tel	+33 (0)5 45 32 28 74
fax	+33 (0)5 45 32 29 53
e-mail	logisdufresne@wanadoo.fr

map 10 entry 188

Château Mouillepied
17350 Port d'Envaux, Charente-Maritime

The stream-fed moat is now mostly dry but this is how the house got its name – 'wet feet'. Many springs still gurgle in the nearby meadows, often flooded by the Charente. The oldest part of the house, the tower, was built in the 15th century, and significant bits added later. Martine and Pierre rescued Mouillepied from a few sorry years and are now restoring the house and grounds; they are a delightful pair. Large airy bedrooms are charming and uncluttered, with original wooden floors or new boards suitably wide; walls are white, curtains cotton. There are more rooms in the cottage beyond the lily pond, these with terracotta floors... and chicken nesting holes in an exposed stone wall. Breakfast – stewed fruit, croissants, all the coffee or tea you'd like – is in the vast orangery overlooking the gardens. (If you are staying in the cottage, have it delivered to your door.) The beautiful grounds contain the old laundry, bread oven and wine store. Pick up a fishing licence at the local bakery, stroll along the banks of the Charente, visit the Roman city of Saintes and one more castle that inspired *Puss in Boots*, the Castle of Crazannes.

rooms	6 + 1: 3 doubles, 2 triples, 1 suite for 4. 1 cottage for 3, weekly rental.
price	€46–€69. Triples €72–€84. Suite €69–€114. Cottage €300-410.
meals	Breakfast €7.50. Good choice of restaurants 2km.
closed	Rarely.
directions	Exit A10 at Saintes; 2km on N137 then right until Ecurat; right for Taillebourg 5km. In St James, right for 500m.

	Pierre & Martine Clement
tel	+33 (0)5 46 90 49 88
fax	+33 (0)5 46 90 36 91
e-mail	chateau-mouillepied@voila.fr
web	www.chateaumouillepied.com

Château de la Tillade

Gemozac, 17260 St Simon de Pellouaille, Charente-Maritime

You can tell that Michel and Solange, the present Vicomte and Vicomtesse, like people and love entertaining. Their impressive château sits at the end of an avenue of lime trees alongside the family vineyards that have produced grapes for cognac and *pineau de Charentes* for over two centuries. Much of the original distillery equipment is on display and well worth a visit. Your hosts make you feel instantly at ease in their comfortable, friendly home, even if you're secretly terrified of dropping the fine bone china. Solange's talents as an artist (she also holds painting courses in her art studio) are reflected in her choice of fabrics, while traditional French beds with rolled headboards capture the elegance of your surroundings. Meals are a delight, with good conversation (in English or French) round the family table while you are waited on lavishly but without stuffiness. The de Salverts provide colourful descriptions of local sites or restaurants to visit, and golfers, too, will be spoiled for choice. Expect an open fire in the salon as Monsieur's philosophy is *"bon vin, bonne bouffe, bon feu."*

rooms	5: 4 doubles, 1 triple, 1 children's 'dormitory' with 4 singles.
price	€75–€90. Triple €120.
meals	Dinner with drinks €35, book ahead.
closed	Rarely.
directions	From A10, exit 36 right for Gémozac. At roundabout take Gémozac bypass for Royan, right on D6 for Tesson. Entrance approx. 3km on left, signed (château not in village, but on D6).

**Vicomte & Vicomtesse
Michel de Salvert**

tel	+33 (0)5 46 90 00 20
fax	+33 (0)5 46 90 02 23
e-mail	la.tillade@t3a.com

map 9   entry 190

Château des Salles

17240 St Fort sur Gironde, Charente-Maritime

A pretty little château with great personality, Salles was built in 1454 and scarcely touched again until 1860, when it was 'adapted to the fashion' (profoundly). One hundred years later, the enterprising Couillaud family brought the estate guest house, its vineyard and stud farm into the 20th century. Behind its fine old exterior it exudes light, harmony, colour and elegant informality with spiral stone stairs, boldly-painted beams and warm, well-furnished bedrooms bathed in soft colours and gentle wallpapers. Salles is a friendly family affair: sister at guest house reception, brother at vines and horses, mother at her easel – her watercolours hang in the public rooms, her flowers decorate bedroom doors – and in the kitchen. At dinner, refined food made with local and home-grown produce is served with estate wines. Sylvie Couillaud will help you plan your stay – she knows it all and is almost a mini tourist office. It's a congenial, welcoming house: people come back again and again and one guest said: "She welcomed us like family and sent us home with goodies from her vineyard".

rooms	5: 4 doubles, 1 triple.
price	€ 73–€ 115.
meals	Breakfast € 8.50. Dinner € 30.
closed	15 October–March.
directions	A10 exit 37 Mirambeau. Château between Lorignac & Brie sous Mortagne at junc. of D730 & D125.

Sylvie Couillaud

tel	+33 (0)5 46 49 95 10
fax	+33 (0)5 46 49 02 81
e-mail	chateaudessalles@wanadoo.fr

Résidence de Rohan

Parc des Fées, Route de St Palais, 17640 Royan (Vaux sur Mer), Charente-Maritime

A gloriously peaceful place: the pool sits lazily on the low cliff, the gardens drop down to the sea, you can lie secluded under the umbrella pines with the water lapping below or enjoy the fashionable beach. The hotel, built in typical Belle Époque style by the Rohans as a seaside cottage, has many of its original features – floors and fireplaces, cornices and carvings, a seductive staircase twisting up to the top floor – and smells deliciously of floor polish. This is one of the very few houses in Royan to survive the bombs of the Second World War. There are buffed armoires and upholstered chairs in the big, recently decorated rooms, skilfully matched fabrics and wallpapers and excellent bathrooms with big old-style basins. Breakfast at low tables indoors or out; dine in small, exclusive Vaux or big, bustling Royan, much favoured by Parisian families. There's masses to do: take bike and ferry to the Médoc vineyards, visit "the best zoo in Europe" at La Palmyre or historic La Rochelle. There's even a surfable Atlantic wave on the Côte Sauvage.

rooms	43: 39 twins/doubles, 4 triples.
price	€ 75-€ 124. Triples € 124-€ 141.
meals	Breakfast € 10.50. Many restaurants nearby.
closed	11 November-20 March.
directions	From Royan follow signs to Pontaillac, then Casino, then coast road to St Palais. Signed.

	M & Mme Seguin
tel	+33 (0)5 46 39 00 75
fax	+33 (0)5 46 38 29 99
e-mail	info@residence-rohan.com
web	www.residence-rohan.com

map 9   entry 192

Domaine de la Baronnie

21 rue Baron de Chantal, 17410 St Martin de Ré, Charente-Maritime

Creaky back? Or simply looking for some effective pampering? Pierre is a successful author, osteopath and dietician who runs a summer practice here and a winter one in Paris. This secluded retreat is only 100m from the bustling nightlife and fun beaches of Saint Martin so you can either come here with others sharing your plans or with large or small people whose idea of a good time is sandcastles or bodysurfing and hanging out. Walking down this side street from the port you could easily miss the Baronnie. The Ile de Ré is a very busy, though charming, place in the summer but the big iron gates lead to a calm green haven. Built as government premises in the 18th century, La Baronnie became a private house but passed from owner to owner, becoming gradually more dilapidated. It was rescued in 1996 by Pierre and Florence – a former model who has been coming to the island for 35 years – and turned into a sanctuary for healthy living. You can come for a 'normal' seaside holiday, with the odd massage, or you can book a special package with a week of treatment and advice, in English, of course. *Minimum two-night stay, a no-smoking property.*

rooms	6: 3 doubles, 3 suites.
price	€ 150–€ 195.
meals	Breakfast € 12.
	Many restaurants in town.
closed	November–March.
directions	Over bridge from La Rochelle to St Martin harbour. Street on left going down to port.

	Pierre & Florence Pallardy
tel	+33 (0)5 46 09 21 29
fax	+33 (0)5 46 09 95 29
e-mail	info@domainedelabaronnie.com
web	www.domainedelabaronnie.com

Hôtel de l'Océan

172 rue St Martin, 17580 Le Bois Plage en Ré, Charente-Maritime

Seasoned travellers, Martine and Noël tried to find a hotel that felt like a home. Although they had worked in antiques and interior design, they realised after a spell running a restaurant that this was what they should be doing – but where? They knew it had to be on an island and after toying with Corsica and the Ile de Ré, they stumbled upon a rather sad old hotel, the Océan, and knew they had found 'their' hotel. Set back from the dunes in a garden pungent with rosemary and lavender, the hotel has 24 bedrooms: some around an inner courtyard, others like tiny cottages among the hollyhocks. They are all different. Children will love the curtained cabin bed set in a buttercup yellow alcove. Floors are covered in sisal matting and Martine and Noël's ships, lighthouses and shells are dotted around against cool, soothing colours. After your *pastis* on the decked terrace, your supper will involve a lot of fresh fish and herbs. The dining room is another success, with cream boards on walls and ceiling and palest greeny-grey carved chairs. It's fresh without being cold and clean without being clinical.

rooms	24 doubles.
price	€ 61–€ 91.
meals	Breakfast € 9. Lunch & dinner € 21–€ 30. Restaurant closed Wednesdays except during school holidays.
closed	5 January–5 February.
directions	A10 exit 33 for La Rochelle. N248 then N11 Rocade round La Rochelle for Pont de l'Ile de Ré. At Le Bois Plage hotel in town centre.

	Martine & Noël Bourdet
tel	+33 (0)5 46 09 23 07
fax	+33 (0)5 46 09 05 40
e-mail	ocean@iledere.com
web	www.re-hotel-ocean.com

 map 9   entry 194

Hôtel Le Chat Botté

2 place de l'Eglise, Ile de Ré, 17590 St Clément des Baleines, Charente-Maritime

Are you de-mineralised? Need some coddling? A pine-panelled, pale-chaired house decorated with pastels and peace, this is part of a family circle: one sister is your hotel hostess, another has her beauty salon right here where you can be wrapped in seaweed and reflexologised, a third has a B&B nearby and two brothers have a restaurant each, one of them next door. You can choose to have your *énergétique* breakfast on the sweet little patio in the garden, with three types of flowering jasmine to stimulate your morning senses, or in the grey-blue dining room... before shiatsu and a bicycle tour of the island. The garden provides fresh flowers for the house, the sea and sky that limpid light that filters into the simple, country-furnished, quilted bedrooms which give onto the church square, the garden or the patio; we preferred the patio aspect but all are havens from the heat of the summer beaches. Bathrooms and linen are of excellent quality. The island has lots to offer – salt marshes, one of Europe's biggest bird sanctuaries, and the Baleines lighthouse for a stupendous view. A charming, peaceful place.

rooms	23: 20 twins/doubles, 3 suites.
price	€63–€108. Suites €185–€230.
meals	Breakfast €8.50–€12. Family-owned restaurant next door.
closed	Last week of November–15 December; 5 January–12 February.
directions	From A10, exit 33 onto N248 then N11 for La Rochelle. Over bridge to Ile de Ré & take northern itinerary towards Le Phare des Baleines. Hotel opposite church.

	Mmes Massé-Chantreau
tel	+33 (0)5 46 29 21 93
fax	+33 (0)5 46 29 29 97
web	www.hotelchatbotte.com

photography by Michael Busselle

aquitaine

Villa Prémayac

13 rue Prémayac, 33390 Blaye, Gironde

The house is down a quiet back street of Blaye, a bustling little town with a pretty hilltop citadel. There's not a huge amount to do here – apart from quaff some famous wines – but the place is perfect for golfers. There are six courses within a put of the villa *and* Roger, your host, was a player of repute. He now edits a golfing magazine. This is a new enterprise for him and Léa who have furbished five bedrooms for guests in the oldest part of the house. It's a bit of a rabbit warren, albeit a well-renovated one. Big bedrooms, named after Greek gods, are plushly carpeted. Ceres is golden with a flowery canopied bed, Aphrodite spring-green with rose-strewn drapes; they overlook small enclosed terraces. Bathrooms are perfectly tiled, with shiny fittings, and are vast, big enough to swing a putter in. There are two small gardens, one Roman and one zen, with bonsai trees. The south-facing hills of Blaye, on the banks of the Gironde, have been lined with vines since the Romans came. Set off for the wine villages and châteaux of Pauillac and Medoc – a 45-minute drive – or catch the ferry from Blaye. Cognac is even nearer.

rooms	5 doubles.
price	€79–€85.
meals	4-5 restaurants within walking distance.
closed	Rarely.
directions	In Blaye, follow Centre Ville signs.

	Léa Golias
tel	+33 (0)5 57 42 27 39
fax	+33 (0)5 57 42 69 09
e-mail	premayac@wanadoo.fr
web	www.villa-premayac.com

Château Julie

Naudonnet, 33240 Virsac (Nr St André de Cubzac), Gironde

Even if bordeaux is not your favourite tipple, this is a superb place to stay. Viticulture is the business here and if you come at the right time you have a grandstand view. Château Julie is Dutch-owned, run by Jos and Wim. Rebuilt in the 18th century to charming proportions, the house is surrounded by 80 hectares of land, half of them glistening with vines. Stay in the château – rooms are simple and uncluttered, with big bathrooms and oodles of towels – or in the self-catering cottage opposite; it sleeps six comfortably, has a big kitchen and two shower rooms. Breakfast is on the terrace in summer, or in the more sombre setting of the hall, beside an impressive wooden staircase. Pop into Bordeaux for dinner where you will be spoiled for choice. In the day play tennis, fish or explore the grounds, on foot or by mountain bike. Children can fish or swim in the lake; they even have their own playroom if it rains. Jos and Wim can also arrange for you to visit a sister château near Saint Emilion. A great place for an active break. *Cash or cheque only. French, Dutch and German spoken.*

rooms	9 + 1: 9 doubles. 1 cottage for 6.
price	€ 70–€ 80.
	Cottage € 400–€ 450 per week.
meals	Fabulous eating nearby.
closed	Rarely.
directions	A10 Paris/Bordeaux, past toll Virsac. 1st exit for Angoulême; signed.

Jos & Wim van der Eijk

tel	+33 (0)5 57 94 08 20
fax	+33 (0)5 57 94 08 23
e-mail	josvandereijk@wanadoo.fr
web	www.chateau-julie.com

map 10 entry 197

Château de Viaud

33500 Lalande de Pomerol, Gironde

The Romans planted the first vines here. Viaud is one of the oldest properties of the Lalande de Pomerol appellation, the grapes grow on 20 hectares of gravelly soil and the vineyard is shown in maps as old as 1784. Wine buffs – and those wanting to learn – will be fascinated to see the latest equipment and the rows of oak barrels maturing their nectar in immaculate, air-conditioned cellars. The bedrooms, named after flowers, are huge, light and inviting. Jasmine is white: twin beds in crisp cotton, light pouring in through French doors; Lavender has a vast bed and views of the vines. You can have breakfast – a French affair but with yogurt and cereal as well – either at a long table in the kitchen or immediately outside on a sunny terrace. Mary aims to make the château warm and welcoming, to children as well, and has plans for a pool. Meanwhile, there's yoga, new recipes to learn, wines to try, you can ride nearby and the World Heritage site of Saint Emilion is a 10-minute drive, with its troglodyte village and 70 hectares of underground tunnels. *Children over six welcome.*

rooms	4: 2 doubles, 1 twin, 1 suite.
price	€ 140–€ 155.
meals	Dinner by arrangement. Use of kitchen possible. Restaurants in St Emilion & Libourne.
closed	Rarely.
directions	From Libourne, N89 for Montpon. After 2km left on D245 to Lalande de Pomerol. Signed at 1st crossroads.

Mary Wakefield

tel	+33 (0)5 57 51 17 86
fax	+33 (0)5 57 51 79 77
e-mail	marywakefield@free.fr
web	www.chateau-de-viaud.com

Château Le Lout

Avenue de la Dame Blanche, 33320 Le Taillan – Medoc, Gironde

If the dusky pink walls, first-floor loggia and green windows give Le Lout the look of a somewhat patrician Italian villa rather than a French château, this is because its original owner chose an architect from Siena to build his country retreat. When Colette and Olivier bought it, the house had been empty for 18 years and was in need of a lot of attention. Colette not only brought a feel for period detail but plenty of elbow grease: she did much of the work herself. A flight of stone steps leads into a white stone hall, sparsely decorated with tapestries and the odd old chest. One side leads to the kitchen and office, the other to a dining/breakfast room with fine *chinoiserie* wallpaper framed by soft green panelling. A stone staircase leads to the bedrooms which are a treat. All have wooden floors; you may find rich orange walls with contrasting cool bedding, or soft cream walls set off by fresh green-patterned cotton, enhanced by lace and rugs. Children will be happy with the pool and huge grounds. Book in advance and Colette will cook you a five-course dinner while Olivier knows all about wine and golf.

rooms	6: 3 doubles, 3 suites for 3.
price	€95–€135. Suites €155–€195.
meals	Breakfast €11. Hosted dinner with wine, €43, book ahead.
closed	Rarely.
directions	Rocade for Bordeaux/Merignac (airport). Exit 7 N215 to Lesparre/Lacanau. After 1km on D2 for Blanquefort/Pauillac. After 2.5km, left at lights to N33 for Le Taillan 1km. Signed.

Colette & Olivier Salmon

tel	+33 (0)5 56 35 46 47
fax	+33 (0)5 56 35 48 75
e-mail	chateau.le.lout@wanadoo.fr
web	www.chateaulelout.com

map 9   entry 199

Château de Sanse

33350 Ste Radegonde, Gironde

What do you do while raising three young boys in Aberdeen and running a successful pizza and sandwich business? You dream of your own hotel and end up buying a run-down 12th-century château in Bordeaux wine country. Mad, courageous – and the right choice to boot! Trish and Mark have worked miracles and done much of it themselves. A stunning entrance hall, white and minimalist, sets the tone for the whole place: a beautiful teak desk, a colonial wickerwork sofa with white on white cushions. Colour comes from the occasional plant and splash of mauve, Trish's theme colour and hugely successful. The off-white and oatmeal theme continues upstairs with sisal in the corridor and coir in some of the bedrooms, a play of texture rather than colour. Lots of thought has been given to families – triples can be arranged and some rooms interconnect – and there's a child-friendly pool. Most rooms have private balconies big enough to sit out on in comfort with lovely views. Mark heads up the kitchen and turns out some very inventive dishes. Book early in season. *A no-smoking property.*

rooms	14: 12 doubles, 2 suites.
price	€ 90–€ 125. Suites € 150–€ 185.
meals	Breakfast € 12. Picnic € 15. Dinner from € 26.
closed	February.
directions	A10 exit St Andre de Cubec to Libourne; towards Castillon La Bataille; D17 right Pujols; D18 left Gensac; D15e right to Coubeyrac. Hotel signed on right.

	Mark & Trish Tyler
tel	+33 (0)5 57 56 41 10
fax	+33 (0)5 57 56 41 29
e-mail	sanse@chateaudesanse.com
web	www.chateaudesanse.com

Auberge de l'Etang Bleu

24340 Vieux Mareuil, Dordogne

The Inn by the Blue Pond… it's actually a small lake, dreamed up by Pierre's father. Forty-odd years ago he bought 10 hectares of wasteland within easy reach of the delightful villages of Saint Jean de Côle and Brantôme (the 'Venice of Périgord') and had the pond dug. The Auberge came next, then the garden running down to the water. Anne was once an English teacher and speaks it perfectly; Pierre is great fun and full of ideas for you. Explore the lovely grounds – the odd duck or swan may choose to join you – or hire bikes and investigate further. The Auberge feels older than it is, with its dark oak beams and traditional furniture. Bedrooms are not huge but carpeted and comfortable; those at the front have a balcony, those at the back park views. But you are here for the food and the well-established restaurant takes it very seriously, in this region famous for its cuisine. Dine in comfort in a rustic, stone-walled room stuffed with fresh flowers and hunting memorabilia, or on the romantic terrace that overlooks the lake. Breakfasts are a treat too, with omelettes, croissants and homemade jams.

rooms	11 doubles.
price	€ 50–€ 62.
meals	Breakfast € 7. Lunch & dinner € 26–€ 45. Children's menu € 12. Restaurant closed Sundays evenings 15 November–April.
closed	1st week in January.
directions	From Angoulême, D939 for Perigueux. After approx. 45km, left on D93 at Vieux-Mareuil. Signed on right.

Anne & Pierre Colas

tel	+33 (0)5 53 60 92 63
fax	+33 (0)5 53 56 33 20
e-mail	contact@perigord-hotel.com
web	www.perigord-hotel.com

map 10 entry 201

Château de la Côte
Biras Bourdeilles, 24310 Brantôme, Dordogne

For four centuries the du Lau family owned the château and the new young owners are equally passionate about the place; they are modern in outlook yet deeply aware of the privilege of history. Not only that, but they have created some of the grandest bathrooms we've seen; in the top-floor suite you may star-gaze through the glass ceiling as you soak. There's much panache, without the place looking as though an international designer has got at it. It is thoroughly French, with a huge range of styles and sizes in the bedrooms... some walls are papered, some show the old stone, some show their age, some are worthy of several stars. The panache carries over to the food — try *magret de canard en croute de fruits secs* — served in a lovely, formal, half-panelled dining room with an open fire. You can play snooker in a panelled sitting room — formal again and very French. It is all utterly quiet, thanks to the six hectares of parkland. There are some very beautiful places to visit nearby so you have a clutch of good reasons for staying here.

rooms	16: 8 doubles/triples, 8 suites.
price	€68–€88. Suites €98–€150.
meals	Breakfast €10. Lunch & dinner €28–€49. Children's meals €12. Restaurant closed Sunday evenings.
closed	15 November–15 March (but open 2 weeks over Christmas).
directions	From Périgueux D939 for Brantôme; left before Brantôme onto D106E1. Château 3.5km on right. Signed.

Michel & Olivier Guillaume

tel	+33 (0)5 53 03 70 11
fax	+33 (0)5 53 03 42 84
e-mail	chateau@chateaudelacote.com
web	www.chateaudelacote.com

L'Enclos

Pragelier, 24390 Tourtoirac/Hautefort, Dordogne

Robert and Dana, who live half the year in Mexico, will welcome you, and he will tell the intriguing history of house and village. L'Enclos encompasses the manor, six stone cottages, the former bakery (two bread ovens remain) and the chapel in a skirt-roofed, blond-stone huddle round the courtyard – enormous personality! The sensational cobbled floor in the hall demands admiration; the dining room, marble floored and rustic walled, dark beamed and Turkish-rugged, conjures up the Ornsteens' natural yet sophisticated style. Light bathes the American potted plants in the salon. Each cottage has its own character, all use bright fabrics that lift and give vibrancy to the bare stone or off-white walls; there are fridges for your drinks, and most have their own terraces. You can have supper served in your cottage, possibly foie gras, salads and cheese; or dinner (reservation is essential) candlelit and convivial, in the dining room. A lush, quiet place for Dordogne explorers, with space for all in its gorgeous garden and a pool that overlooks fruit and walnut trees. *A no-smoking property.*

rooms	6 cottages for 2, 2 with kitchenettes.
price	€ 70–€ 140.
meals	Breakfast € 8. Dinner € 20–€ 30, book ahead.
closed	October–May.
directions	From Limoges N20 for Uzerche 2.5km. Right D704 for St Yrieix la Perche. Before Hautefort right on D62 for Tourtoirac; right on D67. Pragelier signed approx. 1km on left.

Robert & Dana Ornsteen
tel +33 (0)5 53 51 11 40
fax +33 (0)5 53 50 37 21
e-mail rornsteen@yahoo.com
web www.hotellenclos.com

map 10 entry 203

Manoir d'Hautegente

24120 Coly, Dordogne

The ancient manor, first a smithy, later a mill, has been in the family for 300 years but is paradoxically just 50 years old: burned down in the Second World War, it was rebuilt. The millstream has become a fabulous waterfall feeding a pond that shimmers beneath the bedroom windows and the thoroughly kempt garden is a riot of colour. Hautegente is rich inside too, like a private house, with two sumptuous dining rooms clothed in silk and hung with well-chosen paintings and prints. There's a cosy drawing room where a large fireplace and a vast array of cognacs summon the sybarite. Lavishly-decorated bedrooms have fine thick curtains, antiques and pretty lamps; some are small, some enormous and the soft, expensive feel of padded wall fabrics contrasts with the lovely old staircase leading up from the hall. The rooms in the converted miller's house are more modern; four have mezzanines and the ground-floor room is vast. Bathrooms are all beautifully tiled and properly equipped. Madame rules this empire with regal authority, with her more relaxed son and daughter-in-law. A splendid and peaceful place.

rooms	15: 11 doubles, 4 triples.
price	€82–€210. Triples €219–€307. Half-board mandatory June–mid-September €89–€159 p.p.
meals	Buffet breakfast €13. Picnics available. Dinner €45–€58.
closed	November–April.
directions	From Brive N89 for Périgueux through Terrasson. Left at Le Lardin on D704 for Sarlat, then left at Condat on D62 to Coly.

Edith & Patrick Hamelin

tel	+33 (0)5 53 51 68 03
fax	+33 (0)5 53 50 38 52
e-mail	hotel@manoir-hautegente.com
web	www.manoir-hautegente.com

Auberge de Castel Merle
24290 Sergeac, Dordogne

This hidden paradise has been in Anita's family for five generations. Her grandfather archeologist added stones from his own digs; Eyzies, the capitol of prehistory, is nearby. Husband Christopher is British and also devoted to this atmospheric place. They have renovated the old buildings with consummate care, keeping the traditional look, using wood from their own land to restore walnut bedheads and oak doors. Christopher is an enthusiastic truffle hunter and head chef; there's a vast cast-iron cauldron in the banquet room in which he once conjured up a cassoulet for the entire village. This is *sanglier* (wild boar) country and cooking the beast is one of his specialities. Flowery curtains, pelmets and hand-painted flowers on the walls prettify the dining room; bedrooms have a straightforward country look, with Provençal prints and exposed stone walls. Some rooms overlook the courtyard, others the woods. And the views: the glory of the place is its position, high above the valley of the Vézère, with river, forests and castles beyond – best admired from one of the check-clothed tables on the large, leafy terrace.

rooms	6: 5 doubles, 1 twin.
price	€42–€46. Half-board €42–€45 p.p.
meals	Breakfast €6.50. Lunch & dinner €15–€26. Restaurant closed Mondays & Tuesday lunch.
closed	November–mid-March. Reservation essential for March & October.
directions	From Brive A20 or Perigueux A89 to Montignac, then D706 for Les Eyzies. At Thonac left over bridge then right to Sergeac. Signed.

	Anita Castanet **& Christopher Millinship**
tel	+33 (0)5 53 50 70 08
fax	+33 (0)5 53 50 76 25

map 10 entry 205

La Métairie

24150 Mauzac, Dordogne

If you love horses you'll be in your element: you can relax on the terrace and watch them in the next field. You can also ride close by. La Métairie was built as a farm at the turn of the last century and converted into a hotel some 40 years ago, a U-shaped building smothered in wisteria and Virginia creeper. There's no road in sight and you really do feel 'away from it all' – yet the Dordogne and its cliff top villages are just minutes away. Borrow bikes if you're feeling energetic! Bedrooms are large and cheerful, full of sunshiney yellows; beds are huge. They have room for a couple of comfy chairs, too. Bathrooms match – large and cheerful – and three ground-floor rooms have French doors and a semi-private patio. The pool is big enough for a proper swim and when you come out you can read under the trees – there are plenty right by the pool. In summer you can eat out here, or on the flowery terrace. The dining room has black and white floors, washed stone walls and well-spaced tables.

rooms	10: 9 doubles, 1 suite.
price	€99–€135. Suite €160–€210. Reduction of 25% for single occ. Half-board mandatory in high season €116–€150 p.p.
meals	Breakfast €13. Lunch €18–€25. Dinner €38; Périgourdine menu €45.
closed	November–April.
directions	From Lalinde, D703 for Le Bugue. At Sauveboeuf, D31 through Mauzac. Signed.

	M Ostereich
tel	+33 (0)5 53 22 50 47
fax	+33 (0)5 53 22 52 93
e-mail	metairie.la@wanadoo.fr
web	www.la-metairie.com

Hôtel Restaurant Le Château

1 rue de la Tour, 24150 Lalinde, Dordogne

Overhanging the river Dordogne – a lovely restaurant and hotel in a spectacular position – the narrow terrace and swimming pool built into the rocks above the river have views of both the rising and setting sun across the water. The entrance is up a one-way street then through an old arched doorway. You are in the town here but insulated from it. The reception area is small and unpretentious; what is sensational is the stone staircase that winds up from the foyer to an understatedly elegant sitting area. Then come the bedrooms: from the smallest attic room to the biggest suite with balcony, they have pastel-painted walls and simple furnishings. Most overlook the river, others have windows on two sides and overlook the pool and entrance cul-de-sac. Bathrooms are impeccable, with either white or champagne tiles or terrazzo marbled walls. The dining room couldn't be more inviting; it's light and airy with stone and soft apricot-coloured walls, beautiful china, linen napkins, fresh flowers and a spectacular river view through the French windows. Monsieur Gensou cooks, very well. A great place.

rooms	7: 6 doubles, 1 family room for 4.
price	€50–€155.
meals	Breakfast €12. Lunch & dinner €25–€40. Restaurant closed Mondays & Tuesday noon; Sundays from November–March.
closed	3rd week September; 11 November–15 February.
directions	From Bergerac D660 to Lalinde; right at post office, hotel at end of street.

Guy Gensou

tel	+33 (0)5 53 61 01 82
fax	+33 (0)5 53 24 74 60

map 10   entry 207

Hôtel Les Glycines

4 avenue de Laugerie, 24620 Les Eyzies de Tayac, Dordogne

Potential for name-dropping here: Prince Charles stayed for several days in the 60s with his Cambridge tutor. Les Glycines has been lodging people since 1862, when it was a *relais de poste*. It has been enlarged over the years, with the stables being turned into more rooms once they were no longer needed for horses. The gardens are fabulous: they were planted by the son of a head gardener at Versailles. You meander down to the pool under arches laden with roses and honeysuckle and there is even a vegetable garden too. Just past the lobby you enter the dining room which runs the breadth of the building and overlooks the garden. The Lombards took over Les Glycines five years ago, threw themselves into decoration and have renewed the bedrooms again this year. Pascal leads the orchestra in the kitchen; do try his roast veal with choice local ham and truffled polenta. Don't be put off by the busy road and the station nearby: once in the garden you could be in the country, though you might ask for a room at the back or in the annexe. Families can have interconnecting rooms, which sleep five comfortably.

rooms	23: 19 doubles, 4 triples.
price	€ 70–€ 220.
meals	Breakfast € 12. Picnic lunch € 9–€ 23. Lunch € 22–€ 47. Dinner € 33–€ 47. Restaurant closed Mondays, Tuesdays & Saturdays.
closed	November–April.
directions	From Perigueux, D47 to Sarlat. Over river, on left immediately before Les Eyzies station.

	Pascal Lombard
tel	+33 (0)5 53 06 97 07
fax	+33 (0)5 53 06 92 19
e-mail	les-glycines-aux-eyzies@wanadoo.fr
web	les-glycines-dordogne.com

Le Relais du Touron

Le Touron, 24200 Carsac Aillac, Dordogne

Such an attractive approach up the drive lined with neatly-clipped box hedges and spiræa – it is all very elegant-looking, surrounded by broad lawns and handsome, mature trees. Reception is in the main entrance hall, by the high open fireplace, but only the big triple bedroom is actually in the main house: all the other rooms and the dining room are in the modern converted barn and stable block with the pool just below. The new dining room has one all-glass wall overlooking the pool and garden beyond and is flooded with light. Madame, with 14 years experience in Arcachon, is building a reputation for good, interesting food. Bedrooms are above the dining area and have the same decoration in straightforward style: plain carpets and walls, bright bedcovers and curtains and decent lighting. The nearby road is well screened by thick trees and shrubs. Indeed, the three-hectare garden, which also contains a small pond, is a great asset with lots of private corners to be explored and exploited. A delightful bicycle and foot path of six kilometres will take you right into Sarlat.

rooms	12: 11 doubles, 1 triple.
price	€50–€61. Triple €73–€83.
meals	Breakfast €6.50.
	Lunch & dinner €14.50–€34.
closed	15 November-April.
directions	From Sarlat, D704 to Gourdon.
	Hotel signed on right before Carsac.

	Viala Family
tel	+33 (0)5 53 28 16 70
fax	+33 (0)5 53 28 52 51
e-mail	contact@lerelaisdutouron.com
web	www.relaisdutouron.com

map 10 entry 209

Manoir du Soubeyrac

Le Laussou, 47150 Monflanquin , Lot-et-Garonne

Those high, wrought-iron courtyard gates dignify you as you pass through them and you never know quite what to expect. Here there's white paving, a central statue, climbing and potted plants. Walk into the well-planted garden and there's one of those amazing infinity pools that looks as if it spills over the edge of the hill. Most bedrooms have that same beautiful hillside view; their décor is opulently traditional with themed colours, chintzy touches, lots of paintings and prints, some genuine old furniture, and rugs on wooden or tiled floors. Bathrooms have all the cosseting extras; jacuzzi-type massage sprays, hairdryers, colour coordinated dressing gowns and essential oils. The courteous Monsieur Rocca has thought it all through with great care and enthusiasm and cooks gastronomic dinners too. Exposed beams, stone and brickwork and an open fireplace in the dining room set the scene for those candlelit meals and there is plenty of space to relax (with books, games and music) in the huge living room above. Just the place for an up-market country holiday.

rooms	4: 3 doubles, 1 suite.
price	€70-€120. Suite €145.
meals	Breakfast €8. Dinner €28.
closed	Mid-September-mid-May.
directions	From Villeneuve sur Lot D676 to Monflanquin, then D272 for Laussou. After bridge, left to Envals for 3km; left for Soubeyrac.

Claude Rocca

tel	+33 (0)5 53 36 51 34
fax	+33 (0)5 53 36 35 20
web	www.manoir-du-soubeyrac.com

Château de Méracq

64410 Méracq Arzacq, Pyrénées-Atlantiques

Madame will give you a warm welcome in excellent English and is always happy to help or just to chat. She is very proud of her château, her dog, her hens and her husband's cooking. He has established a menu that combines the south-west's predilection for foie gras and duck with exotic sprinklings of spices and rose petals. If you take the half-board option, you can juggle your meals around as you like: even by eating more the next day if you miss one. The pretty château is at the end of a long and inviting driveway through large grounds with chairs under shady trees. One oak, just as you reach the château, is 200 years old, perhaps planted by proud new owners. The eight bedrooms are an unusual mix: some in fresh stripes or flowers, others with bold turquoise or rose walls, with contemporary patterns on the beds. The first-floor rooms are grander, with bath and shower, while those on the second floor are simpler but all have their own shower. Rooms have lace-trimmed sheets, bowls of fruit and flowers and even bathrooms have plants. There are no numbers on the doors. As Madame says: "It wouldn't feel like home".

rooms	8: 6 doubles, 2 suites.
price	€ 70–€ 110. Suites € 140–€ 195. Half-board € 75–€ 97 p.p.
meals	Breakfast € 8–€ 11. Lunch & dinner € 30–€ 50, book ahead.
closed	Rarely.
directions	20 min north of Pau. N34 for 12km towards Aire & Mont de Marsan then left on D944 through Thèze. Château on edge of Méracq.

M & Mme Guerin-Recoussine

tel	+33 (0)5 59 04 53 01
fax	+33 (0)5 59 04 55 50
e-mail	chateau-meracq@wanadoo.fr
web	www.chateau-meracq.com

map 15   entry 211

Château d'Agnos

64400 Agnos, Pyrénées-Atlantiques

Originally an aristocratic hunting lodge, Agnos was a convent for 30 years until this exceptional couple converted it into a fabulous guest house. Heather, warmly communicative, and Desmond, a talented retired architect, both widely travelled and with a great sense of fun, have done wonders with cells and refectory – and still do all the cooking. The black and white bathroom with the antique cast-iron bath and vaulted ceiling used to be the château's treasure room – it is now attached to the gilt-furnished Henri IV suite. The whole house left us agape: high ceilings framing remarkable mirrors, original paintings set into panelling, a cunning mixture of period and modern furniture and a panelled dining room with a superb floor of ancient yellow and stone-coloured tiles and a black marble fountain. Look out for the medieval kitchen, the old prison. Your hosts would be grateful if you could find the secret passage which King François I is said to have used (he stayed here and he had regular amorous escapades). A place of great style, much history and refined food. *Children over 12 welcome.*

rooms	5: 2 twins, 2 suites for 3, 1 suite for 4.
price	€ 70–€ 120.
meals	Hosted dinner € 20, book ahead.
closed	Occasionally.
directions	From Pau N134 to Oloron Ste Marie; through town. South on N134 for Saragosse for 1km. In Bidos, right for Agnos.

Heather & Desmond Nears-Crouch

tel	+33 (0)5 59 36 12 52
fax	+33 (0)5 59 36 13 69
e-mail	chateaudagnos@wanadoo.fr

Hôtel de Charme les Hortensias du Lac

1578 avenue du Tour du Lac, 40150 Hossegor, Landes

Hossegor is such an unusual name: the locals tell us a Royal Horse Guard was stationed under the pine trees before there was a real town. The memory lived on and, *voilà*, Horse Guard has become Hossegor. Second Empire engineers enlarged the basin of the lake, hence the birth of a saltwater lake and, later, this 30s building in 'Basco-Landais' style. Monsieur Hubert has a distinctive style and recently renovated this jewel with an eye to feng shui; soft yellows and oranges, beiges, whites and off-whites, caramels, chocolates and natural fabrics. There are lots of lamps, archways, curves, candles and bunches of those long thin sticks that are said to direct energy. The rugs and lamps were designed by him and made by artisans. All this and the proximity of the lake create a peaceful, harmonious atmosphere. The basic double is not big but impeccable; some rooms have views of the lake. The suites have balconies for in-house meditation. There are six kilometres of jogging paths around the lake, and tea and coffee are served in the salon every afternoon at 4.30pm. *Taxi service provided for airport and train stations.*

rooms	24: 12 doubles, 8 duplexes for 2-4, 2 suites for 2, 2 large suites for 4-6.
price	€ 105-€ 165. Suites/duplexes € 110-€ 340.
meals	Champagne breakfast until noon € 17.
closed	November-March.
directions	A63, exit 7 Bennesse Marenne & Cap Breton follow signs for Hossegor. In centre for beach; 1st right after bridge over canal.

M Frédéric Hubert

tel	+33 (0)5 58 43 99 00
fax	+33 (0)5 58 43 42 81
e-mail	reception@hortensias-du-lac.com
web	www.hortensias-du-lac.com

map 14 entry 213

Maison Garnier

29 rue Gambetta, 64200 Biarritz, Pyrénées-Atlantiques

In glamorous Biarritz, playground of royalty and stars, a jewel of sophisticated simplicity. Pristine-white bathrooms have huge showerheads, bedrooms are done in subtle white, eggshell, dark chocolate and soft coffee with the occasional splash of brilliant colour. The bright breakfast room has Basque floorboards setting off pale walls, white linen as a foil for lovely tableware, light pouring in from great windows. Guests are enchanted by hotel and owner: both have real charm and warmth. Monsieur Garnier was in tourism and fashion. Then in 1999, having fallen in love with Biarritz, he decided to turn this old boarding house into a smart and friendly little hotel. So, no hall counter, just a gorgeous wrought-iron stair rail, a 1930s-feel salon with a deep sofa, an old fireplace and a magnificent oriental carpet – the tone is set the moment you arrive. And you will soon be at ease with your delightful, engaging host. On a quiet side street, five minutes' walk from that fabulous surfing beach, this is remarkable value.

rooms	7 twins/doubles.
price	€80–€115.
meals	Breakfast €9. Lunch & dinner available locally.
closed	Telephone ahead.
directions	From A63 exit Biarritz & La Négresse for Centre Ville & Place Clémenceau. Straight ahead for large, white bank building with clock; left onto Rue Gambetta. Free parking on side street.

	Jean-Christophe Garnier
tel	+33 (0)5 59 01 60 70
fax	+33 (0)5 59 01 60 80
e-mail	maison-garnier@hotel-biarritz.com
web	www.hotel-biarritz.com

Hôtel Laminak

Route de St Pée, 64210 Arbonne (Biarritz), Pyrénées-Atlantiques

The style is country cottage, with all the floral designs, stripes and neatly controlled flourishes that one might expect... almost English. The setting is gorgeous, with all the lush greenery of the Basque countryside at your feet and views up to the mountains. The hotel is on a quiet road outside the village of Arbonne, with a few discreetly screened neighbours and a big, handsome garden filled with mature shrubs and trees. In summer it is a delight to eat breakfast on the terrace. Rooms are neat and attractive, carpeted, wallpapered and with antique pine furniture. You will sleep well here, and be looked after with a quiet and warm efficiency by the owners for whom this place has been a long-cherished dream. You can, too, settle round the open fire in the evenings, warmed by the easy comfort of the place and the satisfying sag of the leather furniture. It is an easy hop to the coast and the throbbing vitality of Biarritz. Those mountains are worth a week's effort in themselves; just below them, the fish await your line.

rooms	12 twins/doubles.
price	€54–€96. Children up to 10 free.
meals	Breakfast €9.15. Dinner €10–€17, book ahead.
closed	Mid-November–January.
directions	A63 exit 4 La Négresse and follow signs to Arbonne; signed.

M & Mme Proux

tel	+33 (0)5 59 41 95 40
fax	+33 (0)5 59 41 87 65
e-mail	info@hotel-laminak.com
web	www.hotel-laminak.com

map 14 entry 215

Hôtel La Devinière

5 rue Loquin, 64500 St Jean de Luz, Pyrénées-Atlantiques

Louis XIV married the Spanish Infanta here and the church door was walled up forever! In the middle of this historic border town, Bernard first renovated his fine old mansion as a private home and then decided to "let outsiders in too": become an insider and feel welcome. In the salon with its sumptuous antique books, grand piano and lovely old French armchairs, you will want to curl up with a book and peek through the richly-draped curtains at the little green haven of a garden, so unexpected in the city centre. You can sit and read here too, in summer, after breakfast among the flowers. Your room has the same atmosphere: fine fabrics and antique furniture, wrought iron, brass or beautifully renovated wooden Basque beds, coordinated bathrooms, excellent sound insulation, attention to detail. The Carrères are a generous, artistic family; Bernard's daughter's paintings enhance salon and staircase, he's passionate about his region, writes about the Basque country and will entrance you with his tales.

rooms	10 twins/doubles.
price	€ 100–€ 140.
meals	Breakfast € 10. Many fine restaurants in town.
closed	Rarely.
directions	From A63, exit St Jean de Luz Nord for town centre. Hotel signed but ask in advance for exact dirctions through pedestrian areas.

M Bernard Carrère
tel +33 (0)5 59 26 05 51
fax +33 (0)5 59 51 26 38
web www.hotel-la-deviniere.com

Lehen Tokia

Chemin Achotarreta, 64500 Ciboure, Pyrénées-Atlantiques

The extraordinary name of this house means 'The First Place' in Basque, and the place is as extraordinary as its name implies. Built in the 1920s by the Basque architect Hiriart, for a British gentleman and his Mexican-Basque wife, it is a monument to Art Deco. Indeed, Hiriart himself invented the expression to describe the style the house epitomises. With stained glass by Gruber, marble and parquet floors, furnishings, carpets and pictures custom-made, it feels, the owner suggests, as if it has been preserved *dans son jus*, like confit of goose. And here it is now for us to enjoy. The bedrooms, like the rest of the house, make you feel as if you are in a luxurious private home: the panelling, furnishings and fabulous bathrooms have tremendous style. As if the architecture isn't enough, the house has the most stunning views over the bay of St Jean de Luz, a rose garden and sumptuous breakfasts. Perfect for those who appreciate Art Deco style.

rooms	7: 6 doubles, 1 suite.
price	€80–€150. Suite €180–€215.
meals	Breakfast €9. Excellent restaurants in the area.
closed	Mid-November–mid-December.
directions	From A63 exit St Jean de Luz Sud to Ciboure. After sign to Kechiloa, left; signed.

Yan Personnaz

tel	+33 (0)5 59 47 18 16
fax	+33 (0)5 59 47 38 04
e-mail	info@lehen-tokia.com
web	www.lehen-tokia.com

map 14   entry 217

Château d'Urtubie

Urrugne, 64122 St Jean de Luz, Pyrénées-Atlantiques

The Chateau d'Urtubie was built in 1341 with permission from Edward III. The keep is still intact, except for the roof which was changed in 1654 to resemble Versailles, using the expertise of local boat builders. Your host, Laurent, is a direct descendant of the builder of the castle, Martin de Tartas, and opened Urtubie as a hotel in 1995 to make sure he can keep it alive. The castle is classified and also operates as a museum: *The Antiques Roadshow* could run an entire series here. You can have a 'prestige' bedroom on the second floor, very grand and imposing: not 'light and airy' which we often praise, but a touch sombre and totally in keeping with the age and style. Upstairs, you have the 'charm' bedrooms, which are slightly smaller. Bathrooms are a mix of ancient and modern, with stylish touches such as airy mosquito nets draped over old-fashioned baths. On the outskirts of a pretty little Basque town, only five minutes' drive from the beach, Urturbie is also set in beautiful gardens. Don't be worried it might be stuffy: Laurent couldn't be more friendly and families are most welcome.

rooms	9: 1 single, 8 doubles.
price	€60–€130.
meals	Breakfast €10. Good restaurants in town.
closed	Mid-november–mid-March.
directions	A63 Bayonne and St Sebastien, exit St Jean de Luz Sud onto N10 for Urrugne. Right just before roundabout entering Urrugne.

	Laurent de Coral
tel	+33 (0)5 59 54 31 15
fax	+33 (0)5 59 54 62 51
e-mail	chateaudurtubie@wanadoo.fr
web	www.chateaudurtubie.fr

photography by Michael Busselle

auvergne
limousin

Au Pont de l'Hospital

B.P. 38, L'Hospital, 19400 Argentat sur Dordogne, Corrèze

Beside the little trout-rich Maronne that rushes over rapids towards its destiny in the great Dordogne stands a house that is run with a minimum of constraints by people who trust that guests will understand it is a family home. With a relaxed and helpful atmosphere and space for all to spread, it is ideal for fishing buffs and families (young children need supervision by that untamed water). Jovial Jim Mallows advertises snacks for passers-by, knows the area backwards and will tell you exactly where to eat great meals of remarkable value – he and Fiona are the most delightful hosts. Bedrooms are small but adequate, some with bathroom, some without. Fiona's anatomical portraits of fish and Jim's watercolours hang in the attractive breakfast room with its wooden tables and woodburning stove. With warning, they will do a barbecue and salad meal on the wooden pontoon projecting over the river. Come for the fantastic position in great walking country with five fishing rivers within 20 minutes, lots of places to visit and such unspoilt simplicity.

rooms	10: 5 doubles; 2 doubles, 3 family rooms sharing 2 showers.
price	€ 24–€ 37.
meals	Breakfast € 5–€ 8. Picnic € 7. Good restaurants in town.
closed	Mid-November–March.
directions	From Tulle, N120 through Argentat for Aurillac. 1st right towards l'Hospital for 2km. Hotel on right after bridge over Maronne.

Jim & Fiona Mallows

tel	+33 (0)5 55 28 90 35
fax	+33 (0)5 55 28 20 70
e-mail	au-pont@wanadoo.fr
web	www.argentat.co.uk

La Maison des Chanoines

Route de l'Eglise, 19500 Turenne, Corrèze

Originally built to house the cannons (*les chanoines*) of Turenne, this ancient restaurant-hotel has been in Monsieur Cheyroux's family for 300 years! No wonder the family held on to it – this 16th-century, honey-stoned house is one of the loveliest we have seen in a village full of steep-pitched slate roofs. Madame, young, charming, *très soignée*, is a fan of fine English fabrics and has used them lavishly for curtains and cushions. Bedrooms are divided between this house and another (equally ancient) opposite, approached via a little bridge from the garden. These well-lit rooms have plain carpets and white walls; bathrooms are luxurious with fluffy towels. The breakfast room is stone-flagged with wickerwork chairs padded in duck-egg blue. The dining room is in the old cannon cellar: small and cosy, with white-clothed tables and vaulted ceiling. You can dine under a fairy-light-strewn pergola in the garden covered with honeysuckle and roses. And the food is a delight; monsieur is chef and will use only the freshest, most local ingredients, including vegetables and herbs from the garden. An enchanting place.

rooms	6: 2 doubles, 2 twins, 1 triple, 1 family.
price	€60–€85.
meals	Breakfast €8. Lunch & dinner menu €30–€36. Open for lunch Sun & holidays. Closed Wed in June.
closed	15 October–week before Easter.
directions	From Brive, D38 to Monplaisir, then D8 for 8km to Turenne. Left uphill following château sign. Hotel on left before church.

	Chantal & Claude Cheyroux
tel	+33 (0)5 55 85 93 43
fax	+33 (0)5 55 85 93 43
e-mail	maisondeschanoines@wanadoo.fr
web	maison-des-chanoines.com

map 10 entry 220

Au Rendez-Vous des Pêcheurs
Pont du Chambon, 19320 St Merd de Lapleau, Corrèze

The proof of the fishing... is in the 15-kilo pike hanging in the bar of this delectable place – it isn't called Fishermen's Lodge for nothing. The house and its exquisite lakeside setting are intimately linked. Fifty years ago, the Fabrys built a house on the banks of the Dordogne; at the same time a dam was started just downstream. Madame opened a kitchen for the site workers – and the house became an inn, which she now runs with her daughter-in-law. This being Perigord, food looms as large as that great fish. The restaurant, a fine room full of light and plants and Limoges china, overlooks the view reaching off to the distant wooded hills of the gorge; menus are brilliantly short and to the point. Bedrooms are differently decorated in simple, pleasing country style with coordinated bathrooms. The terrace is generous, the garden pretty, the view to treasure. Remarkable value in one of France's gentlest, loveliest pieces of country. Take a trip down the river in a traditional long boat – dismantled in Bordeaux, they were 'walked' back to the region to ship out yet more oak for the wine barrels.

rooms	8 twins/doubles.
price	€ 38–€ 44.50. Half-board mandatory in summer, € 41 p.p.
meals	Breakfast € 6. Picnic available. Lunch € 13–€ 25. Dinner € 16–€ 35. Restaurant closed Sunday eves & Mondays, except July & August.
closed	12 November–mid February.
directions	45 minutes' drive east of Tulle: D978 to St Merd de Lapleau via Marcillac la Croisille, then D13 to *lieu-dit* Pont du Chambon.

Madame Fabry

tel	+33 (0)5 55 27 88 39
fax	+33 (0)5 55 27 83 19
e-mail	contact@rest-fabry.com
web	www.rest-fabry.com

Domaine des Mouillères

23250 St Georges la Pouge, Creuse

A small backwater of a village, a big clearing in the Limousin forest – here is a walker's paradise. On a south-facing slope with only distantly rolling hillsides, fine trees and a couple of donkeys to disturb the eye, the long stone hotel was built in 1870 as a farmhouse for Madame's great-great-grandfather and feels as solid as her lineage. Inside, you get that sense of long-gone days of endless country peace: leather-bound tomes, gilt-framed sepia photographs of Grandmamma or great-aunt Gladys as a baby, palely gentle floral designs on wallpapers and bedcovers. But the warm carpeting, the neat little bathrooms, the stripily plush modern furniture in the lounge betray a thoroughly contemporary care for comfort. And there's a lovely terrace outside. The delightfully friendly owners and their children, the geese and their goslings, the donkeys and their foals (summer population, of course) welcome you and your family into their rural world and Madame will serve you dinners of high authenticity: old family recipes made with fresh local produce. After which, peace will descend. *A no-smoking property.*

rooms	6: 4 twins/doubles; 1 double with shower & separate wc; 1 single with separate bath.
price	€55–€80. Single €24.
meals	Breakfast €8. Picnic available. Dinner €15–€30. Two restaurants at 3km & 7km.
closed	October–March.
directions	70km from Limoges for Bourganeuf & Aubusson N141. Left at Charbonnier to St Georges la Pouge.

Madame Elizabeth Blanquart–Thill

tel	+33 (0)5 55 66 60 64
fax	+33 (0)5 55 66 68 80

map 11　entry 222

Château de Maulmont

St Priest Bramefant, 63310 Randan, Puy-de-Dôme

This extraordinary place, built in 1830 by Louis Philippe for his sister Adélaïde, has long views and architecture: medieval crenellations, 16th-century brick patterning, Loire-Valley slate roofs, neo-gothic windows, even real Templar ruins – a cornucopia of character. The Dutch owners provide endless activities (golf driving range, riding, swimming, rowing on the pond) and cultivate a certain 'formal informality'. They have preserved original features – carved inside shutters, the old spit, the astounding banqueting hall with its stained-glass portraits of Adélaïde in various moods – and collected some stunning furniture. Bedrooms go from small to very big, from plain honest comfortable with simple shower room to draped and four-postered château-romantic with marble bathroom (the *luxe* rooms are worth the difference). And do visit the King's Room, a round blue and white (original paint!) 'tent' in a tower, for a brilliant whisper-to-shout effect. Dining rooms are tempting, there are evening entertainments – wine-tasting, music, spit-roast dinner – and staff are alert and eager.

rooms	16 + 3: 15 doubles, 1 suite for 4. 3 apartments for 4-6.
price	€70–€165. Suite €215. Apartments €215–€245.
meals	Breakfast €9.50. Lunch & dinner €17–€44.
closed	January–mid-February.
directions	N209 for Vichy, then to Hauterive on D131. Right after Hauterive to St Priest Bramefant Les Graveyrons, château signed, on D55; right at crossroads on D59 to château.

Mary & Théo Bosman

tel	+33 (0)4 70 59 03 45
fax	+33 (0)4 70 59 11 88
e-mail	info@chateau-maulmont.com
web	www.chateau-maulmont.com

Château de Collanges

Le Bourg, 63340 Collanges, Puy-de-Dôme

Wander down from the Chambre Verte (your medieval-style bedroom) for aperitifs in the salon – very French with its formal antiques, high wooden ceilings and dark striped silk wallpaper. Pascale and Denis will join you before he pops into the kitchen to finish off dinner. A talented cook, Denis is also a doctor (three days a week at a local surgery) and a dab hand at DIY: he is currently restoring a music pavilion in the garden. You dine in a stone-vaulted room with red walls, on the best local produce and vegetables from Pascale's potager. This is a family enterprise and the couple's son Loïc has recently joined the team. Most bedrooms look onto parkland and are named after colours; beds, all a good size, are draped, canopied or four-postered, dressed in lovely embroidered antique sheets and pillowcases. Ivoire has steps up to a bath in a curtained alcove: over the top for some, maybe, but certainly dramatic. There's billiards indoors, and, in a quiet corner of the lovely English garden – Pascale's domain – a new swimming pool beckons.

rooms	5: 3 doubles, 1 triple, 1 suite.
price	€79–€139. Suite €169–€199.
meals	Dinner €38, by arrangement except Mondays & Thursdays. Restaurants 10 minutes' drive.
closed	18 November–18 December; 5 January–5 February.
directions	A75 exit 17 for Ardes sur Couze dans St Germain Lembron; 3km further to Collanges.

	Pascale, Denis & Loïc Félus
tel	+33 (0)4 73 96 47 30
fax	+33 (0)4 73 96 58 72
e-mail	chateau.de.collanges@wanadoo.fr
web	www.chateaudecollanges.com

map 11 entry 224

Hôtel de la Poste

Le Bourg, 15190 Marcenat, Cantal

For a touch of France at its most profound, try this inauspicious little hotel and bistro at the head of a spectacular valley – at 1,200m , smack between two volcanos. This is not a fancy area – although Marie-José and her mother serve up some prize-winning fare on their gingham-topped tables along with an interesting selection of little known wines from the area; things are down to earth and the folk are friendly. We arrived on market day and there was a splendid gathering of locals sitting out on the terrace in front of the hotel, nursing their *petit ballon* before lunch. There are unexpected surprises however: just over the hill a Russian Orthodox monastery, where the art of icon painting by the resident nuns can be watched once a week; and where else could you find a permanent exhibition on lightning but at the local *mairie*? There's more thunder and lightning here than in the rest of France, so a talented local photographer sniffs the electrical storm and sets his lenses. Good value and a humble hub for all the beauty that surrounds. *Marie-José speaks perfect English.*

rooms	8: 3 doubles, 2 triples, 1 family room; 2 doubles sharing shower.
price	€ 28–€ 62.
meals	Breakfast € 5. Lunch € 10. Dinner € 25.
closed	Christmas & New Year for 2 weeks.
directions	A75 exit 23; N122 for Aurillac; right on D679 for Allanche & Condat. Marcenat is between them on the main road.

	Mme Marie-José Andraud
tel	+33 (0)4 71 78 84 78
fax	+33 (0)4 71 78 80 70
web	www.cantal-hotels.com/ marcenat/hoteldelaposte

Hostellerie de la Maronne

Le Theil, 15140 St Martin Valmeroux/Salers, Cantal

Silence and rolling green space! In glorious country where the little Maronne hurtles towards its gorge and brown cows echo the russet of autumn, this 1800s manor looks out to wooded hills and dark mountains. You will meet its charming, subtly humorous owner and be well fed by his wife in a dining room with soft quiet colours and pretty rugs. The lovely double drawing room has deep sofas, two fireplaces, more rugs, some intriguing Madagascan furniture. Bedrooms, all with excellent bedding, vary in size and are on different levels in a small warren of buildings, past flowering terraces and an indoor flower bed. Nearly all have the sweeping valley view (two rooms at the back are up against the hillside); the best are the terrace rooms. Sober décor is enlivened by exotic pieces – framed textiles from India, a solitaire table from Madagascar – and bathrooms are a good size. The pool is ideal for landscape-gazing, there's fabulous walking and you will be made to feel very welcome in this house of silence: no seminars, no piped music and headphones for telly – bliss.

rooms	21: 18 doubles, 3 suites.
price	€ 85–€ 125. Suites € 130–€ 152.
meals	Breakfast € 11. Lunch & dinner € 25–€ 70.
closed	November-Easter.
directions	From Aurillac, D922 north for 33km to St Martin Valmeroux, then D37 towards Fontanges.

	M & Mme Decock
tel	+33 (0)4 71 69 20 33
fax	+33 (0)4 71 69 28 22
e-mail	maronne@maronne.com
web	www.maronne.com

map 11   entry 226

Auberge de Concasty

15600 Boisset, Cantal

Half a mile high stands the river-ploughed plateau, the air is strong, the country wild, the space immense. Here, a good square family mansion, built 300 years ago and proud beneath its curvy shingle roof. Over the last 40 years, the Causse family have restored it, bringing everything thoroughly up to date: jacuzzi, Turkish bath and organic or local-grown produce to keep you blooming (lots of veg from the sister's farm next door). The dining room, dominated by a great inglenook fireplace where a fine plant collection lives in summer, and the covered patio overlooking the pool and the valley beyond, are the stage for great shows of foie gras and asparagus, scallops and confits, where the supporting cast is an impressive choice of estate wines; a fine breakfast spread, too. Guest rooms, some in the main house, some in a restored barn, are stylishly rustic with space, good floral fabrics, new mattresses and an evocative name each – no standardisation here, except for the great view. You will love the smiling, attentive staff and the warm family atmosphere they generate. *Some rooms with balcony or terrace.*

rooms	13 twins/doubles.
price	€ 58–€ 108.
meals	Breakfast € 14. Picnic available. Dinner € 28–€ 39.
closed	Mid-December–mid-March.
directions	From Aurillac, N122 for Figeac, left to Manhès on D64. From Figeac, N122 then D17 after Maurs.

Martine & Omar Causse-Adllal

tel	+33 (0)4 71 62 21 16
fax	+33 (0)4 71 62 22 22
e-mail	info@auberge-concasty.com
web	www.auberge-concasty.com

Château de Varillettes

15100 St Georges par St Flour, Cantal

The latest addition to the collection of historical buildings rescued from dilapidation and neglect by Monsieur Savry — he's unstoppable in his passion for things bigger, and in slightly worse condition, than stamps or vintage motor cars. His philosophy is not to 'interior decorate' but instead to recreate as closely as possible the atmosphere of times past. Whether he haunts auction rooms to clothe his collection or has purchased the buildings to ease his urge for wall tapestries, four-poster antique beds, carved armoires and one-of-a-kind side tables, will remain his secret. This 15th-century defense tower, transformed first into a gentleman's country house, then into a residence for the evêque of Saint Flour, is coming along nicely as a comfortable hotel in a medieval livery of blues, yellows and reds. Fabric-lined walls for the bedrooms and princely fireplaces, one in the arched dining room, another in the salon are a good balance for the large expanses of stone walls. Nicely tiled, thoughtfully integrated, the bathrooms have been admitted into this century, for comfort's sake.

rooms	12: 10 doubles, 2 suites.
price	€ 78-€ 123. Suites € 123-€ 242.
meals	Breakfast € 12, lunch & dinner € 15-€ 42.
closed	November-March.
directions	A75 exit 29. At roundabout, immediately after leaving autoroute, follow signs to Varillettes.

Nelly Mestre

tel	+33 (0)4 71 60 45 05
fax	+33 (0)4 71 60 34 27
e-mail	varillettes@leshotelsparticuliers.com
web	www.chateaudevarillettes.com

map 11   entry 228

Les Deux Abbesses

Le Château, 43300 St Arcons d'Allier, Haute-Loire

No carpeted corridor to your room: instead, a path paved with shiny river pebbles and lined with hollyhocks. When much-travelled Laurence found herself paralysed after a riding fall she vowed, should she recover, to fulfil a childhood dream – to cook, and create beautiful rooms. On a trip to the Auvergne she called on an old friend, mayor of Saint-Arcons-d'Allier, whose dream was to see this hilltop village live again. Their twin visions have met – perfectly. The reception, restaurant and communal rooms of the 'village hotel' are in the 12th-century castle; the bedrooms are in 10 little houses, each with a garden or terrace and its own personality. Be simple or sober, lively or luxurious: you could stay in the Painter's Studio, red, ochre and plum, with a four-poster bed, or sleep in an alcove surrounded by lace. The Rabbit Warren, just down from the church, has a balcony room for children. Clamber down to the river, swim in the pool (not for children after 3.30pm), gaze at the view... this is your own little village and you are one of a privileged few. Food is delicious, influenced by Laurence's time in Japan.

rooms	14: 1 twin, 6 doubles, 1 single, 6 suites.
price	€ 150–€ 250. Single € 100. Suites € 200–€ 350.
meals	Breakfast € 20. Dinner € 45. Restaurant closed Sun, Mon & Tues except during high season.
closed	11 November–9 April.
directions	In Langeac for St Flour; D585 for Saugues & Prades; pass Chanteugues. After 1km left to St Arcons. Over bridge, then right.

Madame Laurence Perceval-He

tel	+33 (0)4 71 74 03 08
fax	+33 (0)4 71 74 05 30
e-mail	direction@les-deux-abbesses.fr
web	www.les-deux-abbesses.fr

Le Pré Bossu

43150 Moudeyres, Haute-Loire

The silence is part and parcel of this fabulous setting in the depths of the countryside. A hotel for the past 30 years, Le Pré Bossu oozes warmth and solidity. Bedrooms are fairly basic but each has at least one piece of fine furniture. Its Belgian owners are passionate about the environment – they have carefully sown wild flowers in the verge opposite the hotel – and they organise mushroom-hunting weekends in the spring and autumn. Monsieur Grootaert handles the cooking, inspired by his own vegetable garden or the fresh produce he brings back from his regular trips to Lyon. Specialities include a vegetable menu (not called 'vegetarian' since he doesn't consider it a philosophy) as well as wild pike when available. Well-behaved children are welcome and it's an ideal spot for either a quiet stay or an adventure holiday taking in canoeing, ballooning and lots of country hikes. At an altitude of 1,300 metres it can get chilly at any time of the year so a huge fire is lit every morning in the library/breakfast room where you are served freshly squeezed orange juice and a choice of homemade jams. *A no-smoking property.*

rooms	6: 1 double, 5 suites.
price	€ 90. Suites € 120–€ 140.
meals	Breakfast € 12–€ 15. Picnic lunch on request. Dinner mandatory € 38–€ 58.
closed	November–Easter.
directions	From Le Puy en Velay D15 for Valence for 15km. At Les Pandraux D36 towards Laussonne for 6km. Left for Moudeyres. Hotel at village entrance.

M & Mme Grootaert
tel	+33 (0)4 71 05 10 70
fax	+33 (0)4 71 05 10 21
web	www.leprebossu.fr.fm

map 12 entry 230

photography by Michael Busselle

midi-pyrénées

Domaine de Rasigous

81290 St Affrique les Montagnes, Tarn

The drawing room is the magnet of this exceptional house: gentle colours, fabulous furnishings and, in winter, log fire in marble fireplace. The soft yellow and white dining room is full of modern art collected in Fons and Ben's native Holland. Never twee, the tables are beautifully decorated for good-looking, varied food and local wines (especially the delicious Gaillac). Natural light, bare floorboards with fine rugs or luxurious plain carpets give that country-house feel to the large, heavenly bedrooms, sensitively decorated with rich colours and interesting furniture. The three suites are elegantly unfrilly. Luxurious bathrooms have been ingeniously fitted into odd spaces – the free-standing bath is most handsome. Even the single room, with its sleigh bed, lovely linen and bathroom in a walk-in cupboard, is on the 'noble' floor, not under the eaves. The courtyard is ideal for summer breakfast; gaze at the water-lilies in Ben's water garden, eight different types of frogs will sing and jump for you. The owners' artistic flair and hospitality make this a wonderful place to stay – try to give it at least three nights.

rooms	8: 4 twins/doubles, 1 single, 3 suites.
price	€75–€90. Single €45–€65. Suites €115–€120.
meals	Breakfast €10. Dinner €25. Restaurant closed Wednesdays. Good restaurant nearby.
closed	Mid-November–mid-March.
directions	From Mazamet D621 for Soual for 16km; left on D85 to St Affrique les Montagnes. 2km further on D85. Green sign on left.

	Fons Pessers & Ben Wilke
tel	+33 (0)5 63 73 30 50
fax	+33 (0)5 63 73 30 51
e-mail	info@domainederasigous.com
web	www.domainederasigous.com

map 16   entry 231

Hôtellerie de l'Abbaye-Ecole de Sorèze

Le Logis des Pères/Le Pavillon des Hôtes, Rue Lacordaire, 81540 Sorèze, Tarn

In the quaint village of Sorèze on the pilgrims' route to Santiago de Campostela, you turn into an avenue lined with huge plane trees. Founded by the Benedictines in 754, Notre Dame de la Sagne Abbey was pillaged and destroyed several times, before the order set up a school there in 1682: you can still see the pond where pupils took an icy dip. In 1776, Louis XVI named it a Royal Military College. Saved from closure after the Revolution, La Sagne reopened as a school under a Dominican in 1854 and closed only in 1991. It is now a peaceful retreat for exploring the Black Mountains: on foot, mountain bike or by horse. Eighteen bedrooms in the Pavillon des Hôtes manage to look spartan while really being very comfortable: white walls, crisp white sheets, simple desks and chairs. The lovely new rooms in Le Logis des Pères, ranging from large to enormous, are up a sweeping stone staircase from a central terrace, all very in keeping with the feel of the place. The grounds are huge so there is no fear of overcrowding. Wonderful meals are served in the pink and green restaurant, or in a shaded courtyard.

rooms	70: 52 doubles in Le Logis des Pères; 18 standard doubles in Le Pavillion des Hôtes.
price	€50–€140.
meals	Breakfast €10.50. Patio restaurant meals €12–€15 (summer only). Traditional restaurant lunch & dinner €20–€35. Restaurant closed Tuesdays.
closed	Rarely.
directions	From Toulouse, A61 exit Castelnaudary, then towards Revel & Sorèze.

	M Jean-Patrice Bertrand
tel	+33 (0)5 63 74 44 80
fax	+33 (0)5 63 74 44 89
e-mail	contact@hotelfp-soreze.com
web	www.hotelfp-soreze.com

Château de Salettes

Lieu-dit 'Salettes', 81140 Cahuzac sur Vère, Tarn

The vines run virtually to the edge of the pool – a delicious spot from which to gaze at the lazy views of hilltop villages as they fade into the distance. Not for nothing is this area known as 'the Tuscany of the Tarn'. Dominating the ancient Gaillac vineyards, Salettes was built in the 17th and 18th centuries and was once home to a junior branch of the Toulouse-Lautrec family. It has recently been renovated from top to toe, in a confidently minimalist style that complements the pale old stones and timbers perfectly. All is cream, white, stone or pale wood; light floods in through floating curtains, floors gleam, pressed white bathrooms towels are serried high. The bedrooms are all sited within the massive outer walls or towers, and look over miles of open country; curtains have been dispensed with where windows are 'castle' not 'château'. You can play tennis, swim, borrow a bike, explore. The whole place is immaculate, and the restaurant a triumph of simplicity – sample the Salettes wines, accompanied by exquisitely presented local produce.

rooms	18: 12 doubles, 1 triple, 5 suites.
price	€ 115–€ 145. Suites € 229–€ 267.
meals	Breakfast € 14. Lunch & dinner € 22–€ 80
closed	Rarely.
directions	From Toulouse A68/N88 exit Gaillac for Cordes sur Ciel; signed.

	M Yorrick Pellegri
tel	+33 (0)5 63 33 60 60
fax	+33 (0)5 63 33 60 61
e-mail	salettes@chateaudesalettes.com
web	www.chateaudesalettes.com

map 16 entry 233

Château de Gandels

81700 Garrevaques, Tarn

Roles are clearly divided here: Philippe devotes his time to the magnificent grounds while Martine, who is as friendly as she is elegant, spent five years doing up the château and now, their five children grown and gone, looks after her guests. An accomplished horsewoman, she is happy to take competent guests out for a ride, but her first love is cooking and she devises the evening menu in the local farmers' market each day. Martine enjoys entertaining guests, but if you fancy something more romantic, she is happy to lay a candlelit dinner for two in a quiet room. Antique dealers in Paris before settling here, Philippe and Martine still dabble in the trade as they love it and their eye has really come into its own in the château. The bedrooms are all huge, all look onto the gardens and are all different. Floors are polished wood or tiled with rugs, but while Baldaquin has *toile de Jouy* and an ornate four-poster, another is painted in soft blue with simple though unusual wooden beds and blue and white covers. *20m-long pool.*

rooms	8: 5 doubles, 3 suites for 4-6.
price	€ 107. Suites € 183.
meals	Snacks available.
	Dinner € 35 with wine, book ahead.
closed	Rarely.
directions	From D622 Revel & Castres road 2km outside of Revel take D45 to Garrevaques. After 2.5km château signed on right.

Martine & Philippe Dupressoir

tel	+33 (0)5 63 70 27 67
fax	+33 (0)5 63 75 22 27
e-mail	dupressoir@chateau-de-gandels.com
web	www.chateau-de-gandels.com

Château de Garrevaques
81700 Garrevaques, Tarn

The walls were breached under fire of bombards and culverins... Then came the Revolution, then the German occupation; but the family is adept at rising from the ashes and the 17th generation of Ginestes is now in charge. Marie-Christine has all the charm and passion to make a go of such a splendid place – slightly faded in parts, full of interest. There are huge reception rooms, magnificent antiques, some original 18th-century wallpaper by Zuber, wood-block floors, a dining room with wood-panelled ceiling. Up the spiral stone stairs is a games room, with billiards, cards, easy chairs and antiques pieces. The Blue Room next door is vast, stunning. All the bedrooms are charming and colourful, some with matching wallpaper and bed coverings. In the new Pavillion: 15 luxury bedrooms, a sparkling new relaxation centre, a second (outdoor) pool and two restaurants, one *gastronomique*, one regional. The garden is studded with old trees as grand as the château. Marie-Christine is unstoppable: cookery courses, itineraries to nearby places of interest, flying lessons next door... you are in good hands.

rooms	23: 7 doubles, 1 suite for 3-5 in château; 15 doubles in Pavillon (opens 2004).
price	Doubles from € 130. Suite from € 230. Half-board from € 100 p.p.
meals	Buffet lunch € 15. Dinner € 30 with aperitif, wine & coffee, book ahead.
closed	Rarely.
directions	From Revel, D1 for Caraman. Opposite Gendarmerie in Revel, D79F to Garrevaques for 5km. Château at end of village on right.

Marie-Christine & Claude Combes

tel	+33 (0)5 63 75 04 54
fax	+33 (0)5 63 70 26 44
e-mail	m.c.combes@wanadoo.fr
web	www.garrevaques.com

map 16 entry 235

Hôtel Cuq en Terrasses
Cuq le Château, 81470 Cuq Toulza, Tarn

Even the name is appealing. Come to the Pays de Cocagne, their brochure says. Where is that exactly, you may wonder, have I drunk that wine? It is in fact an imaginary land of pleasure, from the old French 'land of cakes'. Brochures often stretch the truth, but this place is magical. Philippe and Andonis, who is Greek, gave up good jobs in Paris to buy this 18th-century presbytery after coming here on holiday. Perched in a beautiful garden on the side of a hill, between Toulouse and Castres, the tall, mellow stone house with white shutters looks so inviting. All the rooms, including a two-floor suite by the saltwater pool, are full of character, all different, with old terracotta floors, hand-finished plaster and some antique beds. But it is worth staying here just for the bathrooms – all different, in wood and white or terracotta and with hand-painted tiles. You can have breakfast on a long narrow terrace blending into the garden. If you manage to drag yourself away to do some sightseeing, come back for some real Mediterranean food, bought earlier at the local market. Your hosts speak perfect English and are delightful.

rooms	8: 7 doubles, 1 suite.
price	€90–€130. Suite €145. Half-board available for minimum 4-day stay.
meals	Breakfast €11. Snacks available. Dinner €30, book ahead.
closed	January–March.
directions	N126 to Cuq Toulza. Then D45 towards Revel. After 2km on left at top of hill in old village.

	M Philippe Gallice **& M Andonis Vassalos**
tel	+33 (0)5 63 82 54 00
fax	+33 (0)5 63 82 54 11
e-mail	cuq-en-terrasses@wanadoo.fr
web	www.cuqenterrasses.com

Maison Barbican

25 Grand Rue de la Barbacane, 81170 Cordes sur Ciel, Tarn

A secret garden in paradise, vistas over the Cordes valley, an exquisite cook, a Gaillac wine enthusiast – all in a hilltop village. Bring flat shoes for the cobbled streets – although you may just want to sit with a book in the walled garden. Thank goodness Gilles and Donna, both British, decided to return to the southwest after a brief séjour in the Alps. They found this wonderfully proportioned 1850s house and have renovated the four floors with care. Pale cream stone tiles in the hallway and kitchen area unify the off-white colour scheme and add to the feeling of space, as do the stained-glass windows and doors. Serious gold-rich drapes adorn the double windows in the opulent dining room painted in dramatic raspberry; a deep wooden sideboard reveals its glassware and white crockery. There is a terrace for summer meals, parquet floors, retro sinks and taps, and a large double bedroom with its own entrance. There are other restaurants in Cordes but once you have tasted Donna's sea bass on a bed of new peas and bananas flambéd in rum, you may not want to roam. *A no-smoking property.*

rooms	3 doubles.
price	€ 75–€ 110.
meals	Hosted dinner € 30.
closed	Rarely.
directions	Halfway up to the top of Cordes sur Ciel. Park at Trésor and walk a few hundred yards to the house. Gilles will assist.

Gilles & Donna Thacker

tel	+33 (0)5 63 56 88 95
e-mail	gilles@aol.com

map 16 entry 237

Hôtel du Taur

2 rue du Taur, 31000 Toulouse, Haute-Garonne

Labyrinthine, simple and welcoming, the Taur (the Bull) is as close as you would want to be to the great Place du Capitol, the pink city's throbbing heart. Up the stairs from the student-filled pedestrian street, enter a soft quiet space of crimson carpet and clean-cut 1970s furniture. Prints and paintings are bull-based, some of them by Toutain, a renowned local artist whose monumental sculptures stand in the city squares. The rooms? A good size for their two stars, simply done with white walls and bright contemporary fabrics, new mattresses, bedding and carpets and decent, plain bathrooms; all on the first floor, all giving onto courtyards. One of these is grandly arcaded, others are less decorative, all are blessedly quiet. The pale parquet floor of the breakfast room glows in the light from the three low arched windows that look over the 17th-century street. In about 250 AD, early Christian Saturnin (i.e. St Sernin), refusing to join a pagan bull-worship ritual, was tied to the animal's neck and chased down this very street till he died, thus gaining fame and sainthood. Toulouse is a richly fascinating old city.

rooms	38: 6 small singles, 28 doubles, 4 triples.
price	€45–€66.
meals	Breakfast €8. Lunch & dinner available locally.
closed	Rarely.
directions	From ring road follow Centre Ville to Place du Capitole. Rue du Taur leads off the Place. Underground car park Place du Capitole. Metro: Capitole.

M & Mme Garcia-Beliando

tel	+33 (0)5 61 21 17 54
fax	+33 (0)5 61 13 78 41
e-mail	contact@hotel-du-taur.com
web	www.hotel-du-taur.com

Park Hôtel

2 rue Porte Sardane/13 rue d'Austerlitz, 31000 Toulouse, Haute-Garonne

Right in the centre of old Toulouse, the Park Hôtel is two old red-brick townhouses joined in a charming warren of corridors and rooms with two staircases inside and three little streets outside (all rooms are double-glazed and most are air-conditioned). In contrast to the old brickwork, which can be met again in the very attractive basement fitness and jacuzzi area – and the delicious little antique shop opposite – the rooms are clean-cut and modern with smart grey corridors and pinstripe bathrooms. The owner is the dynamic young soul of her hotel – she and her smiling staff create an atmosphere of warm, relaxed helpfulness – and she has introduced dabs of personality to the renovation with interesting lamps, strong decorative paper flowers, old mirrors, prints and engravings. The smallish, city-hotel rooms are based on lavender or pink tints with functional modern furniture and soft fabrics. You can rely on everything to be perfectly maintained and the welcome to be marvellous. And the hotel has an illustrious, listed neighbour in the form of… a car park, designed by a student of Le Corbusier.

rooms	44: 31 doubles, 10 twins, 3 triples.
price	€59–€66.
meals	Breakfast €7. Wide choice of restaurants nearby.
closed	Rarely.
directions	From ring road towards Centre Ville/Place du Capitole; Place Wilson; Place Victor Hugo. Right into Rue Porte Sardane: 5 minutes to unload then move to Parking Victor Hugo. Metro: Jaurès.

	Ann Beliando
tel	+33 (0)5 61 21 25 97
fax	+33 (0)5 61 23 96 27
e-mail	contact@au-park-hotel.com
web	www.au-park-hotel.com

 map 15 entry 239

L'Oustal del Barry

Place du Faubourg, 12270 Najac, Aveyron

This is an area not to miss. Rolling green hills, cows and more cows, large farms – almost castles – and medieval Najac itself; a scurry of slate roofed houses running up the hill to a fairy-tale fort. The auberge, an 18th-century townhouse, sits smack in the centre. Some rooms have deep views of the château and the surrounding dramatic countryside; others to the back and facing the town square may be a bit noisy. Remy, who has been the chef for years, is now the owner and with the help of his wife, is slowly bringing things out of the time-warped 60s and up-to-date. The rooms will never be luxurious but the revamped ones are modest and good value. The kitchen and the wine cellar are the first priority here: the chef makes his own jams and patisseries, grows his own vegetables and fruit – you can visit the potager – and buys locally what he does not grow. The cuisine, therefore, is seasonal and regional but he adds that *petit grain de folie* which gives the menus their elaborate flavour. Corrine and her friendly staff will advise you on the appropriate local wines.

rooms	20: 17 doubles, 3 rooms for 3-4.
price	€50–€86.
meals	Breakfast €8.50. Lunch & dinner €22.50–€48. Children's meals €10.50. Restaurant closed Mondays & Tuesday noon April-June; October-November.
closed	Mid-November-April. Open for Christmas.
directions	20km south of Villefranche de Rouergue on D922. Right to Najac on D39 for 5km.

M & Mme Remy Simon

tel	+33 (0)5 65 29 74 32
fax	+33 (0)5 65 29 75 32
e-mail	oustal@caramail.com
web	www.oustaldelbarry.com

Villa Ric

Route de Leyme, 46400 St Céré, Lot

Jean-Pierre built his house some 20 years ago, high on a steep hill covered in "proper" trees (not conifers). The view from the terrace, where you eat when it's warm, is of rolling hills as far as the eye can see. Food is an important part of your stay here: Jean-Pierre discusses the menu each evening with guests, most of whom choose half-board. Others do drop by to dine, but the emphasis is very much on a restaurant for residents, and food is fresh and inventive. Bedrooms are Laura-Ashley-pretty, perhaps with broad striped wallpaper and fresh white wicker chairs; many have exposed beams. Bathrooms gleam; each matches its flower-themed bedroom. The hotel is at a crossroads, ideal as a stopover for the Auvergne, Dordogne or the journey down to Spain. But why not linger a little longer? In July and August the old timbered market town hosts a well-established music festival: opera, music in the streets, processions and art exhibitions. Elisabeth is a passionate collector of the ceramics of Jean Lurçat, who settled here in 1945 and whose work is shown at a special workroom-museum in town.

rooms	5 twins/doubles.
price	€79–€105. Half-board €79–€105 p.p.
meals	Breakfast €9. Dinner €35–€55.
closed	November–Easter.
directions	From Paris, A20 exit 52 for St Céré, then Leyne. From Toulouse exit 56. Hotel 2km from St Céré.

Elisabeth & Jean-Pierre Ric

tel	+33 (0)5 65 38 04 08
fax	+33 (0)5 65 38 00 14
e-mail	hotel.jpric@libertysurf.fr
web	www.jpric.com

map 11 entry 241

Hôtel Relais Sainte Anne

Rue du Pourtanel, 46600 Martel, Lot

If conversation should flounder, *un ange passe* – an angel passes by as the saying goes. Perhaps one from the tiny chapel of Sainte Anne, at the centre of this beautiful cluster of ancient buildings, are a reminder of another, quieter time when the hotel was a girls' convent. The chapel is intact and is used occasionally for small concerts and art exhibitions and the whole ensemble has been lovingly and sensitively restored with no jarring architectural mishaps. The large pool is discreetly tucked away and the walled garden, a cunning combination of formal French structure and English informality, manages to retain a strong feeling of the past – young charges playing hide-and-seek in the shubbery, or gathering in the little courtyards or around the fish pond. Inside is equally evocatively atmospheric; warm old stone, fine wallpapers, opulent curtains, heavy rugs and proper attention to lighting. Most of the perfect ground-floor bedrooms have their own terraces. Sophisticated surroundings without any self-consciousness – a rare treat.

rooms	16: 12 doubles, 4 suites.
price	€ 70–€ 140. Suites € 110–€ 205.
meals	Breakfast € 11–€ 13. Great restaurants within walking distance.
closed	Mid-November–mid-March.
directions	From Brive A20 for Cahors exit 54 for Martel; rue du Pourtanel; hotel on right at town entrance.

Pierre Bettler

tel	+33 (0)5 65 37 40 56
fax	+33 (0)5 65 37 42 82
e-mail	relais.sainteanne@wanadoo.fr
web	www.relais-sainte-anne.com

La Terrasse

46200 Meyronne, Lot

A child might build a castle like this: tall and straight, with a mix of round towers, square towers, fat towers and thin towers. It's actually more fortress than château and has stood guard over the Dordogne since the 11th century, though with the scars of much violence. Gilles and Françoise have turned it into an inviting country retreat. Entered from the back through magnificent doors off a pretty courtyard, the entrance lobby has an amazing polished flagstone floor. The more interesting bedrooms are in the oldest part of the building. Most overlook either the river or the pool – set high into the walls with a fantastic view, this is a rare swimming pool with atmosphere. The main dining room is a touch 'interior designed' but you will love the vaulted 'winter' dining room, or eating on the terrace under the vines. Food is real south-west: wonderful concoctions with truffles and top quality ingredients. Save it for dinner or you'll miss seeing Rocamadour, the Lascaux caves or canoeing on the river.

rooms	16: 11 doubles, 5 suites.
price	€ 60–€ 92. Suites € 125–€ 230.
meals	Buffet breakfast € 10. Lunch & dinner € 24–€ 50. Restaurant closed Tuesday noon.
closed	Mid-November-April.
directions	From Limoges, A20 exit 55. At Le Pigeon, D703 for Gramat. Over bridge at St Sozy; hotel ahead.

Gilles Liébus

tel	+33 (0)5 65 32 21 60
fax	+33 (0)5 65 32 26 93
e-mail	terrasse.liebus@wanadoo.fr
web	www.hotel-la-terrasse.com

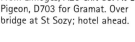

map 10   entry 243

Hôtel Beau Site
46500 Rocamadour, Lot

The perfect way to see Rocamadour: stay in this old hostelry, enjoy the stupendous cliff-hanging view from the restaurant and terrace, visit the historic village in the early morning and leave for the day when it fills with trippers. Rocamadour cracks at the seams between 11am and 7pm so return for dinner and a peaceful evening's stroll along the, by-then, walkable streets. The Beau Site is seriously old with a fairly wild history – stones and timbers could tell many a tale. It has belonged to charming Monsieur Menot's family for five generations and the reception area dazzles with medieval antiquities and shiny brasses on old flagstones worn by endless pilgrims' feet. The salon and games room are in the old vaulted kitchens and pantries, but we found fake leather and spindly legs disappointing. Bedrooms vary in size; recently-renovated rooms have pleasant wooden furniture, rich fabrics and good bathrooms. A friendly, welcoming place in an exceptional position. Hotel guests may drive right to the hotel and park in its private car park. *A no-smoking property.*

rooms	38 + 2: 34 twins/doubles, 3 singles, 1 suite. 2 apartments for 4.
price	€63–€99. Singles €56–€74. Suite €97–€130. Apartment €77–€102.
meals	Buffet breakfast €10. Picnic €7.50. Lunch from €16. Dinner €22–€49.
closed	15 November–6 February.
directions	In Rocamadour take road to Cité. Through medieval gates into village & park in front of hotel. Only hotel guests may use this lane.

	Martial Menot
tel	+33 (0)5 65 33 63 08
fax	+33 (0)5 65 33 65 23
e-mail	hotel@bw-beausite.com
web	www.bw-beausite.com

Hostellerie La Source Bleue

Moulin de Leygues, 46700 Touzac, Lot

If you like the unexpected, here you have it: a three-acre bamboo forest deep in *la France profonde*. Our inspector didn't explain how this came to be... It isn't just any old bamboo, but ranges from dwarf varieties to the 15-foot-high *Phyllostachis violaescens*. Meandering walkways lead to a lake full of koi carp and water-lilies: a magical place for children. The hotel itself is a fascinating ensemble of three old mills – one built in the 11th, one in the 12th and one in the 17th century – beside a spring that sparkles true blue, on any but the cloudiest day. With cars parked near but out of sight, the effect is peaceful and inviting, the rushing water soothing you to sleep and providing a cheerful, cooling background to meals. Bedrooms are spread through three buildings – the restaurant is entirely separate – and vary. Those in the tower are 60s-style but are due to be done up. Numbers Ten and Fourteen are big and traditional, while Number Eight has a private terrace. Despite its size, this is very much a family hotel and would be great for children – though perhaps not the smallest sort.

rooms	15: 12 doubles, 3 suites.
price	€ 69–€ 79. Suites € 125–€ 135.
meals	Breakfast € 6.50. Picnic € 8. Lunch & dinner € 15–€ 36.
closed	8 December-March.
directions	From Villeneuve sur Lot D911 for Fumel & Cahors. By-pass Fumel; after Soturac right for Touzac & follow signs.

M Jean-Pierre Bouyou

tel	+33 (0)5 65 36 52 01
fax	+33 (0)5 65 24 65 69
e-mail	sourcebleue@wanadoo.fr
web	www.sourcebleue.com

map 15 entry 245

Hôtel Restaurant Le Vert

Le Vert, 46700 Mauroux, Lot

The alchemy of family tradition – three generations and 20 years for this young couple – has rubbed off onto the very stone of the walls of this unpretentious, authentic country inn where Bernard's skills shine from the kitchen. All is simplicity with fresh flowers, glowing silverware, old flagstones leading you from the small lobby into the dining room – glance at the blackboard for the day's special to get your appetite going. The local food cognoscenti are greeted as friends here, always an auspicious sign. The rooms in the garden annexe are big, cool and elegant with beamed ceilings, stone walls and antique furniture lightened by simple white curtains and delicate bedspreads. Three rooms in the main house are to be made into two – they will be roomier still and have bigger bathrooms. The pool is hidden on the far side of the garden. In a country where politicians are authors and cooks are philosophers, Bernard's ivory tower is in the kitchen.

rooms	7: 6 doubles, 1 single.
price	€ 50–€ 90.
meals	Breakfast € 7. Dinner & Sunday lunch, menu € 40 & à la carte. Restaurant closed Thursdays.
closed	12 November–13 February.
directions	From Villeneuve sur Lot D911 for Fumel; south of Fumel D139 for Montayral. On past Mauroux towards Puy l'Evêque for approx. 500m. Hotel on right.

	Bernard & Eva Philippe
tel	+33 (0)5 65 36 51 36
fax	+33 (0)5 65 36 56 84
e-mail	hotellevert@aol.com
web	www.hotellevert.com

Domaine de Saint Géry

46800 Lascabanes, Lot

An ancestor unearthed by Patrick's archaeologist mother, and the beauty of the old farm buildings, were enough to inspire this remarkable young couple to purchase a very run-down property in 1986. Now the grassed and paved areas between the buildings are decorated with loads of large-scale exotica – lemon trees, bays, oleanders, olives... and a fountain. A truffle oak and hazelnut forest spreads out behind the buildings. The Dulers also seem to ably manage two small children, a 60-acre cereal farm, an organic vegetable garden and a restaurant – in addition to making and marketing their own sausages, hams, *confits*, and truffle-enhanced foie gras. You can sample all of these delectables and more, as Patrick performs superbly in the kitchen and Pascale handles the divine desserts. Bedrooms are traditionally furnished with solid old wooden bedframes, generous curtains, no frilly bits or clutter – and all come with their own terrace or sitting out space. The delightful pleasures of the table and genuine hospitality are united here in such an intimate and peaceful setting that you may find it difficult to leave.

rooms	5: 4 doubles, 1 suite for 4.
price	Half-board € 158–€ 211 p.p. Suite € 163 p.p.
meals	Half-board only.
closed	5 October–mid-May.
directions	From Cahors, N20 for Toulouse; right for Montcuq & Agen for approx. 500m. D7 left for Labastide Marnhac & on to Lascabanes. Signed.

	Pascale & Patrick Duler
tel	+33 (0)5 65 31 82 51
fax	+33 (0)5 65 22 92 89
e-mail	duler@saint-gery.com
web	www.saint-gery.com

map 15 entry 247

Domaine de Cantecor

La Madeleine, 82270 Montpezat de Quercy, Tarn-et-Garonne

Whether you are in the main house or one of the three outbuildings with their garden-level patios, all the colour-coordinated rooms are bright, unfussy and cheerful. Some of the rooms are spare and small but the property has masses of character and the owners make it clear that they want you to feel at home. On summer nights the floodlit pool is enchanting and during the day you may well be unable to resist a game of boules on the lawn or the delights of a village fête. Comfortable sofas around an open fireplace, bookshelves stacked with paperbacks, a billiard table in the oak-timbered gallery, a country kitchen (the central meeting place) and samples of wine bought from local growers complete this charming picture. This is a good base for exploring the subterranean caves or sampling the full-bodied wines from this area. Mountain bikes are on hand for those so inclined. Lydi and René keep a good supply of information on all the activities in the area and, between them, can hold their own in English, German, Spanish and Dutch, of course. *Cash or cheque only.*

rooms	6: 4 doubles, 1 triple, 1 family.
price	€ 55–€ 70.
meals	Restaurants 600m-2km.
closed	October–March.
directions	A20 exit 58 N20 towards Montauban for 7km; left on D83bis for Madeleine; left after 600m. Signed.

	Lydi & René Toebak
tel	+33 (0)5 65 21 87 44
fax	+33 (0)5 65 21 87 44
e-mail	info@cantecor.com
web	www.cantecor.com

Château de Goudourville

82400 Goudourville, Tarn-et-Garonne

Medieval splendour without the draughts and with hot showers, lashings of atmosphere and romance: Hughes de Gasques established a stronghold here in the 11th century, Simon de Monfort laid siege to Goudourville – in vain – and it was here, after the battle of Coutras, that Henri IV laid 22 flags at the feet of the Countess of Gramont, 'la belle Corisande'. Bedrooms are vast and dramatic with massive four-posters – Clement V, done up in red silk, Charles IX, all stone walls and cream hangings; d'Andouins, with subtle blue-and-cream wallpaper and a pretty, painted four-poster, Gasques, lovely and light in white and cream with a rosy terracotta floor. Baths are deep and bathrooms laden with towels. Muriel gives you the history while Bernard prepares dinner. This is served at small tables in a stone-vaulted dining room with a huge fireplace and you can choose from a selection of medieval dishes or local specialities. There's a tree-filled terrace overlooking the Garonne, a large swimming pool and masses to do and see nearby. Start with the château's beautifully preserved, 11th-century chapel.

rooms	6: 3 doubles, 1 twin, 2 suites.
price	€80–€130.
meals	Dinner €23–€38.
closed	January–February.
directions	From Valence, D953 for Lauzerte. Signed.

Muriel & Bernard Marchegay

tel	+33 (0)5 63 29 09 06
fax	+33 (0)5 63 39 75 22
e-mail	goudourville@wanadoo.fr
web	www.goudourville.com

map 15 entry 249

L'Arbre d'Or

16 rue Despeyrous, 82500 Beaumont de Lomagne, Tarn-et-Garonne

The 'Golden Tree' is Chinese and turn-of-the-century (the previous one); it's a ginkgo biloba, and probably the finest in France. Tony will tell you its story and will explain why he believes Beaumont de Lomagne is the finest example of a bastide town in south-west France; it's certainly very handsome. He and Peggy came here over a decade ago, obviously love the place, and take great care of their guests; they've given thought to disabled access, are happy to look after cyclists and walkers and actively host their evening meals. Peggy's a keen cook and has adopted traditional, regional recipes which you can eat outside in the shaded garden or in the dining room with its tiled floor, open fire and exposed beams. There's a comfortably old-fashioned, lived-in atmosphere in the sitting room – large sofas, books (and TV) – and in the bedrooms too, which are mostly large-windowed; some overlook the garden, some the street and have marble fireplaces, interesting old furniture and pretty decorative touches. A 17th-century gentleman's residence-turned-hotel with plenty of character.

rooms	6 doubles.
price	€45–€55.
meals	Hosted dinner with drinks €20; book ahead.
closed	1-15 January.
directions	From A62 exit Castel Sarrasin. From A20 exit Montauban. D928 towards Auch. L'Arbre d'Or opposite Beaumont post office.

Peggy & Tony Ellard

tel	+33 (0)5 63 65 32 34
fax	+33 (0)5 63 65 29 85
e-mail	anthonyellard@minitel.net

Castelnau des Fieumarcon

32700 Lagarde Fimarcon, Gers

Getting there is almost an initiation. Pass through a large Renaissance portal and spot a music stand and a welcome sign; then ring the gong. If all you hear is birdcall, you are in the right place. Built in the 13th century by local feudal lords, who for a time during the Hundred Year War pledged allegiance to the English crown, this stronghold was left to crumble until 25 years ago when the Coustols family moved in, restored the ramparts, renovated the houses creating gardens for each one and left much of the creeper-clad old stone untouched. The houses are not 'interior decorated', but simple, clever touches lend sophistication: framed dried herbs on the painted walls; mosquito-net baldaquins; terracotta tiles; a massive Louis XV armoire; antique Gascony treasures. Many have their own kitchens. Castelnau is on high ground so the views from every window are astounding, giving off a timeless hazy glow from the low-lying hills and surrounding fields. Stendhal called it the French Tuscany. He would be at home here: no cars, no TVs, no telephones. A rare pearl. *Dinner by arrangement only.*

rooms	12 small houses for 2-9.
price	Rooms: € 110-€ 200; € 550-€ 900 p.w. Houses: € 200-€ 305; € 900-€ 1,972 p.w.
meals	Breakfast € 15-€ 25. Picnic available. Dinner € 38-€ 100.
closed	Rarely.
directions	A61 exit for Auch on N2. From Lectoure D7 for Condom 6km; right on D166 to Nerac. Lagarde signed on left after 4km; village 3km on. Look for large gate; ring gong.

	Fréderic Coustols
tel	+33 (0)5 62 68 99 30
fax	+33 (0)2 47 32 02 52
e-mail	fcoustols@lagarde.org
web	www.lagarde.org

map 15 entry 252

Hôtel les Fleurs de Lees

24 avenue Henri IV, 32150 Barbotan les Thermes, Gers

Barbotan has the only baths in France where you can be treated for arthritis, rheumatism and varicose veins – all at the same time. But if you need a holiday not an overhaul, come to this 17th-century farmhouse, now a beautifully run hotel. Michael is half English, half Chinese and he and Jean have spent their married life working in five-star places in Dubai, Iran, London, Paris, picking up up a few tips along the way. Now they have their own clutch of rooms, a lovely pool lined with loungers, a squash court, a fitness room and a restaurant in which Michael can put into practice his French and international cooking. Interesting bits and pieces brought back from their travels dot the décor; bedrooms, with modern tiled floors and attractive open stonework, are individual and named after flowers. Double rooms are on the first floor, all but one with a large covered terrace, table and chairs; the suites are on the lower ground floor and open to a terrace that leads to the pool. These are themed – African, Oriental, Indian... the honeymoon suite, with drapes over the bed, is a semi-circular symphony in white.

rooms	16: 11 doubles, 5 suites.
price	€65–€85. Suites €115. Full-board November–March, by arrangement.
meals	Lunch & dinner €19–€31.
closed	November–March.
directions	From A62 towards Toulouse, exit 3 Langon for Mont de Marsan; D932 Capitieux; left for Gabarret via D124E, D379, D303 through Maillas & Losse on D24.

Michael & Jean Lee

tel	+33 (0)5 62 08 36 36
fax	+33 (0)5 62 08 36 37
e-mail	contact@fleursdelees.com
web	www.fleursdelees.com

Le Relais de Saux

Route de Tarbes, Le Hameau de Saux, 65100 Lourdes, Hautes-Pyrénées

A dream of a place. Three to five hundred years old, high on a hill facing Lourdes and some dazzling Pyrenean peaks, the house still has a few unregenerate arrow slits from sterner days. You come in through the leafy multi-coloured garden that spreads across lawns and terraces, a splendid first impression, and enter a house where you feel instantly at home. Bernard Hères inherited Saux from his parents and, with the help of his wife's flair and energy has opened it to guests. They are an enthusiastic and interesting couple who can guide you to fabulous walks, climbs or visits before welcoming you back to deep armchairs in the dark old-timbered salon with its peaceful garden view, or a refined meal in the elegant dining room. Bedrooms are in the same traditional, elegant mood with draped bedheads and darkish carpeted or flock-papered walls. One has no fewer than four tall windows, another has a gorgeous old fireplace, the two second-floor rooms are big yet cosy with their lower ceilings. And carpeted, well-fitted bathrooms for all.

rooms	6 doubles.
price	€75–€90.
	Half-board €72.50–€80 p.p.
meals	Breakfast €9. Picnic available.
	Lunch €28–€48.
closed	Rarely.
directions	Left 3km north of Lourdes. Signed but difficult to spot. 1st property 100m from main road.

Bernard & Madelaine Hères

tel	+33 (0)5 62 94 29 61
fax	+33 (0)5 62 42 12 64
e-mail	relais.de.saux@sudfr.com
web	www.sudfr.com/relais.de.saux

map 15 entry 254

Grand Hôtel Vignemale

Chemin du Cirque, 65120 Gavarnie, Hautes-Pyrénées

The site is outstanding, smack bang in the middle of the glacial Cirque de Gavarnie. It is the Mont Blanc of the Pyrenees, surrounded by horse pastures, granite, snow and ice; not even a souvenir shop to spoil the view. Danielle and Christian chanced upon the place a decade ago, when the building was on its last legs – an eccentric edifice built by an Anglo-Irish count in 1903. For the local pair it was love at first sight: not only were they overwhelmed by the surroundings, they loved all the place has to offer: horses, wild animals, hiking. The residence, in spite of its grand name, has not quite recovered its former glory: more Vegas motel than four-star hotel. But rooms are perfectly adequate and the bedrooms carpeted and comfortable, with modern floral bedcovers, drapes and beige-flocked walls. A few have balconies. Your hosts are relaxed and easy, forever running after horses and resident dogs and cats. It's a great spot for a young family. Lots of horseback riding round the Cirque on the famous Meres horses – a species that thrives at high altitude – and truly wonderful walks.

rooms	24: 18 doubles, 4 triples, 2 family.
price	€120–€250.
meals	Picnic on request. Dinner €25, book ahead. Many restaurants within walking distance.
closed	October–15 May.
directions	From A64 exit Soumoulou or Tarbes Ouest for Lourdes; N21 for Argelès Gazost; D921 for Luz. 49km from Lourdes.

Danielle & Christian

tel	+33 (0)5 62 92 40 00
fax	+33 (0)5 62 92 40 08
e-mail	hotel.vignemale@wanadoo.fr
web	hotel-vignemale.com

photography by Michael Busselle

languedoc-roussillon

La Lozerette

Cocurès, 48400 Florac, Lozère

In September 1878, Robert Louis Stevenson set off from Le Monastier with his donkey, Modestine, to walk the 220km to St Jean du Gard. Towards the end of his journey he stopped off at the Cevennes village of Cocurès, on the river Tarn, just above the National Park. Here Pierrette runs the country inn started by her grandmother and passed on to her by her parents. Her father is still around to advise on the best walks. The staff are especially warm and friendly and cope smilingly with all-comers to this busy hotel. Pierrette is very much a hands-on owner, running the reception, taking orders in the restaurant and managing the wine cellar: she is a trained sommelier and will pick you out just the right bottle. Bedrooms are fairly large, with wooden floors and headboards and are done in stripes, checks or flowers: colour co-ordinated but not twee. All have balconies with flower boxes. The whole hotel is spotless without looking clinical. You can play boules in the garden, walk in the National Park or follow Stevenson's trail, either on foot, on a donkey or on horseback. The chestnut in all its forms is the speciality here.

rooms	21 twins/doubles.
price	€ 45–€ 85. Half-board € 48–€ 60 p.p.
meals	Breakfast € 7.50. Lunch € 20–€ 22. Dinner € 27–€ 40. Restaurant closed Tues & Wed noon out of season.
closed	November-Easter.
directions	From Florac, N106 for Mende. Right on D998 for Le Pont de Montvert. After 4km hotel on left, signed.

	Pierrette Agulhon
tel	+33 (0)4 66 45 06 04
fax	+33 (0)4 66 45 12 93
e-mail	lalozerette@wanadoo.fr

Manoir de Montesquiou

48210 Malène, Lozère

Malène is a beautiful little town deep in the spectacular Tarn Gorge; the Manoir sits right in the middle, beneath towering limestone cliffs. When Louis XIII quelled a rebellion in 1652 and ordered all local castles razed, the 15th-century fortress escaped destruction: a royal letter ordered it spared as the Montesquiou family had helped the king. You enter through the original stone gate, into a courtyard dotted with wrought-iron tables and chairs; the greenery creeping halfway up the towers gives a fairy-tale feel. Several terraces are built onto the castle; you can eat out on one, leading off a cheerful yellow and blue dining room. The more formal dining room is in the old vaulted guardroom, with a huge fireplace. Bedrooms are up a spiral stone staircase – traditional and a touch sombre, some with a separate sitting room area which can be curtained off. Evelyne and Bernard run the Manoir with their daughters and use local produce whenever possible; the restaurant has something of a reputation in the area and locals often pop into the bar for a drink and a chat.

rooms	12 twins/doubles.
price	€ 64–€ 125.
meals	Breakfast € 10. Lunch & dinner € 21–€ 40.
closed	November–March.
directions	A75 towards Millau. Exit 42 at Severac for Les Gorges de Tarn. At Les Vignes, D907 for 12km to La Malène. Hotel in middle of town.

Evelyne & Bernard Guillenet

tel	+33 (0)4 66 48 51 12
fax	+33 (0)4 66 48 50 47
e-mail	montesquiou@demeures-de-lozere.com
web	www.manoir-montesquiou.com

map 16 entry 257

Hôtel d'Entraigues
Place de l'Evêché, 30700 Uzès, Gard

When you sit on the wide terrace or swim in the mosaic-lined pool you feel some glorious monument might fall into your lap: Uzès is a perfect little Provençal town and Entraigues, in the shadow of Bishop's and Duke's Palaces, is at the heart of it. The hotel is in fact five cleverly connected 15th- and 17th-century houses: an old building with a fascinating history and lots of stairs and corridors leading off the very French lobby where chairs invite you to rest and breathe in the old soul of stones and antiques. Each bedroom is an individual discovery: here a private terrace, there an eminently paintable rooftop view, and wonderful furniture with personality and interest. The décor is exposed stone and white render, good fabrics and no clutter. We thought the family rooms were terrific, there's outdoor space and a simple buffet/family restaurant as well as the splendid Jardins de Castille for gourmets. Guillaume Savry, the younger generation of this great hotelier family, is quite delightful: cheerful and efficient, unflappable and proud of his hotel. *Book ahead for protected parking in private garage.*

rooms	36 doubles.
price	€ 52–€ 152.
meals	Breakfast € 10.50. Lunch & dinner € 22–€ 49.
closed	Rarely.
directions	A9 exit Pont du Gard on D981 to Uzès. Follow one-way system round towards cathedral. Park in car park in front of cathedral. Hotel opposite.

Guillaume Savry

tel	+33 (0)4 66 22 32 68
fax	+33 (0)4 66 22 57 01
e-mail	hotels.entraigues.agoult@wanadoo.fr
web	www.lcm.fr/savry

Mas de la Treille

30126 St Laurent des Arbres, Gard

Nudge open the shutters and let the morning light filter through the plane trees. All the bedrooms are delightfully unfrilly; just one good Provençal piece of furniture, a painting on the wall, thick white cotton bedspreads, the scents of beeswax and lavender. Bathrooms are unexpectedly glamorous, with round or D-shaped baths and terracotta tiles. By day, views are onto the walled garden to the vineyards beyond, swooping into the middle distance; at night, you can see the lit-up medieval castle of Saint Laurent. The garden, too, is magical when darkness falls – candles are placed around the ancient trees. "Très romantique," says Carl, who takes special care of his guests. He is the proud new owner of the *mas* and has furnished the honey-coloured, blue-shuttered winemaker's farmhouse with carefully chosen antiques. There's lots of space to sit around in, a round pool, a coffee maker for guests, an open fire for chilly evenings and a riding stables down the road. Come for a night and you may stay for weeks. *Carl will pick you up at Avignon train station.*

rooms	5 + 1: 4 doubles, 1 triple (1 room with separate bath). 1 small cottage for 2 with private plunge pool.
price	€70–€130. Triple €125–€155. Cottage €135–€150.
meals	Picnic hamper €15. Restaurants in village 1km.
closed	Rarely.
directions	From Avignon, N580 for Bagnols sur Cèze; left for St Laurent; Chemin St Maurice is a right turn in village. Signed.

Carl Oliveira

tel	+33 (0)4 66 50 62 29
fax	+33 (0)4 66 50 62 29
e-mail	contact@masdelatreille.com
web	www.masdelatreille.com

map 17   entry 259

Domaine du Moulin

Chemin de la Bégude, 30126 St Laurent des Arbres, Gard

The little luxuries of a good hotel and the personality of a B&B in Antoinette's renovated 12th-century mill. She and Otto, both Dutch, have been respectful of age and style: old parquet floors and doors have been revived, a wooden stair polished to glow. Big modern flower paintings and a Belgian tapestry look good on white walls. The river Nizon flows beneath the house and criss-crosses the grounds, several hectares of them – a mill pond flanked by cherry trees (spectacular in spring), an alley of poplars, a lavender field, a pool. And there are swings and slides for the grandchildren, for yours to share. Breakfast is a Dutch feast of hams, cheeses and cherry jams, served at the big table under the tented pergola, or in the all-white dining room with chandelier. Antoinette is lovely and fills the place with flowers. Bedrooms, named after her daughters, have piles of pillows and fine English florals; bathrooms are swish with big showers or two basins; some are air-conditioned, one has a sun terrace of its own. There's a cosy library full of books, and dinners are wonderful.

rooms	8 + 1: 1 single, 7 doubles. 1 apartment for 6 for weekly rentals in summer.
price	€ 50–€ 168. Single € 60–€ 90. Apartment € 800–€ 2,200.
meals	Breakfast € 10. Dinner by arrangement. Restaurants nearby.
closed	Rarely.
directions	A9 exit 22 Roquemaure for Bagnols sur Cèze. After 4km go beyond left turn for St Laurent les Arbres. Left at Rubis, follow road.

J.A. Keulen

tel	+33 (0)4 66 50 22 67
fax	+33 (0)4 66 50 22 67
e-mail	laurentdesarbres@aol.com
web	www.domaine-du-moulin.com

Hostellerie Le Castellas
Grand Rue, 30210 Collias, Gard

Oodles of style at this fabulously restored country house in the centre of a Provençal village. The main house, sturdy, green-shuttered, stone-built, acts as centrepiece to other ancient stone buildings, all of which are linked by gardens, arbours and outdoor pool. Every bedroom is different – one Egyptian in flavour, another Art Deco, a third Provençal – but share terracotta floors, whitewashed walls and pale, polished beams. Luxury without clutter. The place is full of surprises: one bathroom, painted pale ochre, has a floor made entirely of pebbles, a local artist's fantasy; one bedroom has a terrace on its roof. Bathrooms have fluffy towels and impressive toiletries. The illuminated terrace is a delight at night, and the treats continue at table, where meals are taken in a beautifully simple, stone-vaulted dining room. Our inspector loved the delicate flavours (yet decided to forego the foie gras and champagne at breakfast!). Staff are solicitous and discreet, and Madame is gracious and charming, a perfectionist in everything she does.

rooms	17: 12 doubles, 3 singles, 2 suites.
price	Singles & doubles €72–€137. Suites €97–€187.
meals	Breakfast €14. Lunch €27–€84. Dinner €42–€84. Restaurant closed Mon, Tues & Wed noon.
closed	January–February.
directions	A9 exit Remoulins & Pont du Gard for Uzès on D981; left on D12 to Collias. Signed in village.

Chantal Aparis

tel	+33 (0)4 66 22 88 88
fax	+33 (0)4 66 22 84 28
e-mail	lecastellas@wanadoo.fr
web	www.lecastellas.com

map 17 entry 261

Le Château de Saint Maximin

Rue du Château, 30700 St Maximin, Gard

The light of centuries shines from the simple classical façade and the 12th-century tower, the arches and statue-dotted gallery, the vaulted staircase and great fireplace of this noble house. Currents of European civilisation flow through its several levels – white-stoned Italian pool and delightful French fountain, great Anduze jars on the terrace and silver olive trees in the garden, old tapestries and modern art skilfully placed to catch your attention. Jean-Marc Perry collects glass and has a sure eye for interior design, blending aesthetic refinement and creature comfort to perfection. The great classical tragedian Racine stayed and wrote here: generous bedrooms (the suites are vast), subtly elegant in their châteauesque garments and luxurious bathrooms, are called Phèdre, Bérénice... in his honour. One drawing room has a piano, the other, the only (big) television set in the place; tea is served in Sèvres cups, mouthwatering Provençal specialities finish the day. And from the second floor you look straight from exquisite civilisation out to the wild Cevennes landscape.

rooms	6: 3 doubles, 3 suites.
price	€ 145-€ 225. Suites € 180-€ 320.
meals	Dinner € 42. Restaurant closed 16 November-March.
closed	February.
directions	A9 exit Remoulins & Pont du Gard then D981 for Uzès. Right to St Maximin 4km before Uzès. Château in village centre.

	Jean-Marc Perry
tel	+33 (0)4 66 03 44 16
fax	+33 (0)4 66 03 42 98
e-mail	chateaustmaximin@aol.com

L'Hacienda

Mas de Brignon, 30320 Marguerittes, Gard

A warm welcome from your gentle hosts, so proud of their Spanish-style hotel-restaurant, so pleased to be able to share its comforts with you. Russet-shuttered and terracotta-tiled, this two-storey farmhouse has been transformed into a handsomely decorated 12 bedroom hotel in sweeping grounds with restaurant, sauna and pool. Relax under a pink parasol; breathe in the sweet scent of lavender – there are fields of it, as far as the eye can see; take a dip in the heavenly pool. The bedrooms are furnished in a country style, charming, with white walls, polished beams and delicate Provençal prints; most open onto a private terrace. The sitting room too is flounce-free – tiled floors, white walls, floral sofas and chairs. But if you like good food and wine you'll linger in the stylish, candlelit dining room seduced by the flavours of Provence: turbot and mullet, vegetables and herbs from the local markets and mouthwatering sweet creams flavoured with lavender and thyme. Great food, great hosts. *No smoking.*

rooms	12: 5 doubles, 6 triples, 1 family room for 4-6.
price	Half-board only, €95-€110 p.p. June-September. Out of season €85-€100.
meals	Buffet breakfast €12-15. Dinner €30-€55.
closed	Early November-15 December; 7 January-early March.
directions	A9 exit Nîmes Est & Uzès for Marguerittes. There, follow red signs.

Jean-Jacques & Dominique Chauvin

tel	+33 (0)4 66 75 02 25
fax	+33 (0)4 66 75 45 58
e-mail	contact@hotel-hacienda-nimes.com
web	www.hotel-hacienda-nimes.com

map 17 entry 263

La Maison

Place de l'Eglise, 30700 Blauzac, Gard

An 18th-century mellow-yellow stone house in a red-roofed village. Church, tower and château stand guard over the house, and beyond, vines, fields and woodlands. The views are magical. Old vaulted ceilings, shuttered windows and terracotta floors are a stunning foil for contemporary décor; this is a grand old house infused with an informal spirit. Pretty bedrooms are mostly large. The red room has a small private terrace that looks onto the château walls, the suite has a roof terrace with 360° views. Expect warm sandy walls, Indonesian wall hangings, ethnic fabrics, naïve art, a fireplace or two. Breakfast is taken leisurely in the walled garden where an ancient tree casts generous shade, or at a long table in the library with other guests. There's a piano in the salon and a swimming pool in the garden. Christian and Pierre do not do dinner but it's no distance at all to restaurants downhill. Strike out further and visit Nîmes, Avignon, Arles or medieval Uzes. Further still is the Cevennes National Park, staggeringly beautiful, and yet to be discovered by the English! *Children need parental supervision: unfenced water.*

rooms	5: 4 doubles, 1 suite.
price	€95–€160.
meals	2 bistros in village.
closed	January-February.
directions	From Nimes, D979 for Blauzac & Uzès 16km; after Pont Nicolas, left for Blauzac, enter village, house behind church.

Christian Vaurie

tel	+33 (0)4 66 81 25 15
fax	+33 (0)4 66 81 02 18
e-mail	lamaisondeblauzac@wanadoo.fr

Château d'Arpaillargues

Rue du Château, 30700 Arpaillargues, Gard

This noble house, its 15th-century sternness transformed with gracious 18th-century windows, balconies and décor, is a hotel that pampers but does not intimidate. Thick stone walls keep summer scorch at bay, balmy evenings are spent at table in the tree-studded courtyard; refined salons, vaulted dining rooms and a superb staircase are reminders of a more elegant age. History, aristocratic and literary, hangs in the air: Marie de Flavigny, Countess of Agoult lived here, she was Liszt's mistress, mother of Cosima Wagner, and left her husband here for the composer and Paris (an Agoult was also the heroine of *Les Liaisons Dangeureuses*). Rooms are big (slightly smaller in the annexe), very comfortable, with fascinating antiques and features (double doors, fireplaces and mouldings), interesting smallish but mosaic-decorated bathrooms and occasional private terraces. Back through those great iron gates and across the little road are the secluded garden and swimming pool. This is a deeply serene place of ancient atmosphere and modern, not over-luxurious comfort where the welcome is relaxed yet efficient.

rooms	29: 27 twins/doubles, 2 suites.
price	€ 76–€ 107. Suites € 168–€ 229.
meals	Breakfast € 11. Lunch from € 26. Dinner from € 42.
closed	November–March.
directions	Uzès D982 to Arpaillargues, 4km. Château on left at village entrance. Well signed.

Benjamin Savry

tel	+33 (0)4 66 22 14 48
fax	+33 (0)4 66 22 56 10
e-mail	savrychateau30@aol.com
web	www.leshotelsparticuliers.com

map 17 entry 265

Atelier de Calvisson

48 Grand Rue, 30420 Calvisson, Gard

There's a secret to this old townhouse in the little market town: from the narrow street it looks nothing special, but enter the private courtyard and it's another world. The courtyard, a wonderful source of light and greenery, is used for art exhibitions and Monsieur gives lessons: drawing, oil, water colour and pastel. The art studio is at the back of the house. There's a biggish living area for guests and a vaulted dining room for candlelit dinners in a womb-like atmosphere of warm colours and stone walls. Summer breakfast is in the courtyard. Up a spiral staircase, the tempting rooms fan off at different levels – there's a lovely smell of wax-polished stone floors; most are beautifully restored with old doors and good windows that seem to frame pictures. It is all in honest good taste, with simple, solid antique furniture that's genuinely part of the house, and your charming young hostess is eager to help her guests. Nîmes, Montpellier and the Camargue are close by and in summer the house is blessedly cool after the scorching sun. *Weekly courses from April to October (except last two weeks of July). Min two-night stay July and August.*

rooms	6: 4 doubles, 2 suites for 3 (1 with small terrace).
price	€50–€64. Singles €46.
meals	Hosted dinner with wine €18, book ahead; except Saturdays.
closed	December-February except during holidays (by arrangement only).
directions	A9 exit Gallargues. N113 for Nîmes. Just after bas Rhône canal, D1 to Calvisson. In village, along main street, 2 doors from Town Hall.

Régis & Corrine Burckel de Tell

tel	+33 (0)4 66 01 23 91
fax	+33 (0)4 66 01 42 19
e-mail	corinne.burckeldetel@free.fr
web	www.bed-and-art.com

Le Relais de l'Estelou
30250 Sommières, Gard

The last train clattered through some 30 years ago but this clever conversion stops just the right distance short of swamping its railway station origins. As you walk in, the feel is stylishly uncluttered: plain tiled floors, a modern sofa, an understated reception desk. The breakfast room, occasionally used for functions, is a conservatory under the old glass- and iron-girdered awning of the platform waiting room and has smart, pale-cushioned, wrought-iron chairs; it overlooks the tracks, now filled with a burgeoning lavender garden. Opposite are six French-windowed rooms. Bedrooms in the main building are smallish but comfortable (some interconnect for families) and simply dressed – rattan chairs, strong earthy colours; bathrooms are freshly tiled. Second-floor rooms are less minimalist with parquet flooring, *oliveade* and *toile de Jouy* fabrics and long views through prettily arched windows across the plains to the Pic Saint-Loup. Good value, with charming staff, in the olive and grape rich Cévennes countryside and only 35 minutes' drive from Nîmes airport. *A no-smoking property.*

rooms	28 doubles.
price	€ 35–€ 60.
meals	Breakfast € 7.
closed	Rarely.
directions	A9 exit Lunel for Sommières. At roundabout follow signs for Centre Historique; right after bridge for Aubais; 100m after house, Les Violettes, on left; left up hill to hotel.

	Jean-Marc Fauché
tel	+33 (0)4 66 77 71 08
fax	+33 (0)4 66 77 08 88
e–mail	relais.delestelou@free.fr
web	www.relaisdelestelou.com

map 17 entry 267

L'Hutte Éco-eurant

75099 Les Champs Esquissées,

If 'eco' means, among other things, making the best use of available resources, then this place is a minor triumph, and it is set in a gorgeous wildflower meadow. Old bits of pallet have been liberally applied to various parts of the walls, often at engagingly whacky angles. The forest has been ransacked for odd pieces of timber to prop up the cross struts. Nothing has been wasted, no new material used where old can do the job. The shack is 'tucked' under a tree and half-buried in the undergrowth, a clever way of reducing its visual impact and allowing it to grow back into the woods. In an age of obtrusive and self-promoting buildings this is a relief, and a challenge to all town planners. As if that were not enough – there is transport laid on. A three-wheeler stands at the ready for you, painted by the local graffiti artist – again, a clever way of reducing the visual impact of the original design. And there are, of course, serious ecological benefits to having such a small vehicle. Altogether an unusual place, though whether it is for you only you can decide. *Best visited while intact, a no-smoking property.*

rooms	1: Not spacious, but without the clutter of 'facilities'.
price	Inexpensive. Meaning we don't know – well, there was nobody there to ask at the time…
meals	Creative cuisine required. There are trees, if that helps.
closed	Often – it's much more sustainable that way.
directions	Ask a local if you can find one.

K L Khun

tel	+33 (0)9 99 00 00 00
fax	+33 (0)9 99 00 00 01
e-mail	nobodie@reception-pleezewriteletteurs…
web	www.pourquoi-les-multi-vs.eh?/engleesh

L'Auberge du Cèdre

Domaine de Cazeneuve, 34270 Lauret, Hérault

No wonder guests return to this big, bustling house. The lively, charming Françoise and her multi-lingual husband Lutz love welcoming walkers, climbers, cyclists and families. Workshop groups are welcome too: there's a special space, separate from the big and comfy sitting room. The mellow-stoned auberge, adorned by green shutters, iron balustrades and *orangerie* windows at the rear, has been carefully restored. Bedrooms are plain, beamy, white, with the odd splash of ethnic colour and terracotta floors that gleam. Bathrooms are shared; this is not the place for those looking for luxury. Sharing keeps the prices down and there have been no complaints. On the contrary, the atmosphere is one of good humour and laughter. Meals, chosen from a blackboard menu, are served in the *orangerie* or on the terrace. A great place for a family to stay: a swimming pool, lots of space to run around in, and *boules* under the chestnut trees before you turn in for the night. The auberge sits in the middle of the Pic Saint Loup, one of the best vineyards in the Languedoc and Lutz's *cave* makes it a very special place for wine lovers.

rooms	19: 7 twins all share bathrooms 9 triples, 3 quadruples.	
price	€20-€30 p.p. Half-board €32-€42 p.p.	
meals	Light lunch €8. Full choice menu €21-€35 on weekends.	
closed	January-mid-March.	
directions	D17 from Montpellier north for Quissac. 6km north of St Mathieu de Tréviers, left to Lauret, 1km. Through village follow signs for Cazeneuve & Auberge du Cèdre.	

	Françoise Antonin & Lutz Engelmann
tel	+33 (0)4 67 59 02 02
fax	+33 (0)4 67 59 03 44
e-mail	welcome@auberge-du-cedre.com
web	www.auberge-du-cedre.com

map 17 entry 269

Le Sanglier

Domaine de Cambourras, 34700 St Jean de la Blaquière, Hérault

Madame, a Maître Rotisseur, cares for her menus (including wild pig and local fish), while Monsieur cares for his very good wine cellar in their deeply renovated sheepfold (just one stone wall survives from before). In the setting of vineyards and evergreen-clad hills, white outcrops, bright red earth and dense Mediterranean vegetation – strongly beautiful, even starkly wild – the Sanglier's rambling garden is welcoming with its terraces and masses of shade for eating and sitting outside. You can follow a generous breakfast of fresh cheese, cake and *fougace* with a delicious summer lunch and finish with dinner centred on Madame's wild boar speciality or steak grilled on vine stems. But there's lots to do here: exhibitions in Lodève, medieval St Guilhem, watery delights on Lake Salagou. Bedrooms are comfortable, decorated with mottled beige carpets and pastel bathroom suites. There are some lovely black and white photographs of local people, but come not for décor – the scenery is sublime and food is king. One of France's secret places.

rooms	8: 7 doubles, 1 triple.
price	€66–€86.
meals	Breakfast €9. Picnic from €6. Lunch & dinner €17–€37. Restaurant closed Wednesday noon out of season.
closed	November–March.
directions	From Montpellier, N109 through St Félix de Lodez for Rabieux, then D144 for St Jean de la Blaquière.

	Monique Lormier
tel	+33 (0)4 67 44 70 51
fax	+33 (0)4 67 44 72 33
e-mail	hotreslesanglier@aol.com
web	www.logassist.fr/sanglier

La Calade
Place de l'Eglise, 34800 Octon, Hérault

Octon is an unspoilt little village, typical of the flavour and architecture so informed by the Languedoc sun. Right under the old church, the owners have created a colourful atmosphere within the white stone walls of the former presbytery. Don't expect great luxury – the setting is simple, the rooms and bathrooms adequate – but there is a freshness about the place when it's hot, and the beds are comfortable. The terrace, shaded by acacia trees and an awning, is very appealing both at breakfast time and in the evenings – it also serves as the sitting area. The overall feel is bright and clean and the new owners couldn't be more friendly and helpful. They particularly enjoy welcoming families with children. The restaurant is becoming very popular with the locals – always a good sign – so book ahead. There are plenty of places to visit, good paths for hikers, excellent local wines and the fabulous Lake Salagou for swimming and sailing. In short, a great base for daily excursions, where the warm welcome and the authentic atmosphere easily make up for somewhat basic comforts.

rooms	7: 3 doubles, 4 family rooms.
price	€41. Family rooms €57-€73.
meals	Breakfast €6. Lunch & dinner €12-€29. Restaurant closed Tues & Wed out of season.
closed	20 December-February.
directions	A75 exit 54 or 55 (Lake Salagou) for Octon on D148. Hotel in village centre next to church; stone steps lead up to entrance.

Jean-Louis & Martine Methia

tel	+33 (0)4 67 96 19 21
fax	+33 (0)4 67 88 61 25
e-mail	la-calade-octon@wanadoo.fr
web	www.lacalade.com

map 16 entry 271

Hostellerie de Saint Alban

31 route d'Agde, 34120 Nézignan l'Evêque, Hérault

In an enchanting Languedocian village with alleys and archways to be explored, this is a beautifully proportioned, honey-coloured old mansion. The monumental pine tree must have been here before the house; its great twisting branches now hang over the gate. The superbly lush garden surrounds a pool where you can have lunch in summer – fresh local melon, delicious salads – and the lovely old barn is being restored to house all proper pool-side comforts. Indoors, the charming young Swiss owners have gone for less luxuriance: the décor is relaxingly plain, the feel elegant, airy, and well-kept. The biggish, light bedrooms have good pastel carpeting, white bedcovers, translucent curtains and sober colour schemes in beiges, greys and soft pinks. Furniture is modern minimal with moulded chairs and laminated headboards – no drowning in flounces here! There are always fresh flowers on the dining room tables and food is good. The Saint Alban is ideal for seaside and inland visits and many guests cycle out through the vines to the Canal du Midi.

rooms	14 doubles.
price	€67–€105. Triples €92–€103.
meals	Breakfast €9. Lunch €9–€30. Dinner €21. Restaurant closed Wednesdays out of season.
closed	Mid-November–mid-February.
directions	A9 exit 34 for Pézenas & Millau. D13 for 16km to Nézignan l'Evêque. Hotel on right at village entrance.

	Hansruedi Keiser & Niklaus Hürlimann
tel	+33 (0)4 67 98 11 38
fax	+33 (0)4 67 98 91 63
e-mail	info@saintalban.com
web	www.saintalban.com

La Chamberte

Rue de la Source, 34420 Villeneuve les Béziers, Hérault

When Bruno and Irwin set about converting this old wine storehouse, the last thing they wanted was to create a 'home from home' for guests. This is different, and special. The communal spaces are huge, ceilings high, colours Mediterranean, floors pigmented and polished cement. Bedrooms are simpler than you might expect, but with huge beds, often with a step up to them, and dressed in coloured cottons; bathrooms are shower-only, in ochres and muted pinks, perhaps with pebbles set in the cement floor. The cooking is Bruno's domain: "not my profession but my passion". He may whisk you off to the hills early one morning, stopping on the way home for a loaf of bread and a slab of paté to go with the aperitif. In summer you eat on the interior patio, a vast airy space that reaches up to the original barn roof; in winter you retreat to a dining room with an open fire. Guests — eight at most — meet up for a glass of carefully chosen wine and nibbles but dine at separate tables — stylishly decked with flowers, candles and special plates and glasses. Bruno feels dinner is an important moment of the day, to be savoured.

rooms	5 doubles.
price	€84–€98.
	Weekly half-board €750 for 2.
meals	Dinner with wine €25–€31.
closed	Rarely.
directions	A9 exit 35 (Béziers Est) for Villeneuve les Béziers; over bridge over canal to town centre; 2nd left after Hotel Cigale; look for green gate on the right.

	Bruno Saurel
	& Irwin Scott-Davidson
tel	+33 (0)4 67 39 84 83
fax	+33 (0)4 67 39 31 81
e-mail	contact@la-chamberte.com
web	www.lachamberte.com

map 16 entry 273

Les Bergeries de Ponderach

Route de Narbonne, 34220 St Pons de Thomières, Hérault

Monsieur Lentin remembers this *bergerie* when it was full of sheep; he now fills it with contented guests. The whole place is an expression of his cultivated tastes in music, painting (he has a permanent art gallery on the premises), food and wine. You enter your room through its own little lobby, from the freize-painted corridor. Notice the attention to detail in the choice of fabrics and furnishings, take in the luxury of the bathroom, make your way to your own private balcony and take a deep breath; you've arrived in a sort of earthly paradise. Monsieur Lentin offers music – sometimes live, with quartets in the courtyard on summer evenings – but also the most intriguing and carefully chosen regional cooking with a good selection of organic wines. Sculpting your own perfect holiday here is not difficult, given all that's here for you – maybe one third exercise in the Parc Regional with its wonderful walks, one third culture visiting the cathedral and its pink marble choir and one third gastro-hedonism with your feet under the auberge's beautifully laden table.

rooms	7: 6 doubles, 1 suite.
price	€65–€100.
	Half-board €70–€90 p.p.
meals	Breakfast €10. Picnic available.
	Lunches July & August.
	Dinner €25–€43.
closed	15 November–15 March.
directions	From Béziers, N112 to St Pons de Thomières, then left for Narbonne on D907. Hotel 1km further, just after swimming pool on left.

	Gilles Lentin
tel	+33 (0)4 67 97 02 57
fax	+33 (0)4 67 97 29 75
e-mail	bergeries.ponderach@wanadoo.fr
web	bergeries-ponderach.com

La Bastide Cabezac

Hameau de Cabezac, 11120 Bize en Minervois, Aude

The hotel and restaurant are becoming as popular as the Minervois wines that come from the next door Château de Cabezac. The exterior of this old coaching inn – sunflower yellow walls with ocean blue trim – is intense like the sun that beats down on this land that produces its deep purple powerful wines. Hervé directs two restaurants in Paris; he has built himself a magnificent kitchen here and has already planted a kitchen garden next to the pool. The Bastide de Cabezac is still feeling its way but everything is in place. There are good-sized bedrooms, each in different pastel shades with plenty of air and natural light, king-size beds and minimalist accessories. The public areas and the interior *cour* on the first floor are warm yellow and, as is proper in hot lands, terracotta tiles are ubiquitous. The restaurant is named l'Olivier in homage to the working olive orchard nearby; they also transplanted a 300-year-old tree as a symbol of their new endeavor and to add a bit of gravitas.

rooms	12: 8 doubles, 2 triples, 2 suites for 4-5.
price	€ 69–€ 115. Triples & suites € 107–€ 198.
meals	Breakfast € 10. Lunch & dinner € 16–€ 55. Half-board € 25 p.p. Restaurant closed Mon & Tues noon.
closed	Rarely.
directions	From Narbonne, D607 to intersection of D5, D11 & Route de Vins 18km.

	Sabine & Hervé dos Santos
tel	+33 (0)4 68 46 66 10
fax	+33 (0)4 68 46 66 29
e-mail	contact@labastidecabezac.com
web	www.labastidecabezac.com

map 16   entry 275

Le Relais du Val d'Orbieu
Route D24, 11200 Ornaisons, Aude

This looks like a Spanish hacienda deep in the vineyards of Corbières: perhaps not too surprising since the border is only a short drive away. Agnès and Jean-Pierre have spent almost 20 years making the Relais their special place. The rooms and apartments all open onto gardens and terraces; many have their own patio terrace. They are a mix of old and new and one has a four-poster. It is the sort of place where you will find your bed turned down at night and plenty of fresh towels. Jean-Pierre, who can be a bit Basil-Faltyesqe, is everywhere; he is also very knowledgeable about the local vineyards. The food is colourful and Mediterranean with plenty of fish: red mullet with artichokes, baby squid with asparagus and fresh anchovies being regulars on the menu. Hidden among the trees are a fair-sized pool, a tennis court, table tennis and a place to play *pétanque*. The sea is a short drive and there is plenty to explore, with the Cathar castles and the abbeys of Fontefroide and Lagrasse within easy reach, as well as Carcassonne and all the vineyards.

rooms	15 + 4: 14 twins/doubles, 1 suite for 2-4. 4 apartments for 3-4.
price	€95-€145. Apartments & suite €145-€245.
meals	Breakfast €15. Dinner €35-€75.
closed	December–January.
directions	From Narbonne, N113 for Carcassonne; D24 to Ornaisons. 3km to hotel. Well signed.

Agnès & Jean-Pierre Gonzalvez

tel	+33 (0)4 68 27 10 27
fax	+33 (0)4 68 27 52 44
e-mail	relais.du.val.dorbieu@wanadoo.fr
web	perso.wanadoo.fr/relais.du.val.dorbieu

Le Relais de Saint Dominique

Prouilhe, 11270 Fanjeaux, Aude

In the 1800s, this coaching inn was the last stop for a quick mug of ale and change of horse before heading up into the Pyrenees. Today, you won't want to move. Nadine's cheerful greeting is as genuine as her desire that you be pampered while free to come and go as you please. No expense or energy (hers seems endless) has been spared: crisp linens and thick towels in gleaming bathrooms, good beds, sponge-painted walls with a good mix of antique and modern. Unique touches here and there will have you wondering why *you'd* never thought of using Grandma's embroidered tablecloth as a simple cushion cover. American buffet breakfasts in the shaded courtyard in summer are a feast; another terrace for evening meals has decorative touches of old jugs, antique bottles and baskets. Nothing is too much trouble for Nadine, and coming 'home' to sit by the pool a pleasant way to end a busy day. You are near the main road so expect a rumble or two from the junction, but the bedrooms are double glazed and shutters bring added insulation. Some of the regional wines are an absolute 'must'; tastings can be arranged.

rooms	6: 4 twins/doubles, 2 family rooms for 4.
price	€ 49–€ 69. Family rooms € 78–€ 107.
meals	Snacks available. Dinner € 15 in the monastery, book ahead.
closed	Rarely.
directions	From A61 exit Bram onto D4 for Fanjeaux. After 5km, left at roundabout onto D119 for Montréal; entrance immed. on left.

	Nadine Micouleau
tel	+33 (0)4 68 24 68 17
fax	+33 (0)4 68 24 68 18
e-mail	relaisstdominique@libertysurf.fr

map 16 entry 277

Château de Cavanac

11570 Cavanac (Nr Carcassonne), Aude

A quiet place, with birdsong to serenade you. The château has been in the family for six generations and dates back to 1612; Louis, *chef et patron*, has a small vineyard, so you can drink of the vines that surround you. A convivial place, with a big rustic restaurant in the old stables, where hops hang from ancient beams and there's an open fire on which they cook the grills. There are several lovely terraced areas, too. Louis and Anne are justly proud of what they are doing – the hotel is quiet and friendly, with much comfort and an easy feel. Big bedrooms are fairly lavish, with four-posters, dramatic canopies, plush fabrics in soft colours. Chinese rugs cover terracotta tiles, while those rooms most recently redecorated have parquet floors and a colonial feel. Outside you stumble upon (not into, we hope) a delightful swimming pool with underwater lighting for midnight dips. There's a very pretty, sun-trapping terrace with plenty of sunloungers. Beyond the smart wrought-iron gates, Languedoc waits to beguile you; horse riding and golf can be arranged, there are cellars to visit, and medieval Carcassonne is close by.

rooms	28: 19 doubles, 2 singles, 3 triples, 4 suites.
price	€80–€155. Singles €65–€70.
meals	Breakfast €10. Dinner from €36. Restaurant closed Mondays. Other restaurants 2–3km.
closed	January–February.
directions	From Toulouse, exit Carsassonne Ouest for Centre Hospitalier, then take Route de St Hilaire. Signed. Park in restaurant car park.

Anne & Louis Gobin

tel	+33 (0)4 68 79 61 04
fax	+33 (0)4 68 79 79 67

Château de Floure

1 allée Gaston Bonheur, 11800 Floure, Aude

Floure started life as a Roman villa, the Villa Flora, on the Via Aquitania between Narbonne and Toulouse: a peaceful refuge from the military post just a couple of leagues away. In the Middle Ages it became a monastery, until in the reign of Henri IV a local official made it his country retreat. Hidden away behind the austere stone walls, an ivy-draped 18th-century château stands in the centre of matching mellow-tiled cottages and outbuildings, in interesting grounds where you can wander from a formal French garden, through a tree-shaded meadow to the vineyard or the swimming pool. The vaulted bar, complete with grand piano, is in the 12th-century keep. Bedrooms are vast, with beds to match, antique desks and deep comfortable chairs. Some rooms are in the château itself, others gathered around the courtyard. Bathrooms are for luxuriating, with deep baths and attractive tiles. After dinner you can settle in the Bergère drawing room, where one wall was painted by the Vicomte de Laguepie in 1762. Ancient Carcassonne is only ten minutes' drive away, but it may be hard to drag yourself away from these peaceful gardens.

rooms	13 + 5: 10 doubles, 3 suites for 4-5. 5 apartments for 2-3.
price	€ 100-€ 120. Suites € 230. Apartments € 170.
meals	Buffet breakfast € 16. Dinner € 39-€ 59.
closed	4 January-mid-March.
directions	A61 exit 24 then N113 towards Narbonne. Pass Trébes then follow sign to Floure. Hotel in village. Signed.

Madame Dominique Assous

tel	+33 (0)4 68 79 11 29
fax	+33 (0)4 68 79 04 61
e-mail	contact@chateau-de-floure.com
web	www.chateau-de-floure.com

map 16 entry 279

Auberge l'Atalaya
66800 Llo, Pyrénées-Orientales

A place of majestic beauty and wild poetry; a timeless Catalan farmhouse clinging to a rocky hillside; an owner of rare taste and talent – poet, philosopher, musician and lover of beauty. Such is l'Atalaya: a house that captures the imagination and promises riches earthly and spiritual. Family antiques are in all rooms, fine fabrics dress lovely old beds, stained-glass windows illuminate corridors, fresh figs may fill bowls in the intimate little breakfast room and in the big, light-filled dining room, mouthwatering meals are served before that boggling view, while the grand piano awaits its pianist. Your hostess has put her heart into renovating the house she bought long ago as a ruin and it has a quiet, cosy, hideaway atmosphere that is also very elegant: the architecture and décor are in harmony and people of sensitive taste feel utterly at home here. The wonderful little village has hot springs, the river gorges are home to rare butterflies, the hills have sheep and Romanesque churches. What a place!

rooms	13: 11 twins/doubles, 1 triple, 1 suite for 2-4.
price	€90-€140.
meals	Breakfast €11. Lunch (weekends only) & dinner €28-€41. Restaurant closed December-March.
closed	3 November-15 December.
directions	From Perpignan N116 west through Prades to Saillagouse. Left for Llo; left for Eyne. Hotel 1km on right.

	Ghilaine Toussaint
tel	+33 (0)4 68 04 70 04
fax	+33 (0)4 68 04 01 29
e-mail	atalaya66@aol.com

La Terrasse au Soleil

Route de Fontfrède, 66400 Céret, Pyrénées-Orientales

Take at least a weekend, for a splurge of activity and delicious indulgence. It has space: a four-hectare garden, a terrace with olive and mimosa trees, a vineyard; and sports: a big pool and a putting green, a tennis court and three jogging circuits – and deep green views over the hills to Mont Canigou. It's a self-contained retreat of "luxurious simplicity" (the owner's expression) in five connecting villas where the bright colour schemes bring a gay, casual atmosphere – what one might call Southern California in French Catalonia. Rooms are big and airy, each one with terrace or balcony, done in excellent fabrics with custom-made wooden furniture, but not over-filled; suites have two bathrooms. Food counts a lot and delicious meals are served on china made to order in Italy; there's a warm, inviting bar designed for guests to feel pampered. The new spa, outdoor jacuzzi overlooking the hills and massage therapist add to the bliss. A path has even been cut to Céret so that you don't have to walk along the road. Monsieur Brunet is very present and very attentive – you will like him.

rooms	38: 31 doubles, 7 suites for 3.
price	€159–€265. Suites €190–€378.
meals	Picnic available. Dinner from €43.
closed	Rarely.
directions	From Perpignan A9 south to Le Boulou; D115 south-west to Céret. Hotel 2km beyond Céret on road to Fontfrède.

Pascal Leveillé-Nizerolle

tel	+33 (0)4 68 87 01 94
fax	+33 (0)4 68 87 39 24
e-mail	terrasse-au-soleil.hotel@wanadoo.fr
web	www.la-terrasse-au-soleil.com

map 16 entry 281

La Belle Demeure

Auberge du Roua, Chemin du Roua, 66700 Argelès sur Mer, Pyrénées-Orientales

Hard to see from the spic and span interior that this small hotel was once an 18th-century mill. But this is the south, where life is lived *en plein air*. And outdoors at the auberge is so special: you could happily spend all day dozing or reading on the quiet garden terrace by the stone-paved pool surrounded by tropical plants. There is ample opportunity to escape the sun's dazzle under the trees without retreating indoors, and the views of the Pyrenees are splendid. Bedrooms are anonymous but comfortable, and bathrooms a good size. This is a family-run hotel; don't be surprised to see a couple of young children about. The dining room, with its white napery and crystal, is formal and rightly highlights the vaulted ceiling of the old mill – an appropriate setting for the chef's superb *cuisine raffiné*. Unusual to find a hotel hidden away in the middle of the countryside where, in these parts, the whole world is at the beach. If you want to join the crowds, it's a five-kilometre hop to the ocean and a 10-minute stroll to the centre of bustling Argeles.

rooms	20 doubles.
price	€60–€139.
meals	Breakfast €10. Light lunches at poolside. Dinner €29–€75. Restaurant closed Wednesday evenings out of season.
closed	November–6 February.
directions	From Perpignan N114 south for 20km, exit 10 for Argelès sur Mer. In town, right at lights, straight on after underpass, then follow signs.

	Magalie Tonjum
tel	+33 (0)4 68 95 85 85
fax	+33 (0)4 68 95 83 50
e-mail	belle-demeure@fr.oleane.com
web	www.belle-demeure.com

photography by Michael Busselle

rhône valley – alps

Le Moulin de Bathieu

Verclad, 74340 Samoëns, Haute-Savoie

Ski in winter; in summer, explore the mountains – on foot or by bike – or go fishing with Charles. The setting is pure 'Heidi', the views are glorious. In winter snow laps to the door, in summer the terraces tumble with flowers. The Moulin is very much a family affair: she cooks – beautifully; the daughters clean; Charles does the rest. The chalet is pale-pine-panelled, warm and homely and with all mod cons, including a heated garage for your boots and skis. The light, airy dining room has big picture windows that pull in the views, and you can eat on one of a number of terraces – they keep creating new ones! – when it's warm. Three times a week the food is regional, and you can order picnics when you like. Wood-panelled bedrooms are big enough to fit sofas or little sitting areas, and a mezzanine level for the children's beds; all bar one have a balcony with a view. The Moulin is just outside the little town of Samoëns, set well back from the road. It's a brilliant place for an active family holiday – fresh air, good food, lovely people... you could happily spend a week here, or more.

rooms	7: 3 doubles, 1 twin, 2 duplexes for 3-4, 1 suite for 2-4.
price	€ 55-€ 100. Suite € 100-€ 130.
meals	Breakfast € 8-€ 11. Dinner € 20-€ 35.
closed	29 April-15 June; 1 February; 4 November-21 December.
directions	A40 exit 18, D4 for Samoëns. Before entry into Samoëns right on D254 for Samoëns. After 1.5km, on left.

Charles Pontet

tel	+33 (0)4 50 34 48 07
fax	+33 (0)4 50 34 43 25
e-mail	moulin.du.bathieu@wanadoo.fr
web	www.bathieu.com

The Farmhouse

Le Mas de la Coutettaz, 74110 Morzine, Haute-Savoie

Known as the Mas de la Coutettaz – "the old chateau to the locals" – the 1771 farmhouse is indeed the oldest in the valley, sitting at the foot of the slopes of bustling Morzine. Come for summer walks, bike rides and mountain air, or snowbound adventure. It's a perfect staging post for the Avoriaz and Portes du Soleil ski arena, and there's a 'ski host' at the hotel who introduces you to the runs for free. Comfortably rustic bedrooms are reached via stone stairs; the doubles are big and the triples huge, with dark polished beams, massive radiators and old pine doors with original moulding. Ask for a room with mountain views. In the garden is a little chalet for two, nicknamed the Love Nest. Your day starts with a huge – not exclusively French – breakfast: croissants warm from the oven, porridge, perhaps kedgeree. After a hard day on the slopes, it's home to cakes and tea. Smiling, ever-busy Ricardo ensures the evening meal, too, is a sociable affair. After drinks in the bar before a log fire, retire to the old cattle shed – now a magnificent dining room, where long, leisurely candlelit dinners are savoured at the big table.

rooms	8: 3 doubles, 1 single, 3 triples, 1 suite for 6.
price	€75–€175. Single €45–€135. Triples €105–€255. €35 p.p. B&B spring & autumn.
meals	Breakfast €10. Dinner with drinks €30–€40. Restaurants nearby.
closed	May; October–November.
directions	In Morzine, follow signs for Avoriaz. On Ave Joux Plon, left after Nicholas Sport, then right. On left.

	Ricardo Dorrien
tel	+33 (0)4 50 79 08 26
fax	+33 (0)4 50 79 18 53
e-mail	info@thefarmhouse.co.uk
web	www.thefarmhouse.co.uk

map 13 entry 284

Chalet Hôtel La Marmotte

61 rue du Chêne, 74260 Les Gets, Haute-Savoie

A large 30s chalet on the edge of town; it looks onto the slopes in winter, the meadows in summer and is minutes from the lifts. Such a laid-back, child-friendly place to stay, in the family for half a century, now run – beautifully – by a brother and sister team. There's a living room/bar – inviting with log fire, small sofas, big yellow drapes – from which you watch the last skiers trudge home, and a huge, pine-clad dining room (don't miss the special regional menu, served once a week). Bedrooms are cosy with geometric-patterned bedcovers and soft lights. Some have mezzanines, the ones at the back have views across village and valley. Pretty Les Gets is a one-road town that links the valley with Morzine on the other side: a few shops, some bars, a night club; it has also one of the few ski schools in France that uses only British instructors – perfect for families. A bikers' mecca in summer, with marked trails all over the place, even a freshwater lake for swimming, and an adventure playground close by. Back home: a pool, a jacuzzi, fitness room, hydromassage, a smile for every guest and homemade jams for breakfast.

rooms	48 twins/doubles.
price	Half-board only: summer €56–€92 p.p.; winter €113–€185 p.p.
meals	Buffet breakfast & 4-course dinner included.
closed	20 April-28 June; 7 Sept-20 Dec.
directions	A40 exit Cluses for Taninges-Les Gets for 22km. Left at Hotel Chinfrey (green & red hearts), right at 1st r'bout for Centre Station, right at end of road going up.

Josette & Henry Mirigay

tel	+33 (0)4 50 75 80 33
fax	+33 (0)4 50 75 83 26
e-mail	info@hotel-marmotte.com
web	www.hotel-marmotte.com

Hôtel Auberge Camelia
74570 Aviernoz, Haute-Savoie

Roger loves to talk about local history, including stories about the Resistance: the woman who owned the Camelia during the war had strong connections with the clandestines. But the inn was thoroughly modernised by Roger and Sue 10 years ago and now the breakfast buffet is laid out in the old dining room; there's a small, intimate restaurant in the old kitchen, and the bedrooms, carpeted and larger than average, are straightforwardly comfortable with white walls, unfussy furnishings and good big bathrooms. The attractive, open garden has a spring-fed fountain and a sunny terrace where meals are served whenever possible in the sight of impressive hills. Your happy hosts have apparently boundless energy and will take you in their red minibus to the start of some glorious walks. See the spectacular flower meadows, taste wine, ski at all levels – you can even watch the Alpine cattle stroll past your window, their great bells ringing nostalgically. A very welcoming inn with enthusiastic owners and friendly staff who make sure your every need is met, including the need for good food.

rooms	12: 6 twins/doubles, 5 triples, 1 quadruple.
price	€68–€98.
meals	Breakfast €9. Picnic on request €7. Lunch & dinner from €18.
closed	Rarely.
directions	Annecy for Chamonix & La Roche to N203. Right at mini r'bout at Pont de Brogny then under r'way bridge. After 4km right for Villaz on D175. In village keep left, then left for Aviernoz. Auberge on left.

Suzanne & Roger Farrell-Cook

tel	+33 (0)4 50 22 44 24
fax	+33 (0)4 50 22 43 25
e-mail	info@hotelcamelia.com
web	www.hotelcamelia.com

map 13 entry 286

Hôtel Le Cottage Fernand Bise

Au Bord du Lac, 74290 Talloires, Haute-Savoie

Not many cottages have 35 bedrooms; not many have this fabulous setting, either – you might be in a Wagner opera as you gaze at the sun setting over the Roc de Chère across the Lac d'Annecy from the terrace. The three buildings which make up the hotel look, unsurprisingly, like Alpine chalets and are set in pretty, well-planted gardens in which you can wander on your way to meet one of the local millionaires or perhaps Wotan himself. Monsieur and Madame Bise run this welcoming, relaxed establishment with a quiet Savoyard efficiency, which, at its heart, has a proper concern for the comfort of guests. *Douillette* – that lovely word which is the French equivalent of 'cosy' – perfectly describes the atmosphere in the bedrooms, with their floral chintz fabrics and comfortable furniture. Well away from the bustle of Annecy itself, but close enough to everything it offers, this is a wonderfully adult holiday centre, offering multifarious activities for the sporty and inspiration for the arty who wish to follow in the footsteps of Cézanne or Lamartine. Comfort *and* culture – what more could you want?

rooms	35 doubles.
price	€ 100–€ 210.
meals	Breakfast € 14. Lunch € 23–€ 30. Dinner € 35–€ 50.
closed	10 October–20 April.
directions	In Annecy follow signs Bord du Lac for Thônes D909. At Veyrier du Lac follow D909A to Talloires. Well signed in Talloires.

Jean-Claude & Christine Bise

tel	+33 (0)4 50 60 71 10
fax	+33 (0)4 50 60 77 51
e-mail	cottagebise@wanadoo.fr
web	www.cottagebise.com

L'Ancolie

Lac des Dronières, 74350 Cruseilles, Haute-Savoie

L'Ancolie is welcoming and staff are eager to please, reflecting the owner's cheerful efficiency. In a well-kept garden with woods at its back and a lake lapping at its feet, it was custom-designed in 1993 to replace the family's original hotel; they wanted modern comfort in traditional style. So here are wooden balconies and fitted carpets, great log fires in the stone fireplace and a picture window for guests to watch the chefs preparing rich, traditional Savoyard specialities in the kitchen. In summer, the big restaurant opens onto a terrace where you are served before the supremely tranquil lake view. Big bedrooms have lots of wood, of course, and clean-cut modern furniture; some have balconies; luxury bed linen adds a touch of class and bathrooms are as up-to-date as you could wish. As well as fishing in the lake and great walks from the door, there's a good golf course nearby plus delightful little Annecy and cosmopolitan Geneva to be visited (each 20km away). L'Ancolie is ideal for families although small children need supervising near the lake, and excellent value.

rooms	10 doubles.
price	€ 70–€ 102.
meals	Breakfast € 11. Lunch & dinner € 24–€ 50. Restaurant closed Mondays.
closed	2 weeks in February; November.
directions	From Annecy, RN201 to Cruseilles, then D15. Hotel immediately after Institut Aéronautique.

	Yves Lefebvre
tel	+33 (0)4 50 44 28 98
fax	+33 (0)4 50 44 09 73
e-mail	info@lancolie.com
web	www.lancolie.com

map 13 entry 288

Auberge des Chasseurs

Naz Dessus, 01170 Echenevex, Ain

Dominique is a jolly man who is very proud of the Auberge, which his grandparents built as a farm in 1860, and its fantastic sweeping view of the Jura mountains and Mont Blanc. You might be a bit surprised by the African theme in the reception area, but don't let it put you off. Most of the hotel looks more Swedish and this does have an explanation. A Swedish woman who lives nearby was employed to decorate, and spent two years meticulously painting the panelled walls and the ceilings and beams in a typically Swedish style which blends in well here, with the mountain views. The bedrooms are all individually decorated: many once again with panelled and painted ceilings and colour-washed walls, some pale, some in fairly strong colours. The big dining room is panelled in yellow with intricately patterned beams, matching country-style yellow chairs and crisp white cloths. The food is a big reason for staying here and Dominique is an expert on burgundy wines and – rare find – his list is both knowledgeable and suited to any budget.

rooms	15: 10 doubles, 5 twins.
price	€69–€130. Half-board for 3 days or more, €99–€225 p.p.
meals	Breakfast €10. Lunch & dinner €31–€52. Restaurant closed certain days, please check.
closed	Mid-November–February.
directions	Exit A40 at Bellegarde towards Gex. 2km before Gex follow signs to Echenevex. Signed.

	Dominique Lamy
tel	+33 (0)4 50 41 54 07
fax	+33 (0)4 50 41 90 61

Le Clos du Chatelet

01190 Sermoyer, Ain

Washed in barely-there pink, with soft blue shutters, the house was built as a country retreat towards the end of the 18th century – by a silk merchant who must have had a thing about trees. Overlooking the valley of the Saône, with immaculate sweeping lawns, the garden is full of beautiful old ones: sequoias, cedars, chestnuts and magnolias. To one side of the house, an open outbuilding smothered in flowers is home to a collection of antique bird cages. Bedrooms are welcoming havens in elegant muted colours: Joubert in pink-ochre with twin wrought-iron four-posters draped in *toile de Jouy*; Lamartine in palest aqua enhanced by grey and lilac hangings. All have polished wooden floors and gently sober bathrooms. There's much comfort here and an air of calm. A harp stands in the corner of the elegantly comfortable drawing room: we are not sure if it is played but this is the sort of place where it might be. Dinner is by candlelight in the dining room, atmospheric with its old terracotta floor and tinkling fountain in the wall.

rooms	4: 3 doubles; 1 double with separate bath (robes & slippers provided).
price	€79–€95.
meals	Dinner €23–€24, book ahead.
closed	Rarely.
directions	A6 exit Tournus for Bourg en Bresse to Cuisery. Right at Cuisery for Sermoyer/Pont de Vaux. In Sermoyer follow chambres d'hôtes signs.

	Mme Durand Pont
tel	+33 (0)3 85 51 84 37
fax	+33 (0)3 85 51 84 37
e-mail	leclosduchatelet@free.fr
web	www.leclosduchatelet.com

map 12   entry 290

Château Lambert
69840 Chénas, Rhône

Marty's passion for textiles and his eye for detail make this small 17th-century château a heavenly place to be. It sits smack in the middle of beaujolais country on a hill overlooking the village; vines and more vines stretch over the Soâne plain to the snow-topped Alps just visible in the distance. Its front opens to a trellised terrace, below which a vegetable garden is coming back to life: a wonderful setting for a lazy breakfast or an evening aperitif (try their own Moulin à Vent). A fine library takes up an entire wall of the apartment on the ground floor, where neutral walls set off the red plaid chairs on either side of the fireplace and a pair of *vieux rose* antique armchairs render a curvy touch of elegance. All is light green and pale prune with touches of a darker red in the upstairs suite. A magnificent canopied bed in the alcove has matching *toile de Jouy* drapes and bedspread. The high ceilings, good light and muted tones give all the rooms a feeling of airiness and space, like something out of a painting by Vermeer. Dutch Marty is young and enthusiastic – a fine host who will make you feel very much at home.

rooms	4: 2 doubles, 2 suites for 2.
price	€ 98. Suites € 129.
meals	Hosted dinner € 26.50, book ahead.
closed	Rarely.
directions	A6 exit Macon Sud or A40 exit Replonges. N6 towards Lyon. After 12km at La Chapelle de Guinchay, right for Chénas. At church, take street going up on the right. Signed.

Marty Freriksen
tel	+33 (0)4 74 06 77 74
fax	+33 (0)4 74 04 48 01
e-mail	contact@chateau-lambert.com
web	www.chateau-lambert.com

Château de Pramenoux

69870 Lamure/Azergues, Rhône

Climb up into the Mont du Beaujolais hills above Lyon. Rivers pulse down on either side and a great pine forest cleans the air. As you round a curve, gothic pepperpot turrets pop into view. The château sits in a natural clearing and views from the terrace and bedrooms sweep splendidly down the valley; a small pond in front anchors the eye. Emmanuel, a charming young escapee from the corporate world, will point out the bits that date from the 10th century up to the Renaissance; he has lovingly patched and painted a great deal of it himself. Rooms are big, hugely comfortable and have simply elegant bathrooms. Choose the cherrywood panelled room: a gold and white striped bed and Louis XVI chairs dressed in eau-de-nil. Or be King and Queen and slumber under a canopied bed in a room lined with royal blue and golden fleur-de-lys, a textile re-created by Emmanuel himself with the weavers of Lyon. These are most discreet and winsome hosts who light the candelabra in the evening and prepare to end your day in a most romantic manner. A wonderfully peaceful place, run by the warmest people. *Cash or cheque only.*

rooms	4 doubles.
price	€ 110–€ 125.
meals	Dinner with drinks, € 30, book ahead.
closed	Rarely.
directions	A6 exit Belleville; D37 Beaujeu, at St Vincent left for Quincié en Beaujolais & Marchampt D9 for Lamure. Almost through village of Lamure, lane marked Pramenoux facing soccer field & climb.

Emmanuel Baudoin
& Jean-Luc Plasse

tel	+33 (0)4 74 03 16 43
fax	+33 (0)4 74 03 16 28
e-mail	pramenoux@aol.com
web	www.chateau-de-pramenoux.com

map 12 entry 292

Les Jardins de Longsard
Château de Longsard, 69400 Arnas, Rhône

Orange trees in the *orangerie*, an obelisk amid the topiary chessmen, alleys of 200-year-old lime trees... the formal French garden is just one delight here. An English garden surrounds the formal French one and a kitchen garden and orchard add to the charm. In the entrance courtyard are two spectacular Lebanon cedars (one tricentenial) with huge drooping branches that sweep the ground. Your hosts, much-travelled, sophisticated and informal, love sharing their enthusiasm for the area and its wines and will organise tastings, including their own. Bedrooms, pure château, from pastel to bold with hints of Art Deco, some with fine carved door frames and 17th-century beams to guard your sleep, are eclectically furnished (Olivier's brother is an antique dealer). There are panelled rooms and plainer ones all with polished parquet floors, fine rugs, pictures and engravings. Dinner is certainly worth booking – a typical menu might be stuffed red peppers, chicken in cream and morel mushroom sauce, local cheeses and salad, peaches poached in beaujolais. If you want to sample *le grand style*, this may be for you.

rooms	5: 3 doubles, 2 suites.
price	€96–€101.
meals	Dinner with wine €32, book ahead.
closed	Rarely.
directions	From north A6 exit 'Belleville'; N6 for Lyon 10km; right D43 to Arnas. Through village; château on right after 1.5km.

Alexandra & Olivier du Mesnil

tel	+33 (0)4 74 65 55 12
fax	+33 (0)4 74 65 03 17
e-mail	longsard@wanadoo.fr
web	www.longsard.com

Cour des Loges

6 rue du Boeuf, 69005 Lyon, Rhône

Once upon a time, when Lyon was a rumbling, prosperous trade centre, there were four Renaissance houses built for the bankers, printers and spice merchants. Even the king came with his court for lengthy visits and decreed Lyon's quarterly trade fairs to be tax-free. He and the rest of the nobility were entranced by all things Italian. Cour des Loges *is* those four houses, encapsulated under a 20th-century glass roof linking galleries, porticoes, arches and corkscrew staircases; you are inside but feel as if you were in a huge piazza. Jocelyne Sibuet, the owner and decorator, has enhanced that feeling by adding large terracotta pots of sculpted bushes and elegant benches. The bedroom are sensuous with carefully chosen textiles (still a Lyon speciality): red velvets, grey taffetas, mauve linens and silks, each with an eye-catching Renaissance or baroque antique cupboard or trunk. Then there are the hanging gardens overlooking the brick-red roofs – a magical spot for lunch or dinner. The chef already has a reputation for one of the best tables in Lyon, no mean achievement. *Valet parking and porter service.*

rooms	59 + 4: 51 twins/doubles, 8 suites for 2-3. 4 apartments for 3-4.
price	€ 200-€ 320; € 380-€ 520.
meals	Breakfast € 20. Lunch & dinner à la carte € 40-€ 80. Restaurant closed Sundays & Mondays; 5-20 August.
closed	Rarely.
directions	From A42/43 for centre/Place Bellecour. Over Rhône & Saône, right on Quai Romain Rolland; left on Rue Louis Carrand; garage at end.

Véronique Pellicier

tel	+33 (0)4 72 77 44 44
fax	+33 (0)4 72 40 93 61
e-mail	contact@courdesloges.com
web	www.courdesloges.com

 map 12 entry 294

Château de la Commanderie

17 avenue d'Echirolles, 38230 Eybens, Isère

Grand it appears, and some of the makers of that grandeur – Knights Templar and Maltese, princes and prime ministers, presidents and financiers – look down upon you as you eat in the magnificent dining room, a favourite restaurant for the discerning palates of Grenoble. But the atmosphere is of an intimate family-run hotel. The whole place is awash with family antiques and heirlooms, good taste prevails in every room and flowers add that touch of life and genuine attention. Bedrooms are divided among four separate buildings, adding to the sense of intimacy. Rooms in château and chalet are the more traditional with carved wooden beds and gilt-framed mirrors, though some of them give onto a small road. The orangerie's rooms, as you'll discover once you have negotiated the rather plain corridors, look out over fine parkland, and are deliciously peaceful. The least expensive rooms are in the Petit Pavillion, on the road side. But whichever you choose, you will feel thoroughly welcome and pampered, and it's excellent value for families. *Signs for 'La Commanderie' indicate an area of town, not the Château.*

rooms	25 twins/doubles.
price	€ 80–€ 150.
meals	Breakfast buffet € 11. Lunch & dinner € 19–€ 63. Restaurant closed Mon, Satnoon & Sun evenings.
closed	20 December–3 January.
directions	From Grenoble exit 5 Rocade Sud for Eybens, immediately right at 1st lights for Le Bourg; right after Esso garage. Entrance to hotel 300m on left at turning in road.

	M de Beaumont
tel	+33 (0)4 76 25 34 58
fax	+33 (0)4 76 24 07 31
e-mail	resa@commanderie.fr
web	www.commanderie.fr

Michel Chabran

29 avenue du 45 Parallèle, 26600 Pont de l'Isère, Drôme

A tiny jewel, whose main attraction is not the rooms or the setting but the food. Michel Chabran is a prince among restaurateurs, and his sophisticated little hotel, 50 miles south of Lyon, is in France's gastronomic heart. Served on Limoges china dusted with gold… potato purée with Sevruga caviar, *poularde de Bresse*, hot soufflé of Grand Marnier – subtle, original food that has won Michel two Michelin stars. The à la carte menu stretches to four pages, the set menu two, there are 400 wines and the service is exemplary. It all started in 1943 when Michel's grandfather supplied sandwiches to workers heading south on the first paid holidays to the sun; the rest is history. Bedrooms are modest, cosy, flowery and soundproofed – some face the main road, others the garden. Come for a truffle weekend, from November to March: Michel tells you all about the 'black diamonds', then sits you down to a six-course treat, in front of a blazing fire. Work it all off the next day in the Vercors National Park – or visit Chave, producer of the Hermitage wines that most probably seduced you the night before. *Supplement for pets.*

rooms	12 doubles.
price	€ 65–€ 120. Half-board on request.
meals	Breakfast € 16. Lunch € 30. Dinner € 45–€ 120.
closed	Sunday evenings from Nov–March.
directions	A7 south of Lyon exit Tain l'Ermitage or Valence North to N7 for Pont de l'Isère. Restaurant & hotel on main street opp. church.

M & Mme Chabran

tel	+33 (0)4 75 84 60 09
fax	+33 (0)4 75 84 59 65
e-mail	chabran@michelchabran.fr
web	www.michelchabran.fr

map 12 entry 296

Le Clair de la Plume
Place de Mail, 26230 Grignan, Drôme

Famous for its old-fashioned and English roses spilling into winding streets, Grignan is a paradise for rose-lovers. Yet pushing open the wrought-iron gates of this pink-façaded guest house brings into you to something new. Jean-Luc Valadeau has created such a feeling of warmth and hospitality; as he puts it, "a home with all the comforts of a hotel". His bustling staff are equally attentive, leading you through elegant, cosy rooms, antique pieces catching your eye on the way. The small terraced garden adds to the feeling of privacy and light floods in over the original staircase. The bedrooms are quiet, beautifully decorated – Louis Philippe wardrobes in some, country-style wicker chairs in others – and all have luxurious bathrooms. Stencilled walls, ragged walls, original floor tiles or shining oak planks – a great combination of good taste and authenticity. After a generous breakfast, the Salon de Thé is open from 10am to 10pm for exotic selections of tea, sandwiches, mouthwatering patisseries and locally-made traditional ice cream. There are also lots of restaurants nearby. *A no-smoking property.*

rooms	10 twins/doubles.
price	€90–€170.
meals	Good choice locally.
closed	Rarely.
directions	A7 exit Montélimar Sud for Bollène, Nyons & Gap then Grignan. Signed in town.

Jean-Luc Valadeau

tel	+33 (0)4 75 91 81 30
fax	+33 (0)4 75 91 81 31
e-mail	plume2@wanadoo.fr

provence–alps–riviera

Grand Hôtel Nord Pinus

Place du Forum, 13200 Arles, Bouches-du-Rhône

An Arlesian legend, where Spain meets France, ancient Rome meets the 21st century. Built in 1865 on Roman vaults, it came to fame in the 1950s when a clown and a cabaret singer owned it: famous bullfighters dressed here before entering the arena and the arty crowd flocked (Cocteau, Picasso, Hemingway…). Anne Igou keeps the drama alive today with her strong personality and cinema, fashion and photography folk – and bullfighters still have 'their' superb Spanish Rococo room. The style is vibrant and alive at this show of Art Deco furniture and fittings, great *corrida* posters and toreador costumes, North African carpets and artefacts, fabulous Provençal colours and ironwork. Colour and light are deftly used to create a soft, nostalgic atmosphere where you feel both warm and cool, smart and artistic. Each room is differently interesting, some larger – and lighter – than others. And breakfast is a festival of real French tastes – more magic, more nostalgia. As Cocteau said: "An hotel with a soul" – though the tourist invasion may make it noisy and busy during the summer.

rooms	25: 20 twins/doubles, 5 suites.
price	€128–€166. Suites €275.
meals	Breakfast €13–€18. Lunch & dinner from €30.
closed	Rarely.
directions	From A54 exit Arles Centre for Centre Ancien. Take Boulevard des Lices at main post office; left on Rue Jean Jaurès; right on Rue Cloître, right to Place du Forum.

	Madame Igou
tel	+33 (0)4 90 93 44 44
fax	+33 (0)4 90 93 34 00
e-mail	info@nord-pinus.com
web	www.nord-pinus.com

La Riboto de Taven

Le Val d'Enfer, 13520 Les Baux de Provence, Bouches-du-Rhône

Ever slept in a cave? In a bed with ornate cover and hangings, with a luxurious bathroom next door? Here you can. The Novi-Thème family – Christine, Philippe and Jean-Pierre – have farmed here for four generations and still produce olive oil, fruit and wine. In the Val d'Enfer, or Valley of Hell – it would look more like paradise to most people – facing the spectacular cliff-top village of Les Baux de Provence, the property is literally built onto the limestone cliff. The two 'troglodyte' rooms are separate from the others which, along with the apartment, are in the 18th century *mas* facing the garden. Walk up stone steps from the garden to a terrace, where the view is even more amazing than from the rest of the house. There was an olive oil mill here in the 17th century. Now you have Mireille or Vincent with the canopied bed, beautiful furniture handed down the generations and the overhang of the rock face forming half the ceiling. The garden is small but beautiful, with a pool, and the welcome is warm. *Children over 10 welcome.*

rooms	5 + 1: 3 doubles, 2 trogdolyte suites. 1 apartment for 4.
price	€ 152–€ 250.
meals	Breakfast € 16. Poolside lunch € 23. Dinner € 46. Restaurant closed 2 nights a week October-July.
closed	Mid-January-February.
directions	From St Rémy de Provence D5 to Maussane & Les Baux. Past entrance to village & head towards Fontvieille. Hotel on 1st road to right, signed.

	Novi-Thème Family
tel	+33 (0)4 90 54 34 23
fax	+33 (0)4 90 54 38 88
e-mail	contact@riboto-de-taven.fr
web	www.riboto-de-taven.fr

map 17 entry 299

Mas de Cornud

Route de Mas Blanc D31, 13210 St Rémy de Provence, Bouches-du-Rhône

Guest house, cookery school and wine courses combine in a typical farmhouse where two majestic plane trees stand guard and the scents and light of Provence hover. Nito, a nature-lover, cares about how colour creates feeling, how fabrics comfort: she and David, willing American "exiles", have done a superb restoration where every object is clearly the best (hangings from Kashmir, old French tiles). Bedrooms are big and varied, all warm and simple. The atmosphere is convivial and open: you are a member of a family here, so join the others at the bar, choose a book in the library, have a swim in the big pool then a drink from the honesty bar. The kitchen is the vital centre of Cornud: here you eat if the weather is poor – otherwise the garden has some lovely eating spots – and learn, if you have come for cookery lessons; though many stay without following a course. A country kitchen, with cast-iron range, long wooden table, baskets and dried herbs, it also has a non-slip floor and granite worktops – very professional. Come and be part of Provence for a week. *Children over 12 welcome. Minimum stay in studio 5 days.*

rooms	7 + 1: 6 doubles, 1 suite for 2-5. 1 studio with kitchenette.
price	€ 100–€ 200. Suite € 260–€ 380. Studio € 150; € 775 week.
meals	Picnic with wine € 40. Lunch € 21–€ 25. Hosted dinner € 45–€ 65, book ahead.
closed	January-March & November.
directions	3km west of St Rémy de Provence on D99 towards Tarascon. Left on D27 for Les Baux for approx. 1km, then left at sign for mas.

David & Nitockrees Tadros Carpita

tel	+33 (0)4 90 92 39 32
fax	+33 (0)4 90 92 55 99
e-mail	mascornud@compuserve.com
web	www.mascornud.com

Mas de l'Oulivié

Les Arcoules, 13520 Les Baux de Provence, Bouches-du-Rhône

How refreshing to find a modern hotel that brings together old and new so harmoniously and with such impeccable taste. Having fallen in love with the olive groves, lavender fields and chalky white hillsides of Les Baux de Provence, the family built the hotel of their dreams 10 or so years ago: a creamy-fronted, almond-green-shuttered, Provence-style structure, roofed with reclaimed terracotta tiles, landscaped with cypress and oleander. Every last detail has been carefully crafted, from the locally made oak furniture to the homemade tiles round the pool. And what a pool! Temptingly curvaceous, with a jacuzzi and pebble beach for children. Furnishings are fresh, local, designed for deep comfort. Bedrooms are creamy-coloured, country-style with an elegant twist. The bar/living-room has a rustic fireplace, filled with flowers in the summer. The young Achards love to provide guests and their children with the very best and that includes lunches served by the pool; they also sell their own lavender and oil. Mas de l'Oulivié joins the *crème de la crème* of Provence's small country hotels – a stylish retreat.

rooms	27: 16 doubles, 9 triples, 2 suites.
price	€95–€230. Suites €280–€390.
meals	Breakfast €10–€14.
	Poolside lunch €6–€17.
closed	Mid-November–mid-March.
directions	From north A7 exit 24 for Les Baux. Mas 2km from Les Baux on D78 towards Fontvieille.

Emmanuel Achard

tel	+33 (0)4 90 54 35 78
fax	+33 (0)4 90 54 44 31
e-mail	contact@masdeloulivie.com
web	www.masdeloulivie.com

map 17 entry 301

Le Mas des Carassins

1 chemin Gaulois, 13210 St Rémy de Provence, Bouches-du-Rhône

You'll be charmed by the gentle pink tiles and soft blue shutters of the *mas* turned hotel, which settles so gently into the greenery surrounding it. The garden is massive and bursts with oleanders, lemons, 100-year-old olive trees, lavender and rosemary. Carefully tended patches of lawn lead to a good pool with barbecue, and after a swim, there's *pétanque* and badminton to play. Or you could spin off on bikes – the charming town of St Rémy de Provence is no distance at all, down a peaceful road. This is Van Gogh country (he lived for a time nearby, following in the steps of Nostradamus) and an ancient land: the hotel lies within the preserved area of the Roman town of Glanum. Bedrooms are dreamy, washed in smoky-blue or ochre shades; dark wrought-iron beds are dressed in oatmeal linens and white country quilts; some have a light canopy. Ground-floor rooms open to small gardens with table and chairs. The young owners have thought of everything: they will organize collection from the airport or train, car rental, and tickets for local events. *Unsupervised pool. Children over 12 welcome.*

rooms	14: 12 doubles, 2 suites.
price	€95–€120. Suites €150.
meals	Breakfast €10. Poolside lunch €15. Dinner €25, weekdays only. Restaurants 5 minutes away.
closed	January–February.
directions	From St Rémy de Provence centre, over Canal des Alpilles on Ave Van Gogh, then right into Ave J d'Arbaud. Hotel entrance on left after 180m.

	Michel Dimeux & Pierre Ticot
tel	+33 (0)4 90 92 15 48
fax	+33 (0)4 90 92 63 47
e-mail	info@hoteldescarassins.com
web	hoteldescarassins.com

Mas de la Rabassière

Route de Cornillon, 13250 St Chamas, Bouches-du-Rhône

Fanfares of lilies at the door, Haydn inside and Michael smiling in his chef's apron — *Rabassière* means 'where truffles are found' — his Epicurean dinners are a must. Wines from the neighboring vineyard, and a sculpted dancer, also grace his terrace table. Cookery classes using home-produced olive oil, jogging companionship and airport pick-ups are all part of his unflagging hospitality, always with the help of Théri, his serene Singaporean assistant. Michael was posted to France by a multinational, soon became addicted, and on his retirement slipped into this perfect corner of Provence, close to Arles, Saintes Maries de la Mer and Aigues Mortes, the latter built by St Louis in the 14th century. The *calanques*, a series of 'fjords' on the coast to the east of Marseille, are a delight too, as is the Saturday open-air market in Saint Chames. Big bedrooms and drawing room are classically comfortable in English country-house style: generous beds, erudite books, a tuned piano, Provençal antiques. Come savour this charmingly generous and individual house and sample Michael's home-made croissants. *A no-smoking property.*

rooms	5 doubles.
price	€ 115. Singles € 65.
meals	Dinner with wine € 30, book ahead.
closed	Rarely.
directions	From A54 exit 13 to Grans on D19; right on D16 to St Chamas. Just before railway bridge, left for Cornillon, up hill 2km. House on right before tennis court. Map sent on request.

Michael Frost

tel	+33 (0)4 90 50 70 40
fax	+33 (0)4 90 50 70 40
e-mail	michaelfrost@rabassiere.com
web	www.rabassiere.com

map 17 entry 303

Le Mas Blanc

Domaine de Freiresque, 13660 Orgon, Bouches-du-Rhône

What a spectacular pool! It looks like a natural pond – vast, irregular, edged with flat rocks, with a mini-waterfall at one end and long grass growing up to the water. The white *mas* sparkles in the sun in olive groves between Saint Rémy and Cavaillon. This domain produces 3,000 litres of cold-pressed oil a year – savour it in delicious dishes served three times a week. Dinners are sociable affairs at a long table in the dining room, in front of a fire in winter. Before dinner, your hosts gather guests for aperitifs and nibbles on the house and – a generous touch – encourage you to help yourselves to juice, beer or a glass or two of local wine by the pool. Country-smart bedrooms have ancient tiles and high sloping ceilings; beds have heavy cotton spreads. Bathrooms are huge, some with two basins set in natural tiles, showers are big enough for an entire family. We liked Pavot and Pêche, with their views to the Alpilles. Another room is pure lavender; inspired by the fields nearby, its beams are deep mauve, echoed by a paler wash on the walls. Breakfast is relaxed, at a communal table in a sunny old barn.

rooms	6 doubles.
price	€ 180.
meals	Lunch € 17. Dinner € 32, 3 times a week.
closed	15 October–15 May.
directions	A7 exit 25 Cavaillon, D99 for St Rémy de Provence; after 2nd r'bout Plan d'Orgon. Left at 2nd set of lights onto N7 for 1.6km; Domaine de Freiresque on left, mas immediately on right.

Martin & Patricia Bourbonnais

tel	+33 (0)4 90 73 35 99
fax	+33 (0)4 90 73 36 03
e-mail	info@masblanc.com
web	www.masblanc.com

Mas Doù Pastré

Quartier St Sixte, 13810 Eygalières, Bouches-du-Rhône

It's a charming place, gypsy-bright with wonderful furniture, checked cushions, colour-washed walls, fine kilims. Built at the end of the 18th century, this lovely old *mas* belonged to Grandpère and Grandmère: nine months were spent here, three up in the pastures with the sheep. Now Albine has decided to turn the old farmhouse into a hotel and keep it in the family – she and her talented handyman husband, Maurice, have succeeded, brilliantly. Bedrooms have wooden or tiled floors, antique doors and comfortable beds; all are big, some with their own sitting areas. Bathrooms are original with stone floors and beautiful washbasins picked up at flea markets; a claw-foot bath peeps theatrically out from behind stripey curtains. Breakfast is generous 'continental' and Albine will cook a supper as colourful as Provence itself. Chaises longues with their attendant awnings encircle the pool; a Romany caravan sits in the garden. Long views reach to the Alpilles – perfect. Better book early, and for a week. *Unsupervised pool.*

rooms	12: 11 doubles, 1 suite.
price	€ 105–€ 160. Suite € 160–€ 190. Min. 3-night stay during summer.
meals	Breakfast € 10. Lunch € 15–€ 32. Dinner € 32. Restaurant closed Sundays.
closed	15 November–15 December.
directions	From A7, exit at Cavaillon for St Rémy for 10km, then left for Eygalières. Mas on route Jean Moulin, opposite Chapelle St Sixte.

Albine & Maurice Roumanille

tel	+33 (0)4 90 95 92 61
fax	+33 (0)4 90 90 61 75
e-mail	contact@masdupastre.com

map 17 entry 305

Hôtel Restaurant Le Berger des Abeilles

Quartier du Rabet, RD 74e, 13670 St Andiol, Bouches-du-Rhône

You may spot and stroke a friendly llama, goat or pony in the field next door to this welcoming inn. Nicole lends a plot of land to a local educational circus while growing organic vegetables and herbs on another. She knows everything about cross pollination, busy as she was with bees for 10 years before taking over the inn as the fifth generation to do so. As an homage to her ancestors the bedrooms are all named after the previous mistresses of the farm: Alexia, Julie, Rachel, Anaïs… even Maya for herself, the ex-bee keeper. Light, fresh and rag-walled, they are of standard size with – except for the larger two on the ground floor – their own little patios and garden furniture. A vast green parasol of 200-year-old plane trees offers total shade for cool summer relaxing and there is a high-hedged sunny spot for dipping in the pool. Mediterranean and Provençal flavours dominate Nicole's fresh, simple and seasonal menus served outside on the terrace or in her honey-golden dining room. Informal, relaxed and unpretentious, this is a great base for exploring Saint Rémy and the surrounding region.

rooms	8: 4 doubles, 4 twins.
price	€ 72–€ 95.
meals	Breakfast € 10. Lunch & dinner € 24–€ 52. Restaurant closed for lunch except Sundays.
closed	January-14 February.
directions	Exit Avignon Sud on N7 for Aix en Provence for 6km to Verquières. Left at x-roads in Verquières for D74E.

Madame Nicole Grenier Sherpa

tel	+33 (0)4 90 95 01 91
fax	+33 (0)4 90 95 48 26
e-mail	abeilles13@aol.com
web	www.berger-abeilles.com

Hôtel Le Cadran Solaire

5 rue du Cabaret Neuf, 13690 Graveson, Bouches-du-Rhône

A soft clear light filters through the house, the light of the south pushing past the smallish windows and stroking Sophie Guilmet's light-handed, rich-pastelled décor where simple Provençal furniture, stencil motifs and natural materials – cotton, linen, organdie and seagrass – give the immediate feel of a well-loved family home. The simplicity of a pastel slipcover over a chair, a modern wrought-iron bed frame and a white piqué quilt is refreshing and restful – and the house stays deliciously cool in the summer heat. Indeed, the solid old staging post has stood here, with its thick walls, for 400 years, its face is as pretty as ever, calmly set in its gentle garden of happy flowers where guests can always find a quiet corner for their deckchairs. You can have breakfast on the shrubby terrace, under a blue and white parasol, or in the attractive dining room where a fine big mirror overlooks the smart red-on-white tables. A wonderful atmosphere, relaxed, smiling staff, an ideal base for visiting Provence and really good value.

rooms	12 doubles.
price	€ 51–€ 76.
meals	Breakfast € 7.
closed	Open only by arrangement in winter.
directions	A7 exit Avignon Sud for Chateaurenard. D28 to Graveson; signed.

Sophie Guilmet

tel	+33 (0)4 90 95 71 79
fax	+33 (0)4 90 90 55 04
e-mail	cadransolaire@wanadoo.fr
web	www.hotel-en-provence.com

map 17 entry 307

Mas des Comtes de Provence

Petite Route d'Arles, 13150 Tarascon, Bouches-du-Rhône

Homesick for the south of France and looking for a life change after frenetic professional careers in Paris, Frédérique and Pierre fell for this historic hunting lodge and have just settled in with their four young children. The *mas* belonged to King René whose château is just up the road; some say the Germans blocked the underground tunnel that connected the two buildings. A massive, sober, elegant stone exterior dating from the 16th century protects the big interior courtyard overlooked by grey-blue shuttered windows. There is lots of space here and the rooms are regal – the suite and the royal suite are 50m and 100m2 respectively. The suite Roi René is in tones of ivory, brown and beige; Garance in brick and yellow; ironwork chairs and side tables add extra interest. The pool is well hidden from the house in the two-hectare park dominated by 300-year-old plane trees, twisted olive trees, cypress and a profusion of roses. Pierre can direct you to the best canoeing, hiking, cycling, or riding – all just minutes away.

rooms	8: 6 doubles, 1 suite, 1 royal suite for 6.
price	€120–€160. Royal suite €229.
meals	Breakfast €10. Dinner with aperitif & coffee €35, book ahead.
closed	Rarely.
directions	Tarascon towards Arles on D35 'Petite Route d'Arles'. 200m after leaving Tarascon, take small road on left. Mas 600m on left.

	Frédérique & Pierre Valo
tel	+33 (0)4 90 91 00 13
fax	+33 (0)4 90 91 02 85
e-mail	valo@mas-provence.com
web	www.mas-provence.com

Mas des Capelans

84580 Oppède, Vaucluse

Why buy up an old house in Provence and have to do all the work? Here you can lounge by the pool all day, take a leisurely lunch between dips, then wander in to change before enjoying an aperitif as you watch the sun go down behind the hills. Jacqueline and Philippe have been running the Mas des Capelans, the 18th-century home of a silkworm breeder set among the vineyards and fields, for more than 13 years now and their personal touch comes through in the relaxed atmosphere and the house itself. The furniture and bits and pieces in the bedrooms have been collected over the years and not simply bought to give the place the 'right' look. The rooms are largish and simply decorated, with plenty of cushions and flowers. A great place for children: one room has an adjoining room for them and a private terrace while another has children's beds on a split-level. Dinner is under the mulberry trees unless the Mistral is blowing. If you feel like a drink later, simply help yourself from the outside bar and settle up when you leave. *A no-smoking property.*

rooms	9: 5 doubles, 2 triples, 2 suites.
price	€ 122–€ 167. Triples & suites € 145–€ 228.
meals	Buffet breakfast € 10. Poolside lunch € 20. Dinner by arrangement.
closed	November–February.
directions	From Avignon Sud towards Apt on D22, then N100. After Coustellet right for Oppède. Signed.

Jacqueline & Philippe Poiri

tel	+33 (0)4 90 76 99 04
fax	+33 (0)4 90 76 90 29
e-mail	reservation@masdescapelans-luberon.com
web	www.masdescapelans-luberon.com

map 17 entry 309

La Bastide de Voulonne

84220 Cabrières d'Avignon, Vaucluse

This bastide sits in splendid isolation in the lavender fields stretching beneath the ancient hilltop villages perched on the Luberon mountains. The heart of this 18th-century farm is an inner courtyard where you can breakfast to the soothing sound of the fountain. The Bastide has been open for guests since Sophie and Alain rescued it from years of neglect. They have done a fantastic job, sticking to natural, local colours, with tiled floors. The bedrooms are huge. The garden – more like a park – is vast, with a big pool not far from the house. It's a great place for children; Sophie and Alain have three. They grow vegetables in the garden and menus centre round local food. Breakfast is a buffet, in an airy, tiled breakfast room if it's too chilly for the courtyard. Dinner is served at one long table in a big dining hall where the centrepiece is the carefully restored old bread oven. There are loads of places around for a good lunch, or Sophie will prepare a picnic for you. *Two-day truffle courses in January and February, a no-smoking property.*

rooms	8: 7 doubles, 1 suite.
price	€122–€145. Suite €152–€168.
meals	Breakfast €11. Dinner €25 except Tuesdays & Wednesdays.
closed	Mid-November–mid December; open by arrangement only January & February.
directions	After Avignon A7 on N100 for Apt. At Coustellet x-roads to Gordes; at r'bout (Collège de Calavon) for Gordes. After 1km right. Bastide 600m on left.

	Sophie & Alain Rebourg
tel	+33 (0)4 90 76 77 55
fax	+33 (0)4 90 76 77 56
e-mail	sophie@bastide-voulonne.com
web	www.bastide-voulonne.com

Le Mas des Romarins

Route de l'Abbaye de Sénanque, 84220 Gordes, Vaucluse

Michel and Pierre bought this hotel – overlooking one of France's most beautiful villages – in May 2002. Forget the buildings on either side: the secluded pool and garden make you feel away from it all and the hotel even has its own private path into town. The fabulous hilltop view of Gordes with its distant misty-blue mountains and surrounding plains encourages you to linger over a delicious buffet breakfast, usually taken on the terrace. Inside, the sitting room is comfortable without being over-lavish and the warmth of the open fire is always welcome on days when the chilly Mistral wind gets up. The bedrooms are done in ochres and smoky rusts to contrast with stone, oatmeal and cream for the two-toned painted walls. Linens and soft furnishings from a well-known Parisian house are combined with traditional cotton prints. Rooms are small, but cool, comfortable and quiet. Join the other guests when the four-course *table d'hôte* is served; otherwise they will book a restaurant for you and help you explore the local culinary delights (of which there are plenty) on your own. A happy spot, easy living, great walking.

rooms	12: 9 doubles, 3 quadruples, some with private terraces.
price	€92–€145.
meals	Breakfast € 10.50. Dinner 2-3 times a week. Restaurants nearby.
closed	January-February.
directions	From Avignon, east on N7 then left onto N100 for Apt; left to Gordes. Route de Sénanque on left on entering Gordes. Hotel 200m on right. Well signed.

Michel Dimeux & Pierre Ticot

tel	+33 (0)4 90 72 12 13
fax	+33 (0)4 90 72 13 13
e-mail	info@hoteldesromarins.com
web	www.hoteldesromarins.com

map 17   entry 311

La Grande Bégude

Chemin Romieu, 84220 Goult, Vaucluse

The bathrooms are the size of a Paris apartment. Size isn't everything, of course, but what a feeling of space! And such tranquillity. The huge old *mas* sits on the edge of lavender fields and olives. All is serene: pale rosy terracotta tiles, bleached beams, cream or taupe walls, charming old shutters. Bedrooms are special: a huge cream-washed carved bed, a fauteuil unholstered in red check. And those bathrooms: a claw-foot bath by a lightly draped window, basins side-by-side on a stone ledge. Juliette and François are photographers – they've been to Afghanistan, followed the Pope on his travels, recorded world summits. Juliette is happy to cook a delicious supper, but likes it most when there are enough people to create a really sociable atmosphere; if you have the place to yourselves, opt for an evening out. The ground floor is huge and vaulted – a dining room in cool weather; in summer guests gather under the plane tree in the courtyard, or on a terrace overlooking the lavender. The outdoor pool is beautiful but perhaps the best is last: a magical indoor pool under an ancient stone vaulted roof.

rooms	5: 2 doubles, 3 suites.
price	€ 165–€ 215. Suites € 195–€ 250.
meals	Breakfast € 15. Lunch € 25. Hosted dinner € 45, book ahead. Restaurants within short driving distance.
closed	Rarely.
directions	N100 for Apt; D106 for Lacoste. After 500m, left on Chemin Romieu, small road through truffle oaks & lavender for 400m.

	Juliette & François Lochon
tel	+33 (0)4 90 72 29 43
fax	+33 (0)4 90 72 40 13
e-mail	resa@lagrandebegude.com
web	www.lagrandebegude.com

Château La Roque

Chemin du Château, 84210 La Roque sur Pernes, Vaucluse

The first-known stronghold dominating the valley from this craggy lookout held back the Saracens in the eighth century; ceded to the Papal States in the 13th century, it was again an important strategic outpost. In 1741 it settled into peace as a private household. The peace remains blissful, the only interruption coming from the bees buzzing in the acacias. The large square house and its ramparts are in mellow honey-coloured stone; have breakfast on a sunny terrace dappled by vines. Bedrooms are huge, simple bordering on spartan, but never cold. One has a big deep coral bed under high vaulted ceilings, with two antique chairs as bedside tables. Floors are terracotta, interspersed with polished ochre cement in some rooms. Bathrooms continue the theme: roomy, simple, each with big double basins – on old pedestals or perhaps set on tables. Chantal and Jean have a brilliant formula for dinner. Instead of offering a complicated menu, they buy top quality local meat or fish and grill it on request, with organic fruit and vegetables from the village. *Children 12 and over welcome, a no-smoking property.*

rooms	5: 2 doubles, 3 suites.
price	€90–€145. Suites €185.
meals	Breakfast €13. Dinner by arrangement.
closed	Rarely.
directions	From Lyon, A7 exit Orange Sud for Carpentras; for Pernes les Fontaines; for St Didier; for La Roque 2km.

Chantal & Jean Tomasino

tel	+33 (0)4 90 61 68 77
fax	+33 (0)4 90 61 68 77
e–mail	chateaularoque@wanadoo.fr
web	www.chateaularoque.com

map 17 entry 313

Le Mas de Garrigon

Route de St Saturnin d'Apt, Roussillon en Provence, 84220 Gordes, Vaucluse

Christiane, a writer and journalist, settled in the Luberon after years in Africa, bought the plot of land and built the *mas* from scratch in 1979, using local materials and tailoring the house to the hill. The idea was to build a really special place to stay – each room has its own terrace looking out to the wild beauty of the hills. We don't generally recommend piped music… but the classical music Christiane plays does add to the atmosphere. In palest terracotta with lightest blue shutters, the house sits among cypress, olive and almond trees and is perfect in summer, when you can lounge by the pool, and perfect in winter too, when you can settle down by a crackling fire, maybe with a book from the well-stocked library. Inside is in complete and striking contrast to the muted, natural tones used outside: bedrooms are a joyful riot of reds, yellows and blues. Don't worry: Christiane's mix of bold and simple, traditional and daring is never garish, it all works perfectly. Great food too.

rooms	9: 8 doubles, 1 family room for 2-3.
price	€120–€145. Family room €145–€180. Half-board only Easter-October, €260–€286.
meals	Breakfast €16. Picnic lunch available. Lunch & dinner €70. Restaurant closed Mondays, Tuesdays & Wednesday noon mid-November-end December.
closed	Rarely.
directions	From Cavallion on D2 between Gordes & St Saturnin d'Apt.

	Christiane Rech-Druart
tel	+33 (0)4 90 05 63 22
fax	+33 (0)4 90 05 70 01
e-mail	mas.de.garrigon@wanadoo.fr
web	www.masdegarrigon-provence.com

Auberge de la Fontaine

Place de la Fontaine, 84210 Venasque, Vaucluse

Line up your taste buds, and eye and ear will join the chorus to sing praises to this place with a difference. It sits discretely behind the central fountain of one of the most beautiful hill towns of Provence. Enter through a small bistro downstairs, then follow a tiny, wonky staircase to the restaurant where you'll find antique cupboards, rush-bottomed chairs and interesting etchings framed and hung with care. It's all as you might expect – except for a grand piano in the middle of the dining room. If you time it right you will hear it being played during one of Christian's dinner-concerts – about 20 each year – featuring young musicians from all over France and his authentic cuisine. Then up to bed in one of the five suites furnished with modern pieces from young designers of zen-like sobriety, a black and white theme against terracotta tiles. Some of the small private terraces are up on another level. All rooms have working chimneys, air-conditioning, cleverly hidden kitchens (with vegetable peelers and dishwashers!) and sound systems for cassettes and CDs. Outstanding. *30km from Orange and Avignon.*

rooms	5 suites (for up to 4).
price	€ 125 for 1 or 2, € 133 for 3, € 141 for 4.
meals	Breakfast € 10. Lunch & dinner from € 18 in bistro. Dinner from € 34 in restaurant. Bistro closed Sunday evenings & Mondays; restaurant closed Wednesdays.
closed	12 November–19 December.
directions	From Carpentras D4. Hotel opposite fountain, 2-minutes' walk from parking area.

	M & Mme Soehlke
tel	+33 (0)4 90 66 02 96
fax	+33 (0)4 90 66 13 14
e-mail	fontvenasq@aol.com
web	www.auberge-lafontaine.com

map 17 entry 315

Le Château de Mazan

Place Napoleon, 84380 Mazan, Vaucluse

The father and uncle of the Marquis de Sade were born here – an unexpected connection, given the luminosity of the place. Though the infamous Marquis preferred Paris, he often stayed at Mazan and organized France's first theatre festival here in 1772. The château is in a charming village at the foot of Mont Ventoux. Ceilings are lofty, floors are tiled in white-and-terracotta squares that would drown a smaller space, windows are huge with the lightest of curtains. This is a family hotel, despite its size, and Frédéric, who speaks good English, ensures you settle in. His mother, Danièle, is in charge of décor. Ground-floor bedrooms have French windows opening to a private sitting area; first-floor rooms are elegant, with pale tones, antique mirrors and appliqué quilts. Rooms on the top floor, the old servants' quarters, could get hot in summer. There are palms outside, posies within, and secluded spots in the garden – doze in the shade of the mulberry trees. There's also a rotunda and a peaceful pool, and a large terrace for dinner. Do eat in: the young chef has worked in Michelin-starred restaurants and is keen to win his own.

rooms	26: 12 doubles, 13 family rooms for 3-4, 1 suite for 4.
price	€ 120-€ 270. Suite € 400.
meals	Breakfast € 15. Lunch € 30-€ 47. Dinner € 47-€ 61. Restaurant closed Tues; May-October, also Mon.
closed	January-February.
directions	In Carpentras for Sault Ventoux then Mazan. In Mazan, 1st right near Mairie, then left.

Danièle & Frédéric Lhermie

tel	+33 (0)4 90 69 62 61
fax	+33 (0)4 90 69 76 62
e-mail	chateaudemazan@wanadoo.fr
web	www.chateaudemazan.fr

Copyright Captim

La Barjaquière

17 Ancien Chemin de Ronde, 84330 Saint Pierre de Vassols, Vaucluse

There is much more to La Barjaquière than meets the eye. A watery and peaceful world awaits behind this 17th-century edifice set in a small village: blue sky and pots of bougainvillea reflect in a dream of a pool; a second courtyard beckons with another pool, heated this time, flanked by *trompe l'oeil* visions of terracotta vessels spilling with greens and reds. Antique doors, stencilled flowers over the staircase, a quiet sitting space and a book of poetry beckons on the antique side table – Ghislaine has made it all sing with her sense of warmth and colour. Daniel explains that the original primitive structure with its beams, nooks and crannies, mezzanines and terraces inspired this maze of a Provençal interior. You'll even find a sauna on the ground floor. The bright, slant-roofed guest room Soleillant has a beaded curtain and a terrace overlooking the village; apricot floor tiles reflect in the pale yellow, waxed walls. The shimmering ochre walls of Le Parc seem to hold a hundred layers of light which contrast well with a carmine sofa and quilted bedspreads. Add the engaging hospitality of two inventive hosts; you will find it very hard to leave.

rooms	5: 3 doubles, 2 suites for 3.
price	€ 110–€ 150. Suites € 170 for 2, € 195 for 3.
meals	Dinner with drinks € 45, book ahead.
closed	Mid-January–mid February; 20 November–10 December.
directions	A7 exit 22 Carpentras; D950 then D13; left at 2nd aqueduct on D974 to Bedoin & Mont Ventoux for 7.7km. At St Pierre left on D85 to village church. House opposite.

Ghislaine André & Daniel Poncet

tel	+33 (0)4 90 62 48 00
fax	+33 (0)4 90 62 48 06
e-mail	welcome@barjaquiere.com
web	www.barjaquiere.com

map 17 entry 317

Château Talaud

D107, 84870 Loriol du Comtat, Vaucluse

Lavish and elegant – a stunning place and lovely people. Hein has a wine export business, Conny gives her whole self to her house and her guests. Among ancient vineyards and wonderful green lawns – an oasis in Provence – the ineffably gracious 18th-century château speaks of a long-gone southern way of life. Enter, and you will feel it has not all vanished. Restored by the owners to a very high standard, the finely-proportioned rooms have been furnished with antiques, many of them family pieces, and thick, luxurious fabrics. The big bedrooms mix old and new, *Directoire* armchairs and featherweight duvets, with consummate taste and bathrooms are old-style hymns to modernity. The swimming pool is an adapted 17th-century irrigation tank: one goes through an arch to the first, shallow cistern, leading to a deeper pool beyond – ingenious. Guests may laze in the lovely gardens but Conny is happy to help you plan visits in this fascinating area. Then return to one of her delicious meals where guests all sit together. An exceptionally fine, well-kept guest house.

rooms	5 + 3: 4 doubles, 1 suite. 1 apartment for 2, 1 studio for 2, 1 cottage for 5.
price	€ 155–€ 195. Weekly rentals: apartment € 1,350; studio € 1,150; cottage € 1,250.
meals	Dinner € 40 with wine, twice-weekly.
closed	February.
directions	D950 for Carpentras, then D107 at Loriol du Comtat; at r'bout right for Monteux. After 1km, right.

Conny & Hein Deiters-Kommer
tel	+33 (0)4 90 65 71 00
fax	+33 (0)4 90 65 77 93
e-mail	chateautalaud@infonie.fr
web	www.chateautalaud.com

Les Florets

Route des Dentelles, 84190 Gigondas, Vaucluse

The setting is magical, the food imaginative, the greeting from the Bernard family is warm and the walks are outstanding. Les Florets sits just below the majestic Dentelles de Montmirail – a small range of mountains crested with long, delicate fingers of white stone in the middle of Côtes du Rhône country. Over 40km of paths wind through here so appetites build and are satiated on the splendid terrace under the branches of plane, chestnut, maple, acacia and linden trees; the low stone walls are dressed with *impatiens* and hydrangeas (and the peonies were blooming in March!). You'll also be sampling some of the wines that this family has been producing since the 1880s. Bright blue and yellow corridors lead to rooms which are simply and florally decorated; all have big, sparkling, tiled bathrooms. We liked the tiny 50s reception desk dressed with a huge bouquet from the garden; a wonderful ceramic *soupière* brightens one corner, a scintillating collection of delicate glass carafes stands in another. Book well ahead, people return year after year.

rooms	14 + 1: 14 doubles. 1 apartment for 2-4.
price	€ 90-€ 120. Apartment € 120-€ 150.
meals	Breakfast € 12. Lunch & dinner € 24-€ 38. Restaurant closed Mon evenings; Tues & Wed November-December & March.
closed	January-mid-March.
directions	From Carpentras, D7 for Vacqueyras. After Vacqueras right on D7 to Gigondas for 2km. Signed.

M & Mme Bernard
tel +33 (0)4 90 65 85 01
fax +33 (0)4 90 65 83 80

map 17 entry 319

Le Château de Rocher La Belle Ecluse

156 rue Emile-Lachaux, 84500 Bollène, Vaucluse

If you are meandering south, heading for Spain or into Provence, this is a great spot to spend a few days. Bedrooms are big and airy, and the grounds are fun for children: meet the beautiful Anglo-Arab pony, several families of pet rabbits, ostriches, peacocks, even emus. The château is run by Jean-Pierre who describes himself as "a human volcano" and bursts with ideas and enthusiasm; he also speaks several languages. His brother Eric and his Spanish wife, and Jean-Pierre's old friend Rinaldo, also lend a helping hand. The château was built in 1826 when Count Joseph Maurice de Rocher decided to plant the first vineyard in the area; he did it grandly and summoned architects and decorators from Florence. His son was something of a black sheep and gambled away much of the land; his daughter was quite the opposite, offering charitable patronage to local youths and further embellishing the house. Bedrooms are mostly high-ceilinged and multi-floral; one was an old chapel and has an amazing ceiling and stained-glass windows, two connect so are perfect for families.

rooms	19: 12 doubles, 7 triples.
price	€ 54–€ 66.
meals	Breakfast € 9. Lunch & dinner menus € 18–€ 43.
closed	Rarely.
directions	From Bollène towards Suze La Rousse for 1km; right at notice board (lit at night).

Jean-Pierre Carloni,
Eric & Rinaldo Fassetta

tel	+33 (0)4 90 40 09 09
fax	+33 (0)4 90 40 09 30
e-mail	ecluse84@club-internet.fr
web	www.lechateaudurocher.com

Hôtel Arène

Place de Langes, 84100 Orange, Vaucluse

You can drive here, and even park, yet you are in a pedestrian area and it's beautifully quiet in the middle of this ancient town, a stone's throw from the Roman theatre. Monsieur and Madame Coutel have run the Arène for 30 years and have kept all their staff for ages: always a good sign. The entrance hall may be a touch overpowering, but go on in, you won't regret it. Newly-decorated bedrooms are in what our inspector described as "joyful" colours; the older ones are old-fashioned French but most have been transformed with Provençal blues and yellows, with painted cupboards and beds, or possibly wrought iron, and with flowers on the table. The bathrooms are new and white, with coloured tile details and some have big corner baths. Painted furniture, pots and urns and the odd statue add to the Provençal feel, while the stained glass, which looks a bit much in the entrance, is great viewed from the other side and casts a pleasant light into the breakfast room. A special place bang in the centre of Orange, where your children will be made really welcome.

rooms	30: 24 doubles/twins, 6 family rooms for 3-4.
price	€ 77-€ 122. Family € 122-€ 183.
meals	Breakfast € 10. Restaurant next door.
closed	3 weeks in November.
directions	In Orange, left after tourist office along Cours Aristide Briand, 1st right on President Daladier, immed. right on Victor Hugo, 2nd left onto Places de Langes. Cars can get to hotel via this route.

	M & Mme Coutel
tel	+33 (0)4 90 11 40 40
fax	+33 (0)4 90 11 40 45
e-mail	hotel-arene@wanadoo.fr

map 17 entry 321

Hostellerie du Val de Sault

Route de St Trinit, Ancien chemin d'Aurel, 84390 Sault, Vaucluse

This landscape has been called "a sea of corn gold and lavender blue": from your terrace here you can contemplate the familiar shape of Mont Ventoux, the painter's peak, beyond. The charming, communicative owners – she with an artistic background, he a passionate cook – have gathered all possible information, know everyone there is to know on the Provence scene and are full of good guidance; they also provide imaginative food and a special truffle menu in the informal atmosphere of their light, airy restaurant. And… children can eat earlier, allowing the adults to savour their meal in peace. Perched just above the woods in a big garden, this is a modern building with lots of space inside and out; wooden floors and pine-slatted walls bring live warmth, colour schemes are vibrant, storage is excellent; baths in the suites have jets. Each room feels like a very private space with its terrace (the suites have room for loungers on theirs): the pool, bar and restaurant are there for conviviality; the fitness room, tennis court and boules pitch for exercise; the jacuzzi space for chilling out. *Locked shed for bikes.*

rooms	16: 11 doubles, 5 suites.
price	Half-board May–September: doubles €98–€120 p.p.; suites €110–€155 p.p.
meals	Breakfast €11. Restaurant closed for lunch certain days April-October, ex. on weekends and holidays.
closed	November–March.
directions	D1 Col des Abeilles for Sault for 30km, then for St Trinit & Fourcalquier. After big bend, left between fire station & supermarket.

	Yves Gattechaut & Ildiko de Hanny
tel	+33 (0)4 90 64 01 41
fax	+33 (0)4 90 64 12 74
e-mail	valdesault@aol.com
web	www.valdesault.com

Auberge du Presbytère

Place de la Fontaine, 84400 Saignon, Vaucluse

They say "when the wind blows at Saignon, tiles fly off in Avignon": the Mistral blows fiercely down from the mountains to the Mediterranean. This 11th-century village of only 100 inhabitants lies deep in the Luberon hills and lavender fields; the Auberge du Presbytère sits deep in Saigon, half hidden behind an old tree near the village's statue-topped fountain. Unforgettable meals are served under this tree, or in a pretty terraced garden. The bedrooms are striking, a huge fireplace in one, the Blue, with its stone terrace, looks out onto the hills and the simplest of all the rooms, the little one, Pink, has sleigh beds. Lovely Italian stone blocks tile the big bathrooms. A log fire burns on chilly days in the smart but informal sitting area. Jean-Pierre, attentive, and with a disarming sense of humour, will make you feel at home and, though this is perhaps not an obvious choice with children, provides early supper specially for them. A secret, splendid place from which to visit the nearby hill towns. Or if you are fit, rent a bike and follow the cycling signs. Outstanding value and food.

rooms	16: 14 doubles, 2 triples.
price	€52–€115.
meals	Breakfast €8.50. Lunch €21.50. Dinner €32. Restaurant closed Wednesdays & Thursday noon.
closed	Mid-November–early February.
directions	From Apt N100. At r'bout with 1 olive & 3 cypress trees towards Saignon to beginning of village. Left on lane for 'riverains' (residents) to Place de la Fontaine.

	Jean-Pierre de Lutz
tel	+33 (0)4 90 74 11 50
fax	+33 (0)4 90 04 68 51
e-mail	auberge.presbytere@wanadoo.fr
web	www.auberge-presbytere.com

map 17   entry 323

La Bastide Saint Joseph

Chemin St Joseph, 84400 Rustrel, Vaucluse

The delicious, cream-coloured *bastide*, on the route from Italy to Provence, was a natural staging post for the 18th-century traveller and ultimately became a *relais de poste*. After a further spell as a convent, it was abandoned; by the 1950s, trees were coming through the roof. When Meta arrived, five years ago, it had been rescued by an architect... ripe for revival. Gentle smiling Meta, Canadian by birth and well-travelled, speaks perfect French and knows *everything* about her corner of the Lubéron. She has also created a sophisticated yet wonderfully relaxing place to stay. Beautiful big bedrooms have polished, honey-coloured boards and rush mats to soften the tread; bathrooms are as luxurious, if not more so: one has a bath for four! Candles line the elegant sitting room hearth, to be replaced, in winter, by logs. Meta, ever thoughtful, puts exquisite books and flowers in your room and serves you breakfast where you fancy: in the garden, the chapel room or in bed. Stroll through the garden, planted with cypress and 400 lavender bushes, to the pool, perfect with towels and honesty bar. *Cash or cheque only, a no-smoking property.*

rooms	4 large doubles.
price	€ 100–€ 160.
meals	Restaurants nearby.
closed	Rarely.
directions	Avignon to Apt on N100 then D22 for Rustrel; 10 minutes to r'bout for Gignac. House 1 minute up on left, follow stone wall to blue gates.

Meta Tory

tel	+33 (0)4 90 04 97 80
fax	+33 (0)4 90 04 97 80
e-mail	metat@attglobal.net
web	www.bastide-saint-joseph.com

Hôtel d'Europe

12 place Crillon, 84000 Avignon, Vaucluse

Built in 1580 for the Marquis de Graveson, this mansion, a mitre's throw from the Papal Palace, was taken from its noble owner by the Revolution and turned into a hotel. When you stay here, you will be following in the steps of great writers (Victor Hugo, Tennessee Williams), painters (Dali, Picasso), even Napoleon; in earlier times people arrived by boat but as this is no longer possible, the hotel has a car park. René Daudeij has run the Hotel d'Europe for some 24 years – and pretty perfect it is. It is one of our larger hotels but it's still small enough for the staff to take personal care of each guest. This is traditional French hospitality in all its splendour. Bedrooms vary from large to huge, from simply elegant to sumptuous; many have crisp white cotton bedcovers that give a fresh touch among the moulded, mirrored walls, the antiques and the plush-covered chairs. Some have lit-up views of the Pope's Palace. Meals are served at fine tables in the tapestry-hung dining room or on the terrace where the fountain sings.

rooms	45: 38 doubles, 4 triples, 3 suites.
price	€ 120–€ 385. Suites € 580–€ 670.
meals	Breakfast € 20. Lunch & dinner € 33–€ 85. Restaurant closed 13-18 Jan; 18 Aug-2 Sept; 24 Nov-2 Dec.
closed	Rarely.
directions	Exit Avignon for Centre Ville. From ring road around ramparts, onto Porte de l'Oulle for Place Crillon. Signed.

	M Daudeij
tel	+33 (0)4 90 14 76 76
fax	+33 (0)4 90 14 76 71
e-mail	reservations@hotel-d-europe.fr
web	www.hotel-d-europe.fr

map 17 entry 325

Mas du Pont Roman

Chemin de Châteauneuf, 04300 Mane , Alpes-de-Haute-Provence

A land of treasures: Ligurian *bories* – igloo-like dry-stone huts – squat camouflaged in the landscape; Roman churches sit quietly as if time had not passed; a stunning 12th-century Roman bridge spans the river on the edge of this property, a recently renovated 18th-century mill at the end of tree-lined boulevard on the outskirts of a village. Marion graciously watches over your creature comforts while Christian, a most hospitable and jovial host, knows everybody and everything about the immediate area and the intriguing market town of Forcalquier. The sitting/drawing room, with a crackling fire on cool days is an ideal spot to enjoy an aperitif before dinner; Christian will help you pick out your restaurant. An indoor swimming pool and two sauna rooms complement the spanking new bedrooms with their stone quarry tiles, pristine tiled bathrooms and flowery bedspreads. Beautiful grounds, stunning views, flowing water and an outdoor pool and terrace complete the picture. Organise your night watch for shooting star extravaganzas at the nearby St Michel Observatory.

rooms	9 doubles.
price	€ 50–€ 70.
meals	Breakfast € 7; inc. out of season. Two restaurants in village, 2km.
closed	Rarely.
directions	Exit A Marseille & Sisteron for Forcalquier then Apt. Enter village; left, hotel on right at end of avenue of trees.

Christian & Marion Vial

tel	+33 (0)4 92 75 49 46
fax	+33 (0)4 92 75 36 73
e-mail	pont.roman@laposte.net
web	www.ifrance.com/pontroman

Auberge de Reillanne

04110 Reillanne, Alpes-de-Haute-Provence

The solid loveliness of this 18th-century house, so typical of the area, reassures you, invites you in. And you will not be disappointed: you'll feel good here, even if you can't quite define the source of the positive energy. Madame Balmand clearly has a connection to the spirit of the place and has used all her flair and good taste, making all the curtains and bedcovers herself, to transform the old inn into a very special place to stay. Bedrooms are large and airy, done in cool, restful colours with big cupboards and rattan furniture. There are beams, properly whitewashed walls and books. Bathrooms are big and simple too. Downstairs, the sitting and dining areas are decorated in warm, embracing colours with terracotta tiles, white tablecloths and flame-coloured curtains. This would be a place for a quiet holiday with long meditative walks in the hills, a place to come and write that novel or simply to get to know the gentle, delicate, smiling owner who loves nothing better than to receive people in her magical house.

rooms	6: 3 doubles, 3 triples.
price	€68–€72. Half-board €65 p.p.
meals	Breakfast €8.
closed	20 October–March.
directions	N100 through Apt & Céreste. Approx. 8km after Céreste, left on D214 to Reillanne. Hotel on right.

Monique Balmand

tel	+33 (0)4 92 76 45 95
fax	+33 (0)4 92 76 45 95

map 17 entry 327

Le Moulin du Château

04500 St Laurent du Verdon, Alpes-de-Haute-Provence

A sleepy place – come to doze. Your silence will be broken only by the call of the sparrow-hawk or the distant rumble of a car. This 17th-century olive-mill once belonged to the château and stands at the foot of an ancient grove; the vast pressoir is now a reception area where modern art hangs on ancient walls. The Moulin is a long, low, stone building with lavender-blue shutters and the odd climbing vine, and stands in its own gardens surrounded by lavender and fruit trees. In the bedrooms light filters though voile curtains, and shadows dance upon the walls. The feel is uncluttered, cool, breezy, with vibrant colours: turquoise, lilac, lime – luminous yet restful. This is an easy-going 'green' hotel where the emphasis is on the simple things of life – and the organic, Meditteranean cooking is a treat. Boules is played under the cherry tree, poppies grow on an old crumbling stone staircase and views stretch across fields to village and château. There are mountain bikes for gentle excursions into the countryside, and further afield are the Cistercian abbey of Le Thoronet, hilltop villages, local markets, the Verdon Canyon and Digne Les Bains.

rooms	10: 9 doubles, 1 suite.
price	€65–€98.
meals	Breakfast €8. Picnics €9.50. Dinner €30, except Mondays & Thursdays. Restaurant in village.
closed	November-February.
directions	Gréoux les Bains D952 until Riez, then D11 for Quinson; for St Laurent du Verdon; take road after château. Signed.

Edith & Nicolas Stämpfli-Faoro

tel	+33 (0)4 92 74 02 47
fax	+33 (0)4 92 74 02 97
e-mail	info@moulin-du-chateau.com
web	www.moulin-du-chateau.com

La Bouscatière

Chemin Marcel Provence, 04360 Moustiers Ste Mairie, Alpes-de-Haute-Provence

If you ever had a dream of dramatic Provence, this must be it. The cliffs rise indomitably, the water tumbles down, the old village looks as if it grew here. This enchanting vertical house, firmly fixed to the rock since 1765, was originally an oil mill. Its lowest level, in the village centre, houses the oil press; its highest, seventh level opens through the lush secluded garden with its tiny, ancient chapel (now a delicious bedroom with heavily-carved Spanish bed and little terrace) to the top of the village and its perfect Romanesque church. Inside, all is country elegance, antiques and supreme comfort against a backdrop of exposed rock, white limewashed walls, Provençal tiles and original beams. A family home turned guest house, it is decorated in exquisite taste by designer/owner Tonia Peyrot – her son sells his china in the old oil press; her staff are utterly delightful – you'll find deep sofas and an open fireplace in the vast sitting-room. Maïa, the biggest bedroom, is pretty grand, Antoinette has a tracery alcove, all are softly attractive with big, new, Victorian-style fitted bathrooms. Perfect. *A no-smoking property.*

rooms	5 doubles.
price	€ 115–€ 190.
meals	Breakfast € 15. Wide variety of restaurants in village.
closed	Mid-November–20 December; 2 January–February.
directions	A8 from Nice exit 36 to N555 for Draguignan; D557 to Aups. D957 to Moustiers St Marie. Follow road to highest point of village to parking area. Do not drive into village.

Tonia Peyrot

tel	+33 (0)4 92 74 67 67
fax	+33 (0)4 92 74 65 72
e-mail	bonjour@labouscatiere.com
web	www.labouscatiere.com

map 18 entry 329

Les Méans

04340 Méolans Revel, Alpes-de-Haute-Provence

Beds are just for sleeping here as the beauty of the place and its surrounding area will have you up early, climbing mountains – Frédéric is a qualified mountain guide – rafting or canoeing down the Ubaye river or just taking a slow trek on one of the many nearby trails. The Millets (lucky things!) have double lives: ski instructors in the winter and hospitable hosts of this wonderful 16th-century farmhouse in the summer. They have made it a breeze for families by furnishing communal washing machines, a fridge packed with soft drinks, a microwave and a kettle. Elizabeth cooks on the roasting-spit three nights a week – pigeon is one of her specialities – in a wonderful open-plan dining room and kitchen filled with baskets, drying herbs and all sorts of colourful odds and ends picked up over the years. If you insist, a day of doing nothing in particular can be arranged – mountain gazing from the garden is not too strenuous; you could stir yourself to visit the small chapel, or to admire the bread oven, beautifully restored by Frédéric.

rooms	5: 4 doubles, 1 suite for 4.
price	€ 58–€ 62. Suite € 95–€ 140.
meals	Picnic € 8. Dinner € 22 with wine & coffee.
closed	Mid-October–mid-May.
directions	From Gap, D900 for Barcelonnette. After La Fresquière, 10km from Lauzet-Ubaye, do not turn right into Méolans but continue for 500m; left. Signed.

	Elizabeth & Frédéric Millet
tel	+33 (0)4 92 81 03 91
fax	+33 (0)4 92 81 03 91
e-mail	lesmeans@chez.com
web	www.chez.com/lesmeans

Villa Morélia

Vallée de l'Ubaye, 04850 Jausiers, Alpes-de-Haute-Provence

Villa Morélia has a fascinating history: far from isolating themselves in this village deep in the Alps, the inhabitants exported their textile skills first to Flanders, then to the Caribbean and in the 19th century to Mexico, where some 60,000 descendants still live. Many, however, returned and put their money and taste for things foreign to good use, building exotic villas in their valley. With its imposing height, asymmetric façades and coloured chimneys, the Villa Morélia, designed by a renowned Marseilles architect, Eugène Marx, stands out from the rest. Now Robert and Marie-Christine have opened it as a hotel and already established an award-winning restaurant. This charming couple know quite a bit about cuisine, music, dogs and a relaxed style of living. You will love everything inside: high airy ceilings, walnut windows and doors, beautiful tiles and big bedrooms which manage the trick of looking both elegant and welcoming. On top of this, you can ski, go rafting or canyoning, the chef comes from the Eden Roc in Antibes and Robert will pick you up if you don't want to drive.

rooms	6: 4 doubles, 1 triple, 1 quadruple.
price	€85–€180.
meals	Breakfast €12. Picnic lunch available. Dinner from €37.
closed	November–26 December.
directions	7km from Barcelonnette on D900 Gap-Cuneo road. In centre of village.

	Marie-Christine & Robert Boudard
tel	+33 (0)4 92 84 67 78
fax	+33 (0)4 92 84 65 47
e-mail	rboudard@aol.com
web	www.villa-morelia.com

map 18   entry 331

Copyright Eliophot

L'Auberge du Choucas

Monêtier les Bains, 05220 Serre Chevalier, Hautes-Alpes

In an eternity of pure blue air and pure white glaciers, drenched in sunshine 300 days a year, the Alpine village and its old inn, just behind the Romanesque church, pander to your terrestrial appetites. The lush garden is ideal for summer breakfasts with the birds; the sitting room suggests cosy fireside tea – friendly cat and modern pictures – the stone-vaulted dining room with its great open fire is the place to be bewitched by the young chef's magic – "the art of cookery lifted into the realm of poetry," said one guest. But you are summoned by ski slopes, dramatic ice caves, soul-nourishing walks and natural hot springs. Then return to open one of the beautiful doors, painted by an artist friend of Nicole's, into a panelled, carpeted cottagey bedroom with a snug little bathroom. Those with balconies are blissful in the morning sun, duplexes have two (bigger) bathrooms. A brilliant show, led by the amazing whirlwind Nicole who also nurtures a passion for Latin and Greek. Seconded by her charming daughter, Eva, they attend to the minutest details, anxious that it should all be perfect for you.

rooms	12: 8 twins/doubles, 4 duplexes for 4-5.
price	€ 100-€ 260. Half-board € 95-€ 140 p.p.
meals	Breakfast € 14. Lunch & dinner € 19-€ 39. Restaurant closed mid-April-May; mid-Oct-mid-Dec.
closed	3 November-6 December; May.
directions	14km from Briançon on N91. Hotel behind church in centre of village in front of town hall.

**Nicole Sanchez-Ventura
& Eva Gattechaut**

tel	+33 (0)4 92 24 42 73
fax	+33 (0)4 92 24 51 60
e-mail	auberge.du.choucas@wanadoo.fr
web	www.aubergeduchoucas.com

Auberge du Lac
Rue Grande, 83630 Bauduen, Var

Hard to imagine, as you gaze on the blue-green waters of its lake, that the auberge, an inn for hundreds of years, once stood on the old Roman road from Fréjus to Riez. They changed its name in 1973, when the Sainte-Croix Lake was created for the national electricity company, the EDF. The auberge feels genuinely old; the clean smell of beeswax wafts through its maze of corridors, and the rooms are filled with polished Provençal pieces. The young Monsieur Bagarre worked as EDF inspector in Paris but a taste of life in the city persuaded him to return to the peace of the auberge, which he runs with his mother. Enjoy breakfast in your room, perhaps at a little round table by the window overlooking the lake, or on a terrace under the vines. Or, on cooler days, in the dining area, again looking onto the lake; this is a series of beamy, white-walled rooms whose little tables are dressed in warm local colours. Monsieur steps in as chef when needed. A lot of thought has gone into the bedrooms, full of lovely pillows, pictures and flowers. Some rooms have balconies, bathrooms are colourful, and there are enough towels for an army.

rooms	13: 2 singles, 6 doubles, 5 triples.
price	€ 48–€ 75. Half and full-board available.
meals	Breakfast € 6.90. Lunch & dinner € 24–€ 45. Many restaurants nearby.
closed	11 November-15 March.
directions	A8 to Le Muy then N555 for Draguignan; D557 for Flayose then Aups; D957 for Aiguines; after 7km, D49 to Bauduen.

	M & Mme Bagarre
tel	+33 (0)4 94 70 08 04
fax	+33 (0)4 94 84 39 41

map 18 entry 333

Hôtel du Vieux Château

Place de la Fontaine, 83630 Aiguines, Var

Aiguines sits like a belvedere on the flank of Mount Magrès overlooking the Lac de Ste Croix. Once an *oppidum* (hill fort) on the Roman road linking Fréjus to Grenoble, it has never stopped being a place of constant passage. The eye travels unhindered over the lavender-covered Plateau de Valensole towards the blue mountains in the distance. Frédéric, affable and smiley, was born in Aiguines and came home to roost after a busy and peripatetic youth. He is taking his time restoring the hotel, once part of the village's castle. "I want to get it right," he says. Getting it right means no fuss and frills, but a crisp refreshing simplicity. A good sense of colour marries yellow, blue and old rose with Provençal or tartan-patterned curtains; very right in the bathrooms with rich hued Salernes tiles, deep turquoise green, royal blue, salmon, grass-green. Rooms at the front have those views over the rooftops to the lake, others catch a glimpse of a castle and St Pierre's chapel. Bedrooms at the back, looking over a village street, are naturally quieter and may well be cooler in a searing summer. A place with 'soul', intrinsically French.

rooms	10: 8 twins/doubles; 2 twins/doubles with separate wc.
price	€ 47–€ 73.
meals	Breakfast included in high season, otherwise € 6. Lunch & dinner € 20–€ 25. Restaurants in village.
closed	15 October–15 April.
directions	From A8, exit for Draguignan, then D557 through Flayosc & Aups for Moustiers Ste Marie to Aiguines.

Frédéric Ricez

tel	+33 (0)4 94 70 22 95
fax	+33 (0)4 94 84 22 36

Hostellerie Bérard

Rue Gabriel Péri, 83740 La Cadière d'Azur, Var

Fine food, excellent painting and cookery classes, and a building constructed of an 11th-century monastery, an old *bastide* and the 'painter's house'. Danièle and Michel Bérard are true belongers: they grew up in this ancient village in sight of a mountain called the Grand Bérard. They first opened in 1969 and over the years have lovingly restored the place; each bedroom is a surprise. In one, a delicate wrought-iron four-poster, with checked counterpane and *toile de Jouy* curtains, in another, green shutters that open onto olive- and vine-covered hills. In yet another, blue shutters open to the pool. Michel is Maître Cuisinier de France, one of the chosen few, while Danièle is a qualified expert in the local wines. Happy to pursue their own special interests, the couple are gradually leaving the running of the hotel to their daughter Sandra, full of friendly enthusiasm and highly organized. Michel concentrates on Provençal food, using local, seasonal produce, and if you opt for one of his cookery courses you will visit local producers and markets, not just chop and stir... pleasure though this is, in the special kitchen of the old *bastide*.

rooms	40: 36 doubles, 4 suites.
price	€79–€148. Suites €224–€290.
meals	Breakfast €17.50. Lunch à la carte. Dinner €41–€100.
closed	January.
directions	A50 towards Toulon, exit 11. Hotel in centre of village.

M & Mme Bérard

tel	+33 (0)4 94 90 11 43
fax	+33 (0)4 94 90 01 94
e-mail	berard@hotel-berard.com
web	www.hotel-berard.com

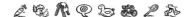

map 17   entry 335

Le Logis du Guetteur

Place du Château, 83460 Les Arcs sur Argens, Var

A vertical rabbit warren of brilliantly renovated old stones around a cobbled courtyard at the top of a medieval village, beneath the keep – the Watchman's House has intimacy, good taste and incomparable views. Below the courtyard, the summer dining room is one of the loveliest stone-flagged terraces we know, with delicious food served on perfectly-dressed tables: gaspacho, salmon marinated with herbs, chicken stuffed with rosemary. Along a secret passage, the winter restaurant in the stone-walled, carefully-lit, 'medieval'-furnished vaults is just as cosy as you'd wish in a snowstorm – and the food as good as in summer. Bedrooms are not large but classically chic and very comfortable with all you'd expect for the price. Each one is different: an elegant wrought-iron bed here, a leather armchair there, modern oils on the walls, beautifully compact bathrooms. The curvaceous pool has more panoramic views – a splendid place to swim. Astoundingly, in the 1960s this beautiful little village was a heap of red-grey stones about to be bulldozed to make way for skyline blocks, then saved by a group of caring Parisians.

rooms	10 + 1: 8 doubles, 2 suites. 1 apartment for 4–5.
price	€ 118. Suites € 149. Apartment € 149.
meals	Breakfast € 13. Lunch & dinner € 26–€ 41. Restaurant closed 20 January–February.
closed	Mid–January–5 March.
directions	A8 exit 36 Le Muy. N7 for Le Luc 3km; right into Les Arcs. Le Logis & Vieille Ville signed at far end of Les Arcs. (5 mins by taxi from station.)

Max Callegari

tel	+33 (0)4 94 99 51 10
fax	+33 (0)4 94 99 51 29
e-mail	le.logis.du.guetteur@wanadoo.fr
web	www.logisduguetteur.com

La Maurette Roquebrune

La Maurette, 83520 Roquebrune sur Argens, Var

If you wonder about the origins of the seven studio houses around the *mas*: yes, there is a story. The previous owner built the first house for his wife when they divorced. Then the same thing happened again. And again... Apparently he still lives nearby and can be found drowning his sorrows. You enter the gates and drive up a steep private road to the car park, leave your car and then climb some more. Don't look for signs, there are none, Wolfgang doesn't want to "make it look like a hotel". The climb is worth it as La Maurette enjoys spectacular 360° views of the red-brown mountain that gave the village its name. You feel miles from anywhere here, but in fact Roquebrune is only a couple of minutes away. Bedrooms all have quarry tiles and a Provençal style but are otherwise very different in size, colour and design; many have a fully equipped mini-kitchen. They also each have their own terrace with table and chairs, and a bottle of wine waiting for their occupants. More a place for a honeymoon than with the children. If you want dinner, the hotel will ring the local restaurant who deliver your choice from their menu. Good idea!

rooms	11 twins/doubles.
price	€ 85–€ 156.
meals	Breakfast € 11. Village restaurants 2km.
closed	Mid-November–March.
directions	A8 exit 37 for Fréjus & Roquebrune onto N7 then D7 at Le Pont du Prieur for Roquebrune sur Argens. Over Argens river, right, then left, left again, pass tree in middle of road. Well signed.

Dr Christine Sckenkelberg & Wolfgang Blumberg

tel	+33 (0)4 98 11 43 53
fax	+33 (0)4 98 11 43 52
e-mail	info@lamaurette.fr
web	www.lamaurette.fr

map 18 entry 337

Centre International Marie Eugénie Milleret

37 avenue du Commandant Bret, 06400 Cannes, Alpes-Maritimes

A convent in Cannes! This unlikely establishment offers the best of two totally different worlds: the peace and quiet of a secluded *maison d'accueil* and, 20 minutes away, the worldly sophistication of the film festival town of Cannes. It is run with the dedication and warmth one would expect from 'the best kind of nuns' who, without promoting their faith, simply allow it to inform everything they do. The rooms, once the cells of the 60-odd nuns who lived here before France became a secular state, are plain but perfectly comfortable, many with views over to the sea; breakfast, which you can have in the somewhat austere dining room or take out to the rather more *sympathique* terrace, is both copious and delicious. Lunch (which can be a picnic if you order in advance) and dinner are unfussy, homely affairs, but at this price you could treat yourself to an occasional blow-out in Cannes. This is a place for refreshment of the soul, whether you find it lying in the sun on the beach, under the trees in the garden, or in the chapel. *A subscription of €8 p.p. to the CIMEM Association is usually requested.*

rooms	65 doubles.
price	Half-board €58–€79. Full-board €72–€93.
meals	Half- or full-board.
closed	Rarely.
directions	A8 exit Cannes Centre Ville. At top of Bvd Carnot, left (after 'lycée' & opp. Hôtel Amarante) into Bvd des Anglais, then right into Bvd de la République. At 2nd T-junc. left into Ave du Commandant Bret; 500m up hill on left.

Reservation service CIMEM

tel	+33 (0)4 97 06 66 70
fax	+33 (0)4 97 06 66 76
e-mail	contact@cimem.com
web	www.cimem.com

Bastide Saint Mathieu

35 chemin de Blumenthal, 06130 Grasse, Alpes-Maritimes

Our inspector gasped as she entered, such is the contrast between rustic simplicity and contemporary elegance. Inge wasn't fazed: "we still do that ourselves," she smiled. A massive stone edifice, the bastide overlooks fields and hills of olive and lemon trees. Retreating here from Malawi as their children grew older, Inge and Arie restocked the grounds with 3,500 plants: 60 new olive trees, lemons, grapefruit, figs, cherries, almonds. This is Arie's domain: he will show you his hands to prove it. Inside is Inge's work and everything is just as she likes it. In one room, the huge canopied bed is placed right in front of the window to catch the early sun. In spite of the luxuries of CD player, internet connection, cashmere blankets and drinks tray, you feel you are staying with a friend – a very attentive one! Bathrooms are decadently gorgeous but never flashy. Choose your soap from Molinard, Fragonard or Galimard: Inge tries to be fair to all the old Grasse houses. Breakfast is as late as you like, watched over by an old painted angel by the fireplace. The pool is huge, or you can settle under an old plane tree with a coffee.

rooms	5: 3 doubles, 2 suites.
price	€230–€340.
meals	Good choice nearby.
closed	Rarely.
directions	A8 exit 42 for Grasse Sud; right until Quatre Chemins r'bout; 2nd right before MacDonald's; left at r'bout; pass Hyper-U; over r'bout; right until Elephant Bleu car wash; right lane; for Opio, St Mathieu, St Jean; to Moulin de Brun; left at T-junc.; immed. right to bastide.

	Arie & Inge Van Osch
tel	+33 (0)4 97 01 10 00
fax	+33 (0)4 97 01 10 09
e-mail	info@bastidestmathieu.com.
web	www.bastidestmathieu.com

map 18 entry 339

La Grande Bastide

Route de la Colle, 06570 St Paul de Vence, Alpes-Maritimes

This 18th-century *bastide* has been turned into a country-house hotel which provides calm luxury, plus the most fantastic views through a sea of palm and olive trees of one of the jewels of Provence: St Paul de Vence. This is not simply an enchantingly 'typical' village, it is also an important artistic centre, still frequented by musicians, writers and painters following in the footsteps of Matisse, Daudet and Pagnol. Despite its proximity to the main road (ask for one of the quieter rooms), the lush gardens keep the exterior world at bay. From the welcoming entrance, along the 'outside corridors' which look out over the gardens, to the rooms, decorated in Provençal style – painted furniture, pretty cotton prints, pastel painted walls – you feel the personal touch of the owners. The pool is overlooked by the terrace where you can eat a breakfast worthy of the setting. You may just want yogurt and honey, or perhaps the full English with a sophisticated French spin appeals? Whatever you choose, a warm welcome and truly painstaking attention to your comfort are guaranteed.

rooms	14: 11 doubles, 3 suites.
price	€ 145–€ 200. Suites € 190–€ 290.
meals	Breakfast € 15. Informal lunch at poolside.
closed	22 November–26 December; 10 January–mid-February.
directions	From A8, exit 47 for St Paul de Vence. After La Colle sur Loup, hotel signed on left.

Heinz Johner

tel	+33 (0)4 93 32 50 30
fax	+33 (0)4 93 32 50 59
e-mail	stpaullgb@voila.fr
web	www.la-grande-bastide.com

Val des Roses

6 chemin du Laurier, 06160 Cap d'Antibes, Alpes-Maritimes

You could drive here, park the car and not touch it until you leave: a sandy beach with a view to old Antibes is a minute away, the old town and market 10 minutes and the shops five. Frederik and Filip are Flemish, in their twenties and found the Val des Roses a short while ago after searching for the 'perfect place'. Filip has all the necessary diplomas; both brothers are charming and sure to make this venture a happy one. They do everything themselves, with the help of one girl, and put on an excellent breakfast, which you can have in your room, on the terrace or by the pool. They will also do a picnic and plan to do light lunches. For dinner, they will recommend a place; phone ahead and make sure you get a good table. A definite find: not cheap, but well worth it. The gracious white house, with white shutters, is enclosed in its garden by high walls in a quiet little road. Inside, fabrics and walls are mostly white, cool and tranquil. Interestingly, the bedrooms are open plan, with a large oval bath giving a sybaritic touch. Many guests are return visitors. *Convenient for Nice airport.*

rooms	4: 3 suites for 2-3, 1 suite for 4.
price	€ 115–€ 130.
meals	Breakfast € 12. Poolside snacks & picnic lunch available.
closed	November–January.
directions	From Antibes towards Cap d'Antibes & Plages to Salis Plage. Keep shops on right, drive south. At old stone archway, Chemin du Laurier on right.

	Frederik & Filip Vanderhoeven
tel	+33 (0)6 85 06 06 29 (mobile)
fax	+33 (0)4 92 93 97 24
e-mail	val_des_roses@yahoo.com
web	www.val-des-roses.com

map 18   entry 341

Villa Saint Maxime

390 route de la Colle, 06570 St Paul de Vence, Alpes-Maritimes

A modern gem, on a site facing St Paul de Vence – a retreat of vast white spaces. The house was built by a British architect during the first Gulf war for an Englishman with "strong Iranian connections"… In an echo of the inner courtyard of eastern dwellings, the main atrium has a retractable roof allowing a cooling breeze to waft through in summer. Bold sweeping lines, marble and terracotta, a white-parasoled pool and, in the central stairwell, a broken-glass garden that sparkles like Ali Baba's jewels. Each air conditioned room has a balcony or terrace to make the most of the view; bath and shower rooms are spectacular. Ann and John spent their early married life in this ancient, fortified village so beloved of Marc Chagall, and have deep emotional roots here. Ann collects modern art; there's a piece or two in your room, more in the famous Maeght Foundation down the road. Breakfast, with champagne if you wish, is any time at all, while a delicious homemade orange aperitif sets the mood for dinner. Immaculate restarants and bars are a step away. *Children over 12 welcome. Unsupervised pool.*

rooms	6: 4 doubles, 2 suites.
price	€ 130–€ 170. Suites € 175–€ 300.
meals	Many restaurants within walking distance.
closed	Rarely.
directions	A8 exit Cagnes sur Mer for Vence then St Paul. Nearing village, left at blue sign for villa. At end of road, blue gate, on left.

Ann & John Goldenberg

tel	+33 (0)4 93 32 76 00
fax	+33 (0)4 93 32 93 00
e-mail	riviera@villa-st-maxime.com
web	www.villa-st-maxime.com

Hôtel Cantemerle

258 chemin Canta Merle, 06140 Vence , Alpes-Maritimes

How appropriate: 1930s sophistication on the doorstep of the Maeght Foundation and Saint Paul de Vence. Much of the furniture came from the old Palais de la Mediterranée in Nice and the feel is pre-war ocean liner — first class, of course! The hotel was built in 1985 in the gardens of Madame Dayan's mother's house, itself the mildly eccentric creation of an Englishman reputedly related to royalty. Rooms are ochre-roofed cottages half concealed by luxuriant garden; the older, duplex quarters have a large private terrace leading to the pool, the newer are on one level, and look to umbrella pines and hills beyond. Colours are muted, relieved by the odd bright kilim or Persian rug and some engravings from the Maeght; the feel is clean but sumptuous. Some rooms have an ethnic touch: nothing heavy-handed, just the odd statue or spear leaning in a corner. A great place for a visit in cooler months: as well as the outdoor pool there's a covered one with luscious green tiles, Moroccan lamps and a hammam. Breakfast is lavish and whenever you like. Lunch or dine in the Art Nouveau restaurant, or outside.

rooms	19: 10 doubles, 19 duplex suites.
price	€ 170–€ 196. Suites € 195–€ 215.
meals	Breakfast € 14. Lunch & dinner € 30–€ 60. Restaurant closed Mondays except in July & August.
closed	Usually October–March.
directions	A8 exit Cagnes sur Mer for Vence. At r'bout (with musical instruments & petrol station) right for 100m.

	Madame Dayan
tel	+33 (0)4 93 58 08 18
fax	+33 (0)4 93 58 32 89
e-mail	info@hotelcantemerle.com
web	www.hotelcantemerle.com

map 18 entry 343

Hôtel Windsor

11 rue Dalpozzo, 06000 Nice, Alpes-Maritimes

A 1930s Riviera hotel with a pool in a palm grove and exotic birds in cages? All that... and much more. Bernard Redolfi-Strizzot has brought the Thirties into the 21st century by asking contemporary artists to do a room each. The result? So many gifts of wit, provocation, flights of fancy, minimalist sobriety and artistic creation: Joan Mas's *Cage à Mouches*, Jean le Gac's blue figures, cosmopolitan Ben's writing on the walls. The other rooms are far from plain, with Antoine Beaudoin's superb frescoes of Venice, Egypt, India – all our travel myths – and Tintin. Plain white beds have contrasting cushions or quilts; furniture is minimal and interesting; delightful little bathrooms, some directly off the room, are all individually treated. All clear, bright colours, including the richly exotic public areas: the much-travelled owners chose their exquisitely elaborate Chinese mandarin's bed for the bar; panelling and colourful plasterwork for the restaurant; a fine wire sculpture, stone and bamboo for the hall. Light filters through onto warmly smiling staff. And there's a stunning Turkish bath, yoga and relaxation centre. Unbeatable.

rooms	57 twins/doubles.
price	€ 105–€ 140.
meals	Breakfast € 8. Lunch & dinner à la carte € 28–€ 38. Restaurant closed Saturday noon & Sundays.
closed	Rarely.
directions	In centre of Nice. A8 exit Promenade des Anglais. Left at museum on Rue Meyerbeer. Right on Rue de France & 1st left Rue Dalpozzo.

Bernard Redolfi-Strizzot
tel	+33 (0)4 93 88 59 35
fax	+33 (0)4 93 88 94 57
e-mail	contact@hotelwindsornice.com
web	www.hotelwindsornice.com

Hôtel les Deux Frères

Place des Deux Frères, 06190 Roquebrune – Cap Martin, Alpes-Maritimes

The oriental blue and gold ceiling of Chambre 1001 Nuits will possibly lull you into one of the best night's sleep you've ever had. Or you may prefer the room in stylish lime green, or the nautical hues of Marine. Most rooms are fairly small but have great views of the coastline, mountainside or the old village square. You'll get a smiling welcome from the young Dutch owner who has combined Provençal comfort with an exotic flavour, down to the seven languages he speaks and his restaurant's innovative dishes. There's also a small café next door for snacks. Dine in summer on the sunshiney terrace with its stunning Riviera views. Long since abandoning suit and tie for less formal wear, Willem hung up his walking stick here and is full of ideas; children simply adore him. After parking in the village, you can either take advantage of the hotel's shuttle which takes guests and luggage up and down the hill, or opt for the short, fairly steep path. Excellent value for money for the area, and ideal for the young and fleet of foot. Book early.

rooms	10 doubles.
price	€65–€101.
meals	Breakfast €9. Lunch & dinner €20–€45. Restaurant closed Mondays & Tuesday noon in summer; Sunday evenings & Mondays out of season.
closed	Rarely.
directions	A8 exit 57 for Menton then Roquebrune Cap Martin. Left at Roquebrune & Vieux Village. Stop at municipal car park & walk 50m.

	Willem Bonestroo
tel	+33 (0)4 93 28 99 00
fax	+33 (0)4 93 28 99 10
e-mail	info@lesdeuxfreres.com
web	www.lesdeuxfreres.com

map 18 entry 345

Hôtel Paris-Rome

79 Porte de France, 06500 Menton Garavan, Alpes-Maritimes

A real find, particularly for those who love gardens. The Paris-Rome was built as a home by Gil's grandfather and has been run as a family hotel for many years. The garden here is actually a courtyard, where you can have breakfast or afternoon tea among the flowers, but Gil has put together a magnificent programme for visiting the gardens along this bit of coast – from Ellen Willmott's Hanbury to an afternoon with the head gardener at Lawrence Johnston's Serre de la Madone and a tour of a rarely-opened botanical garden. Gil also puts on cookery holidays, taking you to the kitchens of leading restaurants, and fishing holidays, when your catch will be cooked to your liking. If you want sun and sand, that's great too: you can have all the comforts of a private beach a short walk away, along the waterfront. As for the hotel itself – rooms are comfortable and traditional and some have a fine view of the sea just across the road. The Castellana family are really friendly and have thought of everything, from a room for rinsing and drying beach things to a little gym.

rooms	22: 18 doubles, 2 singles, 2 triples.
price	€55-€85. Singles €45-€55. Triples €95-€100.
meals	Breakfast €10. Lunch €25. Dinner €30. Restaurant closed mid-November-mid-December.
closed	November-26 December.
directions	A8 exit Menton, head for waterfront and Italian border. Hotel at lights opposite Port of Garavan, 100m before Italian border.

	Gil Castellana
tel	+33 (0)4 93 35 73 45
fax	+33 (0)4 93 35 29 30
e-mail	paris-rome@wanadoo.fr
web	www.hotel-paris-rome.com

WHAT'S IN THE BACK OF THE BOOK?

EUROPE - COURSES & ACTIVITIES

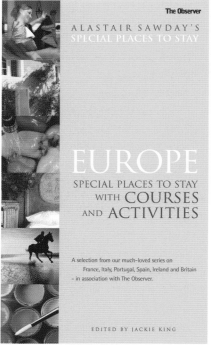

The properties with entry numbers below also appear in our
Europe: Special Places to Stay with Courses & Activities guide (£12.99).

Arts & Culture • 169 • 193 • 196 • Arts & Crafts • 1 • 139 •
181 • 210 • 257 • Cookery • 151 • 153 • 157 • 159 • 162 •
172 • 185 • 188 • 193 • 196 • 197 • 203 • 205 • 206 •
Drawing, Painting & Sculpture • 155 • 169 • 170 • 177 • 188 •
196 • 203 • 206 • 208 • Flora & Fauna • 151 • 169 • 204 •
Food & Wine • 151 • 169 • 174 • 196 • 197 • 204 • 205 •
Gardens & Gardening • 170 • 172 • 206 • 208 • History • 149
• 156 • 159 • 164 • 198 • Languages & Creative Writing • 162
• Mind, Body & Spirit • 151 • 155 • 170 • 188 • Sports &
Outdoor Pursuits • 129 • 151 • 153 • 155 • 156 • 157 • 159 •
164 • 170 • 175 • 177 • 183 • 188 • 198 • 199 • 205 • 208 •
Walking • 156 • 198

FRENCH HOLIDAY HOMES, VILLAS, GÎTES AND APARTMENTS

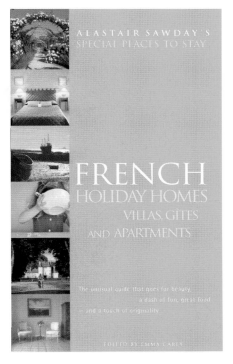

We all know how beautiful the buildings of France can be — so it is no surprise to find some stunners within these pages.

There's a convent school in the Lot, beautifully converted by two painters; a cottage in the grounds of a Burgundian chateau; an old 'bergerie' deep in a forest; a farm in the Loire with 40 goats and its own cheese — and many places with open fires and wood-burning stoves, and even some under-floor heating.

There is a castle whose moat has become a swimming pool. A school has been 'de-classified' into a haven of peace and luxury. There are whole hamlets available, not to mention the huge, and wonderful houses that can take small crowds. We have found tiny flats for two, apartments in Paris and other cities, and exquisite buildings in deep countryside. You can live in style or in charming, rural scruffiness; you may be a minimalist or a traditionalist.

French Holiday Homes, Villas, Gîtes and Apartments (£11.99)

NATIONAL AND REGIONAL PARKS IN FRANCE

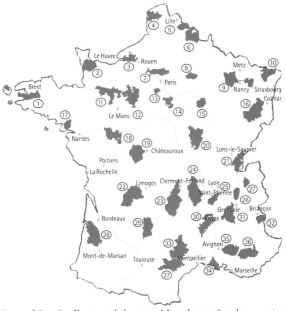

General De Gaulle signed the initial legislation for the creation of its National and Regional Parks in 1967. Forty national and regional nature parks in France now represent 11% of its landmass. Most are off the beaten track and are often missed by the foreign visitor. The motorway network is such that one swishes by huge patches of beautiful countryside without even realising it.

The National and Regional Parks charter promotes:

* Protection and management of natural and cultural heritage

* Participation in town and country planning and implementation of economic and social development

* Welcoming and informing the public, raising environmental awareness

There is a ban on hunting, camping, building and road construction in the six national parks: Cévennes, Ecrins, Mercantour, Port-Cros, Pyrénées and Vanoise. Access can be difficult but the rewards are considerable.

NATIONAL AND REGIONAL PARKS IN FRANCE

There are regional parks to be found in the mountains of Queyras (Hautes Alpes), the plains of Vexin (Ile de France), along the coast of Camargue (Provence), in the woodlands in the Northern Vosges (Alsace-Lorraine), in the wetlands of Brière (Western Loire) and off-shore in Port-Cros (Côte d'Azur).

All are ideal for rambles. Serious walkers can choose from the *sentiers de Grandes Randonnées* (GRs for short) which range through the parks and all park offices can provide maps of local walks.

There are grottoes and museums to visit along with animal parks roaming with bison, yak, greater kudu and a pack of wolves. Activities include: horse-riding, cycling and bike rentals, canoeing and kayaking, canal boating, sailing, fishing, spa treatments, wine tours, bathing, rock climbing, handgliding, ballooning. There are packhorses in Livredois-Forez (Auverge) and donkeys for hire in Haut-Languedoc (Languedoc). A range of activities make them ideal for children and a multitude of crafts are to be observed: clog-making, silk weaving, glass working, stone working in the Morvan (Burgundy), cheesemaking and pipe-making in the Haut Jura (Franche Comté).

www.parcs-naturales-regionaux.tm.fr

This central web site links to all the other parks. All have English language versions.

F. Mulet

FRENCH WORDS & EXPRESSIONS

château	a castle, stately home
bastide	in Provence, another word for *mas*
armoire	free standing wardrobe, often carved
couchettes	bunk beds in a carriage of an overnight train
sympathique	nice, agreeable
maison d'accueil	resting place, safe house
Directoire	furniture with simple flowing lines, 1795-1799
dans son jus	in its own juices
chambres d'hôtes	bed & breakfast
fougace	flat plaits of bread, sometimes with bits of lard, olives, figs, nuts
petit grain de folie	a wee bit mad
lavabo	wash basin
seigneurie	estate of seigneur (feudal lord)
vieux rose	pale rose pink
amuse-bouches	a tasty titbit served before the first course or with the apéritif
tissu textile	fabric
pommeau	a beverage from Normandy, 2/3 apple cider and 1/3 calvados
La vieille France	belonging to the old style
Orangerie	winter garden or conservatory
objets	bric a brac
Moulin	mill
mas	house on two floors, bottom floor originally for sheep or cattle
sanglier	wild boar
la maison musée	museum house
cuisine d'amour	cooking from the heart
pastis	anis flavoured alcoholic beverage
œil de bœuf	round window
à la Petit Trianon	playing at being a shepherdess, as did Marie Antoinette
loggia	an enclosed balcony added to a room, usually an additional bed space
Souleiado	one of the last manufacturers of Provençal fabrics
toile de Jouy	classic French fabrics and wallpapers depicting romantic scenes
maison bourgeoise	house of a solid middle-class citizen
fumoir	a place for smokers
boudoir	lady's private room
logis	the caretaker's lodging
en plein air	outside
cuisine raffiné	refined cooking
cave	cellar
petit manoir	little manor house
pineau de Charentes	a regional speciality made from the white grape and cognac
ciel de lit	canopy over the head of the bed
les chanoines	canons (clergy)
très soignée	very well dressed

FLIGHT ROUTES

Ajaccio (Corsica)
Heathrow

Bastia (Corsica)
Gatwick

Bergerac
Southampton
Stansted

Biarritz
Stansted

Bordeaux
Birmingham
Dublin
Gatwick

Brest
Stansted

Carcassonne
Stansted

Chambery
Gatwick

Clermont-Ferrand
Gatwick
Stansted

Dinard
Stansted

Grenoble
Gatwick

La Rochelle
Stansted

Limoges
Stansted

Lyon
Birmingham
Edinburgh
Heathrow
Manchester
Stansted

Marseille
Gatwick

Montpellier
Gatwick
Stansted

Nantes
Cork
Gatwick

Nice
Birmingham
Bristol
Cork
Dublin
E. Midlands
Edinburgh
Gatwick
Glasgow
Heathrow
Leeds Bradford
Liverpool
Luton
Manchester
Stansted
Teesside

Nimes
Stansted

Paris Beauvais
Dublin
Glasgow
Shannon

Paris CDG
Aberdeen
Belfast City
Birmingham
Bristol
Cardiff
Cork
Dublin
E. Midlands
Edinburgh
Gatwick
Glasgow
Heathrow
Leeds Bradford
London City

Liverpool
Luton
Manchester
Newcastle
Southampton
Teesside

Paris Orly
London City

Pau
Stansted

Perpignan
Stansted

Poitiers
Stansted

Reims
Stansted

Rodez
Stansted

St Etienne
Stansted

Strasbourg
Gatwick
Stansted

Toulon
Gatwick

Toulouse
Belfast City
Birmingham
Cardiff
East Midlands
Edinburgh
Gatwick
Glasgow
Heathrow
Manchester
Southampton

Tours
Stansted

WHAT BOOKS TO TAKE

Suggested books for a holiday read. The editor's recent and dog-eared favourites.

Provence: from Minstrels to the Machine, Ford Maddox Ford, (W.W. Norton)

France on the Brink – A Great Civilization Faces the New Century, Jonathan Fenby (Abacus)

Between Meals, an Appetite for Paris, A.J. Leibling (North Point Press)

French or Foe, Polly Platt (Culture Crossings)

Letters from My Windmill, Alphonse Daudet (Penguin Classics)

French Revolutions: Cycling the Tour de France, Tim Moore (Vintage)

French Country Cooking, Elizabeth David (Penguin)

Charcuterie and French Pork Cookery, Jane Grigson (Grub Street Publishing)

The New France: A Complete Guide to Contemporary French Wine, Andrew Jefford (Mitchell Beazley)

Cathars and Catholics in a French Village, 1294-1324, Emmanual Le Roy Ladurie (Penguin)

An Hour From Paris, Annabelle Simms (Pallas Anthene)

Good Morning, Midnight, Jean Rhys (Penguin Modern Classics Fiction)

Two Towns in Provence, M.F.K. Fisher (Vintage)

Travels with a Donkey in the Cevennes, Robert Louis Stevenson (Northwestern University Press)

The Sun King, Nancy Mitford (Penguin)

French Ways and Their Meaning, Edith Wharton (Berkshire House Publishers)

The Debt to Pleasure, John Lanchester (Picador)

Perfume – The Story of a Murderer, Patrick Suskind (Vintage)

Instructions for Visitors, Helen Stevenson (Black Swan)

Birdsong, Sebastian Faulkes (Vintage)

Fragile Glory – A Portrait of France and the French, Richard Bernstein (Plume)

The Road from the Past: Traveling through History in France, Ina Caro (Harvest Books)

HOW TO CUT THE CHEESE

First of all, a fundamental rule: every portion of cheese should contain some of the rind. This will avoid other tasters being left out because the taste of the cheese is never uniform: it gets stronger the closer it is to the rind due to the mould forming on the surface. Discovering the subtleties is part of the pleasure of tasting cheese.

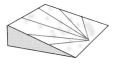

Small sized cheeses
(e.g.: Camembert, Pont l'Evêque…)

Pyramid or coned shaped cheeses (e.g.: Valençay, Pouligny St Pierre…)

Small cheeses
(e.g.: Cabécou, crottins…)

Soft cheeses
(e.g.: Brie or Coulommiers…)

Cheeses with veins of blue mould
(e.g.: Bleus, Roquefort…)

Boxed cheeses
(e.g.: Vacherin or Epoisses…)

Hard Cheeses
(e.g.: Comté, Ossau Iraty…)

Long cylindrical cheeses
(e.g.: Ste Maure, Rouleau de Provence…)

WHAT IS ALASTAIR SAWDAY PUBLISHING?

Twenty or so of us work in converted barns on a farm near Bristol, close enough to the city for a bicycle ride and far enough for a silence broken only by horses and the occasional passage of a tractor. Some editors work in the countries they write about, e.g. France; others work from the UK but are based outside the office. We enjoy each other's company, celebrate every event possible, and work in an easy-going but committed environment.

These books owe their style and mood to Alastair's miscellaneous career and his interest in the community and the environment

These books owe their style and mood to Alastair's miscellaneous career and his interest in the community and the environment. He has taught overseas, worked with refugees, run development projects abroad, founded a travel company and several environmental organisations. There has been a slightly unconventional streak throughout, not least in his driving of a waste-paper-collection lorry, the manning of stalls at jumble sales and the pursuit of causes long before they were considered sane.

Back to the travel company: trying to take his clients to eat and sleep in places that were not owned by corporations and assorted bandits he found dozens of very special places in France – farms, châteaux etc – a list that grew into the first book, *French Bed and Breakfast*. It was a celebration of 'real' places to stay and the remarkable people who run them.

The publishing company grew from that first and rather whimsical French book. It started as a mild crusade, and there it stays – full of 'attitude', and the more appealing for it. For we still celebrate the unusual, the beautiful, the individual. We are passionate about rejecting the banal, the ugly, the pompous and the indifferent and we are passionate, too, about 'real' food. Alastair is a trustee of the Soil Association and keen to promote organic growing and consuming by owners and visitors.

It is a source of deep pleasure to us to know that there are many thousands of people who share our views. We are by no means alone in trumpeting the virtues of resisting the destruction and uniformity of so much of our culture – and the cultures of other nations, too.

We run a company in which people and values matter. We love to hear of new friendships between those in the book and those using it, and to know that there are many people – among them farmers – who have been enabled to pursue their decent lives thanks to the extra income our books bring them.

WWW.SPECIALPLACESTOSTAY.COM

Britain

France

Ireland

Italy

Portugal

Spain

Morocco

India...

all in one place!

On the unfathomable and often unnavigable sea of online accommodation pages, those who have discovered **www.specialplacestostay.com** have found it to be an island of reliability. Not only will you find a database full of trustworthy, up-to-date information about all the Special Places to Stay across Europe, but also:

· Links to the web sites of all of the places in the series

· Colourful, clickable, interactive maps to help you find the right place

· The opportunity to make most bookings by e-mail – even if you don't have e-mail yourself

· Online purchasing of our books, securely and cheaply

· Regular, exclusive special offers on books

· The latest news about future editions and future titles

· Notices about special offers, late availability and anything else our owners think you'll be interested in.

The site is constantly evolving and is frequently updated with news and special features that won't appear anywhere else but in our window on the worldwide web.

Russell Wilkinson, Web Producer
website@specialplacestostay.com

If you'd like to receive news and updates about our books by e-mail, visit the site and at the bottom of every page you can add yourself to our address book.

FRAGILE EARTH SERIES

The Little Earth Book
Now in its third edition and as engrossing and provocative as ever, it continues to highlight the perilously fragile state of our planet.
£6.99
4th edition available April 2004

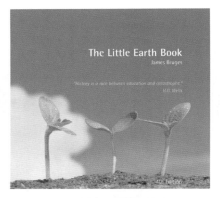

The Little Food Book
Makes for a wonderfully stimulating read — one that may change your attitude to the food choices you make daily.
£6.99

The Little Money Book
Could make you look at everything financial — from your bank statements to the coins in your pocket — in a whole new way.
Available November 2003
£6.99

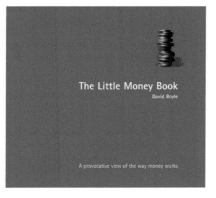

This fascinating series has been praised by politicians, academics, environmentalists, civil servants — and 'general' readers. It has come as a blast of fresh air, blowing away confusion and incomprehension.

www.fragile-earth.com

SIX DAYS

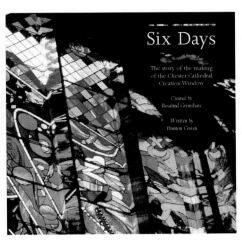

Celebrating the triumph of creativity over adversity

The inspiring and moving story of the making of the stained glass Creation window at Chester Cathedral by a woman battling with Parkinson's disease.

"Within a few seconds, the tears were running down my cheeks. The window was one of the most beautiful things I had ever seen. It is a tour-de-force, playing with light like no other window ..."
                    Anthropologist Hugh Brody

In 1983, Ros Grimshaw, a distinguished designer, artist and creator of stained-glass windows, was diagnosed with Parkinson's disease. Refusing to allow her illness to prevent her from working, Ros became even more adept at her craft, and in 2000 won the commission to design and make the Creation Stained Glass Window for Chester Cathedral.

Six Days traces the evolution of the window from the first sketches to its final, glorious completion as a rare and wonderful tribute to Life itself: for each of the six 'days' of creation recounted in Genesis, there is a scene below that is relevant to the world of today and tomorrow.

Extracts from Ros's diary capture the personal struggle involved. Superb photography captures the luminescence of the stunning stained glass, while the story weaves together essays, poems, and moving contributions from Ros's partner, Patrick Costeloe.

Available from Alastair Sawday Publishing £12.99

ORDER FORM UK

All these books are available in major bookshops or you may order them direct. **Post and packaging are FREE within the UK.**

		Price	No. copies
French Bed & Breakfast	Edition 8	£15.99	
French Hotels, Châteaux & Inns	Edition 3	£13.99	
French Holiday Homes (Jan 04)	Edition 2	£11.99	
Paris Hotels	Edition 4	£9.99	
British Bed & Breakfast	Edition 8	£14.99	
British Hotels, Inns & Other Places	Edition 5	£13.99	
Bed & Breakfast for Garden Lovers	Edition 2	£14.99	
British Holiday Homes	Edition 1	£9.99	
London	Edition 1	£9.99	
Ireland	Edition 4	£12.99	
Spain	Edition 5	£13.99	
Portugal	Edition 2	£8.99	
Italy	Edition 3	£12.99	
Europe with courses & activities	Edition 1	£12.99	
India	Edition 1	£10.99	
Morocco (Dec 03)	Edition 1	£10.99	
The Little Earth Book	Edition 3	£6.99	
The Little Food Book	Edition 1	£6.99	
The Little Money Book (Nov. 03)	Edition 1	£6.99	
Six Days		£12.99	

Please make cheques payable to Alastair Sawday Publishing   Total £ _____ _____

Please send cheques to: Alastair Sawday Publishing,
The Home Farm Stables, Barrow Gurney, Bristol BS48 3RW.
For credit card orders call 01275 464891 or order directly
from our web site **www.specialplacestostay.com**

Title   First name   Surname

Address

Postcode   Tel

If you do not wish to receive mail from other like-minded companies,
please tick here ☐

If you would prefer not to receive information about special offers on our books,
please tick here ☐

FH3

REPORT FORM

Comments on existing entries and new discoveries

If you have any comments on entries in this guide, please let us have them. If you have a favourite house, hotel, inn or other new discovery, please let us know about it.

Existing Entry:

Name of property _____

Book title: _____

Entry no: _____ Edition no: _____

Date of visit: _____

New recommendation:

Name of property: _____

Address: _____

_____

Postcode: _____

Tel: _____

Comments: _____

_____

_____

_____

Your name: _____

Address: _____

_____

_____

Postcode: _____

Tel: _____

Please send the completed form to:

Alastair Sawday Publishing,
The Home Farm Stables, Barrow Gurney, Bristol BS48 3RW
or go to www.specialplacestostay.com and click on 'contact'.

Thank you.

BOOKING FORM

À l'attention de:
To:

Date:

Madame, Monsieur
Veuillez faire la réservation suivante au nom de:
Please make the following booking for (name):

Pour	*nuit(s)*	*Arrivée le jour:*	*mois*	*année*
For	night(s)	Arriving: day	month	year
		Départ le jour:	*mois*	*année*
		Leaving: day	month	year

Si possible, nous aimerions	*chambres, disposées comme suit:*
We would like	rooms, arranged as follows

À grand lit	*À lits jumeaux*
Double bed	Twin beds
Pour trois	*À un lit simple*
Triple	Single
Suite	*Appartement*
Suite	Apartment

Nous sommes accompagnés de   enfant(s) âgé(s) de   ans.
Avez-vous un / des lit(s) supplémentaire(s), un lit bébé; si oui, à quel prix?
We are travelling with   children, aged   years. Please let
us know if you have an extra bed / extra beds / a cot and if so,
at what price.

Nous aimerions également réserver le dîner pour   personnes.
We would also like to book dinner for   people.

Veuillez nous envoyer la confirmation à l'adresse ci-dessous:
Please send confirmation to the following address:

Nom: Name:

Adresse: Address:

Tel No: E-mail:

Fax No:

la réservation — Special Places to Stay

QUICK REFERENCE INDICES

€65 and under

These place offer a double or twin room for two people for €65 or under per night. Check when booking.

The North • 1 • 2 • 3 • Picardy • 9 • Lorraine • 14 • 17 • Alsace • 19 • 20 • 22 • Burgundy • 24 • 25 • 26 • 28 • 30 • 32 • 38 • Paris – Ile de France • 62 • 66 • Normandy • 70 • 75 • 76 • 77 • 80 • 86 • 87 • 88 • 89 • 91 • 92 • 95 • Brittany • 102 • 107 • 116 • Western Loire • 125 • 133 • 134 • 137 • 141 • 146 • Loire Valley • 151 • 155 • 156 • 157 • 160 • 162 • 170 • 171 • 175 • Poitou – Charentes • 180 • 181 • 182 • 184 • 187 • 189 • 194 • 195 • Aquitaine • 201 • 205 • 207 • 209 • 215 • 218 • Limousin • 219 • 220 • 221 • 222 • Auvergne • 225 • 227 • Midi – Pyrénées • 232 • 238 • 239 • 240 • 243 • 244 • 246 • 248 • 250 • 253 • Languedoc – Roussillon • 256 • 257 • 258 • 260 • 266 • 267 • 269 • 271 • 274 • 277 • 282 • Rhône Valley – Alps • 283 • 285 • 296 • Provence – Alps – Riviera • 307 • 320 • 323 • 326 • 328 • 330 • 333 • 334 • 338 • 345 • 346

Wheelchair-friendly

These owners have told us that they have facilities for people in wheelchairs.

Picardy • 6 • 7 • Champagne – Ardenne • 12 • 13 • Alsace • 18 • 21 • Burgundy • 25 • 26 • Paris – Ile de France • 44 • 53 • 64 • Normandy • 72 • 75 • 76 • 77 • 80 • 88 • 89 • 92 • Brittany • 101 • 102 • 109 • 110 • 111 • 114 • 116 • 117 • 122 • Western Loire • 124 • 125 • 132 • 133 • 135 • 136 • 138 • 141 • 142 • 145 • Loire Valley • 158 • 163 • 164 • 165 • 167 • 168 • 173 • 176 • Poitou – Charentes • 180 • 181 • 182 • 184 • 185 • 187 • 188 • 189 • 195 • Aquitaine • 200 • 203 • 204 • 213 • 215 • 227 • 228 • Midi – Pyrénées • 231 • 233 • 235 • 242 • 245 • Languedoc – Roussillon • 259 • 267 • 272 • 275 • 276 • 278 • 281 • 282 • Rhône Valley – Alps • 288 • Provence – Alps – Riviera • 299 • 301 • 307 • 311 • 316 • 318 • 326 • 328 • 338 • 343

Fishing

These places can arrange fishing on or near the premises.

The North • 1 • 2 • Picardy • 4 • 7 • 8 • 9 • Lorraine • 17 • Alsace • 18 • 19 • 21 • Burgundy • 23 • 24 • 27 • 28 • 31 • 37 • 40 • Paris – Ile de France • 64 • Normandy • 72 • 73 • 74 • 80 • 82 • 83 • 86 • 88 • 89 • 96 • 99 • Brittany • 100 • 102 • 103 • 104 • 105 • 106 • 109 • 110 • 111 • 115 • 116 • 117 •

QUICK REFERENCE INDICES

Heated pool

These are places with a heated swimming pool in the grounds.

Mind, body & spirit

Yoga, massage, seaweed wraps etc

Meeting room

These places have rooms suitable for meetings.

QUICK REFERENCE INDICES

Cookery

Lessons available on premises or arranged nearby

Wine

These places are wine-producing properties, will host wine tastings, organise visits to vineyards or any combination of all three.

Wine and cookery

These places can organise cookery lessons and are wine-producing properties, will host wine tastings, organise visits to vineyards or any combination of all three.

QUICK REFERENCE INDICES

Gardens Exceptional gardens nearby. Some places can provide English guides.

Tennis Tennis courts on the premises or within 5km.

QUICK REFERENCE INDICES

Limousin • 221 • 222 • Auvergne • 226 • Midi – Pyrénées • 231 • 234 • 235 • 236 • 240 • 242 • 243 • 244 • 245 • 252 • 254 • 255 • Languedoc – Roussillon • 260 • 262 • 265 • 271 • 273 • 276 • 279 • Rhône Valley – Alps • 286 • 287 • 289 • Provence – Alps – Riviera • 298 • 301 • 307 • 308 • 309 • 314 • 315 • 317 • 321 • 331 • 332 • 335 • 337 • 343 • 346

Secure parking

Secure parking is available at these places.

Picardy • 6 • 7 • 8 • Champagne - Ardenne • 10 • 13 • Lorraine • 14 • 16 • Alsace • 18 • 21 • Burgundy • 23 • 25 • 27 • 30 • 31 • 32 • 34 • 35 • 37 • 38 • 40 • Paris - Ile de France • 44 • 47 • 62a • 65 • 67 • 68 • Normandy • 71 • 72 • 74 • 76 • 81 • 82 • 83 • 87 • 90 • 94 • 95 • 98 • Brittany • 110 • 119 • 121 • Western Loire • 124 • 125 • 126 • 130 • 133 • 134 • 135 • 138 • 139 • Loire Valley • 152 • 156 • 157 • 162 • 164 • 165 • 166 • 168 • 175 • 177 • Poitou - Charentes • 181 • 183 • 185 • 187 • 188 • 189 • 193 • Aquitaine • 197 • 198 • 201 • 203 • 212 • 224 • Midi - Pyrénées • 231 • 235 • 245 • Languedoc - Roussillon • 258 • 260 • 261 • 262 • 263 • 266 • 267 • 270 • 278 • 281 • Rhône Valley - Alps • 283 • 284 • 287 • 290 • 293 • 296 • 297 • Provence - Alps - Riviera • 300 • 301 • 302 • 303 • 304 • 305 • 306 • 311 • 313 • 316 • 318 • 320 • 321 • 324 • 325 • 330 • 331 • 339 • 340 • 341 • 342 • 343 • 345

INDEX - PROPERTY NAME

INDEX - PROPERTY NAME

INDEX - PROPERTY NAME

INDEX - PROPERTY NAME

INDEX - PROPERTY NAME

INDEX - PROPERTY NAME

INDEX - TOWN

INDEX - TOWN

INDEX - TOWN

INDEX - TOWN

INDEX - TOWN

INDEX - TOWN

HOW TO USE THIS BOOK

explanations

❶ rooms

Assume all rooms are 'en suite' unless we say otherwise.

If a room is not 'en suite' we say **with separate,** or **with shared bathroom**: the former you will have to yourself, the latter may be shared with other guests or family members. Where an entry reads 4+2 this means 4 rooms and 2 self-catering apartments or similar.

❷ room price

The price shown is for one night for two sharing a room. A price range incorporates room/seasonal differences.

❸ meals

Prices are per person.

❹ closed

When given in months, this means for the whole of the named months and the time in between.

❺ directions

Use as a guide; the owner can give more details.

❻ map & entry numbers

Map page number; entry number.

❼ symbols

See the last page of the book for fuller explanation.

sample entry

CHAMPAGNE – ARDENNE

La Maison de Rhodes
20 rue Linard-Gonthier, 10000 Troyes, Aube

An exceptional find, a 16th-century timber-framed mansion that once belonged to the Templars. Monsieur Thierry's breathtaking renovation has brought a clean contemporary style to ancient bricks and mortar. Highlights include an interior courtyard of cobble and grass and heavy wooden doors under the coachman's porch that give onto the street. The house sits plumb in the old quarter of Troyes, on the doorstep of the cathedral. Bedrooms are bona fide jaw-droppers – expect the best in minimalist luxury. Huge beds are dressed in white linen, ancient beams straddle the ceilings. Walls are either exposed rough stone, or smooth limestone, often a clever mix of both. Bathrooms, too, are outstanding; most are enormous and have terracotta floors, big bath tubs, fluffy robes. Views are to the cathedral spires, the courtyard or the formal gardens of the Museum of Modern Art, directly opposite. A perfect blend of old and new, an exhilarating architectural landscape. Troyes is full of wonders, though the bibulous may be tempted to venture beyond the city walls. The region is quite well-known for its local tipple – Champagne.

rooms	11: 5 doubles, 2 triples, 4 suites.
price	€95–€179.
meals	Breakfast €15. Great restaurants nearby.
closed	Rarely.
directions	In centre of Troyes, at the foot of the cathedral.

	Thierry Carcassin
tel	(0)3 25 43 11 11
fax	(0)3 25 43 10 43
e-mail	message@maisonderhodes.com
web	www.maisonderhodes.com

❼ 🖼️🖊️🐾🛏️♿🐕🐾   **❻** map 7 entry 13